SUMMIT AT TEHERAN

SUMMIT
AT
TEHERAN

Keith Eubank

William Morrow and Company, Inc. / New York

Library of Congress Cataloging in Publication Data

Eubank, Keith.
  Summit at Teheran.

  Bibliography: p.
  Includes index.
  1. World War, 1939–1945—Diplomatic history.
2. Teheran Conference (1943) I. Title.
D749.E82 1985   940.53′2   84-25538
ISBN 0-688-04336-4

Printed in the United States of America

First Edition

1 2 3 4 5 6 7 8 9 10

BOOK DESIGN BY BERNARD SCHLEIFER

To
Lynn M. Case.
distinguished scholar, dedicated teacher, and good friend

Preface

IN NOVEMBER 1943, Winston Churchill, Joseph Stalin, and Franklin D. Roosevelt journeyed to Teheran for the first of the wartime summit conferences that would determine the outcome of World War II, begin the rearrangement of the political map of eastern and central Europe, and shape forever the history of Europe and the United States.

In the midst of a terrible world war that had yet to be won, the three leaders of the alliance against Adolf Hitler, together with their chiefs of staff, traveled by ship and by plane, in danger from attack by U-boats and the German Luftwaffe, to a distant city rumored to be crammed with German secret agents.

The long trip was necessary because of a crisis in planning the final strategy for the war against Hitler. Stalin, angry over postponements of Operation OVERLORD and suspecting that Roosevelt and Churchill wanted the Russian armies to bleed to death fighting the Wehrmacht, would not disclose Soviet plans to his allies. For their part, they were alarmed over reports that Stalin might conclude a separate peace treaty with Hitler and divide up Europe just as the Russians and Germans had done in 1939. But Roosevelt convinced himself that he, personally, could overcome Stalin's distrust if they could only meet face to face. If such a meeting could save the alliance, bring victory closer, and ensure postwar peace, then the long, dangerous trip to Teheran had

7

to be undertaken because Stalin would meet them nowhere else.

The meeting of the three men became a tale of high drama, including bitter arguments between Stalin and Churchill over the timing of OVERLORD. The arguments were often vicious, with Stalin accusing Churchill of seeking to back out of the operation. Churchill, loath to set a definite date for OVERLORD, was forced by Roosevelt to concede.

The Teheran Conference was unique because here a President of the United States relied on his personal resources, using only his instincts, his political expertise, and his wits to carry out negotiations with Stalin—his only advisers being Harry Hopkins, an admirer of the Russian leader. Since Teheran, no President has gone to a summit conference without briefing books, a host of advisers, and his Secretary of State. No President has ever dared to repeat Roosevelt's solo performance at the Teheran Conference.

Teheran also offers the picture of an American President living in a Soviet embassy because of reports that German agents were planning to assassinate the three men as they moved back and forth across the city. Previously secret military intelligence reports have enabled me to disclose the facts behind the rumored Nazi plot.

It can also be argued that the Teheran Conference was the start of the Cold War because from it arose the present Soviet domination of Poland. For it was at Teheran that Stalin warned his allies that he must have nothing less than a "friendly" government in Poland.

Another product of the Teheran meeting was the notorious Yalta Conference, where, it was later alleged, Roosevelt and Churchill sold out to Stalin. The Yalta Conference cannot be understood without knowledge of the Teheran Conference because much that was decided at Yalta had first been discussed in Teheran, and Yalta completed much of the work begun there.

Here also is the first account of the meeting between Roosevelt and Shah Reza Pahlavi. Thus began the shah's singular relationship with American Presidents that would end only when the Ayatollah Khomeini and his followers drove the shah into exile in 1979.

As the first in a series of summit conferences between American Presidents and Soviet rulers, the Teheran Conference has altered the way American Presidents conduct foreign policy. For these conferences have ultimately become media events enabling American and Soviet leaders to appear before the world as global statesmen.

This is the first complete history of the conference—how it originated, why it was held in Teheran, the arguments, the quarrels, and the secret deliberations that not only fixed the final strategy of the war in Europe but determined the politics of Europe for generations to come.

Acknowledgments

IN RESEARCHING AND WRITING this book, I have amassed a debt of gratitude to all the institutions and to all the people who have aided me. For their help I am indebted to the Paul Klapper Library, Queens College; the New York Public Library; the Archibald Stevens Alexander Library, Rutgers University; the Washington National Records Center, Suitland, Md.; the National Archives; the Manuscript Division, Library of Congress; the Naval War College Historical Collection; Operational Archives, the United States Naval History Division; the George C. Marshall Research Foundation, Lexington; the Masters and Fellows of Churchill College, Cambridge; the Public Record Office, London; and the Franklin D. Roosevelt Library, Hyde Park, N.Y., where it was always a pleasure to work.

I wish to thank the Liddell Hart Centre for Military Archives, King's College, London, for permission to quote from the Alanbrooke diaries. All quotations from the Public Record Office documents are reproduced with the kind permission of the Controller of Her Majesty's Stationery Office.

Edward J. Reese and John E. Taylor, Modern Military Branch, National Archives, were always generous with their knowledge of military records. I am grateful for the assistance given me by Anthony R. Crawford, George C. Marshall Foundation, and Anthony S. Nicolisi, the Naval War College Historical Collection.

I owe a great debt of thanks to those among my colleagues at Queens College who aided me in writing this book. Frank Merli not only read much of the manuscript and gave me wise counsel, but he also was kind enough to seek out documents for me in London; Allen McConnell and Stuart Prall read and commented on portions of the manuscript; Paul Avrich brought relevant articles to my attention.

My special thanks to Sheila Low-Beer who assisted me in the early stages of research; to Bruce Kessler who supplied an important document; and to Warren Henly who, using his fine talent, drew the map of the eastern frontier of Poland.

Research on this book was aided by a City University of New York Research Award, 1976–1977, and by grant recovery funds from Queens College.

I am especially indebted to my editor at William Morrow, Bruce Lee, and to his ever-efficient assistant editor, Elizabeth Terhune, for their aid and advice. My thanks to Ann Adelman who did a masterful job of copyediting the manuscript.

Finally, I am deeply grateful to my wife, Marilyn, who always encouraged me in this project and whenever possible assisted me in archival research. Without her help the task of research would have been more prolonged and laborious.

Contents

Prologue: One Rainy Night

IN WARTIME WASHINGTON, November 11, 1943, had been cold and rainy. Early on that Armistice Day, Franklin D. Roosevelt, accompanied by Navy Secretary Frank Knox and Army Secretary Henry L. Stimson, had paid the customary visit to the Tomb of the Unknown Soldier, but contrary to custom, the President did not speak at the service. As soon as the ceremonies had been completed, he returned to the White House, neglecting his usual banter with the press corps. Later that day, as darkness fell over the nearly deserted rainy streets, few people hurrying homeward paid much attention as black government automobiles came out of the driveway at the south lawn of the White House.

The cavalcade drove through the city, darkened because of wartime blackout restrictions, south to U.S. 1, and continued on until it turned off for Quantico, Virginia, and entered the Marine base. Finally the cars from the White House stopped at the dock where the presidential yacht U.S.S. *Potomac* was ready to get under way. A former Coast Guard patrol boat that had once chased smugglers and rum runners, it had been converted into a yacht for the President's pleasure and convenience. There within an hour after leaving the White House, Roosevelt and his party boarded the *Potomac*. Lines were cast off, the vessel moved out into the Potomac River and sailed downstream through the rainy night; after 3:30 A.M. it dropped anchor off Cherry Point in the Chesapeake Bay. Off in the darkness an American bat-

15

tleship lay at anchor. With the President on board *Potomac* that night were Harry Hopkins, his special assistant; Admiral William D. Leahy, his chief of staff; Rear Admiral Wilson Brown, naval aide; Major General Edwin M. Watson, military aide; and Rear Admiral Ross T. McIntire, the President's physician.

About nine o'clock the next morning, the yacht came alongside the battleship, U.S.S. *Iowa*. Crews of both vessels rigged a gangplank from the after sun deck of the yacht to the *Iowa*'s main deck. Quickly the Secret Service moved the President across, his party following him. At Roosevelt's order, no special honors were rendered as would normally have been the custom when the commander-in-chief boarded an American naval vessel. Already on board and awaiting the President were the Joint Chiefs of Staff: General George C. Marshall, Admiral Ernest J. King, and General Henry Arnold, all of whom had also come aboard without fanfare or ceremony.

With the transfer of the President and his party completed, *Potomac* shoved off, moving upstream accompanied by a submarine chaser. The yacht's skipper had orders to sail to a secret destination and remain secluded there for at least a week in order to give newsmen the impression that the President was enjoying a quiet cruise away from the pressures of wartime Washington.

As the yacht got under way, *Iowa* moved downstream until she reached her berth at Hampton Roads about 6 P.M. There tankers came alongside and began to fuel the battleship because 80 percent of her fuel had been offloaded to permit her to move upstream and rendezvous with *Potomac*. During the fueling, everyone on board whose face and uniform could excite newsmen had to remain hidden. At the same time, watch officers from the White House Map Room came on board bringing mail for the President, including bills for his signature.

That evening, the President dined with the ship's commander, Captain John L. McCrea, formerly Roosevelt's naval aide. But first, Roosevelt had his usual cocktail, although Navy General Orders No. 99, July 1, 1914, barred liquor from American naval vessels. Captain McCrea obeyed the regulations, but not the President, who took the position that because he was commander-in-chief of all American armed forces, rank had its privileges.

During dinner, Roosevelt asked McCrea when the *Iowa* would be getting under way. McCrea estimated that the fuel tanks would be topped off by about eleven-thirty and that the battleship would then be under way. "You know, John," observed Roosevelt, "to-day is Friday. We are about to start on an important mission. Before it is over many important decisions must be made. I am sailor enough to share a sailor's superstition that Friday is an unlucky day. Do you suppose you could delay getting under way until Saturday—this is of course without interrupting your plans too much?"[1] Choosing not to question presidential superstitions, McCrea agreed to his commander-in-chief's request.

Accompanied by three destroyers, at 12:05 A.M. *Iowa* left Hampton Roads for Oran. She dropped the pilot about 2 A.M., and within two hours the battleship and her escorts were steaming eastward. By dawn, with the seas running high, Task Group 27.5 commenced zigzagging, standard procedure in wartime. When the destroyers found it rough sailing in the heavy seas, all hands were ordered below. By 8 A.M., the Task Group had sailed over sixty-five miles from Hampton Roads. *Iowa* steamed on in "Condition of Readiness Three," with one-third of the crew at battle stations at all times.

For Roosevelt, his first day at sea had been a quiet one. In the diary which the President now began for this trip, he wrote: "This will be another Odyssey—much further afield and afloat than the hardy Trojan whose name I used to take at Groton when I was competing for school prizes. But it too will be filled with surprises."[2]

The "Odyssey" referred to the coming meeting with Joseph Stalin and Winston Churchill in Teheran—the first meeting between a President of the United States and a Soviet ruler. This trip would take Roosevelt farther from Washington than any previous President had traveled during his term of office. Already he had sailed outside the territorial limits of the United States on national business when in August 1941 he went to Argentia, Newfoundland, to confer with Churchill; and in January 1943, Roosevelt had journeyed to

Casablanca for another meeting with Churchill.

Now this November Roosevelt had left Washington on a trip that would take him to the Middle East to meet with a genuine Communist ruler, one who as a prominent member of the Bolshevik party had helped overthrow the only democratic government in the history of Russia. In order for Roosevelt to confer with this leader, his ship had to sail through waters where German U-boats lurked, which could sink a vessel bearing the President of the United States. He was risking these dangers so that he might personally meet a Soviet dictator.

Roosevelt would never have undertaken such a tiring journey, and one so dangerous, had not the United States been plunged deep in World War II. Only such a conflict warranted undertaking this arduous journey for a meeting in a far-off city between leaders of countries whose political philosophies had so little in common.

1
Allies Against Hitler

"AIR RAID PEARL HARBOR! THIS IS NO DRILL!" When the message reached Washington in the early afternoon of December 7, 1941, Japanese torpedoes and bombs had begun to destroy the United States Pacific Fleet. After the attackers finally withdrew, the Pacific Fleet had been put out of action, and the United States was at war with Japan even before Congress had acted.

President Franklin D. Roosevelt had been finishing lunch in the Oval Office and talking to Henry Hopkins when he received a telephone call from Navy Secretary Frank Knox. "Mr. President, it looks as if the Japanese have attacked Pearl Harbor."

"No!" cried Roosevelt.

The shocked President, soon consumed by quiet anger, began to issue orders changing the United States from peacetime to war. The next day, after he had recommended a declaration of war, Congress approved it with only one dissenting vote. Now legally the United States had entered into a state of war with the Empire of Japan. On the same day the United States also became an ally of Great Britain in the war against Japan.

Prime Minister Winston Churchill had been spending the weekend of December 7 at Chequers when he heard the Pearl Harbor attack reported on the BBC: "The news has just been given that Japanese aircraft have raided Pearl Harbor, the American naval base in Hawaii. The announcement of

19

the attack was made in a brief statement by President Roosevelt."

At once Churchill telephoned Roosevelt. "Mr. President, what's this about Japan?"

"It's quite true," Roosevelt replied. "They have attacked us at Pearl Harbor. We are all in the same boat now."[1] The next day, His Majesty's Government declared war on Japan. Although Britain and the United States now had a common enemy, the United States remained at peace with Germany.

In Berlin, the news of the Pearl Harbor attack stunned Hitler. But he told the Japanese ambassador, "You gave the right declaration of war." By December 9, Hitler had decided to declare war on the United States. He announced his decision to the world in a speech to the Reichstag on December 11 which was largely devoted to denouncing Franklin D. Roosevelt as a warmonger—a man who for years had hoped for the outbreak of war and who feared peace.

Reichstag deputies rose to their feet, cheering Hitler's announcement that he had ordered passports to be issued to the American chargé d'affaires. Hitler left to Joachim von Ribbentrop, the foreign minister, the duty of reading the declaration of war to the American chargé—"The Reich government therefore breaks off all diplomatic relations with the United States and declares that under these circumstances brought about by President Roosevelt, Germany too considers herself to be at war with the United States, as from today."

By declaring war on the United States, Hitler saved Roosevelt from a bruising battle with isolationist senators and congressmen. Hitler's action turned the United States into an ally of both Great Britain and the Union of Soviet Socialist Republics in the war against Nazi Germany. Despite their differing political philosophies and contrasting economic and social systems, Britain, the United States, and Soviet Russia now had a common enemy—Nazi Germany. By declaring war on the United States, Hitler had hurled these three nations into an alliance. His declaration compelled three nations separated by geography, politics, and economics to join in military coalition. But the task of forging a victorious coalition against Hitler would be painful because in the past

Britain and the United States had had little in common with the Soviet Union. Not only was there the difference in language and culture; there was an almost unbridgeable chasm between Anglo-American political philosophy and Marxist-Leninism. Since 1917, the relations of Britain and the United States with the Soviet Union had been marked by hostility, invective, threats, and even warfare.

The American people welcomed the Russian Revolution, which brought an end to the czar's government in March 1917; they interpreted that revolution as a victory for democracy and the Allied cause. Now the Russian people, led by the new Provisional Government, would fight with even greater zeal. Americans, however, had little understanding of the terrible sacrifices the Russian people had been forced to make for the Allied war effort. Consequently, Americans could not imagine that the Russian people would heed the cries of the Bolsheviks for immediate peace. Yet it was the prospect of peace that helped the Bolsheviks overthrow the Provisional Government in November 1917.

Shocked by the brutal, repressive measures of the Bolshevik government, most Americans believed that the Russian people would quickly come to their senses, repudiate their rulers, and return to genuine democratic government. Willing to let the dust settle in the hope that democracy would emerge victorious, Washington withheld recognition of the Bolshevik government. But instead of democracy becoming the victor, communism triumphed in Russia.

The Communist government, led by Nikolai Lenin, signed the Treaty of Brest-Litovsk with Germany in March 1918 and left the war. Among the Allied powers, Communist Russia had now become a traitor. Because they felt themselves betrayed, Allied governments resolved on military intervention in Russia to prevent German troops from seizing supplies originally shipped by the Allied governments to the czarist armies. In addition, they hoped to establish a second front in eastern Europe to divert the German armies from the western front where victory appeared uncertain.

With limited planning and without clear strategic goals, contingents of the Allied armies intervened during 1918 in what had become a Russian civil war. A small force of British and American troops landed at Archangel in September, only to withdraw in July 1919 after accomplishing little and suffering over five hundred casualties in fighting the hastily formed Red Army. Far to the east, American soldiers landed at Vladivostok late in the summer of 1918. Washington had dispatched these troops to Siberia to aid Czechoslovak prisoners of war who had formed themselves into a foreign legion and were fighting their way out of Russia. When the Americans arrived, the Czechs were no longer in danger. For over a year, American troops remained in Siberia, keeping watch over a large contingent of Japanese forces who had also intervened in the Russian civil war. In addition to the American and Japanese troops, a small British force tried with slight success to aid opponents of the Communist government in Siberia. Eventually all Allied troops left Russia by 1920 except for the Japanese, who lingered on until 1922.

Although the Anglo-American intervention had ended, distrust and suspicion persisted. Soviet propagandists charged the Anglo-American imperialists with planning the intervention for the purpose of overthrowing the revolution of workers and peasants. London and Washington reinforced these charges by continuing to refuse recognition to the Soviet government of Russia. Despite the official policy of nonrecognition, the United States shipped nearly one million tons of food, plus medicines and clothing, to the Russian people during the terrible famine of 1921.

Great Britain took the first step toward healing the breach with the Soviet Union by negotiating a trade agreement in 1921. Under Ramsay MacDonald, the first Labour government restored diplomatic ties with Soviet Russia in 1924, only to break them in 1927 after a raid on the London offices of the Soviet trade delegation revealed it to be a center of Soviet espionage and propaganda. The Moscow press responded with accusations that London planned a militant crusade against the Soviet Union. Diplomatic relations between Britain and the Soviet Union did not resume until 1930, after MacDonald had formed his second government. During the 1930s, even after Hitler had commenced aggressive actions in central Europe, Conservative British governments eyed Soviet Russia with suspicion when Soviet spokesmen exhorted Britain and France to oppose Nazi Germany while the new Soviet ruler, Joseph Stalin, ordered the execution of Russian generals. Soviet Russia seemed a troublemaker bent on mischief rather than a peacemaker concerned with stability in Europe. And many Americans held similar views.

After the failure of intervention, the U.S. government sought to ignore the Soviet Union through a policy of non-recognition. As far as Washington was concerned, officially the Soviet government did not exist. In the Harding administration, Secretary of State Charles Evans Hughes enunciated a policy for the Soviet Union which continued through twelve years of Republican administration. According to this policy, by repudiating debts owed to the United States by the czarist government and by refusing to compensate American corporations for confiscated American property, the Soviet government had forfeited recognition. Moreover, the Communists had made themselves outcasts by sending agents into friendly nations to foment revolution. No political gain could be achieved through recognition of a government whose avowed goals included the overthrow of the American system of government by violence; recognition of government-espoused atheism would only antagonize millions of American church members. Finally, recognition would permit the Communists to open embassies and consulates from which they could dispense their ideology.

The founding of the American Communist party in 1919 frightened Americans who feared the spread of communism. Nor were they reassured when internal social and industrial strife erupted in the same year—industrial strikes, a general strike in Seattle, and a police strike in Boston. These disturbances fed American fears that the whiskered, bomb-throwing Bolsheviks were attempting to undermine the republic. Then the "Red Scare," when Attorney General A. Mitchell Palmer rounded up foreign agitators and deported 249 of them, confirmed the conviction that the Bolsheviks were endangering the United States of America. Because of these Moscow-inspired actions, the Soviet government could not be recognized.

Nevertheless, throughout the 1920s American interest in the story of Soviet Russia persisted as books on Soviet affairs came from the printing presses. The State Department did not budge from its position of refusing all negotiation over the question of recognition. Yet in spite of the official position, trade with the Soviet Union had been permitted and had grown since the end of the war. By 1925, the United States headed the list of nations trading with the Soviet Union. The introduction of the Soviet first Five Year Plan in 1928 led to increased purchase of American products and inevitably had an effect on American attitudes toward recognition of Soviet Russia.

When the Great Depression wrecked foreign trade, American businessmen yearned to participate in greater trade with the Soviet Union, arguing that recognition would open the Soviet market to more American exports and help to relieve unemployment. Recognition might even lead the Communists to moderate their aim of overthrowing capitalism, so the argument went. And when Japanese militarists launched an invasion of Manchuria in 1931, some supporters of recognition argued that it would inhibit Japanese aggression.

American recognition of Soviet Russia came only after the election of Franklin D. Roosevelt in 1932. During the election campaign he had avoided taking any position on the question. After his election, he had a careful examination made of the problem of recognition as well as its effects on voters' attitudes. The research revealed that the majority of Americans favored recognition, with the only hard-core opposition coming from some church groups. Business leaders still favored recognition, as did Roosevelt, believing that such action would contribute to American prosperity through the increase in Soviet-American trade.

Assured that recognition would not arouse a significant number of voters, Roosevelt invited the Soviet government to open negotiations. Moscow dispatched a delegation, headed by Soviet Commissar for Foreign Affairs Maxim Litvinov, to negotiate the agreement. After Litvinov arrived in the United States on November 7, 1933, Roosevelt moved quickly to take a personal role in the negotiations. During the four negotiating sessions at the White House, Roosevelt ignored the State Department's memoranda that he first obtain agreement on the debts owed the United States and on the American claims against Soviet Russia. Instead, he chose to recognize the Soviet Union while postponing final agreement on the settlement of debts and claims to some future date. Roosevelt chose this tactic because he did not want this issue, which appeared unimportant to him, to delay an agreement so close to being completed. In addition, he could not spend any more time negotiating one agreement because of the press of other business—a similar circumstance would later limit his personal negotiations with Stalin.

On behalf of the Soviet government, Litvinov pledged that his government would refrain from aiding or abetting propaganda or subversive activities aimed at the overthrow of the United States government. The Soviet government would also grant freedom of religion to American citizens living in the Soviet Union. Americans would have access to information on economic conditions in Soviet Russia and be guaranteed certain legal rights. The final agreement, signed on November 17, 1933, received approval from the press, business, and labor, as well as some church groups. One Roman Catholic spokesman declared: "Roosevelt has put God back into Russia." For Roosevelt, the resumption of diplomatic relations with the Soviet Union amounted to a personal achievement in diplomacy.

Yet recognition of the Soviet government did not have the expected results. By 1935 the negotiations over debts and claims had collapsed, thanks largely to a document so loosely worded that Litvinov and Roosevelt called it a "gentleman's agreement." The anticipated increase in trade that would help dispel the Great Depression never materialized. The credits desired by the Soviet government were not forthcoming, and Russian hopes for loans from the United States were blocked by the Johnson Act, which forbade loans to nations in default to the United States. Inside the Soviet Union, however, recognition proved beneficial because it seemed to prove that the economic and political influence of the Soviets had compelled the United States to grant recognition. The leading capitalist power had capitulated to the power of the Soviet peasants and workers.

Within a year after American recognition of the Soviet

Union, admittance to the League of Nations gave the Soviet image more respectability. At Geneva, the Soviet Union became the outspoken advocate of disarmament and collective security—a position that won friends among those Americans who feared the march of fascism in Europe. But the Moscow Purge Trials in the late 1930s shook the confidence of such American friends. If the shocking confessions and trials were true, then communism was indeed rotten. If the confessions were false, then the Soviet tyranny far exceeded that of the czars. These same friends were bewildered and shocked when the Soviet Union signed a non-aggression pact with Nazi Germany in August 1939, which enabled Hitler's armies to invade Poland and permitted Stalin to send Soviet occupation armies into eastern Poland.

Shortly after the fighting in Poland had ended, Soviet armies attacked Finland in November 1939, arousing American sympathies for a small nation that had become the victim of a bully. Even Roosevelt condemned the Soviet action in a speech on February 10, 1940: "The Soviet Union, as a matter of fact, as everybody knows, who has got the courage to face the fact . . . is run by a dictatorship, a dictatorship as absolute as any other dictatorship and it had invaded a neighbor so infinitesimally small that it could do no conceivable, possible harm to the Soviet Union, a small nation that seeks only to live at peace as a democracy and a liberal forward looking democracy at that."[2] Within weeks of his speech, Finland made peace with the Soviet Union. American sympathy could not save Finland from defeat.

Concern in the United States over the plight of Finland was soon forgotten when German armies invaded and conquered Denmark and Norway in April 1940. After Nazi forces had opened the offensive against France and the Low Countries in May 1940, Soviet armies occupied the Baltic States in June, and by August they had become integral parts of the Soviet Union. The U.S. government promptly froze the assets of the Baltic States, and to show sympathy for their cause continued to recognize the Baltic diplomats and to pay their salaries from the frozen assets. Throughout the Battle of Britain, which followed the Germany victory in western Europe, Stalin aided Germany by providing supplies and raw materials as well as a naval base near Murmansk.

Fearing Japanese support of Hitler's cause in Asia, in April 1941 Stalin concluded a five-year neutrality pact with Japan. Washington, regarding the pact as a move aimed at turning Japan south toward the Philippine Islands and away from Siberia, froze Soviet funds in retaliation and withheld export licenses. By the spring of 1941, however, Hitler's armies had intensified preparations for the invasion of Soviet Russia.

Through their intelligence services, the British and American governments obtained information about Hitler's plans. Both governments warned Stalin of the impending catastrophe, but ignoring their warnings, he did all within his power to avoid or postpone the German attack. He increased the shipment of supplies to Germany, vetoed all criticism of Germany in the Soviet press, and withdrew recognition of the ambassadors and the governments whose states had fallen victim to Hitler's armies. The Anglo-American intelligence reports proved accurate: German armies crossed the Soviet borders in the early morning hours of June 22, 1941. The sudden attack rendered Great Britain and Soviet Russia unwilling allies.

Stalin wanted his newfound ally to supply Russia not only with war materials but also with troops who were to establish a front in northern Russia or in France. To the United States, Stalin sent a request by June 30 for more than a billion and a half dollars worth of equipment and munitions, including three thousand bombers and three thousand fighter planes.

Stalin's lengthy shopping list failed to receive wholehearted approval. Within the United States a debate erupted over aiding Soviet Russia. Why not let the Nazis and Communists kill each other off, argued some in the strong congressional isolationist bloc. Measures were offered in Congress to prevent or impede American aid for Soviet Russia. Professional military men in Washington did not expect the Red Army to hold out against Hitler's armies for more than three months at the most. Opinion in London concurred. In these circumstances, why should Soviet Russia be given aid that might soon be lost in combat?

But on June 24, Roosevelt had told a press conference,

"Of course we are going to give all aid that we possibly can to Russia." And in London, Churchill had already declared, "Any man or state who fights on against Nazism will have our aid. Any man or state who marches with Hitler is our foe."[3]

Before these pledges could be fulfilled and help in the form of war materials shipped to Russia, both Roosevelt and Churchill required first-hand knowledge of Russian needs. Yet such knowledge was in short supply because American and British ambassadors remained uninformed about Soviet military needs and deficiencies. As no Soviet bureaucrat dared release such information, a better source of information had to be found. The best source was of course Stalin, whom someone must now contact. Ordinary ambassadors were inadequate. One man, because of his close connections with President Roosevelt, might have greater clout than an ambassador.

In July 1941, Harry Hopkins, Roosevelt's special assistant, went to London to prepare the way for the first meeting between Roosevelt and Churchill, scheduled for later that summer. Since the fate of Soviet Russia would be high on the agenda of that meeting, accurate information about Soviet needs had to be obtained. Hopkins proposed that, as Roosevelt's personal envoy, he make a quick trip to Moscow to see Stalin and find out from him whatever he could about Russian needs. Roosevelt approved the visit and requested Stalin "to treat Mr. Hopkins with the identical confidence you would feel if you were talking directly to me." Churchill in turn instructed Hopkins personally to tell Stalin "that Britain has but one ambition today, but one desire—to crush Hitler. Tell him that he can depend on us."[4] Hopkins left Churchill to board a train that would take him to Loch Lomond. From there he would begin the uncomfortable, dangerous flight to Russia.

Since 1940, Harry Hopkins had been living at the White House. By now he had become Roosevelt's closest friend, his confidant, someone without any personal or political ambitions except to serve "the Boss." Roosevelt confided in him, showed him confidential papers and, when Hopkins's health permitted, sent him off as his trusted agent. The son of an

Iowa harness maker, a former social worker, Hopkins had first worked for Roosevelt during his term of office as governor of New York State. Following Roosevelt's election triumph in 1932, Hopkins became head of the Federal Emergency Relief Administration, the first of many jobs that he would hold in the Roosevelt administration. In April 1941, Roosevelt put Hopkins in charge of Lend-Lease, the program to make the United States the "arsenal of democracy."

Hopkins had dreamed of becoming a presidential candidate for the 1940 election, but his poor health ended that dream. Not only did he suffer from ulcers, but cancer required surgeons to cut away much of his stomach; subsequently he developed a condition which made it difficult for his system to absorb protein. In spite of his repeated illnesses, Hopkins never hesitated to travel anywhere that "the Boss" asked him to go. Now he was off to Moscow, because Roosevelt trusted him fully, confident that Hopkins would faithfully follow instructions, which in this instance were unwritten.

Upon his arrival in Moscow on July 29, Hopkins received VIP treatment from Stalin. The Soviet ruler granted him lengthy private meetings in which he disclosed information he had denied the American and British ambassadors, including the military needs of the Soviet armed forces. In one three-hour meeting, Stalin reviewed with Hopkins the military crisis facing the Soviet forces. Stalin confessed that only a declaration of war by the United States would defeat Hitler. He assured Hopkins "that he would welcome the American troops on any part of the Russian front under the complete command of the American Army."[5]

Hopkins explained that the American and British governments would be unwilling to dispatch large quantities of munitions and equipment to the Soviet Union until a conference had been held between the three governments at which the strategic and military interests of all three nations could be fully explored. Until they knew the outcome of the battle then raging in Russia, the conference could not be held. Stalin welcomed such a meeting but told Hopkins that he could not leave Moscow to participate in it. He would be glad to make available to the U.S. government all the required information, including designs of Soviet guns and tanks. Stalin promised Hopkins that such a conference would receive his personal attention. With this promise, on August 2 Hopkins left Moscow.

The meetings with Stalin convinced Hopkins that a conference of the three governments could be held only with Stalin present. No one in the Soviet government dared release the necessary information except Stalin. Hopkins had learned in Moscow that Stalin would not disclose anything vital about Soviet plans and needs to the British ambassador, nor to Laurence Steinhardt, the American ambassador, but only to the personal representative of the President of the United States. The information which the British and American governments needed in order to aid Soviet Russia in the war against Germany would only be revealed by Stalin—and only to very special people. Hopkins's experience in the discussions with Stalin would ultimately influence Roosevelt's decision to seek a personal meeting with the Soviet leader.

After leaving Moscow, Hopkins returned to London, then set sail on August 4 for the United States with Churchill on H.M.S. *Prince of Wales*. They were bound for Argentia Harbor, off the Newfoundland coast, where Roosevelt and Churchill would hold their first official meeting of the war.

At Argentia, Roosevelt and Churchill discussed Britain's needs, mutual problems, the extent of American aid to Britain, and a common policy toward Japan. Out of their meeting came the Atlantic Charter, a statement of war aims, noble and selfless, which received more publicity in the press than it deserved and which would ultimately create problems for both men when Stalin began enunciating his territorial demands. Another result of the Argentia meeting was an invitation to Stalin for a conference in Moscow to consider the apportionment of supplies. Stalin immediately accepted the proposal of the meeting, as he had promised Hopkins he would.

To meet with Stalin in Moscow—as he insisted—Roosevelt and Churchill designated Averell Harriman and Lord Beaverbrook, respectively, as their representatives. Harriman, a partner in the banking firm of Brown Brothers Harriman & Company, chairman of the board of Union Pacific, and chairman of the executive committee of Illinois Central, had voted Democratic and worked in the Roosevelt administration in the 1930s. Max Aitken, Lord Beaverbrook, Canadian-born, had made his fortune in the cement business, bought the *Daily Express*, and become an energetic figure in British politics. He was currently the British minister of supply. The standing of both men in Anglo-American politics should have given them enough prominence to convince Stalin that he ought to confide in them about Russian needs and plans.

Their meeting with Stalin in Moscow, held late in September, proved to be a great disappointment, however. Instead of confiding in Harriman and Beaverbrook, Stalin presented a list of demands which he wanted fulfilled immediately. No general discussion took place about the Soviet potential for producing weapons or about Soviet future needs. Stalin showed no interest in planning, only in demanding. Not only did he volunteer little information to the Anglo-American delegation, he rejected all discussion about strategy with General Hastings Ismay, chief of staff to Churchill, dismissing him after ten minutes of general conversation.

The Moscow Supply Conference had not fulfilled the original hopes of those who conceived it. The Russians had proven to be very secretive. For much of the time Stalin maintained a surly attitude, continually criticizing the British for their failure to launch an invasion of France that would relieve the pressure on the Red Army. Although Harriman and Beaverbrook had been designated as special agents for their respective national leaders and had brought distinguished advisers and officers with them to Moscow, Stalin would not open up and discuss broad strategy with them. He appeared to be reneging on his promises made to Hopkins in July. Stalin's attitude could be blamed on his preoccupation with the course of the war. There was also another reason for his attitude: he would talk frankly only with Churchill and Roosevelt. Little would be gained by dispatching additional special agents to confer with Stalin even though the agents had the full confidence of Churchill and Roosevelt.

While Stalin had been conferring with Harriman and Beaverbrook, he had learned that Hitler was preparing a final assault aimed at taking Moscow. Every resource had to be mobilized to repel the attackers. The Nazi offensive against Moscow, launched in October, brought German troops to the outskirts of the Soviet capital. The Red Army counterattack on December 6 eventually halted the forces advancing on Moscow. No one on the battlefield knew it, but Moscow would not fall and the German armies would be driven back at a frightful cost.

Even as the guns roared before Moscow, the bombs began to fall on Pearl Harbor. Unlike Churchill, Stalin sent no message to Roosevelt recording his reaction to the news of the Pearl Harbor attack or to the news that Hitler had declared war on the United States on December 11, 1941. Stalin did not even send a message to Roosevelt upon learning that the Soviet Union now had a second ally. Though the two leaders had begun corresponding after the Moscow Conference, at Harriman's suggestion, the first exchanges were routine. But thanks to the Japanese attack and Hitler's declaration of the war, the tone of the correspondence did change.

Roosevelt was first to communicate with Stalin after the United States had become a Soviet ally. Writing on December 16, he explained how important he thought it to be that they take immediate steps not only for joint operations in the near future, but also for the final defeat of Hitler. "I should like very much to see you and talk it over personally with you"; but Roosevelt realized that his wish was an impossible dream because Stalin, directing the defense of Moscow, could not leave the Soviet Union for such a long, dangerous journey.[6] Likewise Roosevelt himself, caught up in the multitude of tasks required to turn the United States from peace to global war, could not leave Washington for a top level conference. Only Churchill dared leave British shores to sail for America. He surprised Roosevelt on December 9 with a proposal to come as soon as possible by warship to the United States for a conference to review Allied war plans on the highest executive level. Roosevelt replied with an invitation for Churchill to stay at the White House. After an eight-day voyage on H.M.S. *Duke of York*, Churchill and his staff arrived to confer with the Americans for the first time as Allies.

The Washington Conference, code-named ARCADIA, lasted from December 22, 1941, to January 14, 1942, and resulted in a basic agreement to defeat Hitler's armies before turning all of the Allied forces on Japan. A difference over the method of achieving this victory soon appeared. The American chiefs of staff preferred a direct assault on the continent of Europe as soon as a force could be trained and assembled. To mount such an assault would require a huge force with correspondingly high battle casualties. The British plan, drafted by Churchill during the Atlantic crossing, called for throwing a defensive ring around Europe, the capture of North Africa, and a series of landings at widely separated points in western Europe, the French coasts, the Balkans, and Italy. The American planners argued against launching such widely dispersed attacks, which would fritter away Allied strength through the failure to concentrate effort in a major offensive. The prospect of a landing in North Africa troubled them greatly because Roosevelt, eager to involve American troops in action across the Atlantic, seemed to side with Churchill and his staff. However, defeats in the Pacific and British losses to Erwin Rommel's Afrika Korps in North Africa forced the postponement of any immediate invasion of Africa. But the debate over the indirect versus the direct assault of Europe had only begun and would continue until a final settlement between Roosevelt, Churchill, and Stalin at the Teheran Conference.

At the ARCADIA Conference, British and American planners agreed on the creation of the Combined Chiefs of Staff—a standing committee that combined the United States and British chiefs of staff with headquarters at Washington. A Joint Staff Mission would represent the British chiefs of staff in Washington. Whenever Roosevelt and Churchill held conferences, the Combined Chiefs of Staff would meet at the same site to review the war situation and make any necessary plans, based upon the recommendations of the President and the prime minister. In the plenary sessions of their conferences, the Combined Chiefs of Staff would act in the role of advisers to Churchill and Roosevelt. The Combined

Chiefs of Staff helped to direct Anglo-American military strategy, to achieve unity of command, and so ensure a smoother functioning of the two separate military establishments. This unique device provided Britain and the United States with the means to achieve the close cooperation which military alliances had so often lacked.

Two Allies had joined in the Combined Chiefs of Staff; one Ally—the Soviet Union—had been omitted. The omission made the Russians feel left out of the decision-making process: whenever Roosevelt and Churchill met with the Combined Chiefs of Staff and without Stalin and his staff, the Soviet ruler could argue that Russia and her interests had been ignored. But geography, suspicions, conflicting political philosophies, and Stalin's personal domination of the entire Soviet system made integration of the Soviet staff into the Combined Chiefs of Staff an impossible task. The alternative to integration into this scheme of command was to fall back on ambassadors (whom Stalin ignored), special missions to Moscow, or as the last resort, meetings of the three government leaders. Until conditions permitted the three to confer, and until they could agree on the time, place, and need for such meetings, it would be necessary to use personal deputies such as Hopkins, Harriman, and Anthony Eden.

Before the Pearl Harbor attack and Churchill's voyage to the United States, it had become imperative for him to send Eden, his foreign secretary, on a long trip by sea and rail to Moscow to confer with Stalin. Anglo-Soviet affairs had deteriorated severely since September. Stalin's demand that Britain establish a second front in France or failing that send an army to Russia had gone unfulfilled. Consequently, new suspicions took root: the British would fight to the last drop of Russian blood and then make an Anglo-American peace without Russia. Because Churchill had to prevent any cause for Stalin accepting a separate peace should that be offered by Hitler, his grievances must be examined. Stalin's list included a clarification of British and Soviet war aims; plans for postwar organization for peace; an agreement on mutual aid against Hitler; Britain's failure to declare war on Finland, Hungary, and Rumania; and of course the standing demand for British troops in Russia failing the establishment of a second front in France. Eden's task of pacifying Stalin, given this list of grievances, would not be easy. He left London for Moscow on December 7, 1941.

When Eden arrived in Moscow on December 15, the United States Pacific Fleet was wrecked, Guam and Wake Island were under attack, and Japanese troops had landed on the northern Philippines. H.M.S. *Prince of Wales* and *Repulse* had been sunk off Malaya, Hong Kong was under siege, and Japanese forces were advancing on Singapore. Under these conditions, Britain and the United States had to resupply their own forces; little remained for the Soviet Union.

Eden's trip to Moscow launched him on his most important diplomatic mission since returning to the Foreign Office. Elected to Parliament after fighting in the trenches in World War I, he became the glamour boy of international diplomacy during the 1930s when he appeared in Geneva as spokesman for the British government. In 1935 he became foreign secretary at the age of thirty-eight, only to resign in 1938 after quarreling with Neville Chamberlain over appeasing Benito Mussolini. During the thirties Eden gained an undeserved reputation as a hardliner on the issue of appeasement. After Churchill became prime minister in 1940, he recalled Eden to the cabinet as secretary of state for war; later Eden replaced Lord Halifax as foreign secretary.

Eden arrived in Moscow weak from battling influenza during the trip on board ship. At his first meeting with Stalin, the Soviet ruler produced drafts of two treaties: one a military alliance, and the other an agreement on common action in dealing with European postwar problems and with the future of Germany. The second treaty contained a secret protocol in which Stalin had set forth his requirements for the postwar frontiers of the Soviet Union. They included restoring the Baltic States to the Soviet Union along with the territory taken from Finland in 1940 and from Rumania. The basis for the future Soviet-Polish frontier would be the Curzon Line. (Originally proposed at the time of the Paris Peace Conference in 1919, the Curzon Line ran farther to the west of the 1921–39 Russo-Polish frontier, but it generally corresponded with the Ribbentrop-Molotov line of 1939.) Poland would obtain East Prussia, and if France emerged from the war weakened, Britain could have bases in Boulogne and in Dunkirk. Stalin also suggested that Britain garrison bases in Norway, Sweden, Belgium, and the Netherlands.

Eden could not sign such an agreement without consulting his colleagues in London. Moreover, as he pointed out to Stalin, the British government could not enter into any secret arrangement relating to the postwar period without first consulting with Roosevelt. Stalin had no objection to Eden informing the U.S. government so that the Americans would also participate in his agreement.

Churchill, who learned of Stalin's proposals while he was on board ship bound for the United States, vetoed any frontier proposals. "We are bound to the United States not to enter into secret and special pacts," he telegraphed Eden. "To approach President Roosevelt with these proposals would be to court a blank refusal, and might cause lasting trouble on both sides."[7] Backed by his prime minister, Eden continued to resist Stalin's arguments for restoring the 1941 Soviet frontiers, and he left Moscow without any agreement on the question.

Eden's encounter with Stalin over the postwar frontiers of the Soviet Union foreshadowed a problem that would bedevil Russo-American relations for years, creating hostility and misunderstanding. Before the German armies had been driven from Russian soil, Stalin wanted to specify Soviet postwar claims to European lands and to nail down British consent to his demands without awaiting the end of the war; because the British needed Russia as an ally, they ought to accede to Stalin's demands. Moreover, if the British could neither send an army to Russia, as he had requested earlier, nor land armies on the continent of Europe to establish a second front, they ought not to begrudge him changes in frontiers favorable to Soviet interests. He would not be put off with arguments for postponing frontier claims until after the war had ended and a peace conference had convened. He wanted his claims recognized as quickly as possible, while Britain and the United States had greatest need for Soviet armies to battle the German armies. If the capitalists were truly sincere, they would accept his frontier demands.

Eden returned to London convinced that Britain and the United States ought to show their sincerity. He instructed Lord Halifax, British ambassador in Washington, to consult President Roosevelt and to propose that Britain and the United States assure Stalin of their support for Soviet acquisition of bases in territories close to the Soviet Union. The question of the Soviet Union absorbing the Baltic States, as well as portions of Finland and Rumania, ought not to be postponed to the peace conference. Eden wished to impress on the Soviet government that in matters of war and peace aims, the three nations should work for a tripartite solution. If the precedent of a three-nation agreement could be established for the postwar arrangements, Britain and the United States would be in a stronger position in dealing with Stalin. Eden feared that a refusal of Stalin's frontier demands could eventually mean the end of all prospects of Soviet cooperation in the future.

When Halifax, who had been the foreign secretary when Neville Chamberlain made his ill-fated journey to Munich, talked with Roosevelt, the President seemed favorably inclined toward Eden's proposals. Then Roosevelt's attitude hardened, and he rejected a secret agreement reestablishing the 1941 frontiers of the Soviet Union. This topic would be considered only at the end of the war when the Soviet Union would obtain full and legitimate security. Roosevelt planned to take up the matter directly with Stalin, but he could not travel to Moscow nor could Stalin leave the Soviet Union at that time. Roosevelt would handle the matter through Litvinov and Admiral William Standley, the new American ambassador in Moscow.

Because Roosevelt's optimism did not satisfy Eden, the foreign secretary convinced Churchill to make a direct appeal to the President. Already the Soviet ambassador, Ivan Maisky, had been prodding Eden about the delay in drafting an agreement on frontiers that would satisfy Stalin, who was now growing impatient. The order of the day issued to the Red Army on February 23, 1942, reflected this impatience in that it omitted all references to Anglo-American help for the Soviet Union—Soviet war aims were limited to the liberation of Russian territory but not the destruction of the Nazi regime. Stalin appeared to hint that unless the frontiers he wished were guaranteed by his allies, when the Soviet armies reached those frontiers, they would halt. Consequently on March 7, Churchill appealed to Roosevelt, insisting that because the war had reached so grave a stage, with disasters such as the fall of Singapore, they ought not to allow the Atlantic Charter to stand in the way of recognizing the Soviet frontiers as they had existed on June 22, 1941, even though the Russians may have liquidated some "hostile elements" when the Soviet armies occupied the Baltic States earlier in the war. (Here Churchill was alluding to mass executions.) He asked Roosevelt "to give us a free hand to sign the treaty which Stalin desires as soon as possible." He excused his appeal on the grounds that the German invasion of Russia would be renewed in the spring, and little could be done to help the only country that was heavily engaged with the German armies.[8]

Roosevelt replied by calling Litvinov to the White House on March 12 to inform him of his opposition to recognizing the 1941 Soviet frontiers. Disturbed by reports of negotiations concerning the postwar frontiers of Russia, Roosevelt said that he wanted "to explore more thoroughly what might be in Stalin's mind regarding this question." The President felt "put out by the fact that Stalin did not approach him directly in regard to a question in which he was necessarily vitally concerned." Refusing to subscribe to any treaty, even a public treaty dealing with definite frontiers, until the war had ended in victory, Roosevelt maintained that he was "100% in favor of facilitating the complete security of the Soviet Union." He promised Litvinov that "when the appropriate moment came after the successful conclusion of the war, the United States would support the efforts of the Soviet Union to achieve such measures of legitimate security." The President recognized the Soviet Union's need of a guarantee against being put in a position in which Germany once more would be able to attack her, fifteen or twenty years after the end of the war.

But Litvinov should call Stalin's attention to the provisions of the Atlantic Charter, which provided for the dismemberment of Germany. "What was involved was a basis of confidence and trust between the United States and the Soviet Union." According to Roosevelt, "the immediate and most important objective was to win the war." He would await, "with interest," whatever reply Stalin would send him through Litvinov.[9]

There was little here that would serve to cheer Stalin. He would just have to trust Roosevelt to support his claims regarding frontiers when the war ended. Roosevelt the politician dreaded negotiating over frontiers and territories before victory had been won because the negotiating process could lead to wrangling among allies. Who could know in 1942 what the political conditions might be when the shooting stopped? Roosevelt preferred to keep his options open and to await the outcome of the war before making commitments about Russia's frontier demands.

He imagined that he could avoid promising Stalin territorial concessions before a peace conference because of his own special relationship with the Soviet dictator. To Churchill, Roosevelt wrote: "I know that you will not mind my being brutally frank when I tell you that I think I can personally handle Stalin better than either your Foreign Office or my State Department. Stalin hates the guts of all your people. He thinks he likes me better, and I hope that he will continue to do so."[10] Churchill never commented on this strange message. Neither did Roosevelt ever explain the source of his information about Stalin liking him so much.

Roosevelt's boasting reflected arrogant confidence in his ability to persuade people to change their minds. He believed that his unique ability to charm people into accepting his point of view would work with Joseph Stalin. If his technique had worked so often with hardheaded American politicians, why not with Stalin? He could employ that charm best in a face-to-face meeting, but at the moment such a meeting was impossible. Roosevelt could only use Litvinov to pass on to Stalin his objections to making the frontier changes at this time.

But the President's opposition to Stalin's demands did not deter Eden, who believed that the haggling between London and Moscow in 1939 before the outbreak of war had pushed Stalin into making a deal with Hitler. Eden would not be responsible now for driving Stalin once more toward any agreement with Hitler. He believed the British government could not allow this matter to drag on any longer— "Anglo-Russian relations cannot be left in suspense at this critical moment in the war,"[11] he wrote to Halifax. Eden feared antagonizing Stalin by avoiding negotiating the frontiers. If Roosevelt could not approve of British actions, Eden could only hope that he would understand.

He drafted a short treaty which recognized the integrity of the territories of Britain and the Soviet Union prior to Hitler's attack on Russia; both nations would promise not to intervene in the other's affairs. Eden had already offered Stalin a treaty containing promises similar to Roosevelt's pledge of security for the Soviet Union to be delivered after the war had ended and Stalin had rejected it. The new treaty was necessary because Britain could not create a second front on the continent of Europe, nor could she ship vast quantities of war materials to the Soviet Union in 1942. But a treaty that pacified Stalin ought to be drafted and signed. It would have to serve as a substitute for the second front and the supplies.

By March 1942, Eden believed that he must defy Roosevelt and reach agreement with Stalin over the frontier question because he feared that if Stalin were denied the frontiers of June 22, 1941, he might make peace with Hitler or else become so hostile toward the Churchill government that it would fall. That Stalin might feel driven to such extremes could not be ruled out even in 1942 because in 1939 he had shocked the world by making a pact with Hitler. To Stalin, the frontiers he wanted could mean so much that he would choose any method to obtain a guarantee. Rather than risk Stalin's anger in 1942, Eden chose to defy Roosevelt.[12]

Stalin's frontier demands frustrated Roosevelt because in his conceit he thought that if he could only arrange a face-to-face meeting, he would charm Stalin into changing his demands and into accepting his promise to satisfy Soviet security needs after the guns had ceased firing. Roosevelt had convinced himself that he alone could bring about this change in the Soviet ruler's thinking. Once they had that meeting and talked about the frontier problem, there would no longer be any need for a treaty that could only antagonize allies fighting Hitler. But the conflict prevented the direct discussion that appeared so vital within four months after the Pearl Harbor attack and Hitler's declaration of war. Since they could not meet, Roosevelt had to find some means to circumvent the need for a treaty that would alter the frontiers of countries still occupied by German forces.

2

Invitation to a Conference

WHILE THE ALLIES QUARRELED over Soviet frontiers, a global war raged. Off the Florida coasts, U-boats sank American ships in broad daylight. Half a world away, Japanese troops took Singapore—the greatest symbol of British power in Asia. From that defeat British imperial strength would never recover. To the north, on Bataan Peninsula, Japanese troops at last compelled the surrender of the sick, weak American and Filipino soldiers. In Berlin, Hitler and his generals drafted plans for a spring offensive against the Soviet armies. In London and in Washington grave doubts arose over the survival of the Soviet regime in the face of the coming German assault.

During that gloomy spring of 1942, Franklin Roosevelt was concerned about the balance of power that would exist when the war at last had ended. By then British power would have been eroded, and the once great empire would be greatly diminished in size. (Already Roosevelt had suggested changes in the government of India which irritated Churchill.) With Britain weakened, he would have to deal with a powerful Soviet Russia. Consequently, in the argument between the Allies over the Soviet frontiers, Roosevelt chose to pacify Stalin by offering an invasion of the continent of Europe which he hoped would entice Stalin into dropping his frontier demands. Roosevelt found the means to appease Stalin through the results of American military planning.

The newly appointed chief of War Plans Division was a balding, quick-tempered little known man, General Dwight

D. Eisenhower, who late in February 1942 recommended, "We should at once develop, in conjunction with the British a definite plan for operations against northwest Europe." A month later, in a memorandum to Army Chief of Staff General George C. Marshall, Eisenhower argued that the principal target for the first major offensive should be Germany, to be attacked through western Europe. That same day at a White House luncheon, Marshall sold the President on the value of a plan for a cross-Channel invasion of Europe.

Immediately Roosevelt informed Churchill: "I have come to certain conclusions which are so vital that I want you to know the whole picture and to ask your approval." To explain the new plan, he would send Marshall and Harry Hopkins to London. "It is a plan which I hope Russia will greet with enthusiasm and, on word from you when you have seen Harry and Marshall, I propose to ask Stalin to send two special representatives to see me at once."[1]

In the plan for a second front, Roosevelt thought he had found the means to relieve the pressure on the British to accede to Stalin's demands for an immediate promise of frontiers and territory. For Roosevelt it was urgent that Stalin be diverted from his persistent demands that London and Washington concede to him now the Baltic States and other areas. If he could promise Stalin a second front, then he would defer his territorial and political demands until the end of the war. Unpleasant arguments with other allies, such as Poland, could be avoided. Moreover, the promise of a second front might keep Stalin from negotiating with Hitler in order to escape a losing war. This fear persisted, refusing to go away because in 1939 Hitler had been able to reach an agreement with Stalin. It must not be allowed to happen again.

Roosevelt also had domestic political considerations in mind when he decided on the plan for a second front. He needed military action in 1942 to galvanize American public opinion and to serve as evidence that the American people were committed to an all-out war against Germany. He feared that the series of defeats in the Pacific would generate a powerful demand that U.S. forces should concentrate only on victory in the war against Japan. Finally, American troops in action on the European continent would also quiet criticism

of Roosevelt's seeming ineffectiveness in directing the mo-
bilization of the nation's combat forces.

Marshall and Hopkins, bearing the second front plan, arrived in London on April 8. In the discussion which began
immediately with Churchill and his military chiefs, Marshall presented the plan, soon labeled the "Marshall Memorandum," to an audience that appeared sympathetic.
According to his memorandum, an Anglo-American force
would invade France between Le Havre and Boulogne some
time after April 1, 1943. However, should the war in Russia
become so desperate that the Soviet armies seemed on the
brink of collapse, or should the German armies in western
Europe suddenly weaken, then a modified, smaller Anglo-
American attack should be launched during September–October 1942.

The British military leaders, headed by General Sir Alan
Brooke, the precise, competent chief of the Imperial General Staff, accepted the Marshall Memorandum in principle,
but they had their private reservations about launching an
attack in the fall of 1942. They hesitated because, as a result
of the severe shortage in shipping, American troops would
not be available in large numbers by the fall of 1942. Consequently any Anglo-American invasion force that might then
land on the French beaches would be predominantly British
and the casualties also would be predominantly British. The
nightmare of Dunkirk and the slaughter on the Somme in
1916 were remembered all too painfully. To underline these
fearful memories, Churchill and his staff daily received reports of British losses and defeats in other theaters of war. A
daring German general, Erwin Rommel, with limited forces,
was chasing the British Eighth Army across the sands of North
Africa. The island fortress of Malta endured continuous air
attacks and suffered grievous losses. Japanese planes were
attacking Ceylon; in the Indian Ocean Japan's naval forces
outgunned units of the Royal Navy. Because of these peril-
ous conditions, British military and civilian leaders dreaded
a landing on French shores if it were to be a largely British
show. Nevertheless, Churchill and his generals did not reveal their reservations to Marshall and Hopkins but concealed them and expressed agreement in principle because

they wanted to promote harmony with their allies.

Back in Washington, the reports from Hopkins to Roosevelt implied that the talks were progressing smoothly and that the Marshall Memorandum had been accepted. Roosevelt received Hopkins's first report on April 11. That same day the President set in motion his plan to cool Stalin's demands. In a message to the Soviet leader, Roosevelt explained that distance, to his regret, made it practically impossible for them to meet at that time: "Such a meeting of minds in personal conversation would be greatly useful in the conduct of the war against Hitlerism. Perhaps if things go as well as we hope, you and I could spend a few days together next summer near our common border off Alaska. But in the meantime, I regard it as of the utmost military importance that we have the nearest possible approach to an exchange of views."

Roosevelt went on to explain that he had "a very important proposal involving the utilization of our armed forces in a manner to relieve your critical western front. This objective carries great weight with me."[2] Roosevelt meant the plan then being debated in London, which he hoped would take Stalin's mind off frontiers. Accordingly, the President asked Stalin to consider dispatching Vyacheslav Molotov and a reliable general to Washington as soon as possible. He offered to supply the transport plane in order that the Soviet visitors could make the round trip within two weeks.

After pondering the proposal for a week, Stalin agreed to send Molotov and the general for a meeting with Roosevelt no earlier than May 10–15, but on the way to Washington, Molotov would stop off in London for talks. As for the personal meeting with Roosevelt, Stalin commented: "I have no doubt that I shall be able to have a personal meeting with you to which I attach great importance, especially in view of the big problem of organizing the defeat of Hitlerism that confronts our two countries."[3] Roosevelt, not accustomed to being easily turned aside when he proposed personal meetings, tried again.

The new American ambassador, Admiral William Standley, brought Stalin another invitation from Roosevelt on April 23. Although there had been misunderstandings between the two nations, Standley told Stalin, the President believed that if he could only "sit down with Stalin and talk over problems there would never be lack of understanding." The President had instructed Standley to "suggest that he and Stalin meet somewhere in Alaska or Siberian waters sometime this summer to discuss the whole problem of world affairs."

Stalin thanked Standley for the message from Roosevelt, observing only that the proposed meeting had been discussed in their cables and that "he still had hopes that it could be brought about."[4]

Roosevelt never disclosed to Churchill that he had attempted to arrange a private meeting with Stalin because the blow to Anglo-American relations at that time could not be sustained. Roosevelt did not wish Churchill to be present since the prime minister could interfere with that personal relationship he so wanted to establish with Stalin. At that meeting, Roosevelt would have offered the second front as a substitute for frontier changes. Stalin, however, did not intend to meet with Roosevelt as long as he was in the position of seeking help and favors from the Americans. He would meet Roosevelt only after he had secured a better bargaining position. Why should Stalin meet Roosevelt, who had not produced a second front and who opposed the Soviet demands for frontiers of 1941? It would be more advantageous for Stalin to send his loyal henchman, Molotov, to discover what the American President had to offer. As for Roosevelt, he would have to be satisfied with meeting Molotov.

On his way to the United States, Molotov stopped off in London, even though Roosevelt would have preferred to meet with him first. Molotov, who arrived in London in a surly mood, brought up with Churchill and Eden the Anglo-Soviet treaty which Eden had debated with Stalin during the last days of December 1941 within the Kremlin walls.

Since their meeting, stories about the Soviet demands contained in the proposed treaty had leaked, prompting angry comments among the Tory members of Parliament. Churchill's private parliamentary secretary sent him a sampling of these comments:

"This is Munich again, but worse!"

"We are acquiescing in an aggression."

"Why have a treaty now? Why not wait to see the result of the German spring offensive when Russia may not be in such a strong bargaining position?"

He warned Churchill that the treaty was a matter that could develop into a major crisis. But Eden was not alarmed. "Opposition so far comes mainly from the most ardent supporters of Munich, but I agree that it may become serious," he wrote Churchill. "Munich was a collapse before a foe, and the betrayal by France of an ally. It has, of course, no resemblance to the present project."

But Churchill did not take the treaty so lightly after receiving a letter from Lord Chancellor Sir John Simon, who advised against signing an agreement with anyone that did not have the approval of the United States. He feared that the American contribution to Russia would suffer because of the resentment among Americans of Polish descent. "I really do not know how, if such a transaction came to be debated in the House of Lords, I could defend it." As the grumbling mounted, Churchill realized that even within the cabinet there was growing opposition to the treaty with the Soviet Union. "I do not want to face a bunch of resignations," he wrote Eden.[5]

From Washington there had even come reports that bad publicity in the United States over the treaty could strain relations between the three Allied powers. Churchill, unwilling to face unpleasantness with the Americans, directed Eden to produce a new draft that would be more satisfactory to Washington.

In response to these pressures, both parliamentary and American, Eden drafted a new version of the Anglo-Russian treaty, which amounted only to a twenty-five-year mutual assistance treaty without any mention of Soviet frontiers. Of course this proposal displeased "Mr. Brown," the code name for Molotov during his London stay, and he would not make any concession. "It was not sufficient simply to restore what existed before the war," he announced in a meeting at No. 10 Downing Street; "the Soviet government must secure their territory on their north-western and south-western frontiers."[6] Molotov had his instructions from the Kremlin and would not change.

Meanwhile, the American ambassador in London, Gilbert Winant, had been trying to arrange a meeting with Molotov through Ivan Maisky, the Soviet ambassador. Molotov rebuffed all of Winant's requests until late in the evening of May 25, when his appeal was at last granted. When Winant arrived at the Soviet Embassy, he announced to Molotov that he wanted to "talk turkey," which confused the Soviet interpreter who thought Winant wanted to talk about Turkey. After Winant had educated the interpreter about American colloquialisms, he began educating Molotov about the American view of the Soviet Union. In Britain, Winant explained, the public was ahead of the government in friendliness toward Russia, whereas in the United States the government was far ahead of the public in wishing to aid Russia. But in Washington, the best friends of Russia were bitterly opposed to recognizing Russian territorial demands, Winant explained. If the Russians persisted in their territorial demands in this treaty with Britain, it "would create the most serious embarrassment to the government of the United States and to Russia's best friends in America."

Here Molotov interrupted Winant. "I will substitute the Eden agreement for the treaty we had intended to sign," he said. "You can advise your government that we will not insist on the treaty."[7] It was a good moment for Winant to leave the Soviet Embassy. The next afternoon, Molotov appeared at the Foreign Office prepared to discuss Eden's treaty, which they finally signed on May 26.

Molotov had not changed his mind on his own initiative. Certainly he had asked his master in the Kremlin for fresh instructions. By the sudden shift in the Soviet position Stalin signaled a concession in the hope that Roosevelt would give a firm promise of launching a second front soon. Before Molotov left London for Washington, however, he received little in the way of a promise of a second front from Churchill. The matter was being studied and preparations were being made for a possible landing in 1942.

Vyacheslav Molotov, who arrived in Washington on May 29, was a genuine Bolshevik and a thorough believer in Marxist-Leninism: he had helped plan the revolution that overthrew the Provisional Government in November 1917.

Siding with Stalin in the struggle for power after Lenin's death in 1924, Molotov had worked his way into the Politburo, the elite group who governed the Soviet Union. His appointment as foreign minister in May 1939, succeeding Litvinov, signaled a change in Soviet foreign policy. In August 1939, Molotov negotiated the Nazi-Soviet Pact with Ribbentrop that allowed Hitler to begin World War II.

Molotov was the perfect assistant for Stalin, carrying out his master's orders with relentless tenacity. As a negotiator, said one observer, "Molotov had all the grace and conciliation of a totem pole."[8] A sour little man, with a bulging forehead, his cold, suspicious eyes peered out through a pince-nez. Whenever he traveled abroad, a squad of bodyguards protected him, and in Blair House and at Chequers he always slept with a loaded revolver beside his bed. It would take all of Roosevelt's charm to thaw Molotov.

At their second meeting, Roosevelt briefed Molotov on his concept of "The Four Policemen"—Britain, Soviet Russia, China, and the United States—who would police the postwar world and punish any nation that menaced the peace. All other nations would be disarmed and the four policemen alone would enjoy the use of armaments. Molotov observed that some nations, such as Poland and Turkey, not to mention France, might be cool to such an arrangement. Roosevelt obviously hoped that the "Four Policemen" concept would appeal to Stalin. It was a topic they could discuss privately whenever they had their personal meeting.

Molotov then asked the President if he was acquainted with the terms of the treaty which he recently had signed with the British in London. Roosevelt knew the treaty well. He expressed delight that the frontier question had not been mentioned in the document because "there might be a proper time for raising this question, though the present was not the moment." But Molotov reminded him that the Soviet government had a very definite conviction in the opposite direction. Nevertheless, they "had deferred to the British preference and to what he understood to be the attitude of the President." Molotov hinted that Stalin still expected a second front because of his deference to the President's position on the frontier question by dwelling at length on his government's view of the vital need for a second front to draw off the Nazi forces for the Red Army.

In the session on May 30, with Chief of Naval Operations Admiral Ernest J. King and General Marshall present, the discussion focused on the second front. Molotov warned that if the Russian armies could not hold out against the Nazi onslaught, German strength would only grow, helped by the food and raw materials from the Caucasus. "The war would thus become tougher and longer," observed Molotov. But if the Allies could draw off forty German divisions in 1942 through a second front, the balance of power would be so changed that the Soviet Union might even defeat Hitler's armies that same year. "His government wanted to know," Molotov reported, "in frank terms what position we take on the question of a second front, and whether we were prepared to establish one. He requested a straight answer."

With his chiefs of staff present, Roosevelt put the question to General Marshall: Could they tell Stalin that a second front was being prepared? Marshall, caught between the grim Molotov and the smiling President, could only answer, "Yes." Roosevelt added that Molotov could tell Stalin to "expect the formation of a second front this year." Marshall tried to qualify the statement that the President had dragged out of him by underlining the shortage of shipping created by the need to send troops and equipment to the British Isles while at the same time using ships to transport supplies and equipment to Russia by way of Murmansk. But Marshall's qualification failed to lessen the impact of what seemed to Molotov a promise of a second front.

In the final meeting with Molotov, on June 1, Roosevelt declared: "We hoped and expected to set up a second front in 1942." Later he again declared that the Americans expected to set up a second front in 1942, and as the meeting ended, he repeated the expectation of establishing a second front in 1942. Only once did he try to qualify his promise by stressing the need for more shipping to help the buildup for the second front, shipping that would have to be diverted from carrying munitions to Russia. "The Soviets could not eat their cake and have it too," he reminded Molotov.[9] With a promise of a second front thrice repeated, Molotov left Washington to return to Moscow by way of London.

Roosevelt had hoped that his assurance of a second front in 1942, which he repeatedly promised to Molotov, would curtail Stalin's demands for a treaty negotiated and signed during the war that would set down the Soviet postwar frontiers. If Stalin's wishes about territories were to be met during the war, suspicions and tensions among the other Allies could grow and divide the United Nations. But Stalin's acceptance of the Anglo-Russian treaty without specific frontiers merely postponed a crucial question. Roosevelt would encounter it again at Teheran.

The meeting with Molotov disappointed Roosevelt, for he had never negotiated and conferred with anyone exactly like him. In the discussions with Molotov, the famous Roosevelt style was cramped by the need to work through two interpreters, Samuel Cross and V. N. Pavlov, and by the interminable periods waiting for the interpreters to finish their work.

For Roosevelt, a meeting with Molotov was a poor substitute for the one he wanted with Stalin. At lunch on May 30, he told Molotov that "there was, however, one Russian whom he looked forward to meeting, and that was Mr. Stalin, whose masterly leadership was carrying his country through so serious a crisis." There is no record of Molotov's reply. Roosevelt could only hope that his compliment would help to bring about the meeting for which he yearned.

When Molotov returned to London after his Washington visit, Churchill, with the full support of the War Cabinet, gave him a note stating: "We are making preparations for a landing on the Continent in August or September 1942. . . . It is impossible to say in advance whether the situation will be such as to make this operation feasible when the time comes. We can therefore give no promise in the matter, but provided that it appears sound and sensible we shall not hesitate to put our plans into effect." Then Molotov flew to Moscow, where he commented to the British ambassador about "Anglo-Saxon promises," and hinted at the cruel disillusionment if these promises were broken. Apparently Roosevelt's promises had their effect on him because there were reports that he had been talking about the establishment of a second front in 1942.

As a result of the promises made to Molotov about a second front, Churchill considered it wise to fly to Washington for another meeting with Roosevelt and the Combined Chiefs of Staff. Sweltering through hot June days, the two men at last agreed that Allied forces would land in Europe in 1942 if a sound plan could be devised that promised success. If such a plan could not be devised, then an alternative must be found. To that end, they ordered more study of Operation GYMNAST—an invasion of North Africa. But in the midst of their deliberations, word came that Tobruk, the British fortress in Libya, had fallen to Rommel. Action was indeed required.

When Churchill and his staff returned to London, they intensified their study and soon concluded that an invasion of France in 1942 (code-named SLEDGEHAMMER) had little chance of success. Later in July there was more argument over the invasion with General Marshall and Admiral King in London. Before the month was out, a planning decision had been made: North Africa in 1942. At that time, Churchill, lacking confidence in the British Army after a string of disasters and fearing another Tobruk or Singapore, would not agree to SLEDGEHAMMER, for which Britain would have to provide the bulk of the troops.[10] Because Churchill, the British chiefs of staff, and the War Cabinet opposed SLEDGEHAMMER, there would not be any invasion of France in the fall of 1942 as Roosevelt had promised Stalin. The decision meant that someone would have to undertake the task of informing Stalin that Roosevelt's promise would not be kept.

This unpleasant task fell to Churchill. He must travel to Moscow and there inform Stalin about the broken promise and change in plans. Roosevelt, who had claimed that he understood Stalin so well, never mentioned the change in plans in his correspondence with him. Instead, Churchill had to endure an angry, bitter encounter with Stalin in August. With Averell Harriman representing Roosevelt, Churchill had to withstand taunts and insults from Stalin over the Allied failure to fulfill the promise of a second front in France in 1942. Great was Stalin's anger because he had dropped his demands for frontiers and land in return for a promised second front and now there would be none in 1942.

At their first meeting, Stalin asked why the British and Americans were afraid of the Germans. Patiently, Churchill explained the reasons for the Allies' decision not to open a second front in France in 1942 because it would not help the Russians. More important, a great offensive was being planned for 1943. Gradually Churchill swung the discussion around to the new invasion, TORCH, planned for late October in North Africa. After listening intently to Churchill's description of the invasion plans, "May God prosper this undertaking," exclaimed the atheist Stalin.

On the night of August 14, Stalin hosted a Kremlin banquet. The mood, however, was not festive but somber and quiet. Stalin ate some cheese, a single potato, and sipped wine from a small vodka glass. During the toasting session, Harriman explained to Stalin that Roosevelt hoped to meet him soon. Stalin conceded that it was important that they meet. When could Stalin meet the President? "In the winter I am not so preoccupied," Stalin replied. "Perhaps in the Far East, perhaps in western Europe." Harriman explained that Roosevelt disliked flying and would not want to leave the United States until after the congressional elections in November. "Perhaps Iceland in December," said Stalin. Harriman agreed that December would be suitable for Roosevelt but dangerous for Stalin. Such a flight did not worry Stalin because he had good airplanes.[11]

On Churchill's last night in the Kremlin, August 15, Stalin invited him into his private apartment for a late night supper where Churchill met Stalin's pretty daughter, Svetlana, who would one day flee to the United States.

During the talk—which lasted until two-thirty in the morning—when the possibility of a Roosevelt-Stalin meeting again surfaced, Churchill tried to promote an invitation for himself. His host graciously consented to Churchill being present. Before the late supper ended, Churchill had invited Stalin to visit England on the way to Iceland for his meeting with Roosevelt.

To Roosevelt, Churchill later reported: "I feel that I have established a personal relationship which will be helpful. On the whole, I am definitely encouraged by my visit to Moscow. I am sure that the disappointing news I brought could

not have been imparted except by me personally without
leading to really serious drifting apart. It was my duty to go." [12]
These words could only have irritated Roosevelt, who had
tried and failed to arrange a meeting with Stalin. Churchill
had gotten in first.

Churchill's news that there would be no invasion of the
continent of Europe in 1942 angered Stalin because the Soviet Union desperately needed supplies which he thought
the capitalist Allies owed the Soviet Union, now under assault by Hitler's armies. But U-boat attacks on convoys to
Russia were so deadly that the Admiralty had suspended
transporting supplies until the long Arctic days became
shorter. One of the worst attacks came when Convoy PQ 17
lost 22 ships out of 33. Such losses meant little to Stalin when
German armies were advancing into the Russian interior.

A German offensive had been launched on June 28, and
by late July German armies held the Don River for its entire
length. On August 23, the 16th Panzer Division reached the
Volga north of Stalingrad. Many Russian units had disinte-
grated under the shock of the German onslaught as officers
deserted their troops and soldiers fled from the battlefield.
Panzer units had even pushed deep into the Caucasus
Mountains. Yet convoys to Russia were resumed, only to be
canceled again in October because of the sinkings. In addition to the U-boat attacks, shortages in Allied shipping, the
supply needs of American and British forces, production
problems, and bureaucratic mistakes all combined to restrict
the flow of supplies to the Soviet Union during the fall
of 1942.

In a letter to Henry Cassidy—an Associated Press correspondent based in Moscow—which was printed on the front
page of *Pravda* on October 5, Stalin lashed out at his allies:
"In comparison with the assistance which the Soviet Union,
drawing off the main forces of the German fascist troops is
rendering to its allies, the assistance from the Allies to the
Soviet Union is meanwhile of little effect. To expand and
improve this assistance only one thing is required: complete
and timely fulfillment by Allies of their obligations."

Stalin's outburst reflected his frustrations and fears over
the battle raging at Stalingrad, which threatened to become

a German victory. Stalin needed a scapegoat and the Allies were available, particularly the British, who were denounced for treating Rudolf Hess as a prisoner instead of a war criminal. (Deputy leader of the Nazi party, he had flown to Britain on May 10, 1941.) Stalin could also blame the Allies because Roosevelt's promise to Molotov about a second front in 1942 had gone unfulfilled. The Soviet public had been led to believe that a second front was imminent and that it would compel the Germans to withdraw.

At this point, communication with the Soviet leader all but ceased. Churchill cabled his worries to Roosevelt when messages to Stalin brought only a cryptic "Thank you." Less concerned than his British ally, Roosevelt thought the Russians "do not use speech for the same purposes that we do." Eventually Stalin replied to Roosevelt, explaining that he had fallen behind in his correspondence because of the Stalingrad battle.

By the time that Stalin wrote his next letter to Cassidy, British and American forces had begun landing in North Africa on November 8. To Cassidy's written question about the Soviet view of the Allied campaign in North Africa, Stalin answered: "The Soviet view of this campaign is that it represents an outstanding fact of major importance demonstrating the growing might of the armed forces of the Allies and opening the prospect of disintegration of the Italo-German coalition in the nearest future." The anti-British campaign in the Soviet press stopped, and Soviet writers began to call the United States and Britain "Our Allies."

Roosevelt, buoyed by the presence of American soldiers at last fighting across the Atlantic, proposed to Stalin that "before any further step is taken, both Churchill and I want to consult with you and your staff" over future operations in the Mediterranean. Stalin responded: "I share your view that the time is ripe for appropriate consultations between the general staffs of the U.S.A., Great Britain, and the U.S.S.R." To Churchill, Roosevelt went further: it should be a "military strategical conference," to be held within the next month or six weeks in either Cairo or Moscow. The three leaders would be represented by a small group, with General Marshall representing Roosevelt. Each delegation was to have no more than three members. The conference would plan for the next step in the assault by the Allies. It would also ensure that Stalin could not complain that he had been ignored.

But Churchill, with more experience in face-to-face dealings with the Russians, poured cold water on Roosevelt's idea. A Russian delegation in Cairo would be so tied up that it would have to refer every point of substance back to Stalin, whereas a conference in Moscow would suffer much less delay. However, Churchill wanted the British and American missions to reach a joint, agreed viewpoint before traveling to Moscow.

In advance of such a meeting, Churchill knew the Soviet views. "They will say to us both 'How many German divisions will you be engaging in the summer of 1943? How many have you engaged in 1942?' " The Russians would demand a second front in 1943, with an Anglo-American invasion of the European continent. These demands could only be met by national leaders or by shipping experts who would be present. He did not see how the chiefs of staff could be spared for so long a time.

Then Churchill proposed a conference of the three leaders. "Stalin talked to me in Moscow in the sense of being willing to come to meet you and me somewhere this winter, and he mentioned Iceland. I pointed out that England was no farther and more convenient. He neither accepted nor rejected the idea." Churchill suggested a conference held on ships lying alongside each other off Iceland. A suitable vessel would be provided for Stalin from which he could fly the Soviet flag. It seemed to Churchill that Stalin had appeared eager to travel in one of the Soviet airplanes, and such a conference would provide him with the opportunity. "Only at a meeting between principals will real results be achieved."

The prospect of deciding strategic problems personally with Stalin delighted Roosevelt. To Churchill he proposed to take a small staff—Army, Air, and Naval chiefs of staff—Harriman and Hopkins. No State Department representative; no press. Roosevelt suggested that they meet some time after January 15, 1943, in Algiers or near Khartoum. Iceland or Alaska would be impossible for him, and for Stalin as well.

He rejected anything resembling a joint Anglo-American meeting prior to conferring with Stalin—"I do not want to give Stalin the impression that we are settling everything between ourselves before we meet him." After all, he insisted, they understood each other so well that "prior conferences between us are unnecessary." When the meeting with Stalin opened, they would "work things out from day to day."

The prospect of meeting with Stalin so pleased Roosevelt that he sent the Soviet leader a message the same day as his message to Churchill. "I believe that he will accept," Roosevelt wrote Churchill. "I prefer a comfortable oasis to the raft at Tilsit," alluding to the meeting of Napoleon and Czar Alexander I in July 1807, when they met on a raft in the Niemen River to make peace and decide the politics of Europe.

Churchill, overjoyed at Roosevelt's proposal, replied, "It is good of you to come and I will meet you anywhere." He too sent a message to Stalin urging him to join in the meeting. He asked Roosevelt if Marshall, King, and Arnold could come to London for advance preparations, "Otherwise Stalin will greet us with the question, 'Have you then no plan for the second front in Europe promised me for 1943?'" Churchill also wanted to bring Anthony Eden and an assortment of people, including chief of staff, personnel from the cypher staff, a map room staff, and secretaries, totaling about twenty-five.[13]

Roosevelt dispatched Harriman to London with instructions to inform Churchill that Eden could not come to the meeting. If Eden came, as foreign secretary, then Roosevelt would have to allow Cordell Hull, the Secretary of State, to attend. This was not a prospect that Roosevelt relished because Hull was often a nuisance. He could be rigid and stubborn, and he would have his set of questions to be answered that would not suit Roosevelt. Hull would so cramp Roosevelt's style that he would be unable to achieve that longed-for private meeting with Stalin. No one would attend from the State Department. Above all, Harriman must make Churchill understand that Roosevelt rejected any preliminary conference with the British before the meeting with Stalin.

After three talks with Churchill, Harriman felt "thoroughly beaten up," but he had convinced the prime minister that Eden must be dropped from the meeting to ensure that Hull would be absent. But Roosevelt's refusal to reach an agreement in advance on plans to propose to Stalin still troubled Churchill.

On December 2, Roosevelt told Stalin that because of the need to reach strategic decisions soon, "you, Churchill and I should have an early meeting." A conference of military leaders from the three nations would be insufficient because of the need to refer final decisions to their superiors. Roosevelt wanted tentative decisions about procedures to be adopted if the German armies collapsed. He confessed that the compelling reason for the meeting "is that I am very anxious to have a talk with you." Roosevelt proposed that the three leaders meet secretly in a secure place in Africa that would be convenient to all three men. The meeting ought to take place between January 15–20, 1943. He considered Iceland or Alaska out of the question at that time of year. Perhaps they could meet in southern Algeria or near Khartoum—places that could be easily put "off limits" to visitors and to the press. He hoped that Stalin would favor his proposal because "I can see no other way of reaching the vital strategic decisions which should be made soon by all of us together."

Stalin replied quickly, explaining that although he had said that he favored such a meeting, he could not leave the Soviet Union. "I must say that things are now so hot that it is impossible for me to absent myself for even a single day," he wrote Roosevelt. "Just at present important military operations of our winter campaign are developing and they will not diminish in January. More probably the contrary will be true."

Still Roosevelt did not give up his quest for a meeting with Stalin. He suggested North Africa, about March 1, because "there were matters of vital importance to be discussed between us," questions relating to Germany, North Africa, and the Far East. Roosevelt wanted a discussion that would be concerned with political matters which might suddenly become critical, should there be a sudden collapse of German might. But Stalin ignored Roosevelt's request for a meeting about such political questions. Once more he refused to leave the Soviet Union "in the immediate future, or even in early March." He based his refusal to meet with Churchill and with Roosevelt on the press of matters at the front—Stalingrad. What subjects were so important that he must leave the Soviet Union when the terrible battle still raged around Stalingrad? As for the second front, Stalin expressed confidence that the promise of a second front made by Roosevelt and by Churchill would be kept in the spring of 1943.[14]

Stalin's excuse that the direction of the battle at Stalingrad prevented him from meeting with Roosevelt and Churchill also concealed a search for a negotiated settlement between the Soviet Union and Germany. Such an arrangement seemed justified because the second front had not developed and because Britain and the United States preferred that Russia and Germany destroy each other—so Stalin may have argued. As the Soviet armies encircled the Sixth German Army at Stalingrad, in a public speech on November 6, 1942, Stalin declared that "it is not our aim to destroy all organized military force in Germany, for every literate person will understand that this is not only impossible . . . but . . . also inexpedient from the point of view of victory."[15] Here Stalin was signaling to the German military class: those who had arranged the deal with the Soviet government in the 1920s which allowed the German army to begin secretly rearming on Soviet territory in order to bypass the restrictions in the Treaty of Versailles. More than any group in Germany, the military caste should have realized by then the cost of the conflict which Hitler had thrust on Germany. A negotiated settlement with the Soviet Union, similar to that reached during the Weimar Republic, could bring peace.

In December, Peter Kleist, an official in the German Foreign Ministry whose duties often took him to Sweden, learned through German friends in Stockholm that a man in the city with close connections to the Soviet Embassy in Stockholm wanted to meet him. On December 14, in a log cabin on a cliff overlooking the Baltic, Kleist met Edgar Clauss, a businessman who had lived in Latvia, Lithuania, and Germany. According to the story which Clauss told Kleist, the Soviet leaders were ready to reach a settlement with Germany in order to end the fighting. "I can guarantee that if Germany agrees to the 1939 frontier, you will have peace in a week." [16]

Within weeks, a Soviet-sponsored "German People's Radio" reported that a strong peace movement was growing among Germans of every class. The Moscow press carried reports of a secret conference of these Germans, who were said to be seeking peace. All of these developments, real and imagined, amounted to signals from the Soviet Union for peace negotiations.

So while Stalin awaited a reply from the Germans about his signals for peace negotiations, he refused to meet with Roosevelt and Churchill. To have joined in a meeting with them could very well have undermined any negotiations that could have led to a cessation of fighting and the restoration of the 1941 frontiers between Germany and the Soviet Union. These were the same frontiers that Roosevelt and Churchill refused to recognize in a treaty. Now with German forces losing the battle of Stalingrad, it was a good moment to learn if Hitler was inclined to negotiate a deal similar to that reached in August 1939. Any meeting with Roosevelt and Churchill would only have wrecked the negotiations.

Had Stalin left Moscow in the final phase of the Stalingrad battle to join Roosevelt and Churchill in a conference, the results might well have been a badly strained alliance. Churchill and his generals were unwilling to hazard a cross-channel attack in 1943. As for Roosevelt, he was unsure of where the next major blow ought to be struck by the Anglo-American forces. In a meeting of the three leaders in January 1943, Stalin would have argued fiercely for a second front in 1943 and insisted on an unconditional promise, which Churchill would have been unwilling to give. Any promise to invade the Continent from the west in the summer of 1943 would have required the suspension of operations in the Pacific theater in order to build up sufficient forces for an invasion of western Europe. Such a change in American operations could have brought charges that Roosevelt was about to betray the American soldiers and sailors in the Pacific and that he had forgotten those who had died at Pearl Harbor and on Bataan.

Consequently the meeting in North Africa now became a meeting of two—Churchill and Roosevelt, at Casablanca in January 1943, during the final days of the battle for Stalingrad. The news of the decisions reached by Roosevelt and Churchill did not cheer Stalin. In the first communication sent by them to Stalin, they announced their intention of clearing Axis forces out of North Africa, followed by opening up the Mediterranean for military traffic and coupled with a heavy air attack on Axis targets in southern Europe. Large-scale amphibious operations would be launched in the Mediterranean as soon as possible. Strong American forces would be concentrated in the British Isles which, together with British troops, would prepare "to re-enter the continent of Europe as soon as practicable." They also planned to increase the day and night bombing offensive against Germany. Of course they would also increase operations against Japan. But it was a vague plan that did not please Stalin. "I should be grateful," he wrote, "if you would inform me of the concrete operations planned and of their timing."

The reply, dispatched by Churchill, still did not satisfy Stalin. Roosevelt and Churchill hoped that the Allied forces would drive Axis forces from Tunisia by April 1943; the Allies expected their troops to seize Sicily in July and begin clearing the Mediterranean of enemy troops, while at the same time bringing about the collapse of the Italian government. Such operations, however, would utilize all of the landing craft and the shipping that could be collected in the Mediterranean area, as well as all of the troops that had been trained in assault landings. Still, Churchill promised that the Allies would push preparations for a cross-Channel operation in August 1943, although he noted that shipping and assault landing craft shortages could delay the operation. If that happened, the cross-Channel attack would be prepared with stronger forces for the autumn. Even then its timing would depend upon the strength of the German defenses along the coast.

The news that a second front could come no earlier than August 1943, and then only if conditions were favorable, led Stalin to warn his allies that the German army had intensified preparations for operations against the Soviet Union in the spring and summer. He thought it essential "that the blow from the west be no longer delayed," and warned his allies "of the grave danger with which further delay in opening a second front in France is fraught."[17] The vague promises of a second front did not lessen Stalin's mistrust of Roosevelt and Churchill.

Already he had signaled his irritation with his allies through the twenty-fifth anniversary celebration of the Red Army, late in February 1943. In his pronouncements, broadcast throughout the Soviet Union, Stalin purposely omitted any mention of the aid the United States and Britain had given to the Soviet Union, stressing that, "in view of the absence of a second front the Red Army alone is bearing the whole weight of the war." London and Washington carefully noted the omission. Having rejected all invitations to a high-level conference, Stalin now publicly ignored the contributions of the Allies to the common cause. More strikingly, there was a sudden lessening in the offensive operations of the Soviet armies in March 1943. Did the lull in the fighting mean that the Russian armies would stop at the 1941 frontiers?

3
A Second Mission to Moscow

IN THE LIBRARY OF Spaso House, the American Embassy in Moscow, Admiral William Standley spoke with a few American reporters on the afternoon of March 8. The ambassador told them about his recent trip to Kuibyshev and about living conditions there. (During the fall of 1941, when German troops were advancing on Moscow, the diplomatic corps and many government departments had been evacuated to that city.) None of the reporters took notes as Standley spoke because they had heard about Kuibyshev before. It was not news.

Eddy Gilmore of the Associated Press asked: "We're sending quite a lot of stuff over here, aren't we, Mr. Ambassador?" Standley replied that Gilmore was correct.

"Ever since I've been here," Standley then said, slowly, "I've been carefully looking for recognition in the Russian press of the fact that they are getting material help not only through Lend-Lease, but through Red Cross and Russian-American Relief, but I've yet to find any acknowledgement of that."

Edward Page, the second secretary of the embassy, swallowed twice and suddenly looked very ill.

"Is that off the record, Mr. Ambassador, or may we use it?" asked Henry Shapiro of United Press.

"Use it," replied Standley, as the reporters scrambled for pencils and paper to take down the ambassador's statement. He told them that the American public knew relief and other supplies were being shipped to the Soviet Union, but the Russian people did not realize this. It was unfair, he declared, to mislead the American people, who were giving millions of dollars and thought they were aiding the Russian people. At the same time the Russian people did not realize that the aid came from the Americans, acting out of friendship for the Russians, who were unaware of this fact.

There was a pause. A reporter asked why the Soviet government had not informed the people about the aid.

"The Soviet authorities," Standley answered, "seem to be endeavoring to create the impression at home as well as abroad that they are fighting the war alone and with their own resources rather than to acknowledge aid from anyone else."

There was a question about the status of the Lend-Lease legislation. Standley thought that the bill had only just passed the Foreign Affairs Committee. "Congress is rather sensitive," he said as the reporters took down his remarks. "It is generous and big hearted so long as it feels that it is helping someone. But give it the idea that it is not—there might be an entirely different story."

Then a reporter asked if there had been any change in the situation regarding the exchange of military information with the Russians. Standley replied: "There is no obvious change in the Russian attitude regarding the exchange of information on the conduct of the war."[1] His news conference ended at that point.

The reporters scrambled from Spaso House to the Moscow subway and from there to the Foreign Ministry, where they handed their hastily written stories to the censors. Surprised, confused, and angry at the stories, the censors telephoned to higher authorities before passing them. Five hours later, after approval probably came from the Kremlin, the chief censor, his face white with anger, passed the stories. (His mother had starved to death in Leningrad.)

Even before the stories of Standley's press conference had appeared in the American newspapers on March 9, Sumner Welles, Acting Secretary of State, cabled Standley: "A United Press report alleges you have stated in press interview that the Russian people had no knowledge of Lend-Lease, Red Cross, and other incidental services rendered to Russia by this country. Please telegraph substance of any such remarks if made."

At his press conference on March 9, Welles had no comment to reporters' questions about Standley's remarks other than to state that the ambassador had spoken without prior consultation with the State Department. To the reporters, Welles announced that understanding and trust existed among the United Nations and whatever Standley may have said had never been intended to cast doubt on that trust and understanding.

That evening in Russia, Soviet citizens listening to the radio heard an official statement featuring a report by Edward Stettinius, Lend-Lease administrator, on the fulfillment of the Lend-Lease Act. The official statement had been read at dictation speed so that editors of provincial Soviet newspapers could take it all down. On March 15, *Pravda* devoted half of its foreign news coverage to discussing the Stettinius report.

When Molotov talked with Standley on March 10, the usually grim old Bolshevik was quite mild but to the point. The Soviet press, he maintained, had printed all the statements published in the United States and in Britain about military aid to the Soviet Union. The Soviet people knew first hand about the aid from the United States. Stalin and he had often expressed their gratitude.

Standley explained that he wanted recognition for the relief supplies that had been paid for, not by the government, but by the American people. Lend-Lease, he argued, was a business deal between governments, but relief represented the goodwill and friendship of the American people. However, since Molotov wanted to bring up the question of Lend-Lease, as American ambassador, he had no direct official information on that topic except for the statement which Stalin had made to the newspaper correspondent, Cassidy, in October 1942. Aside from that statement, Standley told Molotov, he had failed to obtain any information about the benefit of Lend-Lease to the Soviet Union. When Standley voiced his hope that his remarks would not harm American-Soviet relations, Molotov replied: "No, I do not believe so; perhaps they will have a useful effect in America." The effect of his remarks would be felt most by the ambassador.

William H. Standley, a California rancher's son, and a Naval Academy graduate, had seen his first action in the Philippine Insurrection at the turn of the century. He had retired from the United States Navy in 1937, after a career that had taken him from commanding destroyers to Chief of Naval Operations. His retirement ended in 1939 when Roosevelt appointed him a special naval adviser to the President. In 1941, after visiting the Soviet Union as a member of the Harriman mission, Standley returned an admirer of the Russian people in their battle against the Nazi invaders. When Washington decided it needed a new man in the Moscow Embassy, Roosevelt called on his old friend. It seemed a wise choice, for he was a naval officer with broad experience who could help speed aid to Russia.

Arriving in Moscow in February 1942, Standley soon learned about the frustrations and the aggravations in dealing with Soviet officials. They made promises but seldom kept them. Complaints came quickly if American supplies were late or incomplete, while Standley's requests for information were ignored. The Soviets doled out information reluctantly but wished to be fully informed of Allied intentions. Russian armies had gained knowledge of German weapons, tactics, and methods which could save the lives of American soldiers, yet Soviet authorities refused to share this information with either the British or American Allies. Such seeming ingratitude led an old sailor like Standley to act in a most undiplomatic way.

Western diplomats sympathized with Standley's outburst. From London, Averell Harriman reported that his British and American friends were secretly pleased that Standley had spoken out in Moscow even if he had been indiscreet. Harriman sensed a growing feeling in London that "we are building up trouble for the future by allowing the Russians to kick us around." In Moscow, Standley's words delighted the British ambassador, Archibald Clark Kerr, who could not help being pleased by his American colleague's statement. "This may teach the Russians to be a little more grateful than they have been in the past for all they have been getting." Standley had reacted to a "growing sense of frustration and irritation which is common to all here," Clark Kerr noted. "Today the ambassador is in doubt whether he had been altogether wise. His mood is a mixture of school-boy-ish mischief about the sensation he has made and of wonder whether it will lead to his recall."[2]

Standley's press conference aroused the Washington politicians. Sol Bloom, chairman of the House Committee on Foreign Affairs, took the floor of the House to denounce him. Senator Tom Connally, the powerful chairman of the Senate Committee on Foreign Relations, declared: "It does not lie with me to criticize the ineptness of our ambassador to Russia. . . . But the information which has come to me—not in a great volume—convinces me that the Russian people and the Russian government do know of the aid which the United States is undertaking to get to Russia." At his press conference on March 13, Roosevelt declined to comment on Standley's statements.

Russians resented Standley's comments because they were suffering heavier casualties than either the British or the Americans. The Soviet government, however, did not want to admit publicly its dependence upon western capitalists for supplies and equipment. One Russian growled: "We've lost millions of people, and they want us to crawl on our knees because they send us spam. And has the 'warmhearted' Congress ever done anything that wasn't in its interests? Don't tell me that Lend-Lease is charity."[3]

But the March 8 press conference meant that Standley had to be replaced. First, however, Roosevelt and Hopkins needed someone to repair the damage they believed Standley had done to Soviet-American relations through his remarks to reporters. They turned to a lawyer-diplomat whom they believed would be welcomed in Moscow and who would pacify Stalin: Joseph E. Davies, American ambassador in Moscow in 1937–38, and the author of *Mission to Moscow*, which had only recently been made into a film.

The son of a Wisconsin wagonmaker, Davies became a successful lawyer after entering politics and helping swing Wisconsin to Woodrow Wilson in the 1912 election. While working in Washington for the Wilson administration, Davies met a tall, handsome young politician from New York,

Franklin D. Roosevelt. Davies lost the race for a Wisconsin Senate seat in 1918, so he established a Washington law firm specializing in tax cases and became a millionaire. In the election of 1932, he campaigned enthusiastically for Roosevelt but did not ask for a cabinet post as did many who had worked for the victor. Davies's divorce after over thirty years of marriage cost him more than a million dollars, and his remarriage to Marjorie Post Hutton, the General Foods heiress, in 1935 gave him headlines in the tabloids. In 1936 Davies worked hard for Roosevelt's reelection, contributing generously to the campaign fund and expecting an ambassadorship as reward. When the hoped-for call came from the White House, he was asked which post he would like. He wanted Russia or Germany. Roosevelt told him that he could go to Russia and prepare to go to Germany later. The President wanted Davies to improve Soviet-American relations and to wrestle with the debts still owed the United States while gathering information on Russian political, industrial, and military affairs.

Within twenty-four hours of Davies's arrival in Moscow, he had driven the professional diplomats on his staff to consider resigning in a body when he shocked them by his cocksure attitude that he could settle Soviet-American problems where everyone else had failed. He handled his new job like a good lawyer: he had a new client, the Soviet Union, and he would defend his client with all of his talent and knowledge. However, as an ambassador, Davies was more suited to act as Roosevelt's personal agent, someone outside the State Department who would work wholeheartedly for "the Boss" and report directly to him. For such a task, Davies was ideal. His mission: to win Stalin's confidence and make the Soviet Union appear more appealing to the American people. Soon Davies and his wife were eager advocates of Stalin's regime.

The new American ambassador became a conscientious observer of the show trials which Stalin staged during the 1930s to rid himself of every potential opponent and to show Soviet citizens the dangers of opposing his rule. While Davies watched the trials, George Kennan, embassy secretary, whispered a translation into his ears. Although he was a trained lawyer, Davies ignored the obvious fakery in the show trials and announced to American journalists that the defendants were all guilty as charged. Eager to be loyal to Roosevelt, Davies often wrote reports that were misleading and biased.

Life in Moscow was not always pleasant; occasionally it was grim. Davies and his wife left the Soviet Union in June 1938 and arrived in Brussels in time for the outbreak of World War II. In 1940, Davies returned to Washington and to his private law practice.

When the invasion of Russia came in June 1941, Davies was among the very few who prophesied that the Red Army would withstand the German attack. Consequently, with the approval of Roosevelt and Hull, by 1942 he was maintaining an unofficial liaison with Litvinov, the Soviet ambassador. In January 1942, Davies published *Mission to Moscow*, a collection of his official reports to the State Department, diary entries, excerpts from his journal, and personal letters. Here, with presidential blessing, Davies presented a brief for Soviet-American friendship, again arguing his case like a good, high-priced Washington lawyer. Warner Brothers bought the rights to the book and made it into a motion picture starring Walter Huston as Davies. In March 1943, a second mission to Moscow loomed for Davies when he received a message that "the Boss" wanted to see him.

After Davies had been ushered into the Oval Office on March 13, Roosevelt came quickly to the point: he wanted Davies to go to Russia because Standley had "messed things up, speaking out of turn." His usefulness was ended, and he would have to come home. The President explained that he and Churchill had been trying for some time to get Stalin to a meeting but they had gotten nowhere. Now Standley's flare-up about American aid and Russian ingratitude had worsened the situation. The damage had to be repaired because "nothing was more important than to keep the Russians fighting and working with us to win the war." If anyone could iron out this misunderstanding, it would be Davies. The President wanted him to replace Standley as American ambassador in Moscow. Because Davies had health problems, Roosevelt insisted that he go to the Lahey Clinic in Boston for a checkup. But even if the doctors refused permission for him to become ambassador, Roosevelt asked him to take a C-54 plane, a doctor, his own food, and be off to Moscow in late April or May. There Davies would "cool it off and secure a meeting of the Big Three."

Davies suggested that Roosevelt send Harry Hopkins. "No, I can't spare Hopkins," replied the President. "I need him here. Besides, they have confidence in you, and I will see to it, if they do not already know it, that they know you have my full confidence." Because Standley had impaired his influence through his comments to the press, Roosevelt believed that Stalin and Molotov would talk more frankly with Davies alone than if Standley were present.[4]

After the meeting with the President, Davies talked with Hopkins later on March 13 and urged him to go to Moscow as ambassador. But Hopkins felt that he could be more useful in Washington. There were, he said, "as you know, rumors of all kinds current of the 'all out effort' which Hitler is making through the Japanese Embassy in Moscow and through the German Embassy in Sweden, to work out a separate peace with Stalin, offering to compensate the Soviets practically on their own terms. . . . It was vital that their confidence in us or our attitude towards them should not be impaired. If they arrived at the conclusion that we were not on the level with them, there was no telling what might happen." In this crisis, according to Hopkins, Davies was "the ace in the hole." Davies then left Washington for the Lahey Clinic; he would not return until April 12.

While Davies was having his health checked out, Anthony Eden came to Washington for meetings with Roosevelt, Welles, Hopkins, and Hull. On March 15, Eden dined with Roosevelt and Hopkins, and during four hours of conversation, the President gave Eden a frank account of his views about European problems. Roosevelt's wide-ranging comments both perplexed and alarmed Eden. The President "seemed to see himself disposing of the fate of many lands, allied no less than enemy. He did all this with so much grace that it was not easy to dissent. Yet it was too like a conjurer skillfully juggling with balls of dynamite, whose nature he failed to understand."[5]

In his talk with Eden, Roosevelt did not appear hostile toward Soviet demands regarding Poland—"He thought that if Poland had East Prussia and perhaps some concessions in Silesia, she would gain rather than lose by agreeing to the Curzon Line." Roosevelt believed that the three powers should decide on a just and reasonable solution which Poland would have to accept. To him the big question concerned continued postwar cooperation. As for the Baltic States, Roosevelt "realized that, realistically the Russian armies would be in the Baltic States at the time of the downfall of Germany and none of us can force them to get out"; he wanted to urge Russia not to absorb the Baltic States without another plebiscite. It was up to the "Big Powers . . . to decide what Poland should have." The President "did not intend to go to the Peace Conference and bargain with Poland or the other small states." He wanted Poland set up so that it would help maintain the peace of the world, and he wanted to move the Prussians out of East Prussia the way that the Greeks had been moved out of Turkey after World War 1.[6]

Roosevelt's comments surprised officials in the Foreign Office when they received Eden's dispatch reporting this conversation. In one year Roosevelt's views had completely altered—he seemed to have come around to the opinions held in the Foreign Office concerning the Soviet Union. His changed viewpoint could be traced partially to his fear that Standley's outburst had not only destroyed prospects for a personal meeting with Stalin but wrecked all chances to establish close relations with him in order to ensure that the Soviet government would not undermine postwar peace-keeping measures. Consequently, Roosevelt sought some concession that might pacify Stalin and induce him to cooperate with the United States and Great Britain. But even though he might make such statements to Eden, it was not the same as pinning him down to an agreed, written statement about the future of Poland. At the same time, there was the hope that Davies might be able to smooth over Standley's gaffe.

When Davies returned to Washington on April 12, he had another meeting with the President. (By then Davies knew that his health would not permit a second tour in Moscow as ambassador.) Both Roosevelt and Davies agreed that the Russians had greater confidence in American good faith and purposes than they had in Churchill and the British Empire. If a friendly broker were required, it should be Roosevelt, not Churchill, Davies said. Roosevelt replied that because of the rivalries between Russia and the British Empire, it would be hard to keep the team of Churchill and Stalin together.

"I like the Prime Minister," Roosevelt said. "He is a very great man, but at times he is difficult. But we understand each other and will get along." Neither the President nor Churchill could secure Stalin's agreement to a meeting of the three leaders. The Standley press conference had only worsened the situation.

Davies should travel to Moscow and try to repair the situation. If anyone could do it, Roosevelt thought that Davies could. Furthermore, if Roosevelt met Stalin personally and informally, he thought he could convince him that "we had no ulterior purposes and that differences could be cleared up." On the basis of Stalin's public statements, Roosevelt believed that the Marshal was "a man who understood practicalities and would give weight to such considerations." The United States was not hostile toward Russia. The primary concern of the United States was to cooperate with Russia and with Britain in defeating Hitler and the Axis powers, and then to secure peace for the three nations. Roosevelt stressed that America had no ulterior purposes, asking only to attend to her own affairs and not to meddle in the internal affairs of other countries.

The President had concluded that he must see Stalin and talk personally with him because he could discuss any differences with Stalin better alone. Stalin knew that as far as Roosevelt was concerned, the United States had no hostility toward the Russian people. American people were concerned with the security of the United States, Britain, and Russia, peace, and a decent world after the fighting had ended.

Roosevelt instructed Davies to arrange for a private meeting limited to Stalin and himself. Later arrangements could be made for the three leaders to meet. "Churchill will understand. I will take care of that." After Davies had arranged the meeting, he should seek Stalin's views on the organization of postwar Europe, the Mideast, the Mediterranean, and especially of Poland, Finland, Rumania, Bulgaria, and Germany. Davies should familiarize himself with the recent diplomatic correspondence. They would meet again in Evansville, Indiana, on April 26.

Davies went then to the State Department on April 14 for conferences, including one with Loy Henderson, who was in charge of the Russian desk. The same afternoon, Davies met General Marshall, who had already been briefed on Davies's mission. Marshall advised him to fly the longer route—North Africa and Iran—rather than the northern route to Moscow by way of Iceland. Their discussion turned to the Russian problem. Marshall declared that Davies could tell Stalin that as far as the American armed forces were concerned, the sole purpose was to defeat Hitler in the most direct way and in the shortest time. Marshall promised Davies that his former valet, now a corporal in the United States Army, would be assigned to him for the trip to Moscow.

On April 13, Cordell Hull informed Standley that the President was planning to send Davies to the Soviet Union for the purpose of delivering an important and secret message to Stalin. Davies, while carrying out the direct orders of the President, would report to Standley upon his arrival. Hull, anticipating discord between Davies and Standley, added that he was certain that both diplomats would cooperate fully. Standley would arrange for a meeting of Davies with Stalin within a month.

Davies spent April 19 with Harry Hopkins, a confirmed believer in the need for personal discussions between Roosevelt and Stalin. Hopkins urged complete frankness in approaching Stalin in order to secure the meeting with the President. To this end, Hopkins outlined the topics which Davies ought to explore with Stalin: postwar world organization for peace, ways to prevent anarchy in subjugated enemy countries before peace had been restored, the future of Germany, the status of eastern Europe, as well as Stalin's views on Italy, France, Bessarabia, the Dardanelles, and China.

Fearing that Stalin might confront Davies with a long list

of complaints, Hopkins reviewed possible answers to such a list. Why had the cross-Channel invasion of France been delayed? Why had Soviet leaders not been invited to conferences over global strategy? Why were Soviet leaders always confronted with readymade decisions? Why had the United States failed to sever diplomatic relations with Finland? Why had American officials said they would fight alongside the Polish army to prevent Polish frontiers from being pushed back? Why were officers known to be hostile to the Soviet Union sent to represent the United States in Moscow? But even as Hopkins and Davies prepared for the mission to Moscow, the alliance suffered a severe injury.

On April 13, Radio Berlin broadcast reports of the discovery of a mass grave near Smolensk containing the uniformed bodies of approximately four thousand Polish officers. Berlin announced that these officers had all been slain by the Soviet secret police. Moscow denounced the report as a "base lie," claiming that the Polish officers had fallen into the hands of German-Fascist hangmen in the summer of 1941.

The newly discovered remains were from among the approximately fifteen thousand Polish officers missing since the early weeks of the war and thought to have been taken prisoner by the Soviet armies when they invaded Poland in 1939. Moscow had always dismissed requests from the Polish government for information on the whereabouts of the missing officers, alleging that they had all been released, or they had escaped, or they were still traveling somewhere, or they might have been detained in Soviet labor camps as enemies of the Soviet Union.

For the Germans, the mass grave in the Katyn Forest was a godsend because these bodies could weaken the alliance and accelerate an anti-Soviet propaganda comapign in Europe. Had not the war begun over Poland? Now one of the Allies had been murdering Polish prisoners by the thousands. This propaganda windfall came just as preparations were under way for a great German offensive aimed at pinching off the Kursk salient and gaining a quick victory before the British and American armies landed on European shores.

The Poles, in reaction to the discovery in the Katyn Forest, called for an on-the-spot investigation by an impartial body such as the International Red Cross. The Russians struck back. Shortly after midnight on April 26, the Polish ambassador entered the Soviet Foreign Ministry, summoned there by Molotov, who accused the Poles of conspiring with Hitler in a propaganda campaign aimed at the Soviet Union. Accordingly, the Soviet government was breaking off diplomatic relations with the Polish government.

Stalin defended the action to Roosevelt as necessary because the Poles were in collusion with Hitler. Since they had adopted a hostile attitude, they had in effect broken diplomatic relations themselves. They had become the tools of Hitler. But Roosevelt could not believe that the Polish government had collaborated with the Hitler gang. Stalin ought to judge the request to have the Red Cross investigate as a mistake. The President reminded Stalin that several million Poles, serving in the American Army and Navy, were bitter against the Nazis. A break between Moscow and the Polish government would affect their attitude toward the war.

But the break with the Poles was not a sudden, off-the-cuff decision by Stalin. Moscow and the Polish government had been haggling and quarreling for months. The argument grew more intense after Moscow announced in January 1943 that all Polish nationals within the Soviet Union would be considered Soviet citizens because they had come from eastern Poland, an area which Moscow claimed as its own; next, the Soviet government forbade Polish relief agencies to operate among Poles living in the Soviet Union; finally, families of Polish officers and soldiers already outside the Soviet Union were barred from leaving the country to join their loved ones. At last the Katyn discovery had provided Stalin with a convenient excuse to break off diplomatic relations with the Polish government-in-exile. The break gave him an advantage in his campaign for eastern Poland. If the Poles in London believed the Nazis, they must give way to Poles who accepted the word of the Soviet leaders.

For Roosevelt and Churchill, the Katyn discovery and consequent rupture of Soviet-Polish relations proved embarrassing; they wished it would all quickly disappear. Now more than ever, Roosevelt had to meet alone with Stalin, and only Davies could reach him to arrange this.

The President canceled the Evansville meeting with

Davies on April 26 because of a news leak. He did not see
Davies again until April 29, when at a luncheon meeting,
Roosevelt told him that he would draft a letter to Stalin containing his proposal for a meeting of the two men. Davies
would deliver the letter to Stalin in person and present Roosevelt's proposal on the spot. He should also explore the
topics which the President might confront if the meeting with
Stalin eventually took place. Standley must not deliver the
letter. Davies had to do it because Roosevelt believed that
sending a personal envoy would add more weight to the
proposal.

As to arrangements for the actual meeting, it would be
advantageous for them to meet in some remote spot, away
from populated areas, perhaps on a ship or on an island, or
at a site without easy access. The place must have privacy
and not be subjected to interruptions from the press. Then
Roosevelt, taking a globe on his desk, measured the distance
from Moscow to Alaska, comparing it to the distance from
Alaska to Washington. He determined that Alaska was halfway between Moscow and Washington. "Why not meet
there?" he asked Davies. He would be willing to meet Stalin across the Bering Straits in Siberia on Russian soil or on
a warship—Russian or American—in the Bering Sea. Conditions would be primitive but he would enjoy them. Davies
must cable him directly about the time of the meeting, using
a code which Roosevelt worked out on the spot. Later, Davies returned to the White House for the letter he would deliver to Stalin. Roosevelt read it to him, asking for his
comments, but Davies had nothing to add.

Even before his plane took off, *The New York Times* in a
front-page story reported that Davies would leave on May 5
for Moscow as a special representative of Roosevelt to extend an invitation to Stalin to meet Roosevelt alone. At his
news conference on May 7, Roosevelt stated that Davies was
carrying a letter from him to Stalin but that he did not know
the contents. Only Roosevelt and his secretary, Grace Tully,
knew them. Davies would learn the contents only after Stalin had read the letter. A reporter asked if the letter had been
written in English. Roosevelt quipped that it was in Irish.

Davies left Washington on May 6, flying by way of Miami,

Trinidad, Natal, where he went for a swim, Dakar, Kano, Khartoum, Karnak, Luxor, and Cairo. At every stop he received VIP treatment as the personal representative of the President. From Cairo he flew on to Teheran, Kuibyshev, Stalingrad, and finally to Moscow, arriving on May 19.

"Davies arrived yesterday," Standley wrote his wife, "clowning as usual, but he is a friendly clown, and if I have to put up with clowns and publicity hounds, I'd rather it be a friendly one; Davies knows the problems and is cooperating with me."[7] Soon after his arrival, Davies held a press conference at which he rehashed ideas from his book and described his stopover in Stalingrad where he had placed a wreath on the grave of the unknown Russian dead. Following the instructions of Hull, Standley had contacted Molotov about an appointment for Davies to see Stalin. When Standley and Davies paid a courtesy call on Molotov on May 20, he told them that Stalin would see them at nine o'clock that same evening. The speed in scheduling an appointment amazed Standley, who had become accustomed to the customary Soviet delays in such matters.

The purpose of the appointment was to deliver the letter from Roosevelt. Davies infuriated Standley by his refusal to discuss the contents of Roosevelt's letter because he would show it to no one but Stalin. Moreover, Davies informed Standley that he could not be present when that moment came. At the appointed hour, Standley accompanied Davies to the Kremlin and there explained to Stalin the purpose of the visit. "Our President," declared the ambassador, "has intimated that he does not want me to be present when his letter is delivered. With your permission, Mr. Stalin, I will withdraw." A puzzled Stalin replied, "As you please."

Alone now with Molotov, Pavlov, the interpreter, and Stalin, Davies explained that Roosevelt had sent him as his personal envoy to deliver a note to Stalin and to discuss the general situation with him and with Molotov. Roosevelt, deeply concerned about the deteriorating relations between the Allies, urged repair or otherwise a disaster could occur. Because of Standley's press conference, the situation had grown more acute. The President wanted Stalin to understand that the attitude of the United States had not changed and that although the American people opposed the Communist ideology as a form of government, Congress and the American public were "unequivocally devoted to winning the war over Hitler and the Japs and preserving the peace of the world from the threat of either Hitler or the Axis." Roosevelt was convinced that Stalin's word was good, and that with mutual confidence, both nations could get along and keep the peace.

"I was directed to state," said Davies, "that the President believed that there are no differences which cannot be worked out with mutual self-respect to preserve the physical securities of each of the allies, through discussion and mutual effort." Unfortunately the three chiefs of state had not been able to meet earlier. Davies's principal mission, he declared, was to urge the speedy agreement on a meeting. Speaking from a personal point of view, based on his knowledge of Roosevelt, whom he had known intimately for many years, and from his previous contacts with Soviet leaders, he was convinced that the differences threatening the unity of the Allies could be composed and confidence strengthened if the chiefs of state could meet and know each other. Ultimately they would see eye to eye and find agreement to win the war and to preserve the peace. Davies had been sent as a personal envoy—as a mark of America's profound respect for Soviet contributions to the war effort. At this point Davies presented the President's letter to Stalin, who handed it to Pavlov for translation. While Pavlov read, Stalin doodled on a sheet of paper.

Roosevelt had written:

> I want to get away from the difficulties of large staff conferences or the red tape of diplomatic conversations. The simplest and most practical method that I can think of would be an informal and completely simple visit for a few days between you and me.

He understood Stalin's desire to keep in daily touch with Soviet military operations because he himself felt it unwise to be away from Washington for a long time. Yet there was always the possiblity that after the Russian troops went on the offensive, Germany might crack up during the next winter. Because they were unprepared for that possibility, it was Roosevelt's belief that Stalin and he ought to meet during the summer.

But there was a problem—where to meet. Africa was too hot in the summer, and Khartoum was British territory. Iceland was unsuitable because of the difficult flying conditions, and more important, if they met in Iceland, Churchill would have to be invited. Roosevelt suggested that they meet on either side of the Bering Straits. Neither would bring a staff; only Hopkins, an interpreter, and a stenographer would accompany him. Then Stalin and he could talk very informally and get "what we call 'a meeting of minds.'" No official agreement would be necessary. They could discuss military and naval matters without staffs being present.

The President hoped that by the end of May, Anglo-American forces would be in complete control of Tunisia. Consequently, Churchill and he would soon be working on the next phase of the offensive. The American estimate of the situation was that Germany would attack Russia in the summer and the attack would be directed at the center of the Russian lines. The President closed his letter, "You are doing a grand job. Good luck."

Stalin looked grim as Pavlov read. He interrupted only once, when reference was made to Churchill not being invited. "Why?" asked Stalin. Davies explained that both men trusted each other. Roosevelt would advise Churchill about the meeting. Discussion between Roosevelt and Stalin over their views of the world would take up less time than if the same were to be attempted with Churchill present. A meeting between Roosevelt and Stalin would create no more suspicion that had been created by the meeting of Churchill and Stalin. If Stalin and Roosevelt met, they would surely understand each other.

"I am not sure," said Stalin.

"Well, from what I know of what you both have done, I am sure," Davies replied.

"But, understanding alone is not enough," Stalin protested. "There must be reciprocity and respect." Davies assured him that was what he would get and what he was receiving at that present moment.

Davies attempted to enlighten Stalin on the President's

thinking about international affairs. Stalin interrupted to launch into a monologue aimed at setting forth his goals. Germany's future war potential had to be destroyed and Germany must repair the destruction she had caused to Russia. He wanted autonomous, independent governments in Finland, Poland, and Bulgaria, with some advantageous territorial adjustments to these states at the expense of Germany and the other enemy states as compensation for injuries. Britain might require military bases in Europe and the Mediterranean, and the United States might want them in the Pacific Ocean and in other places for security. The Soviet government "wanted all European peoples to have the kind of government they themselves chose, free from coercion." The Soviet Union should have access to warm waters, and on the western borders there should be really friendly countries, not secretly hostile, as they had been in the recent past. Stalin lashed out at the old Polish government of generals, rich landlords, and politicians, whom he claimed had stabbed Russia in the back.

Stalin continued to doodle. Then, looking up at Davies, he said: "I think your President is right. I think he represents America, as I understand it. He is a great man. I believe in him. You may tell your President I agree with him and it is necessary that we meet, as he suggests." Calling for a map, Stalin measured the distance between Moscow and Washington as Roosevelt had already done. He understood that the President had difficulty in walking and that it would be trying for him to travel by airplane. Stalin would be happy to meet Roosevelt at Nome or Fairbanks, whichever he preferred. The meeting would be informal and military staffs would not be needed. He set the date tentatively for July 15 or early in August. Davies explained the President's code, and Stalin promised that a letter, prepared for Roosevelt, would be given to Davies at a second meeting.

After having agreed to the President's request for a personal meeting, Stalin suddenly pressed for more war materials. Davies must tell the President that the Soviet armies were in need of high octane gasoline as well as pursuit planes. Stalin asked how many troops on both sides were fighting in Africa, and just as quickly answered his own question: a total of 700,000. "How many, on the other hand, are fighting on our 2,000 mile front? Approximately, altogether over 4,000,000 Germans, Spaniards, Italians, Rumanians, Finns, and Russians. The Red Army is fighting on their front alone, and suffering under the occupation of a large part of our territory by a cruel enemy." He reminded Davies, "We are waiting for a real offensive in the west to take some of the load off our backs. We need more fighting planes, more locomotives, more equipment, more rails, more food, more grain." Abruptly the monologue halted. "Advise the President that our resolution remains indomitable." Throughout all of this meeting, Molotov had sat quietly by saying nothing.

The next morning Davies informed Standley, with a straight face, that he did not know what was in the letter he had handed to Stalin because it was written in Russian and he had not discussed it with Stalin. To infuriate Standley further, Davies refused to tell the ambassador what Stalin had discussed with him for an hour and a half.

Later that day, Davies held a press conference with Eddy Gilmore, and two war correspondents, Quentin Reynolds and Bill Downes. Although he told them about his meeting with Stalin, he refused to reveal the contents of the letter. "It was a secret letter, boys. I can't tell you its contents," he said.

Gilmore asked: "Did you discuss with Mr. Stalin the apparent lack of Russian cooperation, particularly with regard to giving us information about German military and naval matters, which might help to save the lives of many American soldiers and sailors?"

Davies's face flushed. "No, I did not discuss any such thing with Mr. Stalin. I'm here to deliver a personal letter from President Roosevelt to Premier Stalin, not to air a lot of opinions." And he went on to say that there always had existed the fullest cooperation on the part of the Russian authorities, who were furnishing the American government with all the information that had been asked for. The correspondents ought to reexamine their attitudes and have faith in Russia because they could do tremendous harm to the United States by criticizing the Soviet Union in their stories.

According to the British ambassador, Davies insisted on "throwing in a lot of sobstuff and making little speeches which turned the correspondents hopping mad." He angered them with his "platitudes about our great ally and how she is bearing the entire burden of the war!" The press conference became a shouting argument which ended only when Standley showed the newsmen out. A day later, on May 22, Davies called in the correspondents to apologize for his display of anger, but that did little to appease them.[8]

The correspondents had been puzzled by the need for Davies and an entourage—private plane, nine-man crew, nephew, valet, personal physician—all to deliver two ounces of mail which Standley could easily have done. Despite Davies's precautions, they guessed that the letter contained an invitation for a meeting of the three leaders. They could not imagine that Roosevelt would omit Churchill from the discussions.

The evening of May 23, Stalin hosted a dinner in the Kremlin for Davies and Standley, who described it as the dullest Kremlin dinner ever attended. The menu was elaborate for a nation in which people caught in the war starved to death. The eating had to be halted for the required toasts. Molotov opened with a salute to American-Soviet solidarity, and greeted Davies "as a real friend" who had greatly contributed to closer friendly relations between both countries. Davies's toast became a long oration on the "horrors of war, the glories of Stalingrad and the greatness of the Soviet armies, peoples and leaders." He proposed that Stalingrad, now in ruins, be left as a monument to the atrocities which had been committed by the German armies. A new city would be built five or six miles away from the ruins. "His speech was drenched with tears but the tears were all his own, Russian eyes remained dry. . . . Stalingrad has become rather a back number now."

After toasts from Standley and Clark Kerr, Stalin hailed the Allied armed forces in a short toast. Then Molotov started on his toasts, but when he was about a third through his list, with much of the menu yet to be eaten, Stalin, leaning across the table, told him he had had enough. Rising to his feet, Stalin announced: "We will adjourn immediately to the projection room where we will see our guest of honor's motion picture, *Mission to Moscow*." So instead of spending "the traditional two hours of boozing around those green and gold tables in the anteroom, we were hurried cold sober to the movie theater to see Mr. Davies' film about himself," wrote Clark Kerr.

The picture dealt at length with the Moscow Purge Trials—a period of history that the Soviet hierarchy would like to have forgotten. It was loaded with blatant propaganda and historical errors. The script writers had telescoped two trials into one, and the actor who played Andrei Vyshinsky, the mustached vitriolic prosecutor, wore a great black beard. Hollywood made the British ambassador, Lord Chilston, appear a halfwit. "Walter Huston was fine," a British diplomat commented later (Huston played Davies). "But he couldn't compare with Stalin. Do you know that Stalin kept a straight face throughout the showing? He didn't laugh once!" Those British and Americans in the audience who knew their Russian history were embarrassed. The Russian viewers were quiet although now and then they giggled at the historical absurdities. Litvinov muttered, "Silly." Stalin, buried in a large chair, said nothing except to grunt once or twice. As soon as the film was finished, he announced: "One more drink boys and then home." Clark Kerr, quite amazed at the early hour, wondered if something was wrong; but Stalin had other more important matters than listening to an evening of toasts. After all, he had given Davies the required promise.[9]

As Davies left a luncheon given by Molotov on May 26 to celebrate the Anglo-Soviet treaty of 1942, the foreign commissar told him that Stalin would see him in the Kremlin that evening. That night, accompanied by his nephew, Davies called on Stalin, who gave him his reply to Roosevelt's letter, handing him an English translation to read. Then Molotov placed the translation and a Russian version in an envelope, sealed it, and handed it to Davies for transmission to Roosevelt.

The reply would please Roosevelt because Stalin was in full agreement that they ought to meet without Churchill. Stalin proposed that they meet in Fairbanks about July 15, subject to a possible delay because of the expected German attack. Stalin would advise Roosevelt using a code. If his message read "Will begin operations from Moscow—July 28," Stalin explained, such a message would mean he would arrive in Fairbanks or Nome fourteen days before the named date, July 14. Then Stalin went off again on another monologue dealing with intelligence and international affairs.

Soviet intelligence sources had learned that information about the sailing of convoys for Murmansk was reaching the German High Command. It was being sent by diplomatic pouch from the Finnish legation in Washington to the Finnish Foreign Office and from there to the German minister in Helsinki. Here was a hint that the United States ought to expel the Finnish diplomat.

Turning to international affairs, Stalin declared that the Soviet Union wanted to maintain peace and ensure collective security and that this would have to be done by three or four of the big powers. An organization in which peace would be maintained by twenty or thirty very small countries such as Haiti would be disastrous. Russia must be assured that the power of any world organization would not be directed against her if the great powers fell into a dispute. After victory the Soviet Union would rely on its own strength and its own outposts. Once more he reminded Davies that the Soviet Union must have friendly neighbors. Poland, Finland, Rumania—autonomous, independent states—could have mutual defense pacts with the Soviet Union, with each other, and with other nations, but they should be "friendly" governments. The present Polish government was hostile to Russia, although professing friendship and an interest in a world organization as a second line of defense. At that point, Davies's evening with Stalin ended with a picture-taking session.

For Davies, the trip had been a physical ordeal. Often he had to receive visitors at the American Embassy while he was in bed. Clark Kerr, the British ambassador, had a number of bedside chats with him, talking chiefly about his stomach problems and his intimacy with Roosevelt. On one occasion Davies gave Clark Kerr a copy of his book, and a box of vitamin pills and laxative pills on which the ambassador could rely absolutely.[10]

But Davies could not leave soon enough for Ambassador

Standley, who found him pretentious and too eager to impress everyone that he was the special representative of the President. "The whole show reeks of the oil of publicity for Mr. Joseph E. Davies and his film and book, *Mission to Moscow*. I think the Russians sensed it too," Standley wrote to his wife. When Standley inspected Davies's plane shortly before takeoff on the morning of May 29, he found it "very lush"; he noticed that Davies now had the title of his book and movie, *Mission to Moscow*, painted on the nose in English and in Russian.[11]

After a farewell visit to Molotov, Davies's plane left Moscow early in the morning. Flying eastward, it brought Davies to Washington by June 3. When news of his arrival reached the President, he canceled a press conference and ordered that Davies come immediately to his office. There Davies and his wife were taken directly to Roosevelt, and after a short chat with Marjorie Davies, she excused herself so that her husband could make his report to "the Boss."

Davies handed the President Stalin's reply, in which he agreed with Roosevelt's prophecy of a "large scale offensive of Hitlerites" on the eastern front. Despite shortages in planes and fuel, the Soviet armies were preparing to meet the new offensive. Much would depend on the Anglo-American operations in Europe. Stalin agreed that a meeting ought not to be postponed. As he could not foretell developments on the eastern front during June, it would be impossible for him to leave Moscow then; instead, he suggested a meeting in July or August. If Roosevelt agreed, he promised to inform him two weeks before the date of meeting. Davies would communicate the place. Stalin also agreed on limiting the number of advisers to be present. He concluded by thanking Roosevelt for sending Davies, who had knowledge of the Soviet Union and who could make judgments without bias.

For two hours Roosevelt questioned Davies about his talks with Stalin. What were his viewpoints and his plans? What did he ask? The envoy replied that it had taken some time to penetrate the "suspicious, almost hostile attitude of Stalin." As Davies interpreted the Soviet attitude, Churchill was stalling on the cross-Channel attack in order to save British strength for domination of Europe after the end of the war.

He sought to divert Allied attacks from the assault through France in order to launch an attack through the Balkans and Italy so as to control the area after the war had ended. It was part of a plan to "bleed Russia white and to make a British peace and have the power of a strong British military at the peace table in Berlin." As their meeting ended, Roosevelt exclaimed, "Joe, you have done a grand job."

Davies wrote a report on his mission for the President which certainly influenced Roosevelt's thinking. Davies concluded that if the British and the United States failed to deliver on a cross-Channel attack during the summer of 1943, "it will have far reaching effects upon the Soviets that will be effective both on their attitude and in the prosecution of this war and in their participation in the reconstruction of peace." Unless the attack on Germany were to be a concerted effort carried on simultaneously by all of the Allies, Davies predicted that the Soviet armies would "stop at their western boundary and be content with driving the invader out of their territory if they can do so." He believed that a legacy of suspicion of the western Allies was still strong. "The belief exists in some quarters that the United Nations want a weakened Russia at the peace table and a Red Army that is bled white." As to relations with other nations, the Soviets would "insist upon a return of their old boundaries as a restitution of an ancient wrong." They would take back from Poland what they considered wrongfully taken from them. Davies avowed that the Soviet government would scrupulously avoid any interference in the internal affairs of other governments. Most of all, the Soviet government wanted a peaceful world, but it was prepared to go to the limit in making it impossible for Germany ever again to break that peace. The Soviet Union wanted a strong, not a reactionary Poland, but would never relinquish the Curzon Line. Davies concluded his report: "As to the particular mission I was engaged upon, I believe that the result thereof has been completely successful."[12]

After reading Davies's report, Roosevelt wrote Stalin to thank him for the courtesies extended to his envoy during his visit. "I am happy that you and I are in complete agreement in principle on all matters contained in your letter. And

I will await your further communication in accordance with your letter and your understanding with Mr. Davies."

To Standley, Davies may have been a clown, but he had done the job for Roosevelt. His obvious bias toward the Soviet Union had been an asset in gaining access to Stalin on such short notice. Moreover, Stalin had agreed to come to a meeting on American soil, without Churchill at which Roosevelt could establish that personal relationship he believed so necessary to break down Stalin's suspicions of the capitalist United States. Of course Standley could just as easily have handed the letter to Stalin; it would have been cheaper to have done that than to dispatch a military crew and a plane to Moscow and to provide Davies and his party with per diem for the trip. But Roosevelt, fearing the effect of the Standley press conference on his invitation to Stalin, had turned instead to Davies for a second mission to Moscow.

For Roosevelt, the prospect of such a meeting—the first in American history—was so tantalizing that he chose Davies as his special representative. He surmised that because he had sent Davies, famed as a defender of the Soviet regime, Stalin would grant him a hearing when he arrived in Moscow as Roosevelt's special emissary. Most important, Roosevelt knew that Davies would present his views faithfully and accurately.

If the meeting between the two leaders took place as planned, Roosevelt believed that he could convince Stalin that the United States could be trusted and that the long-held suspicions ought to be discarded. Through a private meeting, Roosevelt thought he could persuade Stalin to collaborate with him in creating a peaceful postwar world. The break with Poland and the rumors of secret negotiations between Germany and the Soviet Union made this meeting imperative. If all these goals could be achieved, then the cost of the crew and Davies's entourage had been worth every penny.

Yet, why had Stalin changed his mind and agreed to see Roosevelt? Why had the leader of the Communist party of the Soviet Union suddenly promised to meet the leader of the capitalist United States outside the Soviet Union? Obviously Stalin had not been as deeply affected by the Standley press conference as Roosevelt and Hopkins had imagined. If Stalin had made any comment to Davies about the outburst, Davies would certainly have recorded it in view of his opinion of Standley as a diplomat—"He would never take a prize pumpkin as a negotiator or a diplomat," he wrote his wife. Stalin probably interpreted Davies's appearance in Moscow as a signal from Roosevelt of a change in American attitudes. Only a major proposal could warrant sending one man so far in a government airplane in wartime to carry a single letter. Could it mean that Roosevelt would accept Stalin's desires concerning the western frontiers of Russia? Did he wish to abandon the Polish government?

Stalin may have believed that Roosevelt had a very important proposal to discuss which he wished to conceal from Churchill. Through this invitation, Roosevelt was offering Stalin an opportunity to isolate one Ally from the other. It was a maneuver which Stalin had often practiced and certainly appreciated, particularly now when the more powerful of the western Allies chose to practice it against the weaker.

When the prime minister had come to the Kremlin in August 1942, the arguments had been bitter and Stalin had fathomed the combative nature of Churchill. In his absence, Roosevelt might be easier to maneuver, to flatter, to convince, and to manipulate. Without Churchill, Stalin would have an opportunity to explore the motives and character of the President. To accomplish that, however, he would have to undertake a lengthy trip and leave the Soviet Union.

Since rising to the summit of Soviet power, Stalin had never dared leave the center of power and journey beyond the Soviet frontiers because of the potential risk to his person and his position. Indeed, he feared to travel even within the Soviet Union. But under the circumstances, it might be worthwhile for him to risk going to Fairbanks if the President of the United States seemed so eager to meet privately with him that he had sent a messenger bearing a personal invitation. The journey to American soil and the meeting might well be worth the gamble of leaving the security of the Kremlin and entering a foreign land.

4
Stalin's Conversion

GERMAN U-BOAT CAPTAINS seeking a target in May 1943 would have found the best possible one in the *Queen Mary*, then the world's largest passenger ship, as she sailed westward across the Atlantic Ocean. On the passenger list were five thousand German prisoners of war and "Colonel Warden," better known as Winston Churchill, His Majesty's Prime Minister and First Lord of the Treasury, on his way to confer once again with President Roosevelt. Churchill's doctors had vetoed a bomber flight because he was recovering from pneumonia and pressurized cabins in airplanes were not yet available. So the *Queen Mary* was chosen because she happened to be in England, preparing to embark German prisoners for camps in the United States. The pride of the Cunard Line, the *Queen Mary* had been launched in 1934 and drafted for war in 1940. The fine paneling had been removed, sanitary equipment installed, and tiered bunks erected in cabins, in the chic cocktail bars, swimming pools, and every other possible location. Soldiers ate and slept in shifts as the liner crossed the Atlantic without escorts because of her speed. Hitler offered a reward to the U-boat skipper who sank the ship, but her speed enabled her to evade them all.

Churchill and his entourage traveled in comfort; with two decks sealed off from the rest of the ship, they had quarters and offices for work. A detail of Royal Marines guarded Churchill's suite around the clock. He ordered a machine gun installed in the lifeboat to which he had been assigned because he did not intend to allow a U-boat to capture him without a personal fight.

The *Queen Mary* sailed on May 6, 1943—but not before being cleansed of some unwelcome passengers, insects that came aboard with troops from Australia. On board now were Churchill ("Colonel Warden"), the British chiefs of staff, Harriman, Beaverbrook and his new bride, assorted admirals and generals, and a host of clerks. Churchill and the chiefs of staff used the voyage to plan for the upcoming meeting in Washington with the American chiefs and the President. There a major question of strategy had to be decided. Where would the Allied armies strike next?

During the voyage, Churchill and his chiefs agreed that preparations should begin at once to establish a bridgehead on the toe of the Italian boot. If Italian forces appeared on the verge of collapse, then the Allied armies should invade Italy. Germany could not hold all of Italy and the Balkans without risking a collapse on the Russian front, Consequently, the Allies ought to be ready to exploit any weakening of the German position in the Balkans, and they ought to be prepared to invade southern France and at the same time attack across the Channel. All of these possibilities depended upon a substantial weakening of German forces. The British chiefs were convinced that the Mediterranean theater of operations offered the best opportunity for the Allies. Fighting in that theater, instead of transporting troops and weapons back to the United Kingdom, would lay the groundwork for the cross-Channel attack. However, Roosevelt and his chiefs of staff had a different view of strategy.

Already the Americans had come to a decision: At the next meeting with the British, their principal objective would be to "pin down the British to a cross-Channel invasion of Europe at the earliest practicable date and to make full preparation for such an operation by the spring of 1944."[1] The Joint Chiefs resolved that nothing should delay or jeopardize the basic strategy against Germany, which entailed preparing and launching the cross-Channel invasion in 1944. If the British insisted on involving the United States in military operations to the east of Italy, they would fight alone while the American forces would expand operations in the Pacific theater.

After the *Queen Mary* dropped anchor off Staten Island on May 11, Harry Hopkins, representing Roosevelt, came aboard to welcome Churchill and to escort him to Washington on a train. The two Allied staffs, which functioned as the Combined Chiefs of Staff, debated strategy in the capital during May until they reached a compromise. The final blow against Germany would come across the Channel. Resources would be concentrated in Britain in order to launch an invasion with a target date of May 1, 1944. A bomber offensive would be launched against the German installations, aimed at weakening the morale of the German people. But the American members of the Combined Chiefs had to concede somewhat to their British colleagues on operations in the Mediterranean area. The actions there would be planned to eliminate Italy from the war. Nevertheless, the Americans gained a victory: commencing in November 1943, seven divisions would be returned to the United Kingdom from the Mediterranean. By this decision, the Americans hoped to limit the strength available for any future Mediterranean operations. The results of the debates of the Combined Chiefs received the approval of Churchill and Roosevelt on May 25. Now it would be necessary to report the results to Stalin.

The President and the prime minister took on the task of drafting the statement to be dispatched to Stalin. After the final meeting, they labored until two o'clock in the morning, drafting and redrafting the message which could only disappoint and infuriate Stalin. Drafts were typed, corrected, and then retyped. Churchill volunteered to take the message with him when he left the next day and to work on it as his plane flew toward Newfoundland, where he would send it to Roosevelt. The weary President agreed gladly. Later in the morning of May 26, as soon as he was airborne, Churchill settled down with the assorted drafts of the message to Stalin. Because he soon found himself making little headway in the revision process, he turned the task over to George Marshall, who was aboard the plane bound for North Africa. After two hours' work, the general presented Churchill with a clean typed copy which so pleased him that he forwarded it to Roosevelt as soon as the plane touched down at Gander. Roosevelt made two slight changes, then forwarded the message to the American Embassy in Moscow, and on June 4 Standley presented it to Stalin.

The message explained that at the recent Washington Conference the Allies had decided to intensify the air offensive against Germany, and to force Italy out of the war at the earliest possible moment. After Operation HUSKY (the invasion of Sicily), Eisenhower had been directed to plan an offensive aimed at achieving the collapse of Italy. Now that the Allies controlled North Africa, they would concentrate American and British forces in the United Kingdom where an Anglo-American staff constantly revised plans in order to take advantage of German weaknesses in France or in Norway. By the spring of 1944, sufficient men and matériel would be concentrated in the British Isles to attempt a full-scale invasion of the European continent when the air offensive would be at its peak. German forces would be compelled to disperse in order to guard against attacks. Should the Axis weaken, they would be prepared to exploit this condition.

From Moscow, Stalin replied quickly. He reminded Roosevelt and Churchill that on February 12 the prime minister had announced preparations for a cross-Channel attack in August 1943, and that, if weather or some other cause hindered the operation, an attack would be prepared for September 1943. Now in May Roosevelt and Churchill had decided further to postpone the invasion of Europe, already delayed from 1942 to 1943. The postponement would strain the resources of the Soviet army, fighting alone for its own country and for its allies against a strong and formidable enemy. The news of the fresh delay and the withholding of support for the Soviet army would dishearten both the soldiers and the Soviet people. The Soviet government could not join in a decision adopted without its participation and without any joint discussion of so vital a matter that could severely affect the outcome of the war.[2]

Churchill, replying first, observed that Russia would not be helped if the Allies threw away a hundred thousand men in a disastrous cross-Channel attack such as he thought would certainly occur. He saw no point in sending these men to defeat in a cross-Channel attack if it were to be attempted with the forces then available to the Allies. If the Anglo-American force landed, it would be driven into the sea because the Germans were not only too strong but could also easily bring up reinforcements by rail.

How could slaughtering British troops help the Soviet armies? "I would never authorize any cross-Channel attack which I believed would lead to only useless massacre," wrote Churchill. The greatest help would be to win battles as the Anglo-American forces had done in Tunisia, where they had been aided by their seapower. By knocking Italy out of the war in 1943, they would draw more German troops away from the Russian front than by any other available means. After Italy had been defeated, Churchill thought that the Germans would then have to establish a new front on the Alps or on the Po River, and at the same time they would have to draw upon their reserves to replace the thirty-two Italian divisions. The bombardment of Rumania could be increased while the air offensive over Europe would cause more havoc in Germany. Expected victories in the U-boat war would speed the movement of American forces in Europe. Churchill believed that victory in North Africa had dislocated the German strategy and would delay Hitler's plans for a great summer offensive in Russia.

Turning to Stalin's complaints that he had not been consulted about these decisions, Churchill accepted his reasons for not attending the recent meetings. For his part, Churchill would go at any risk to any meeting place agreeable to Stalin and to Roosevelt. To that end, he proposed that Stalin fly to Scapa Flow for a meeting during the summer of 1943. There a hearty welcome would await him.[3]

Churchill had given Stalin what he considered a soft answer, but he would not allow a useless massacre of British troops on French beaches simply to remove Stalin's suspicions. Tired of these "repeated scoldings, considering they have never been actuated by anything but cold-blooded self-interest and total disdain of our lives and fortunes," he had tried to hint that Stalin had offended the western powers, whose strength was growing and who could play a helpful role in Russia's future.[4] Roosevelt, unwilling to undermine his planned meeting with Stalin minus Churchill, would only concur in Churchill's message. But the argument continued with messages back and forth.

Stalin replied that he thought Churchill and Roosevelt

were aware of the dangers involved in launching an invasion and were prepared for them. He listed the dates in messages received from Churchill in 1942 and early in 1943 promising a cross-Channel operation in 1943. Because conditions for the operation had improved, he could not imagine that the British and American governments would go back on their decision to invade Europe by 1943. Moreover, the Soviet government was entitled to expect an invasion in 1943. Churchill's unwillingness to throw away a hundred thousand men in a disastrous cross-Channel attack did not move Stalin because in previous messages Churchill had spoken of an Anglo-American force of more than one million troops and on another occasion of an "adequate force." Churchill had contradicted himself because he feared to lose men yet had prepared a mighty invasion force. Stalin reminded him that the decision revoking previous promises of an invasion had been made without Soviet participation and without inviting Soviet representatives to Washington. By this action he and Roosevelt had disregarded vital Soviet interests in a war against a common enemy. No longer was it a matter of being disappointed in his allies. Now it had become a question of the Soviet government preserving confidence in the Allies—a confidence subject to great stress. Stalin ended with a warning. They ought not to forget that when it was a question of saving the lives of millions of people suffering in Europe and in Russia, and of reducing the losses of Soviet armies, the Anglo-American sacrifices became insignificant in comparison.[5]

This message so offended Churchill that he thought it would end all correspondence and personal contact between Stalin and himself. For Stalin had implied that the British feared to sacrifice troops in the invasion of France, preferring that Soviet soldiers fight and die for them, forgetting that for a year Britain had stood alone while Stalin frantically appeased Hitler. Churchill, who dreaded the losses in British soldiers, would not sacrifice them until there was no alternative. But Roosevelt, eager to meet with Stalin alone, avoided the argument.

When Stalin had referred to losing confidence in the Allies, whose sacrifices were insignificant when contrasted with those of the Soviet people, he signaled that if they were about to let the Soviet Union fight Hitler alone, he could always make peace with Hitler to halt the Russian sacrifices. It may have been coincidence, but during the same month in which these exchanges occurred, rumors of negotiations toward that end circulated in Europe. A Swedish newspaper reported that Soviet and German officials had been negotiating not far from Stockholm. Such reports of course reached London and Washington. Indeed, there had been another meeting on June 18 in Stockholm between Edgar Clauss, the East European businessman on good terms with the Soviet Embassy in Stockholm, and Peter Kleist, the official in the German Foreign Ministry. Clauss, who claimed to be relating conversations with the Soviet Embassy staff, reported that the Soviet Union did not want to fight one minute longer than necessary for the British and Americans. Germany held areas which the Red Army would have to win back with great losses, but these areas were negotiable and a deal could be concluded immediately.[6] The negotiations went nowhere, but rumors were leaked, probably deliberately, to embassies and to newspapers.

These stories, coupled with Stalin's anger over the decision to postpone the invasion until 1944, only increased Roosevelt's longing for a personal meeting with Stalin. Churchill, however, had yet to be informed about the meeting Roosevelt sought. Although the President had conferred with Churchill repeatedly in Washington during May, he dared not explain to him that Davies had been dispatched to Moscow to convince Stalin to attend a meeting without the prime minister. Churchill imagined that Davies had been trying to convert Stalin to the idea of meeting with both leaders. "I will of course come anywhere you wish to have a rendezvous," he assured Roosevelt, "and I am practising every day with my pistol to make head [sic] against the mosquitoes."[7] He proposed that they meet during the summer at Scapa Flow, the President sailing there in a battleship. It was the moment to approach Stalin about a meeting.

The President realized that the unpleasant task of telling Churchill could not be postponed any longer, but instead of telling him himself, Roosevelt sent Averell Harriman as the messenger with the bad news. (Harriman had recently been chosen as the American ambassador in Moscow because Davies's health was not up to the ordeal of wartime life there.)

Harriman arrived in London late on June 23, and after he and his daughter, Kathleen, had dined that evening with Churchill and Lord Beaverbrook, he broke the news to Churchill that the President had asked Stalin to meet him without the prime minister. Churchill the politician argued fiercely against such a meeting because of the reaction in Britain, where the public would regard such a meeting as a snub to him and a sign of mistrust. Harriman insisted that a more intimate understanding could be achieved when only two men met. Then he stressed the favorable American reaction to a Roosevelt-Stalin meeting in contrast to a meeting on British soil, which would imply that Churchill was the host who had arranged it.

For Churchill, Harriman's announcement was a calamity. It implied that Roosevelt and Stalin sought to shut him out of the top-level Allied planning conferences. But what was worse, it signaled a change in the reality of world power: The United States and the Soviet Union were drawing closer at the expense of Great Britain.

Instead of reproaching Roosevelt for concealing his negotiations with Stalin, Churchill took the line that the world expected and the Allied nations desired a meeting of the three leaders. Together they could plan for future moves in the war and seek the foundations of postwar peace. A meeting of the three men at Scapa Flow or anywhere else in the world would be one of the "milestones of history." On the other hand, enemy propagandists would make much of a meeting between Stalin and Roosevelt without Churchill because it would imply a serious breach in the alliance, alarming and bewildering many people. His trip to Moscow in August 1942 had been on a lower level for the purpose of explaining why Britain and the United States could not establish a second front. "Nevertheless," he concluded, "whatever you decide, I shall sustain to the best of my ability here."[8]

Even though Churchill, for the sake of the common cause, tried to be gracious, Roosevelt did not hesitate to lie. He claimed that Stalin had proposed a meeting without the prime minister. According to Roosevelt, Stalin had "told Davies that he assumed that we could meet alone and that he agreed that we should not bring staffs to what would be a preliminary meeting." Roosevelt tried to squirm out of his disloyalty to his old friend by blaming Stalin for the idea of the two leaders meeting alone, without their staffs, in what should be considered the preliminary to a later full dress meeting of the three men and their military staffs. He discovered advantages in what he had labeled a "preliminary meeting" in the opportunity to allow Stalin to be more frank with him than he would have been if the three leaders and their staffs were present. In such intimate circumstances, Stalin would be less inclined to push for the second front, argued Roosevelt; and would be more open in expressing his views about a variety of topics than if Churchill were to be present. "I want to explore his thinking as fully as possible concerning Russia's postwar hopes and ambitions and to cover much the same field with him as did Eden for you a year ago." To pacify Churchill, Roosevelt proposed a meeting with him in Quebec soon after the visit with Stalin. Later, in the fall of 1943, there would be a full dress conference with the Russians. "I have the idea that your conception is the right one from the short point of view," Roosevelt wrote, "but mine is the right one from the long point of view."

By June 29 Churchill had conceded, agreeing with Roosevelt that "if you and Uncle J. can fix up a meeting together I should no longer deprecate it. On the contrary, in view of his attitude I think it important that this contact should be established."[9] Churchill's concession resulted partly from Stalin's last message denouncing the decision to postpone the second front. Churchill's change also reflected concern that the relationship with Stalin might deteriorate until he would make a deal with Hitler. To add to Churchill's fears, he found an ominous meaning in the cessation of the German offensive on the Russian front. Could it be linked to the rumors of peace negotiations?

Despite the rumors and the recall of the Soviet ambassadors from London and Washington, the quiet along the central eastern front did not in fact mean that Hitler was contemplating a negotiated peace with Stalin; rather, it existed because intense and detailed preparations were under way for Operation CITADEL, an attempt to have the German armies drive into the Kursk salient from two directions. The Kursk salient between Moscow and Kharkov extending 130 miles wide, and, thrusting 80 miles to the west, offered a tempting target for a classic pincer movement, with the Ninth Army attacking from the north and the Fourth Panzer Army from the south. The spearheads of these two armies were planned to meet east of Kursk. Such a victory would not wreck the Soviet armies nor would it attain a great strategic goal. Why then attack? Because the salient was there, and because after the Afrika Korps had suffered defeat in Tunisia, any victory looked inviting. A victory at Kursk could also disrupt the Soviet forces enough for Hitler to order the movement of troops westward to block an invasion of Italy or an Allied movement into the Balkans. Finally, a victory would arouse the neutrals and encourage halfhearted German allies.

After preparations had begun for Operation CITADEL late in March 1943, Hitler ordered it postponed three times in order to permit the stockpiling of guns and tanks. The Soviet forces, forewarned by their intelligence sources, had prepared carefully for the attack with parallel fortifications in the manner of World War I. The area to be defended was heavily mined and covered by thousands of guns. To the rear beyond the salient, Russian strategic reserves waited to counterattack after the Germans had committed themselves. Both sides massed thousands of tanks for what would become the greatest tank battle of the war.

The opening salvoes came late in the afternoon of July 4, and at dawn the next day, the entire German front opened up on the massed Soviet forces. During the next five days, the German armies gained little while suffering heavy losses. Late on July 9 the news reached Hitler at his headquarters at the Wolf's Lair that an Allied invasion had been discovered in the Mediterranean bound for Sicily. By the morning of July 10, Operation HUSKY—the invasion of that island— was under way. Over 160,000 Allied soldiers landed in Sicily by July 12, and the same day, the Soviet armies launched a counteroffensive in the Kursk salient. After a high-level conference on July 13, Hitler canceled CITADEL because he feared that the loss of Italy and the threat to the Balkans might endanger his southern flank. He could not know that the Kursk battle would be the last great German offensive in Russia.

The German armies after Kursk would never again be strong enough to mount such an offensive on the Russian front. Hereafter they would be fighting on two European fronts. Units of the Wehrmacht would be shunted back and forth across Europe to plug gaps in the German defenses. Kursk, not Stalingrad, was the decisive battle in the East. It was a set battle piece, a great attack prepared with care, in which the German armies massed all their strength for one great assault; but it failed to produce the hoped-for results. Kursk showed that Soviet tanks and artillery could halt the vaunted Panzer units; it showed the results of changes in the Soviet High Command and the improvement in the morale and training of Soviet troops since the summer and fall of 1941 when entire Soviet armies fell apart. The last great German offensive in Russia had been halted by defeat.

Thanks to the victory at Kursk, there was a new cocky spirit in Moscow as artillery salvoes and fireworks celebrated the victories. Moscow was no longer in danger and the entire diplomatic corps was allowed to return from Kiubyshev. No longer was the second front a matter of life and death as Soviet armies made spectacular gains following the victory at Kursk. The Soviet assault swept on toward the Dnieper River, the last great barrier before the vital raw materials of the Ukraine and Rumania. The Russians would continue to lose thousands of men daily, but it began to be taken for granted that the war would eventually be won.

In future dealings with Churchill and Roosevelt, the Kursk victory would mean that Stalin was no longer a beggar, appealing for a second front. He possessed an advantage over the other two Allies: the Soviet armies had defeated the mighty Wehrmacht in a battle Hitler had prepared. The Anglo-American armies had only landed on Sicilian beaches, whereas the Soviet armies had decisively defeated the Germans and gone on the offensive. Stalin could now exploit his advantage in negotiating with Churchill and Roosevelt.

They had heard nothing from him since the message on June 23 which so infuriated Churchill. Roosevelt cabled him on July 15 asking to hear from him soon "about the other matter which I still feel to be of great importance to you and me."[10]

Davies, troubled by Moscow's silence over the projected Roosevelt-Stalin meeting in Fairbanks, telephoned the White House repeatedly in July seeking information. Hopkins telephoned him on July 24 to report nothing from Moscow. What did Davies think? "I didn't like it; it looked bad. We should have heard something before this." He continued to call the White House. Finally on August 4, he called on the Soviet attaché, young Andrei Gromyko, to inquire if any information had come from Moscow. Gromyko claimed that Stalin's whereabouts were unknown from day to day, and that he could not communicate with him until he returned to Moscow. Sensing a stall, Davies asked Gromyko to forward a message to Stalin urging him, regardless of the second front problem, to cooperate and to "further the idea of a meeting of the Chiefs of State or their representatives. The essentials as to the situation were still as I stated them in Moscow, and it is vital to peace that there should be a meeting." In view of Davies's status within the Kremlin, Gromyko promised to forward the message to Stalin.[11]

At last from Moscow news came to Washington on August 8; by that time Stalin had probably read Davies's message. He informed Roosevelt that the situation along the eastern front, requiring all his attention to direct the action and necessitating trips to various sectors, had prevented him from replying. Roosevelt, he hoped, would understand that at the present time he could not make a long journey and consequently would be unable to keep the promise made to Roosevelt through Davies in May. Stalin considered a meeting of "the responsible representatives" of both countries would be expedient. It could be held either in Astrakhan or Archangel. If Roosevelt found this personally inconvenient, then he might wish to send someone to the meeting place whom he fully trusted. Next they should decide on the proposals to be discussed at the meeting. He had no objection if Churchill came and made it a tripartite meeting.[12]

Stalin had vetoed the kind of meeting so dear to Roosevelt, and instead had suggested sites that would be totally inconvenient. He had hinted for the first time at the possibility of a conference of the three heads of government—a prospect less than pleasing to Roosevelt. If there were to be any meeting, Stalin had indicated that the site had to satisfy him. At the same time, he had opened the way for a meeting on a lower level. But he had lied when he claimed that the war required him to make frequent trips to the front. In truth, he carefully avoided the battlefront, preferring the safety of the Kremlin where elite troops, constantly rotated, protected him not only from the enemy but also from his own people.

Stalin tailored his message to Churchill to fit the prime minister's case. He omitted any mention of a personal meeting with Roosevelt, agreeing only that a meeting of the three heads of government was "absolutely desirable" and that it should be achieved at the first opportunity, but he could not absent himself from the front for even a week. As a result, he could not travel to Scapa Flow or any other distant place. Instead, he proposed the meeting of "the responsible representatives of our states" at a time and place which should be agreed upon. Before this, agreement ought to be reached on the questions to be discussed.[13]

Churchill received this message after he had reached Quebec, where he was soon to·have another high-level meeting with Roosevelt. (The President had proposed this in June when Harriman revealed to Churchill that he had not been invited to the proposed Roosevelt-Stalin conference.) After Roosevelt arrived in Quebec, the two men sent a message to Stalin reiterating their wish for a meeting of the three leaders and suggesting Fairbanks as the site. Churchill would remain on the western side of the Atlantic as long as might be necessary to arrange for the Fairbanks meeting. If it could not be arranged for the three heads of government, then they favored a meeting at the foreign ministers' level, which could be exploratory in character.[14]

Stalin claimed that he could not leave the front for so distant a point as Fairbanks, convenient though it might be for Roosevelt and Churchill. Hitler was sending fresh divisions to the Russian front, and in the opinion of Stalin's colleagues he could not leave. He too favored a meeting on the foreign ministerial level, but he wished for one that was practical and preparatory, not merely "exploratory." He wanted the questions to be considered by the three representatives to be defined in advance and the proposals to be drafted before the discussions took place.

Churchill and Roosevelt informed Stalin of their eagerness to get a foreign ministers' meeting under way. Roosevelt suggested that the ministers meet September 25; Churchill wanted them to convene in London during October. London, however, did not please Roosevelt, who saw it as advantageous for Churchill, and so he suggested more remote sites: Casablanca, Tunis, or Sicily. The meetings must be strictly limited; none of the participants could have extensive powers. Roosevelt planned to send Sumner Welles, Under Secretary of State, in place of Hull, if Molotov and Eden represented their governments. Stalin accepted Churchill's time but said that the meeting could take place only in Moscow.[15]

Roosevelt would have preferred to meet with Stalin. But since he would agree only to the foreign ministers meeting, that would have to suffice. They would have to act as substitutes until an arrangement could be found satisfactory to the three leaders.

At last, on September 8, Stalin sent Roosevelt the news he had so long desired. He was prepared to arrange for a meeting of the trio between November 15 and December 15 (dates originally proposed by Roosevelt). He thought it "expedient to choose as the place of the meeting the country where there are the representatives of all three countries, for instance, Iran."[16] Here was the hoped-for breakthrough—for the first time Stalin had actually proposed a time and a place for the three men to meet.

What had converted Stalin? A month earlier he had rejected not only a meeting alone with Roosevelt but also all of the earlier invitations. In May he had agreed to meet Roosevelt in Fairbanks without Churchill. Then came the Washington Conference, when Roosevelt and Churchill postponed the invasion of France until 1944. Stalin must have thought that Roosevelt had double-crossed him, after agreeing to the

Fairbanks meeting, by conspiring with Churchill to deny him the second front to which he believed he was entitled. Why should he be treated in this manner by such a notorious capitalist? If the President chose to be devious, Stalin would show him that a promise to meet in Fairbanks did not entitle Roosevelt to connive with Churchill at postponing the invasion.

Always prudent in his scheming, Stalin may have had second thoughts about traveling to a foreign country, the wealthiest among the capitalistic nations. The symbolism would imply that the leading Communist must go to the capitalists. Better to let them come to him. Moreover, it would have been a long journey, taking Stalin far from the center of Soviet power and at the same time making him dependent upon a long line of communications which the Americans could tap. The risks of distancing himself from the Soviet nerve center were just too great.

On August 8, Stalin rejected the meeting with Roosevelt in Fairbanks but at the same time opened the door to a meeting on the foreign ministry level where the ground could be prepared for a future meeting of the three leaders. And by September 8, he had become amenable to a date and site for a conference with Roosevelt and Churchill. His stonewalling appeared to have ended.

Stalin's change in policy can be traced to the aftereffects of the Battle of Kursk and the landing of Anglo-American forces on the beaches of Sicily on July 10. Victory at Kursk meant that Soviet armies would be on the attack and that Stalin's earlier excuses for remaining away would no longer be valid. If he wished to capitalize on this victory, he must meet with both men. If he refrained from meeting with them, he would lose the advantage given him by the Kursk victory. There, Soviet forces had defeated the Germans in a great land battle and taken the initiative from them. In the future Allied leaders would need Soviet help more than ever, particularly when the Anglo-American forces landed in France in 1944; at that time a Soviet offensive would be essential to draw the German troops away from western Europe. So now they must come to Stalin and negotiate with him as the leader of armies that recently had defeated the Germans in Europe.

Neither Roosevelt nor Churchill had such an advantage. Until Kursk, the advantage had been theirs; now it was Stalin's.

He had become converted to the idea of meeting the two leaders also because of the landings in Sicily and the effects of that success. Mussolini's government fell on July 25, and after negotiations carried on in Madrid, the Italian government surrendered on September 3. On that same day, the British Eighth Army began to cross the Straits of Messina, landing on the toe of Italy. At last an Allied army had reached the mainland of western Europe. Here was proof of their intention to invade Europe, if only through the Italian peninsula. As a result of their recent meeting in Quebec, Roosevelt and Churchill had once more, in a report to Stalin, declared their intention of launching the invasion of 1944. With Allied forces on the shores of southern Europe, and with preparations increasing for the invasion from the west, more than ever Stalin wanted to know the future plans of the Anglo-American leaders about the war and the postwar world. He must have such information because Italy was closer to Soviet Russia than the English Channel and the French beaches.

Stalin also claimed to have been highly displeased by not being privy to the negotiations between the Anglo-American negotiators and the representatives of the Italian government. On August 22 he complained that the United States and Britain had always reached agreement between themselves, "while the U.S.S.R. is informed of the agreement between the two powers as a third party looking passively on. I must say that this situation cannot be tolerated any longer."[17] After the Allied landings in Sicily and Italy, Stalin realized that the policy of refusing to meet with Roosevelt and Churchill no longer paid dividends. He could learn more and bargain better by conferring with them than by remaining within the Kremlin. But he dared not enter a meeting with the two capitalists without first making careful preparations.

Stalin feared being faced with unexpected issues or disagreeable demands. In advance of the meeting with Churchill and Roosevelt, he had to sound out their intentions. He needed to measure the strength of their demands and to test their flexibility about concessions to his own demands. As a seasoned Communist, such precautions were necessary in dealing with capitalists because Stalin had never negotiated personally with two such men at the same time. Moreover, he believed that such precautions would guarantee the maximum chances of success. For these reasons he had initiated the idea of a foreign ministers' meeting prior to the meeting with Churchill and Roosevelt. By insisting that the foreign ministers come to Moscow, Stalin would be in a position to monitor and control events. Molotov could confer quickly with him about any question that might arise, and, if necessary, the conference room could be bugged. With the foreign ministers in Moscow, the meeting would proceed according to this timetable and in the direction he desired.

Although Stalin had been converted to the prospect of meeting with his capitalist allies, he still remained the prudent, suspicious Bolshevik who had survived the struggle for power after Lenin's death, destroying his enemies and thousands of potential enemies only by careful and thorough planning. Part of a similar planning process would be to use the foreign ministers' meeting as a means of testing the Allies for surprises before he met with Churchill and Roosevelt.

At last it appeared that the three leaders would come together, thanks to Stalin's realization that little could be gained by refusing such a meeting. For the first time in history, the Soviet ruler would meet with the President of the United States. Much though remained to be decided, chiefly the site of the meeting. On this question, Churchill and Roosevelt would soon learn how tough and persistent a negotiator Stalin could be. Because he had consented to meet with them did not mean that he would accede easily to their positions. He had consented to meet because he knew that they would need his help in the future—and that would give him an advantage in bargaining with the capitalist Allies.

5

Is This Trip Necessary?

DURING WORLD WAR II, American travelers often saw posters in railroad stations asking, "Is this trip necessary?" The question reminded them that seating space on overcrowded trains was limited if not nonexistent; they might very well spend the entire journey standing or seated on their luggage. The sign was intended to discourage citizens from traveling unless the journey would aid the war effort. This phrase might have haunted Roosevelt during the weeks after September 8 when he argued with Stalin over the site of their proposed meeting. Was a trip necessary in wartime which would require that the President of the United States travel to the Middle East, even to the western portion of Asia?

Although Stalin apparently had finally agreed to a meeting of the three leaders, the question of the site troubled the President. Never before in the history of the American presidency had a President gone farther from Washington than Casablanca, and now Stalin wanted Roosevelt to attend a meeting in Teheran. The distance from Washington to Teheran would involve long flights and possible delays if vital documents had to be dispatched to the President. The trip to Teheran would also cause a constitutional problem for Roosevelt. "My Congress will be in session at that time and, under our constitution, I must act on legislation within ten days," he wrote Stalin.[1] Bills passed by Congress would have to be flown to Roosevelt for his signature and then returned to Washington—all within ten days. Bad weather could

lengthen the flying time beyond the ten-day period and produce a constitutional crisis. Always mindful of congressional
sensitivities, Roosevelt did not want his absences from
Washington to create a constitutional problem at that time;
after the war, when discussions over the peace settlement
were held, he would be free to attend such meetings without congressional complaints. Consequently, he proposed
Egypt, a neutral state, as a site for the meeting. But Stalin
found Egypt inappropriate because the Soviet Union had no
representative there. However, he had no objection to Teheran.

In deference to Stalin's wishes, Churchill had already
consented to meet in Teheran although he would have preferred Cyprus or Khartoum. Nevertheless, he told Stalin that,
"on this meeting of the three of us, so greatly desired by all
the United Nations, may depend not only the best and shortest method of finishing the war, but also those good arrangements for the future of the world which will enable the British
and the American and Russian nations to render a lasting
service to humanity."[2]

Churchill liked the idea of using ships, one for each of
the three leaders, anchored in a harbor in Egypt, Syria, or
Cyprus. Each leader could use his vessel as a headquarters
and communications center. Roosevelt thought the idea excellent but he doubted that Stalin would consent, and so
Churchill dropped the proposal. Next, he suggested that arrangements be made for a meeting in Cairo, which would of
course become known. "Then perhaps only two or three days
before our meeting, we should throw a British and Russian
brigade around a suitable area in Teheran including the airfield and keep an absolute cordon till we have finished our
talks." The Persian government would be kept in the dark
until the moment to act. "Thus we shall have an effective
blind for the world press and also for any unpleasant people
who might not be as fond of us as they ought." For the future, Churchill suggested that the phrase "Cairo 3" be used
instead of Teheran in their correspondence, and that the code
name for the meeting of the three leaders should be "Eu-
reka," which "I believe is ancient Greek." While not opposed to Churchill's diversionary tactics in Cairo, Stalin

regarded the throwing of brigades around an area in Teheran before the meeting as "inexpedient as it would cause an unnecessary sensation and would decamouflage the preparations. I suggest that each of us should take with him a sufficient police guard."[3]

While the top-level debate over possible sites continued, through telephone calls to the White House and the Soviet Embassy Joseph E. Davies learned that the Roosevelt-Stalin meeting had been canceled and that a foreign ministers' meeting had been proposed as a substitute. Throughout August and into September, Davies had been unable to talk at length with Roosevelt, who had been away from the capital much of that time. And Davies could not talk with Harry Hopkins until September 25, after he had emerged from another stay in the hospital. Then Davies briefed him on Stalin's case for doubting American sincerity.

Stalin suspected the Americans because they had reneged on signing a treaty relating to his demands for a new Polish frontier, which he considered "as vital to his defenses against repetition of German aggression." To Stalin, the continued presence of the Finnish minister in Washington was suspicious. Why did the President permit the sabotaging of Lend-Lease by a few in the War Department and in the State Department through the propaganda that the United States would ultimately have to fight Russia? "The Quebec Conference," said Davies, "again showed Churchill and Roosevelt 'cheek to jowl,' planning military and possibly political strategy. This combined with the knowledge of common language, tradition and ideology, indicated a closer union between them than he had with either." At least Stalin knew that he had a treaty with Churchill. He would fear being placed in between Churchill and Roosevelt in a conference which would settle vital interests unless he was reasonably assured that Roosevelt would go along. Probably he would not consent to any meeting with Roosevelt until he felt reasonably certain as to the President's attitude on one vital security concern: his western frontier. The Soviet Ministry believed that powerful forces inside the State Department never lost an opportunity to disparage and fight the Soviet Union. An example was the "alleged shooting of Polish soldiers" at Katyn. All of these suspicions or facts made Stalin reluctant to meet with Roosevelt or with Roosevelt and Churchill (whom Stalin disliked, according to Davies) unless there were reasonable assurances beforehand as to how each man regarded matters vital to Stalin.

Hopkins asked what should be done. Davies replied that Roosevelt ought to get word to Stalin that regardless of what might occur at the foreign ministers' meeting, he would guarantee that when Stalin and he got together, some method satisfactory to Stalin would assure that his vital interests would be accommodated. Stalin's vital interests were equitable and right and "should be acceded to in the common interests of world peace." The smaller nations had to make sacrifices. "Who would fight the Red Army, once they were in possession?"

Hopkins asked if Stalin would make a separate peace. Davies felt confident that Stalin would not do so unless convinced that the capitalist nations were ganging up on him and that he would not get a square deal. There was "grave danger that just as Britain and France drove him into making terms with Hitler in 1939, there was danger that we would do it again, only this time [we would] convince him that for the Russians the only safe way out was to go it alone."[4]

After talking with Hopkins, Davies had a lengthy discussion with Roosevelt in the White House on September 27. The President asked the reason for Stalin's reluctance to meet him. Davies replied that Stalin welcomed a meeting with Roosevelt, but he was not keen on Churchill, "they got into each other's hair." It was clear to him that no meeting between the three men would be agreed upon until Stalin felt reasonably sure that he would not be confronted by two against one on the question of Soviet security in Poland and on matters affecting his vital interests. Stalin resented the American position on the Polish issue and would not surrender his "vital security" or meet with Roosevelt and Churchill until he knew where the Americans stood on that issue.

Davies then asked Roosevelt point-blank where he stood on that question. "Why of course we will not fight Russia for Poland," replied Roosevelt, "but I do want to talk to him about it and see whether I cannot convince him as to the manner in which his aims could be obtained without offending democratic public opinion, i.e., possibly through a plebiscite or possibly through giving all inhabitants the right of election to opt as to which government they wanted."[5] As a result of this discussion, Davies was sent off on another mission for the President.

Three days later he left for Mexico City to talk with his old friend Constantine Oumansky, the Soviet ambassador, who was believed to have influence with Stalin. In Mexico City on October 2, they strolled in the embassy garden discussing Soviet-American relations. There Oumansky explained that the Soviet ambassadors in London and Washington, Maisky and Litvinov, had recently been recalled to Moscow because of resentment over the failure to launch the cross-Channel invasion, which would have relieved pressure on the Red Army, and because of lack of confidence in Churchill, who was blamed for thwarting American efforts to launch the invasion. British influence had intensified suspicion and ill-will in the United States against the Soviet Union. The Standley incident had only proved the insidious influence of Britain on American diplomacy. Oumansky had found other changes in American attitudes. State Department subordinates were openly critical and hostile toward the Soviet Union—their comments had been overheard by the Soviet staff at official diplomatic and social functions in Mexico City. "In the State Department, in some circles of the Army and Navy," he said, "there were not only words, but acts hostile to the Soviets."

The Soviet government had been ignored in the matter of world planning when their country was killing more Germans than any other of the Allied nations. Repeatedly Moscow's leaders had been confronted with actions on vital questions of military and political strategy on which as partners they should have been consulted in advance. Oumansky continued with his list of complaints, ending with the question: "Why does the United States government not recognize the validity of the Curzon Line? Britain has done so." To do so would be to rectify a wrong done to Russia. Because of all these complaints, in the Soviet view, "the West

was hostile and intent upon bleeding their Soviet ally white."
Davies's visit to Moscow had helped to repair some of the
deterioration in American policy toward Russia, but Oumansky had not been surprised when the Roosevelt-Stalin
meeting had not taken place. "The forces hostile to Russia
had been again effective. They did not want Stalin and Roosevelt to meet."

As to any future meeting of the three leaders, before Stalin put himself in the position of being overruled two to one,
he would have to deal at arm's length. His confidence in
American goodwill had been shaken. Moreover, vital questions could not be discussed informally between diplomats
because American representatives in Moscow had been unfriendly, almost openly hostile, with the single exception of
Davies's tenure as ambassador.

Davies had not tried to interrupt Oumansky's monologue. When he finally finished, Davies agreed that he
understood much of what Oumansky was trying to say, but
there were always two sides to every question. They were
unjustified in distrusting the motives of the American government, the top officials, and the President, who was concerned with beating Hitler as quickly as possible and with
developing "a durable, just peace in the world based upon
law, order, fairness and equity and a live-and-let-live policy
among nations." The President had been happy that Stalin
had agreed to the meeting in Fairbanks, but in Davies's absence at the Washington Conference the second front had
been postponed. Oumansky should not misunderstand the
situation because on military matters Roosevelt was governed by his advisers. He was vitally concerned with preserving the unity of the three nations since he knew that
without it, neither the war nor the peace could be won. Roosevelt had valid reasons—shipping and the Pacific situation—for agreeing to the delay in the second front. But that
did not mean he did not want to meet Stalin so that they could
know and measure each other as Churchill and Stalin had
already done.

Then Davies came to the reason for his present visit. He
asked Oumansky to send a message to Stalin in an effort
to repair the damage. Stalin should accept Davies's personal guarantee that if he and Roosevelt met, they would

come to a complete and final agreement upon matters that would preserve the vital interests of each nation and promote world peace.[6] Their personal meeting, Davies guaranteed, would result in an understanding that "Roosevelt would not ultimately object to the Curzon Line" or to the annexation of the Baltic States. He urged Stalin to agree to a meeting with Roosevelt in the Mediterranean area.[7]

On his return to Washington, Davies immediately reported to "the Boss," who was particularly interested in Oumansky's revelations of indiscretions on the part of members of the American diplomatic service. Davies told him that he had given Oumansky "the special 'message to Garcia,' " who had replied that because of Stalin's personal confidence in Davies, the meeting was assured.[8]

Roosevelt's concessions to Stalin about the Curzon Line and the Baltic States did not result from a sudden lapse in direction of American foreign policy but represented changes in policies he had pondered for months. As early as March 1943, when Anthony Eden had come to Washington for consultation with American leaders, he had dined with Roosevelt and Cordell Hull. That evening, March 15, Roosevelt had surprised Eden with his views on the Polish question, because he "thought that if Poland had east Prussia and perhaps some concessions in Silesia, she would gain rather than lose by agreeing to the Curzon Line." At the appropriate time, Britain, the United States, and Russia should decide on a reasonable and just solution, and if all were agreed, Poland would have to accept it. Roosevelt did not object to the Russian claim to the Baltic States. "His view of this is that if Russia takes these states nobody is going to turn her out." And he thought "it might be desirable if at some stage we, Russia, and the United States were to try to come to an agreement about Poland."[9]

Seven months later, because he wanted Stalin to come to their meeting at a convenient site, Roosevelt had used Davies to signal Stalin that he would make a change in foreign policy in order to obtain a meeting. By hinting at concessions on the Curzon Line and the annexation of the Baltic States—two matters very dear to Stalin—Roosevelt had sought to reassure him about Soviet-American relations. In conceding these demands, Roosevelt would show Stalin that there was no cause for suspicion and that at their meeting he would not line up with Churchill in opposition to him. Thanks to this concession, there ought to be no more barriers to Stalin's accepting the final details.

Roosevelt's change in policy was an error in strategy, for he had given away a major bargaining point before being certain that Stalin would concede. If Roosevelt would concede so easily, why should Stalin give in? He need only maintain his position and the arrangements would all ultimately satisfy him. Such a concession could only convince Stalin that Roosevelt and Churchill would need Soviet help when the second front got under way. Nevertheless, the argument over meeting sites continued.

Uninformed about Roosevelt's concession to Stalin, Churchill next put forward another site for their meeting: a Royal Air Force training school near Habbaniya in Iraq that would provide isolation and security, and would be only a few hours flying time from Cairo. To Roosevelt, he proposed that they "put up three encampments and live comfortably in perfect seclusion and security." He referred the President to Matthew, chapter 17, verse 4: "Then answered Peter and said unto Jesus, Lord it is good for us to be here; if thou wilt, let us make here three tabernacles; one for thee, and one for Moses and one for Elias." Roosevelt thought it an excellent idea. "St. Peter sometimes had real inspirations," he wrote Churchill. "I like the idea of three tabernacles. We can add one later for our old friend Chiang." [10]

Unhappy with Teheran as the site for the long-sought-after meeting, and hoping that the concession would move him, Roosevelt wrote Stalin on October 14 that because of the U.S. Constitution, he did not feel he could really take the risk of traveling so far from Washington: "The Congress will be in session. New laws and resolutions must be acted on by me after their receipt and must be returned to the Congress physically before ten days have elapsed. None of this can be done by radio or cable." Teheran was too far away for the constitutional requirements to be fulfilled. Planes could be delayed—whether flying eastbound or westbound—by the mountains around Teheran. In the past, planes traveling in either direction were often held up for three or four days.

He had other sites to propose. Cairo, an attractive city, had a hotel and villas near the Pyramids in an area that could be isolated. Asmara, the capital of Italian Eritrea, he had heard would be a good site because it had excellent facilities and a landing field. He even adopted Churchill's idea of a ship for each of the three leaders anchored in a Mediterranean port. Then he added Habbaniya, where "we could have three comfortable camps with adequate Russian, British and American guards." (He omitted the three tabernacles.) The press would be banned and the site cordoned off by troops. As to the date for their meeting, he proposed some time between November 20 and 27. "I am placing a very great importance on the personal and intimate conversations which you and Churchill and I will have, for on them the hopes of the future world will greatly depend." [11]

None of the sites suggested pleased Stalin. He replied that Teheran alone was acceptable because the Red Army's offensive, which had opened during the summer, would continue into the winter, and his colleagues demanded that he maintain daily personal contact with the Soviet Supreme Command. Consequently, Teheran would be best because of the telegraph and telephone connections with Moscow. For these reasons Stalin's colleagues insisted on Teheran as the site of the meeting. Of course he wanted the press excluded; he accepted Roosevelt's proposed dates.

Churchill now added a fresh complication to the argument: he requested a full meeting of the Combined Chiefs of Staff after the close of the foreign ministers' conference in Moscow before the meeting with Stalin. The plans for 1944 troubled Churchill and the British chiefs of staff, and they wished to review them. They were concerned that by adhering rigidly to plans made earlier at Quebec, the Allied armies might fail to exploit new successes in the Mediterranean area. Already they feared that not enough German forces would be contained to prevent Hitler from concentrating forty or fifty divisions against the Allied troops that would be landing in France. For a time, Roosevelt balked at a Combined Chiefs meeting, claiming that the results of the Moscow Conference ought to be digested first, and other projected plans, particularly those for the defeat of Japan, had also to be completed. The staffs could meet after the meeting with Stalin.

Then because he feared that Stalin would go nowhere but to Teheran, on October 25, Roosevelt suggested to Churchill that they meet with their staffs in North Africa or at the Pyramids, and at the close of their talks ask Chiang to meet with them for two or three days. At the same time, they would ask Stalin to send Molotov for a meeting at the same site. Roosevelt suggested November 20. Churchill liked the idea but not the date.

Next, the President proposed that they ask Stalin to consider sending a Russian military representative to sit in on the discussions of the Combined Chiefs of Staff. Stalin's representative could make whatever comments and proposals his leader might desire. But Churchill vetoed that proposal because a Soviet officer representing Stalin would be useless unless he spoke English. Moreover, there would be interminable delays because the officer would lack authority to speak without explicit instructions from Stalin. The Soviet representative would block all discussions and call only for the second front. Churchill reminded Roosevelt that the Russians had not informed them about their plans. "I do not think we should open this door to them as it would probably mean that they would want to have observers at all future meetings and all discussions between us would be paralyzed." In the operations which they were now planning, there would not be a single Russian soldier. The interjection of the Russians into the staff discussions would harm the intimacy and friendship established between the two staffs. "If that were broken, I should despair of the immediate future."[12] But a formal conference of the three powers would be different because the Russians would be represented by people with wide-ranging powers, wrote Churchill.

By October 19, when the Moscow Conference of foreign ministers opened, Roosevelt had someone in Moscow to plead his case for a change in the meeting site: Cordell Hull, the Secretary of State. Originally he had not been Roosevelt's first choice to head the American delegation. The President had hoped to use the Moscow Conference as a fitting climax to the career of Sumner Welles, Under Secretary of State. A professional diplomat, and a personal friend of Roosevelt, Welles was an eloquent spokesman for the Wilsonian idea of the postwar world. Preferring to work through Welles rather than Hull, for years Roosevelt had used both men, playing one off against the other so that he could better control foreign policy. Because both men had factions within the State Department, by the summer of 1943 the infighting forced Roosevelt to make a choice. Thanks to Hull's political connections, Welles had to be sacrificed; he resigned on September 25. The Hull faction in the State Department pushed for him to head the delegation. Although he was not the best choice because of his age and because a speech impediment made understanding him difficult, nevertheless, Roosevelt appointed him to head the American delegation. So at the age of seventy-two, Hull left on his first airplane flight to lead the American delegation at the Moscow Conference, which he believed would fail.

Stalin regarded the foreign ministers' conference as a test of the sincerity of Churchill and Roosevelt before he himself joined them in conference. In Moscow, Stalin and his deputy, Molotov, could examine the Allies through their foreign ministers. As the conference was being held in Moscow, they could maintain control over the proceedings and block any unwanted proposals. To avoid antagonizing the visiting delegations, they remained on their best behavior. Never had Molotov been so polite and genteel. He had a superb opportunity to orchestrate the conference because Eden and Hull generally worked at cross purposes. They could not even agree on the temperature in the conference room—Hull insisted on 90 degrees. He did his best to develop a close personal relationship with Molotov but not with Eden. Molotov reciprocated by letting the western statesmen take the initiative whenever they wished, but he carefully blocked any proposal that might injure Soviet policies or hinder Soviet aspirations in a future sphere of interest.

Eager for discussions of plans about the second front, the Russians seemed pleased by the exposition of the preparations for OVERLORD[13] by General John R. Deane, chief of the United States military mission in Moscow, and by General Hastings Ismay, chief of staff to the British minister of defense. Deane was surprised by the friendly tone of the questions put to him by Molotov and the Soviet generals. There were no angry demands for an immediate second front. The Soviet officials seemed to attach less importance to OVERLORD than they had previously. "They may even urge some delay to OVERLORD if it would make more immediate results possible," reported Deane. He advised the Joint Chiefs of Staff, "You may be confronted with insistence that further operations be undertaken in the Mediterranean now such as for the purpose of quickly drawing German strength from the eastern front." [14]

Anthony Eden proposed a self-denying ordinance to block bilateral treaties with smaller countries. His ordinance would prevent the Soviet Union from negotiating treaties with countries such as Czechoslovakia and Poland, thus creating spheres of interest. Eden never made a fight over this issue, perhaps because Molotov accepted the British-sponsored European Advisory Commission, which would have consultative powers in dealing with the surrender of Germany and the future of the occupied countries.

As for Hull, he came to Moscow bearing a Four Power Declaration, superbly vague, and intended to thwart Republican attempts to make a campaign issue in 1944 out of the question of maintaining peace in the postwar world. The Declaration, which had evolved out of discussions at the Quebec Conference, called for a pledge by Britain, the United States, the Soviet Union, and China to cooperate in maintaining postwar peace and security and in establishing an international organization at the earliest possible date. Although Molotov was cool toward any agreement involving China, he eventually accepted the Declaration, but not before he had obtained changes in the wording that left the Soviet government free to act as it wished in building spheres of interest.

The old Tennessean, Cordell Hull, had another task at the Moscow Conference: To persuade Stalin that the President could not travel to Teheran because of the Constitution. Acting under instructions, Hull presented a presidential message to Stalin on October 25. Roosevelt argued that Teheran was impossible as a site because the distances involved prevented him from fulfilling his constitutional obligations, which he once again explained to Stalin. Flights into and out of Teheran might be impossible for days at a time because the approaches to the city involved flying over mountains. Roosevelt could not assume that he would be able to fulfill his constitutional obligation to act on bills within ten days. "Therefore, with much regret I must tell you that I cannot go to Teheran and in this my Cabinet members and the legislative leaders are in complete agreement."

He had a new site to suggest: Basra in Iraq (at the head of the Persian Gulf), where they would be protected by their own troops. A special telephone line could be laid from Basra to Teheran, where it could connect up with a line into Russia. At Basra, Stalin would only be a short distance by plane from Teheran.

Roosevelt argued that he would have to travel six thousand miles while Stalin came only six hundred miles from Soviet territory. "I would gladly go ten times the distance to meet you were it not for the fact that I must carry on a constitutional government more than one hundred and fifty years old." Their meeting would be important "not only to our peoples as of today, but also to our peoples in relation to a peaceful world for generations to come." If Stalin did not like Basra, then Roosevelt proposed Bagdad, Asmara, or even Bakara. Although Turkey was neutral, he was certain that the Turks might welcome the idea of being hosts.[15]

After Stalin had read a Russian translation of Roosevelt's message, he handed it to Molotov without comment. But he promised Hull that he would consider Basra as a possible site and would consult with his colleagues. Molotov spoke up, claiming that civil and military authorities in the Soviet Union were loath to have Stalin absent at all from the country if he went to any place where he could not maintain constant direction of the important military operations now in progress. Stalin interrupted to suggest postponing the meeting until the spring of 1944, when military operations would have to be suspended because of the thaw which turned the Russian roads into rivers of mud. At that time Fairbanks, Alaska, would be an appropriate meeting place.

Hull tried to persuade Stalin of the urgency of meeting.

An announcement that the three leaders were planning to confer "would electrify our peoples and allies and be most disheartening to our enemies." But this prospect did not sway Stalin because he had military operations under way that would inflict a decisive defeat on the Germans. "It was an opportunity which might only occur once in fifty years in warfare," and he could not neglect it.

Hull could only fall back on the possibility of establishing proper communications between Teheran and Basra, which he alleged would be as good as those between Teheran and Moscow. Insisting that he was not being stubborn, nor that he was considering prestige but only military necessity, Stalin could not understand "why a delay of two days in the transmission of any state papers could be so vitally important, whereas a false step in military matters was not a grammatical error which could be subsequently corrected but might cost thousands of lives." [16]

Harriman, who had been present during this talk, outlined the technical arrangements that would be made for communications between Basra and Moscow. Eager to impress his audience, the ambassador described the three camps which would be set up at Basra, guarded by British, Russian, and American troops. But Stalin, not troubled by security but preoccupied with communications, promised to confer with his colleagues before replying.

After the October 25 session of the Moscow Conference, Harriman cornered Molotov and asked if communications was really the only drawback to Basra as opposed to Teheran. Molotov swore that it was the sole reason for Stalin's refusal to meet anywhere but in Teheran. According to Molotov, the Soviet government had direct telephone and telegraph lines to Teheran which were controlled by Soviet troops. That being the case, Harriman argued, could not similar arrangements for communications be made from Teheran to Basra with American and British assistance? Instead of answering the question, Molotov asked why, if Roosevelt flew into Teheran, railroads and highways could not be used to transmit documents, should the weather prevent flying. Harriman replied that even air delivery would tax the ten-day limit and the extra time required for seven hundred miles of ground

travel would make it impossible to stay within the constitutional limit. Harriman asked Molotov to accept Roosevelt's
decision that Teheran was impossible and to concentrate on
finding a solution to the problem of communications between Teheran and Basra. Molotov agreed, but without enthusiasm.

Eden, too, had been drafted into pressuring Stalin to accept Roosevelt's position about meeting in Teheran. When
the foreign secretary brought up the proposed meeting of the
three leaders, Stalin declared that he was prepared to attend
a meeting either late in November or early in December at
Teheran, which was the best site because of communications. His colleagues considered that it would be detrimen-
tal to the Soviet war effort if he were to be out of touch with
operations. This consideration made Teheran the only possible site. He regretted any inconvenience caused the President, but he hinted that he was prepared to postpone the
meeting until spring—a prospect Roosevelt dreaded. To Eden,
Stalin seemed sincere. "I think that he genuinely wants the
meeting," he wrote Churchill, "but I do not believe that he
is prepared to go to a place where he has not a legation
through which he can keep in hourly secret touch with Moscow." [17] He doubted that Stalin would go to any other city
that did not contain a Soviet Embassy in which he and his
staff could work—"They are so suspicious that they would
suspect microphones in every British battleship." [18]

Back in Washington, the information from the commanding general of the Army Air Forces seemed to confirm Roosevelt's fears about the constitutional problem created by the
lengthy journey to and from Teheran. General Henry H. Arnold reported that Teheran lay in a valley with a mountain
range 18,000 feet high on the north, cutting the city off from
the Caspian Sea. To the south another mountain range
reached a height of 16,000 feet between Teheran and Abadan. A railroad line connecting Abadan, Basra, and Teheran
ran through the mountains reaching a height of 7,000 feet.
From Abadan to Teheran, the distance by air was 500 miles
and by railroad 700 miles; flying into Teheran, American
pilots would have to clear 16,000 feet. "German pilots, however, go through the valleys and make the trip at an altitude

not in excess of 7,000 feet. However, the German pilots have been flying down there for years and know every rock and tree, while the American pilots have not been flying down there and do not know the route so well."[19] There were landing fields at Habbaniya, Basra, Abadan, and Teheran that could handle American planes.

Even as Arnold reported on the problems of flying into and out of Teheran, preparations had begun stateside for a presidential trip to North Africa. On October 24, the commanding officer of U.S.S. *Iowa*, Captain John McCrae, had been ordered to report to the Commander-in-Chief, U.S. Atlantic Fleet, for duty in connection with transporting the President, his party, and the Joint Chiefs of Staff to an undisclosed North African port. The next day, work at Pier No. 5, Naval Operating Base, Norfolk, began on *Iowa*'s boilers in preparation for the impending trip. Stringent security precautions were ordered to protect the secrecy of the voyage as strange boxes were loaded on board. A derrick barge from the Norfolk Navy Yard came alongside *Iowa*, now anchored in Hampton Roads, and unloaded heavy objects, including a bathtub. Then after weighing anchor, the battleship moved to another anchorage in Chesapeake Bay where the installation of the special equipment continued while the gun crews ran through antiaircraft drills. When preparations were completed, Roosevelt hoped to sail for North Africa by November 7.

From London, Churchill proposed that he meet Roosevelt in Casablanca between November 15 and 20. "I have a great wish and need to see you. All our troubles and toils are so much easier to face when we are side by side."[20] But Roosevelt vetoed Casablanca because *Iowa* drew too much water. Moreover, before meeting Churchill and the Combined Chiefs of Staff in Cairo on November 20, he wanted to spend time in North Africa.

As for Stalin, Roosevelt had a new idea to propose to Churchill. If Stalin would fly to Basra for a day, they could join him there for the meeting. If he rejected that proposal, Roosevelt wanted to travel to Basra anyway, and there meet with Molotov and a Russian staff, all the while pleading with Stalin to join them in Basra for a day's meeting. "I still think

it vital that we see him, but I simply cannot get out of constitutional communication with my Congress."[21]

Churchill gladly acceded to the President's wish: they
would meet in Cairo on November 20. He even offered to
assume the responsibility for making the arrangements for the
meeting, now code-named SEXTANT, another Churchill
suggestion. A villa, surrounded by woods and about a mile
from the Pyramids, would afford complete seclusion for the
meetings; it could be reached from the airfield in twenty
minutes without traveling through any towns. The entire area
would be easily cordoned off by troops. "There are some very
interesting excursions into the desert which we could make
together."[22] Churchill warned Roosevelt about the dangers
connected with sailing through the Mediterranean because
of air attack from glider bombs. He planned to sail about November 12 and to spend a few days in the Mediterranean.
Churchill welcomed a preliminary meeting with Roosevelt
before SEXTANT began. Although willing to go to Basra to
meet Stalin, he saw no reason to make the trip from Cairo
simply to meet with Molotov and some Russian generals who
could come to Cairo. But he would do whatever Roosevelt
wished him to do in order to obtain that meeting with Stalin.

In Moscow, Hull continued to press for a site more convenient to Roosevelt. One evening at a reception at the
American Embassy, he asked Molotov about a possible trip
to Basra. "Why cannot the Marshal fly down even for one day
and meet the President and Mr. Churchill?" Molotov retorted that if the meeting was so important, why could not
Roosevelt fly a bit further and meet Stalin in Teheran? Once
more Hull asked: "Why could not the Marshal fly down and
meet the President and Churchill for even one day and then
leave you there as his representative?" Molotov rejected such
heresy. He was unfit to substitute for Stalin because he was
not a "military man."[23]

During the evening of October 30 Hull sat next to Stalin
at a Kremlin banquet. Again he argued the case for a meeting of the three leaders because of the effect that it would
have on world opinion. Stalin admitted that Molotov could
represent him at Basra but he would not go beyond Teheran. What did Hull think of the substitution? Hull replied

that he thought the presence of Molotov would not have the effect throughout the world of the news that Stalin had been present at such a meeting.

To Roosevelt, Hull reported that Stalin was "inflexible at this time about attending a meeting with you and Mr. Churchill at any place beyond Teheran." They could only continue to attempt cooperation with the Soviet government and hope that Stalin would eventually join the President and prime minister for a meeting. "There is nothing left as to meeting Mr. Stalin at the moment unless you should have a meeting in any event at some place like Basra and decide to fly to Teheran for a day to meet him, since it is evident that he will not at present take even a day off to fly anywhere beyond Teheran." If the President found that undesirable, then Hull could only suggest that wherever Churchill and the President met, they ought to invite Stalin, and after he declined, invite him to send Molotov and a general of suitable rank.[24]

The next day, Hull and Eden talked together about the problem. "We agreed that it is pretty clear that U.J. [Uncle Joe] will not go beyond Teheran," Eden reported to Churchill. "Hull and I feel that it would be wrong for you and the President to go to Basra and meet Molotov even if you were to meet Chiang Kai-shek later. Therefore the only alternatives we can see are:—(a) For you and the President to make a descent for a day or two on Teheran solely to meet U.J. from Basra or any other place you choose for your headquarters. This is the best we can hope for. (b) If the President is not prepared to do the above then the meeting will have to be postponed."[25]

Eden did not believe that it would be embarrassing if a Russian representative came to the meeting of the Combined Chiefs of Staff. "After all that has been said and done here I am clear that U.J., Molotov and company do not for a moment contemplate that there could be anything in the nature of a full Anglo-American staff meeting to discuss the war in Europe without their being invited."[26] During the conference, he had learned much about the Russians:

So far as I can judge the mood of these incalculable people, they are now in the current to move with us in all matters, provided that they can be made to feel that they are in all things our equals and that we are holding nothing back. . . . I do not think that any of us sufficiently understood, I know that I have not, how much these people have suffered from a feeling of exclusion which the extent and scope of their victories has only served to intensify. However unjustified this feeling may be, it is real.[27]

Back in Washington, Roosevelt awaited Stalin's answer, hoping that Eden and Hull could somehow convince him that the American Constitution prevented him from journeying to Teheran. The distance and the dangers were unimportant to him, but until he had received a reply from Stalin, the presidential departure date could not be set. Before leaving Washington, Roosevelt had wanted to talk with Hull, but unfavorable weather conditions delayed Hull's flight from Moscow.

Any further delay waiting for the weather in Moscow to improve did not suit Churchill. Could Roosevelt consider leaving on schedule and meeting Hull in Egypt? Churchill proposed that his ship tie up alongside *Iowa* in Oran or Gibraltar. There the two men could discuss the results of the Moscow meeting before sailing eastward to Malta, where they could meet with the Combined Chiefs and then go on to Cairo. After reading Eden's dispatches from Moscow, Churchill changed his mind about meeting with a Russian military delegation in Cairo. When they had settled their business about the Anglo-American campaign, they should open the whole war situation frankly and fully to the Russians. After finishing with the Russians, they could then meet with Chiang.

"Uncle Joe will not come beyond Teheran," he wrote. "I see no advantage in going to Basra, though I would gladly do so if a triple meeting could be arranged. I suggest that, when we are at Cairo, we try to wheedle him to Habbaniya, or if the weather is really good, make a six hours' hop ourselves to meet him in Teheran. Failing this, we should ask for Molotov."[28]

Roosevelt vetoed Churchill's proposed schedule. He preferred the original plan because preparations had already been made for the destroyers to escort *Iowa*. Changes would interfere with scheduled convoys which required escorts. He would wait, hoping that Hull would be back no later than November 13. Then *Iowa* would sail and he could meet Churchill in Cairo by November 22 or 23.

One guest had accepted Roosevelt's invitation to meet with him and Churchill in Cairo: Chiang Kai-shek, president of the National Government of the Republic of China. At the President's insistence, Chiang had been invited to confer with him and with Churchill. The invitation to Chiang had originated in the spring of 1943 when reports from China indicated that Chiang's government might collapse. A Roosevelt-Chiang meeting would help to bolster the Generalissimo's regime.

Bearing the rank of "Generalissimo," Chiang was not only president of the National Government but also commander of all the Allied armed forces in the Chinese theater of operations and head of the Kuomintang, the sole official government political party. Slim in stature, with dark eyes peering from a face that often resembled a mask, he was neither a dynamic reformer nor a bold leader who yearned to lead his troops in a campaign to drive out the Japanese. Chiang intended to preserve his armies and to amass supplies from the United States for use in the future struggle with Chinese Communists for the control of China after the war with Japan had been ended.

His closest confidant was Mayling Soong, his beautiful and glamorous wife, a Bryn Mawr College graduate and a member of the wealthy and powerful Soong family. Because her family had been Christian for generations, Chiang was influenced to convert to Methodism, a move that delighted the missionary establishment and made him a great Christian statesman in the eyes of American Protestants.

The American people considered China their favorite ally, the symbol of resistance to Japanese aggression. They believed in the myth that Chinese armies were inflicting major defeats on the Japanese armies. However, because revelations about the corruption and incompetence of Chiang's armies would give aid and comfort to the enemy and undermine confidence in his leadership, newspaper correspondents colored the truth, reporting victories that often existed only in their stories. Nevertheless, American military planners believed that China would eventually become the base for the final attack on the Japanese homeland. Chinese armies would tie down a million Japanese troops and keep them from being used to defeat the American forces advancing across the Pacific Ocean. Consequently, all criticism of Chiang's misgovernment had to be censored and he should have whatever supplies he demanded in order to sustain his government lest it fall and a new regime make peace with the Japanese.

Roosevelt's attitude toward Chiang and China was colored by the American public's view of Chiang as the great democratic, Christian ally of the United States. Any hint that the President did not share this view would have stirred up a political storm that Roosevelt dared not face. Public opinion polls revealed American sympathy for the Chinese, whom they believed to be fiercely resisting the Japanese armies. Roosevelt had no alternative to Chiang. He would not haggle with him over supplies or demand reforms in his government. Because Roosevelt foresaw China becoming one of the great world powers in the postwar era, he feared to antagonize Chiang. China had to be treated as a great power now. Roosevelt was convinced that the day of empires was drawing to an end and that after the war, with the British, French, and Dutch empires gone, a power would be needed to maintain peace in the Far East. China would have to be that power.

By the spring of 1943 concern mounted in Washington over the condition of China, where growing inflation, discontent in the provinces, and Japanese victories over Chinese armies threatened to undermine Chiang's regime. In June, Roosevelt decided that a meeting with Chiang ought to be arranged even if it only involved a friendly exchange of pleasantries because it would bolster the Generalissimo's position and boost Chinese morale. A Roosevelt invitation for a meeting with Chiang would make the Chinese people realize that the powerful United States had recognized that China had equal rank. Hopefully the meeting would restore the confidence of Chinese officials and people in their government. Of course Chiang would never ask for such a meeting because he would lose face and that could weaken his position. So after a lengthy visit by Madame Chiang, during which she moved into the White House, Roosevelt sent an invitation in June 1943. Although Chiang was eager to meet in August or September, that was too early for Roosevelt. Not until October could he invite Chiang to meet with him and Churchill.

On the role of China as a great power, Churchill and Roosevelt were far apart in their thinking. "I cannot regard the Chungking government as representing a great world-power," Churchill noted in November 1942. "Certainly there would be a faggot-vote on the side of the United States in any attempt to liquidate the British overseas empire."[29] Consequently, he left to Roosevelt the task of inviting Chiang to Cairo.

Instead of sending the message through the American ambassador in Chungking, Roosevelt dispatched another personal emissary, Patrick J. Hurley. A selfmade millionaire, Hurley had started work at age eleven in an Oklahoma coal mine. A World War I veteran, he made a fortune in banking, oil, real estate, and corporate law. His leadership in the Hoover presidential campaign in Oklahoma led to an appointment in 1929 as Secretary of War. When the New Deal came to Washington in 1932, Hurley stayed on to practice corporation law. After Pearl Harbor he badgered the War Department for a command appointment, but his age and lack of training ruled out such an assignment. Roosevelt, however, liked him. His muscular figure, close-cropped mustache, blue eyes, square jaw, and gray hair gave the impression of a no-nonsense leader. The United States needed more men like Hurley, Roosevelt told his son Elliott. Hurley spoke plain language, unlike "the men in the State Department, those career diplomats . . . half the time I can't tell whether to believe them or not."[30]

Early in 1942, Roosevelt made Hurley a brigadier general and sent him to Australia to coordinate efforts to ship guns and supplies to the beleaguered American troops in the Philippine Islands. Although Hurley was also appointed U.S. minister to New Zealand, he spent less than six months there because he wanted to escape that backwater of the war. Returning to Washington, he became a roving envoy for the President, traveling to the Soviet Union as a fact finder, where he was one of the first American officers permitted to visit the battlefields. Stalin even honored him with a personal meeting in November 1942. Now in the fall of 1943, Roosevelt dispatched Hurley on another trip to the Middle East and to China. He directed Hurley to discuss the Cairo Conference with Chiang, following his policy of treating China as an ally on a par with the Soviet Union and Britain.

Hurley arrived in Chungking, complete with medals and uniform. The U.S. military attaché, looking at Hurley's rows of ribbons, commented, "General, I see you have every campaign ribbon but Shays' Rebellion."[31] In his talks with Hurley, Chiang voiced his worries about meeting with Stalin, and in view of the troubles with Chinese communism, finally refused to do so. Without success, Hurley tried to calm the Generalissimo's fears that the Soviet Union wanted either to communize China or to conquer and annex portions of the country. According to Hurley, Stalin had renounced world conquest as a basic policy of communism, and Russia no longer subsidized or directed Communist activities in other nations.

Pressed for time, on October 27 Roosevelt asked Chiang for a meeting with him and Churchill in Cairo between November 20 and November 25. "I am looking forward to seeing you because I am sure there are many things that can only be satisfactorily settled if we can meet face to face."[32] Three days later, Roosevelt invited Chiang to meet him and Churchill in Cairo on November 26. Although Chiang accepted the invitation, he insisted that Roosevelt and Churchill meet him prior to their meeting with Stalin. If that could not be arranged, then his meeting with them must be postponed. From Stalin, Roosevelt still had no message.

Forced to make a decision on November 5, the President decided to leave Washington on November 11. By that date, if all went well, Hull would have returned and reported in person on the Moscow Conference and his meetings with Stalin. Roosevelt hoped that *Iowa* would reach Oran no later than November 20; from there he would fly to Cairo. He asked Chiang to arrange to be in Cairo on November 22 so that he and Churchill could meet the Generalissimo before they met Stalin.

News came from Stalin on November 6. Once more he

had rejected Roosevelt's pleas. He could find no place suitable for the meeting with Roosevelt and Churchill other than Teheran. His duties as supreme commander of the Soviet armies obliged him to carry out the daily direction of military operations, and since the summer campaign was extending over into a winter campaign, he claimed that it was more important than ever for him to carry out these duties. Under these conditions, he ruled out any chance of traveling beyond Teheran. "My colleagues in the government consider, in general, that my travelling beyond the borders of the U.S.S.R. at the present time is impossible due to the great complexity of the situation at the front." Consequently he was willing that Molotov substitute for him. According to the Soviet constitution, Stalin explained, Molotov would exercise "all powers of the head of the Soviet government." He thought this solution would end all of the difficulties over a mutually agreeable meeting place.[33]

The same day new information came to Washington about weather and travel between Cairo and Teheran. The British reported that in 1942 travel by air between Cairo and Teheran from mid-November to mid-December was delayed only twice and then only for not more than two days. Harriman, who also looked into the problem, found that the weather was at its worst during January and February, but that weather predictions for late November and early December could be made for at least three days. Moreover, he felt that the risk of bad weather was greater for Stalin than for Roosevelt, who would be flying between Cairo and Teheran. Harriman proposed that, if the weather predictions were favorable, Roosevelt fly from Cairo to Teheran and Stalin come to Teheran from Moscow. They would have thirty-six hours in which to have at least "two 3-cornered meetings and for you to see U.J. alone as well."[34] This was a plan Harriman thought Stalin would accept. If they then failed to meet, it would only be the fault of the weather.

The decision was now up to Roosevelt. He, more than Stalin, wanted the meeting. But Stalin's last message—cool, indifferent—inferred that he did not regard the meeting as important and that it was up to Roosevelt to decide if there would be any meeting at all because he also had objected to

Teheran as the site. Until now, Stalin had opposed every suggestion or fallen back on an excuse. Now he was prepared to meet Roosevelt and Churchill, but only at Teheran.

More than anything, Roosevelt would have preferred to meet alone with Stalin, but it appeared he could only have a meeting with Churchill present and only in Teheran. No American President while in office had traveled so far from Washington. Dare he risk a communications breakdown that would prevent him from signing important bills and provide ammunition for his enemies at home? Should he reject a meeting with Stalin simply because of a clause in the Constitution when so much was at stake? If it became known that he had refused to meet Stalin because of a clause, what repercussions could be expected? In the postwar world, Stalin's cooperation would be essential. How would he react to Roosevelt rejecting a meeting because of a constitutional technicality when great strategic decisions had to be made? In the past Stalin had not been present when Roosevelt and Churchill had met for decision making. What would be his response when Roosevelt rejected a meeting that would at last enable Stalin to participate in that decision making?

If Roosevelt were to go to Teheran, plans would have to be swiftly made. The Secret Service would have to prepare for the trip, checking routes and accommodations. Already in the Norfolk Navy Yard workmen were completing the installation of special equipment on *Iowa* for Roosevelt and his party.

On November 8, Roosevelt conceded to Stalin's demand that the meeting be held in Teheran: "You will be glad to know that I have worked out a method so that if I get word that a bill requiring my veto has been passed by the Congress and forwarded to me, I will fly to Tunis to meet it and then return to the Conference. There I have decided to go to Teheran and this makes me especially happy." Roosevelt added that "the psychology of the present excellent feeling" demanded that the three leaders meet, if only for two days. The Combined Chiefs of Staff could commence working in Cairo on November 22, and he hoped that Molotov and the Soviet military representative, whom he hoped could speak English, would come to Cairo at that time. Then, on Novem-

ber 26, they would all go to Teheran in time for a conference opening the next day. "The whole world is watching
for this meeting of the three of us," he told Stalin. "The fact
that you and Churchill and I have got to know each other
personally will have far reaching effect on the good opinion
within our three nations and will assist in the further distur-
bance of Nazi morale."[35]

As for the constitutional problem, it could be solved by
interpreting Article I, section 7, of the Constitution to mean
that the ten days could not begin until the President had received the bill that needed his signature. ("If any bill shall
not be returned by the president within ten days . . . after
it shall have been presented to him, the same shall be a law,
in like manner if he had signed it, unless the Congress by
their adjournment prevent its return, in which case it shall
not be a law.")

Now Roosevelt had to await Stalin's reply, uncertain
whether he would consent to come to Teheran. In his message of November 5, Stalin had seemed indifferent to the idea
of a meeting. Roosevelt had interpreted this to mean that
Stalin "would not come even to that place—this because his
advisors did not wish him to leave Russian soil."[36]

Late in the evening of November 9, Harriman in Moscow
formally transmitted to Molotov the President's message
agreeing to travel to Teheran. Molotov grilled the ambassador about the Cairo meeting, seeking to learn what military
topics would be discussed so that the Soviet staff could be
prepared. Harriman promised to obtain more detailed information from Roosevelt.

Instead of commenting favorably on the concession, Molotov asked if the President had not noticed that "in Marshal
Stalin's message of November 5 it was stated that his colleagues in the Soviet government did not consider it advisable for Marshal Stalin in general to leave the Soviet Union
at the present time because of the complexity of the operations on the front?" Harriman could only reply that Roosevelt thought Stalin's offer to travel to Teheran still stood.
Molotov could not stop. "The general reluctance to have
Marshal Stalin leave the Soviet Union at all had been clearly
set forth in that message."[37] However, he could not speak

for the Marshal, but he would transmit Roosevelt's message.

For another day, Stalin let Roosevelt dangle. Not until the actual date of his departure from Washington did the President receive Stalin's message agreeing to travel to Teheran and promising to dispatch Molotov to Cairo along with a military representative.

The news that Roosevelt had invited the Russians and the Chinese to come to Cairo at the same time did not suit the prime minister. Churchill complained that Roosevelt had agreed that there would be "many meetings" between the American and British chiefs of staff before either the Russians or the Chinese arrived. He begged for a postponement of the Russian appearance in Cairo until November 25. Roosevelt refused because, he informed Churchill on November 11, he had just received Stalin's promise to meet them in Teheran. Until now he had doubted if Stalin would go through with his offer to travel to Teheran. "Thus endeth a very difficult situation, and I think we can be happy." As for "many meetings" between the British and American chiefs of staff, he would not have Stalin thinking "we had ganged up on him on military actions." The chiefs of staff would only be working on plans. "It will not hurt you or me if Molotov and a Russian military representative are in Cairo too. They will not feel that they are being given the 'run around.'" Roosevelt urged: "Let us take them in on the high spots."

In addition, he wrote Churchill, he now had Stalin's confirmation of the Teheran meeting. So Molotov and the Soviet military representative would travel with them to Teheran and afterward return to Cairo for more talks. "I think it is essential that this schedule be carried out. I can assure you there will be no difficulties. . . . I am just off. Happy landings to us both."[38]

Roosevelt's refusal to concede to Churchill's wishes indicated that Roosevelt was more concerned about Stalin's sensitivities and Soviet-American relations than he was about the Anglo-American alliance and his relationship with Churchill. Even to suit the prime minister, Roosevelt would not alter the schedules for the Cairo and Teheran conferences.

But it was not to be that way. Learning from Churchill's deliberate leak that the Chinese would also be in Cairo, Stalin informed Roosevelt that circumstances of a "serious character" would prevent Molotov from coming to Cairo. Instead, he would be available for the Teheran meeting—where the Chinese would not be present. Stalin had vetoed the Molotov trip to Cairo because a meeting with Chiang Kai-shek could injure relations between the Soviet Union and Japan. So Roosevelt could have the Chinese at Cairo but not the Russians. They would come only to Teheran.

Stalin had won. The conference would meet when and where he wanted it to meet; Roosevelt had been forced to concede to his wishes. However, the President had wanted this meeting so much that he was at last compelled to meet all Stalin's demands. Roosevelt had argued against Teheran as the site because he was worried about the distance that would separate him from Washington—no American President had ever before attempted to carry on the presidency from so far away. Roosevelt could not convince Stalin that there were also political complications as well as a constitutional technicality. The election of 1942 had brought Republican victories in Congress—they came within seven seats of capturing a majority in the House of Representatives. There was a possibility that a coalition of Republicans and conservative Democrats might vote out a bill needing a presidential veto. If a storm or engine trouble delayed the plane carrying the bill, it might not be returned to Washington within the constitutional time limit. The Republicans would be delighted by the spectacle of "that man in the White House" failing in his constitutional obligations. Roosevelt would also be subject to severe criticism for failing to carry on his job at home. Why did he have to travel so far? He should stay at home and work at winning victory.

Stalin had rejected Roosevelt's pleas, however, because in Teheran he would feel more secure and his line of communications with Moscow would be maintained. All of the other sites proposed by Roosevelt and Churchill would have left Stalin isolated, without the security of Russian troops. In Teheran, Stalin would be in a city and in an area occupied by Soviet troops (since August 1941, Soviet troops had controlled northern Iran). Moreover, he would not be cut off from this protection, and he would be able to return safely and quickly to Moscow should events require this. In addition, his line of communications would be under Soviet control all the way from Teheran to Moscow, enabling him to check on his Kremlin colleagues and to direct the course of the war.

But there was more to Stalin's ploy than security. By demanding that Teheran become the site of their first meeting, he forced the President of the capitalist United States to concede to the Chairman of the Council of Ministers of the Soviet Union, and to travel to the site convenient to the leading world Communist. Such a concession placed Roosevelt at a disadvantage even before the conference opened, which had been Stalin's intention ever since September 8. To compel Roosevelt to concede, Stalin had appeared indifferent to the fate of the meeting. By his attitude, he implied that if Roosevelt wanted the meeting, he could have it only at Teheran. The choice of site had become a test of strength between the two men, as far as Stalin was concerned. The more impatient of the pair, Roosevelt, had to capitulate if he were to have the meeting he craved. Because Teheran was Stalin's choice, he had won the first round before the three men sat down at the conference table.

During the past few weeks, Stalin's insistence on Teheran as the meeting place, as well as his earlier refusals to meet with Churchill and Roosevelt, had combined to make his consent to meet at all that much more important. Thus Churchill, and above all Roosevelt, ought to be grateful to Stalin for graciously condescending to meet with them, even in Teheran. If Roosevelt believed so strongly that a meeting with Stalin was necessary, he ought to journey to Teheran in spite of the American Constitution in order to bring it about. Stalin's hard line on the meeting site had brought him a psychological victory before the President's plane had even landed at Teheran.

6
On to Cairo

"THE LUCK HAS HELD," wrote the President in his diary on November 19—"very little sea or wind, though our speed of 24 knots means an occasional drift of spray as I sit on a wide deck forward of my cabin, and I can or do think of nice things—until a plane passes or a destroyer escort is relieved by another and then the war looms up again."

The war came very close on November 14. That afternoon, *Iowa* was practicing an air defense drill, and, for the President's benefit, simulating an air attack from the starboard side. Live ammunition was being fired by the antiaircraft batteries to demonstrate the curtain of fire that could be put up to stop any attack that came close to *Iowa*. Suddenly, amid the barrage, a message reached the bridge: "Torpedo is coming your way!" The destroyer *William D. Porter* had sent the message over TBS (Talk Between Ships) radio.

"General stations" sounded. Over the ship's loudspeaker came the warning: "This is not a drill! Torpedo on the starboard beam!" Throughout the battleship could be heard the pounding of feet as the crew dashed to battle stations, and the clanging of watertight doors being slammed shut. Then over TBS came a further shock: "The torpedo may be ours!"

Captain McCrea at once ordered *Iowa* to turn toward *Porter* so that the battleship, which was only three feet shorter than three football fields, would offer as narrow a target as possible to the oncoming torpedo. But a battleship cannot be whipped around like a speeding automobile. Bells clanged as the great ship went full speed ahead and turned toward *Porter*. The after gun watches reported seeing the torpedo's wake about 1,000 yards away on *Iowa*'s starboard quarter. In the turbulence caused by the ship's high-speed turn, the torpedo detonated with an explosion which to all on board *Iowa* felt as if a depth charge had gone off close by.

Roosevelt had been wheeled from the luncheon table out to the deck to watch the gunnery action. He and all those watching with him had been supplied with cotton for their ears. When the report came about the torpedo firing, an officer on the bridge above the President yelled: "It's the real thing! It's the real thing!" In the confusion, Roosevelt could not at first understand what had happened. Hopkins yelled at him repeatedly asking if he wanted to go inside. "No— where is it?" asked Roosevelt. "Arthur! Arthur! Take me over to the starboard rail. I want to watch the torpedo!" Arthur Prettyman, Roosevelt's valet, did as he was ordered.

For Captain McCrea and Admiral King, it was not only a frightening but a humiliating incident. The United States Navy appeared totally incompetent before an assembled group of top-ranking officers of the Army, not to mention the commander-in-chief. An American destroyer had fired a torpedo aimed at the vessel carrying the chief of staff of the U.S. Army, the chief of staff of the U.S. Navy, the commanding general of the U.S. Army Air Force, the chairman of the U.S. Joint Chiefs of Staff, and the President of the United States along with his personal staff! More embarrassed than angry, Admiral King wanted to relieve the skipper of *Porter* in mid-ocean, but Roosevelt overruled him.

The accidental firing of the torpedo resulted from the failure of the chief torpedoman on *Porter* to remove a primer from the firing lock of the torpedo-launching mechanism. Apparently the primer had been inserted to learn if it was the correct fit, and someone neglected to remove it. During the drill, the destroyer used the battleship as the aiming point in practicing a torpedo attack. Someone touched the firing mechanism, launching the torpedo in the direction of *Iowa* and its distinguished passenger list. Later McCrea ordered that in future none of the escorting destroyers was to use *Iowa* as the aiming point in practice drills.

After the excitement had ended and it was learned that the torpedo had come from an American destroyer, Hopkins joked: "It must have been some damn Republican!" General Arnold asked Admiral King, "Tell me, Ernest, does this happen often in your navy?"[1]

But the torpedo incident was no joking matter to the Secret Service detail who had the responsibility for protecting the President's life. Should McCrea have had to order "Abandon ship," it would be the task of the Secret Service detail to lift Roosevelt into his lifeboat. After the incident the agents annoyed Admiral Brown, Roosevelt's naval aide, by remaining even closer to him. Brown grumbled that Churchill traveled with only one Scotland Yard man. There was a difference: Roosevelt had lost all use of his legs and would have to be lifted into the lifeboat by the Secret Service agents. Further, for the first time in the history of the American presidency, they were responsible for a President who was sailing through waters infested by German U-boats. A U-boat skipper would have risked much to get a shot at the vessel carrying the American President.

The lifeboat could not be redesigned because of his physical condition, but other parts of the battleship were altered to fit Roosevelt's disability. Captain McCrea had turned his cabin over to the President and lived in his sea cabin up on the navigating bridge while his commander-in-chief stayed below. For the convenience of the President, a number of alterations had to be made. An elevator had been installed to enable the Secret Service agents to move him from one deck to another. Ramps had been built over the coamings and deck obstructions to permit him to get about in his wheelchair accompanied by Prettyman, his valet. In the bathroom, a special tub had been installed in the shower with metal railings around the edge. The toilet bowl had been raised to the level of his wheelchair, and the mirror had been lowered to enable him to shave while sitting in his chair. Because he did not like the regulation stiff canvas shower curtains, the President had directed that a decorative shower curtain be installed around the tub.

With Roosevelt had come twenty bottles of Saratoga Springs water and a supply of motion pictures for showing every night. Among the pictures were Walt Disney films, short subjects, newsreels, and motion pictures produced by the Navy. For Roosevelt's reading, his secretary, Grace Tully, had sent a supply of detective stories. In case he had an opportunity for fishing, there were three sets of deep sea fishing gear. As the President would be away from the White House during the Thanksgiving holiday, a supply of frozen turkeys had been loaded on the battleship. For his mess, china and silver had been brought from the White House because there was only enough on board for the ship's officers. The presidential silver and china would also be used to serve meals and state dinners in Cairo and in Teheran. An ample supply of liquor had also been brought from the White House, together with playing cards, poker chips, the presidential flags, and Roosevelt's favorite reclining chair.

During the voyage, McCrea submitted all routine ship's orders to the President: the position, speed, course changes, and fuel on board. Whenever the course was to be altered, McCrea would ask the commander-in-chief's permission. Roosevelt enjoyed the protocol of having ship's information reported to him in the proper naval terminology as would normally be done to any flag officer. At mess he liked to tell stories about "When I was in the Navy."

Whenever weather permitted, Roosevelt sat on the flag bridge deck, dressed in old trousers and a fishing shirt. There he read detective stories, napped, or talked with Harry Hopkins. The area was "off-limits" to all on *Iowa* except a few very important people. Those crew members venturing near the presidential area observed Hopkins leafing through official documents and taking notes. One story went the rounds in the crew's quarters: each evening, Roosevelt, who had been engrossed in his detective stories, would ask Hopkins: "Harry, what have you read today that I ought to know about?" Hopkins would then brief the President on his reading.[2]

The ship on which Roosevelt and Hopkins were traveling was the third one in the history of the Navy to carry the name *Iowa*. Constructed at the Brooklyn Navy Ship Yard, she was launched on August 27, 1943. *Iowa* measured over 887 feet, displaced 45,000 tons, had a top speed of 30 knots, an armament comprising nine 16-inch guns, and a complement of 2,800 officers and enlisted men.

After a shakedown cruise in August 1943, she got under way for Argentia, Newfoundland, and her first assignment, the *"Tirpitz* watch," neutralizing the threat of the powerful German battleship which had been reported preparing to sally forth into the North Atlantic from a Norwegian port. Now assigned to carry Roosevelt and his party to North Africa, she would later see plenty of action in the Pacific theater and years after in the Korean War.

Throughout the voyage, *Iowa* had a screen of three destroyers which had to be relieved frequently for refueling because of her speed. Each group of escorts met the battleship at prearranged rendezvous points during the voyage. Whenever it became necessary for a presidential message to be sent off, one of the destroyers came alongside and the message was passed across. The destroyer then left temporarily in order to transmit the message by radio; on completing the transmission, the destroyer rejoined *Iowa.* Many of the messages were routine, but others were more important, destined for "the Former Naval Person," as Winston Churchill was called in his correspondence with Roosevelt.

A special train carried Churchill and his staff from London to Plymouth, where he arrived after dark on November 12. He boarded H.M.S. *Renown* without displaying the usual "V" sign because he was suffering from a head cold and a sore throat, complicated by the aftereffects of inoculations against typhoid and malaria. Churchill remained in his cabin for most of the voyage. In the party which came on board with the prime minister were Gilbert Winant, the American ambassador, Admiral Sir Andrew Cunningham, First Sea Lord and chief of Naval Staff, and Lieutenant General Sir Hastings Ismay, chief of staff to the minister of defense. By special permission of the cabinet, Sarah Churchill, the prime minister's daughter, serving in the Royal Air Force, accompanied him as his aide-de-camp.

The first day out of port, *Renown* and her escorts sailed through heavy seas with the quarterdeck often under water and at times three inches of ocean in the wardroom. Off Portugal, the weather improved, and on November 15 she sailed into the harbor at Gibraltar. By then Churchill had recovered sufficiently to come on deck.

The next port of call was Algiers, where Churchill conferred on board ship with General Alphonse Georges of the French Committee of National Liberation, and with General Walter Bedell Smith, chief of staff to Eisenhower. Churchill did not go ashore to pay a courtesy call to General Charles de Gaulle, leader of the Free French Forces, because he would surely be recognized and the security of the impending meetings could have been endangered. But De Gaulle, ever jealous of his position, regarded Churchill's failure to call on him as a deliberate insult.

From Algiers, *Renown* sailed at high speed for Malta. Off the island of Pantelleria the crew went to "action stations" when a German reconnaissance plane was sighted, but the Luftwaffe dared not attack because of protection easily available from Malta. When *Renown* at last came alongside the dock at Malta, Churchill was eager to go out on deck. But Admiral Cunningham used one excuse after another to keep him off the quarterdeck. At last after Churchill had become visibly angry, the admiral exclaimed: "I wouldn't go out there if I were you, Prime Minister. It's like a snakes' honeymoon!"[3] Churchill took the admiral's advice and allowed the deck officers to make everything shipshape before making his appearance.

Once ashore, Churchill was taken by a devious route to the governor's palace, "a cold barracks of a place." The governor, Lord Gort, turned his bedroom over to the prime minister, who, still trying to throw off a head cold and temperature, immediately went to bed. The bedroom, on the second floor of the palace, overlooked a street which was a favorite promenade of the Maltese. When Lord Moran, Churchill's physician, visited him on November 18, he complained about the noisy Maltese who walked beneath the windows of the bedroom. Leaping from bed, Churchill rushed to the open window. To those people walking below he shouted: "Go away, will you? Please go away and do not make so much noise."[4] He voiced another complaint: the mooing of the governor's cows disturbed his sleep. Churchill left his bed only for a formal dinner given by Lord Gort, and when he conferred with his chiefs of staff, he remained in bed.

Two of the chiefs of staff, General Sir Alan Brooke, chief

of the Imperial General Staff, and Air Chief Marshal Sir Charles Portal, chief of the Air Staff, had arrived earlier, having flown out to Malta in Churchill's plane. Brooke had the prime minister's cabin, which he found most comfortable—"Bed with sheets, small table, chair and lavatory complete!" Together with the other members of the chiefs of staff, they met around Churchill's bed on November 18 for a conference.

He delivered a bitter tirade on the deficiencies of the Americans, and he bemoaned the losses which Britain had recently suffered in the Aegean and along the Dalmatian coast. (The islands of Cos and Leros had just fallen to the Germans.) Churchill's pleas to Roosevelt to reinforce the British troops on the islands and to help retake the island of Rhodes had been rejected. It had been a painful blow.

Churchill's tirade troubled Brooke. Would he adopt this line at the coming conference with the Americans in Cairo? To Brooke, Churchill seemed inclined to tell the Americans, "All right, if you won't play with us in the Mediterranean, we won't play with you in the English Channel." If the Americans should reply, "All right, then we shall direct our main effort in the Pacific," Churchill would answer, "You are welcome to do so if you wish." Brooke feared that such tactics would not pay.[5]

Brooke saw that underneath his bitterness, Churchill hated to surrender the position of the dominant partner in the relationship which he had enjoyed until now with the President. Churchill was jealous because Roosevelt was becoming the dominant partner. Now the Americans, thanks to their superiority in numbers and armament, would be able to determine Allied strategy and even to veto operations which Churchill supported. But to Brooke, the Americans seemed unable to comprehend British strategy in the Mediterranean. In Churchill's unhappiness, Brooke saw a wish to find a theater in which all of the laurels would go to Britain. Churchill despaired because he realized that ahead loomed a battle with Roosevelt and his staff over strategy, and he lacked the forces to win that battle. Although he and his chiefs of staff were agreed on future strategy, they knew that the Americans were at odds with them.

The British chiefs of staff questioned the "sanctity of OVERLORD." Would the plans and the date for OVERLORD be maintained irrespective of events in the Mediterranean theater of operations? "This issue," wrote the chiefs on November 11, "is clouding the whole of our future strategic outlook, and must be resolved at Cairo." The successful Soviet campaign which had defeated the enemy at Kursk and the subsequent victorious advance of the Red armies, plus the defeat of Italy and the possibility that Turkey might enter the war, all combined to make the British chiefs advocate reconsidering the decisions which had been taken at the Churchill-Roosevelt meetings in Washington and Quebec.

Although the British chiefs claimed to be eager to cross the Channel and to attack the Germans in the spring or summer of 1944, they did not want to "regard OVERLORD on a fixed date as the pivot of our whole strategy on which all else turns." They doubted that achieving a certain strength in the armies by a fixed date would end all their troubles and shorten the war. If followed to its extreme, this policy could paralyze all efforts in other theaters of war. Everything would be fixed on one date and one operation. But at the appointed time, they argued, the German strength might be so great that OVERLORD would be impossible; or the reverse could be true: the Germans could be so weak that other plans would become necessary.

The British chiefs insisted that the best policy for the present was to attack the Germans in every place where the Allies possessed superior forces. Superiority could be achieved only by stretching the German forces and threatening as many of their vital areas as possible. Then OVERLORD could be launched by the summer. But they preferred not to attach overwhelming importance to a certain number of divisions or to a specific date. The date must not become the master, preventing the Allied armies from seizing any opportunity that offered an advantage.

To this end, they formulated a series of goals which ought to be pursued even if that meant postponing the date of OVERLORD. These goals included a unified command in the Mediterranean, continuation of the campaign in Italy, aid to the guerrilla armies in Yugoslavia, Greece, and Albania, the entry of Turkey into the war, the opening of the Dardanelles as soon as possible, and a campaign to further resistance in the Balkans with the aim of increasing chaos and turmoil. Above all they would attack the Germans everywhere, build up the Allied forces, and finally invade Europe as soon as the German strength in France and the general war situation gave good prospect of success. To these goals, Churchill assented with the words: "I cordially agree."[6]

The chief of the Imperial General Staff viewed Europe as a great strategic front in which German troops were distributed around the perimeter according to the threats existing in each theater of war. From France, German forces watched the Channel while other units kept watch in Norway and Denmark. In the east, German armies battled the Russians; in southern Europe, German detachments threatened Turkey and maintained control over the Balkans. A considerable German force held Italy and guarded southern France. All of the German forces were controlled centrally and served by a first-rate railway system, built up during World War I and now augmented by the Autobahn system of roads. It was far easier for the Germans to shift divisions quickly from the eastern front to France than for the Allied forces to move similar units from Italy by sea to France. In Brooke's judgment, the Allied forces ought to draw as many German divisions as possible away from the English Channel and hold them as long as possible in southern Europe. They ought to take full advantage of the conditions existing in 1943 to draw German reserves from the Channel. Should there be any weakening of Anglo-American strength in the Mediterranean, the Germans could then move forces to the Channel coasts.[7] Of course, Brooke's conception of Allied strategy differed from that of the Americans.

For months, American officials and the Joint Chiefs of Staff had considered the British to be uninterested, if not frightened, at the prospect of crossing the English Channel and attempting to land on the shores of France. Memories of the 1914–18 bloodbath deterred them from crossing the Channel and pushed them to look elsewhere for less costly campaigns.

Henry Stimson, a New York corporation lawyer and for-

mer Secretary of State in the Hoover administration, now
Secretary of the Army, after a trip to Britain in the summer
of 1943, returned convinced that Churchill and Brooke had
been influenced by the horrors of Passchendaele and Dunkirk. "Their hearts are not in it," he wrote in his diary. "British theory (which cropped out again and again in unguarded
sentences of the British leaders with whom I have just been
talking) is that Germany can be beaten in a series of attri-
tions in northern Italy, in the eastern Mediterranean, in
Greece, in the Balkans, in Rumania, and other satellite
countries, and that the only fighting which needs to be done
will be done by Russia."[8] Stimson condemned this method
of "pinprick warfare" because Stalin would not be convinced that it represented the fulfillment of the pledge of a
second front. The failure to land in France would only create problems after the war.

The logic of the American Joint Chiefs of Staff followed
a line of thought similar to Stimson's. They complained that
"the United Nations have failed during the past year and a
half to concentrate their forces and to hold on to decisions."
There had only been "verbal adherence to the decision that
the main and decisive effort should be a cross-channel operation and that forces and supplies should be built up in
the U.K. for that purpose." The diversion of resources to the
Mediterranean had only produced a drop in the American
forces that could be brought to bear on Germany and Italy.
The change in plans, from concentrating on crossing the English Channel to landing in North Africa and in Italy, had
only wasted the Allied effort and, if continued, might very
well postpone the victory and produce merely a partial defeat for the enemy.

The American view continued to be that the failure to
practice economy in resources in concentrating their use
would not assure complete victory. To clinch victory, the
American chiefs contended, the United States and Britain had
to decide on a main effort and adhere firmly to that decision.
In contrast to the British view, they argued: "The Mediterranean does not offer an opportunity for decisive military action against the German citadel, does not present an
opportunity to draw continually increasing forces from Rus-

sia, and does not provide the opportunity to place effectively in combat the ground forces of the United States and
Britain."[9] Unless the Soviet armies were supplemented, it
was highly doubtful that the Russian army would be able to
destroy the German forces without an Allied cross-Channel
assault on Europe. These questions and other matters were
now about to be discussed in mid-ocean by the President and
the American chiefs of staff.

On board *Iowa*, now almost halfway across the Atlantic Ocean,
the gin rummy games went on daily among the President's
party. Harry Hopkins and General Arnold were the consis-
tent winners, but in the end, Hopkins won back all that the
general had won. More serious matters concerned the President and his Joint Chiefs of Staff in two meetings held in
his cabin.

On November 15, Roosevelt opened the first meeting with
the announcement that he had summoned Ambassador Harriman from Moscow to attend the Cairo Conference, and he
formally announced that "the big conference would be held
in Teheran." Both Stalin and Molotov would be present.

Then the Joint Chiefs presented the President with their
views on the United Nations strategy in the Balkans–eastern
Mediterranean area, which had so troubled the British chiefs
of staff. The American chiefs of staff regarded the approach
to the European fortress by way of the Balkans and the eastern Mediterranean as unsuitable because of the terrain and
the communications problems. Experience, they argued, had
shown that limited operations, no matter how attractive, inevitably required resources beyond those originally anticipated. Nevertheless, Allied strategy would be served, they
believed, by causing Germany to dissipate her strength in
the Balkan–eastern Mediterranean area. To that end, they
insisted that operations in the area be strictly limited to supplying Balkan guerrillas by sea and by air, small-scale action
by commandoes, and the bombing of vital strategic targets.
They were prepared to bring Turkey into the war but without diverting any resources that might prejudice operations
elsewhere. To this proposed policy, the President replied,
"Amen!" With an "okay" he approved the paper. He wanted

it sent to the British, and announced that the Americans must take their stand on this memorandum.

The discussion wandered to other problems. Roosevelt declared that "it was his idea that General Marshall should be the commander in chief against Germany and command all the British, French, Italian and U.S. troops involved in this effort."[10] Marshall made no response.

As to the upcoming conference in Cairo, Roosevelt announced that the meeting with Chiang Kai-shek and the Joint Chiefs of Staff should be separate from and precede any meeting with the British. He requested that agendas be prepared for the meetings with Chiang, Churchill, and Stalin.

When he next met with the Joint Chiefs, on November 19, they handed him a proposal for the appointment of a supreme Allied commander who would have overall command of operations in the Mediterranean, northwestern Europe, and the Allied air forces. Although Roosevelt concurred in their proposal, he admitted that when he took up the question with Churchill a compromise might be necessary.

Generally it was understood that the supreme commander would be an American officer. Roosevelt wanted an American because of the disparity in the numbers of British and American troops that would comprise the total Allied forces by 1944. It was estimated that by January 1944 the total U.S. forces would be 10,529,000, while the British contingent would total 4,412,000. Already there were more American troops than British in the United Kingdom. By January 1944 the United States would have 12,500 combat airplanes overseas and the British 9,000. These numbers meant that at the coming talks in Cairo and later in Teheran, Britain would become the junior partner in the alliance. Roosevelt was keenly aware of the importance of these figures.

Next, Roosevelt and the Joint Chiefs took up a memorandum about spheres of influence in Germany following the Allied invasion of France and Germany's collapse. He would break Germany up into three large states for the purpose of occupation. One state would be composed of southern Germany, Baden, Württemberg, Bavaria, and everything south of the Main River. Northwest Germany would form a second state, and the northeastern area the third. He thought that Stalin would approve such a division of the defeated enemy. The arrangement desired by the British—the United States controlling France and Germany south of the Moselle River with northwestern Germany under British administration—displeased him because he regarded France as a "British baby." The British should occupy France, Luxembourg, Belgium, Baden, and Württemberg, and the United States northwestern Germany. He opposed U.S. forces occupying southern Germany. As for Berlin, he wanted American troops in the city as soon as possible. Roosevelt expected that there would be a "railroad invasion of Germany with little or no fighting."

The chiefs tried to explain that it would be an impossible task to rearrange the plans for OVERLORD to achieve his desire of American forces in northwestern Germany. For logistical reasons, the American troops would have to advance through Europe on the right of the British. Marshall pointed out that if Roosevelt's goal were to be attained, at some time the Allied forces would have to disengage from the OVERLORD plan in order to achieve the cross-over of British and American troops which Roosevelt desired.

But the President could see only the nefarious British political intrigues at play in their desire to have American troops occupy southern Germany. He ignored the statement from Marshall that the occupation arrangement was logical and that it was based on keeping supply lines as short and as direct as possible. Before the meeting ended, Roosevelt sketched out on a map his ideas about the occupation zones in Germany. Months later, his sketch would create problems for Allied planning staffs.

As for the agendas which Roosevelt had asked to be prepared for his meetings with Churchill and Stalin, they received less consideration than the agenda for the meeting with Chiang. Roosevelt indicated that he would tell Chiang about operations contemplated against China only in general terms. His reluctance to inform Chiang stemmed from the reputation for loose security at Chiang's headquarters.

The agenda for the Churchill meetings brought a blunt announcement from Roosevelt that he did not intend to allow Churchill to rope him into accepting a European sphere of influence, by occupying Yugoslavia, for example. He indicated his concern about the Soviet attitude regarding operations in the eastern Mediterranean and the Balkans. Marshall stated the position of the American chiefs of staff: The Balkan question had to be settled because operations there were unnecessary. If the British tried to ditch OVER-LORD in order to undertake operations in the eastern Mediterranean–Balkan area, then they should be told that the United States would pull its forces out and shift them over to the Pacific. Roosevelt pointed out that the Russians were already only sixty miles from the Polish border and forty miles from Bessarabia; soon they would be entering Rumania. They might say: "If someone would now come up from the Adriatic to the Danube, we could readily defeat Germany forthwith." Marshall said that he would simply explain the implications of such a move to the Russians and offer only air support.

Marshall, as chief of staff, was concerned with coordinating Soviet and American operations. He asked the President how he contemplated doing business with the Russians. Roosevelt, who may not have grasped the complexities of the question, muttered something about using the control commission in London. There was a European Advisory Commission, but its power had been strictly limited at the Moscow Conference.

When the agenda for the meeting with Stalin came up for discussion, Roosevelt commented only on the Soviet demands that they receive some of the Italian shipping. Roosevelt wanted the Soviet Union to have "one-third of the ships as a token of good-will." And with that he was finished discussing agendas.

The proposed agenda for the first meeting between Roosevelt and Stalin called for discussion of Soviet collaboration in strategic bombing, the use of Soviet bases by American forces, and the occupation zones if there was a sudden German collapse. If the Soviet delegates brought up certain items, the American delegates ought to be prepared to discuss them, including the situation of Turkey and Sweden, the Italian fleet and shipping, and Soviet collaboration in the war against Japan.[11]

Roosevelt paid little attention to this agenda because it could be a means of limiting discussion. It was for this reason that he never seriously considered the agenda with the chiefs of staff. He was eager for a freewheeling, off-the-cuff talk with Stalin; agendas belonged to the State Department people, whom Roosevelt had left back in Washington because they only got in his way.

Suddenly a new problem, not on any agenda, had developed: Newspaper and radio correspondents had gotten wind of a big meeting in Cairo. On November 13, a United Press correspondent in Cairo reported that the Mena House Hotel was being closed to the public and would be fumigated in anticipation of visits and conversations in Cairo of great importance. Byron Price, the director of the Office of Censorship, immediately protested and tried to have the dispatch stopped, but it was too late.

On November 15, Wallace Murray, from the State Department, complained to the British ambassador about a United Press story from Cairo, published in the *Washington Times-Herald* and other newspapers on November 14, reporting "indications that an international conference of major import will be held in Cairo shortly" and that the Mena House Hotel was being closed to the public to prepare for the guests who would be expected shortly.[12] More followed, for on the same day RCA received a report that the NBC man in Cairo would "have three men on his hands any way." He suggested the need for "heavy scheduling latter half this week." [13] The *New York Daily News* correspondent in Cairo wanted the quickest link-up between Cairo and New York before November 18.

The leaks had gone so far that Gilbert Winant, the American ambassador in London, had to take up matter with Anthony Eden, who assured him on November 17 that urgent steps were being taken to prevent further leakage through British censorship. The same day in Cairo notices had appeared in the local papers announcing the closing of the Mena House Hotel where the high-level meetings were taking place. In answer to the complaints of the American minister, Alexander C. Kirk, the British assured him that it would not happen again. Censorship had been put into effect, and cover stories had been put out that the meeting place would be either Luxor or Jerusalem. But neither place could be taken seriously because there has been an outbreak of malaria in Luxor and Jerusalem was too politically sensitive a city.

When these messages had all reached Roosevelt in mid-ocean, he radioed Churchill that since the enemy now knew the site of their meeting, thanks to the leakage through press and radio, he proposed that the meeting place be changed to Khartoum. He informed Eisenhower of the security leak and asked him to evaluate the risk of meeting in Cairo. But in Eisenhower's view, the arrangements already in progress afforded the best security that could be provided. If it became necessary, he would lend additional fighter planes, but he recommended that the planned meeting take place. If, however, the President wished to change the site, Eisenhower recommended Malta because he judged the facilities there to be sufficient for Roosevelt's party.

Roosevelt's message about changing the site had found Eisenhower at Malta where he had come from a meeting with Churchill. On November 18, together with the First Sea Lord, Admiral Andrew Cunningham, and the commander-in-chief of the Allied Fleet in the Mediterranean, Admiral John Cunningham, Eisenhower conferred with Churchill about changing the site of the conference. All agreed that the Cairo meeting ought to take place as planned. Any attacking German aircraft would have to fly overland for one hundred miles before reaching the site; already defenses had been strengthened against such an operation. They eliminated Khartoum because accommodations were inadequate and the city was one thousand miles from Cairo, making the movement of staff difficult. But if Cairo were ruled out, Malta would have to be the substitute.

When Churchill investigated Malta as a possibility, it soon proved inadequate. There was no one hotel that could provide even the crudest of services that would be required. Food was scarce on the island, the water supply was questionable, and the weather was hot. *Iowa* could not sail there because the huge battleship would soon be detected and her presence would indicate that some very important people were aboard. Finally, Churchill recommended that they keep to the original plan. Roosevelt concurred.[14]

* * *

On November 18, the President wrote to his wife:

> All goes well and a very comfortable trip so far. Weather good and warm enough to sit with only a sweater as an extra, over an old pair of trousers and a fishing shirt. I don't dare write the route but we should see Africa by tomorrow night and land Saturday morning. All our crowd are getting a real rest, mostly reading—I have had 2 staff meetings. It looks as if I'll be away a little longer than I thought.[15]

On November 19, *Iowa* sighted the fourth escort group—the light cruiser U.S.S. *Brooklyn,* two American destroyers, and three British destroyers. The combined task group's speed was regulated so that it would reach a point about twenty miles west of Cape Spartel around six o'clock in the evening. At that time all ships went to "General quarters" in readiness for an enemy attack by sea or air. The task group traveled through the Straits of Gibraltar under cover of darkness at a speed of twenty-seven knots with the intention of reaching the harbor of Oran at first light.

Roosevelt asked to be informed when the task group passed the Rock of Gibraltar because he wanted to see it. Later, he wrote in his diary: "On Friday night, with additional escorts and higher speed we passed through the Straits of Gib. and though it was dark I saw the 'loom' of Gibraltar. Can I truthfully say hereafter that I have 'seen' it?"

Iowa entered the harbor of Oran on November 20 and anchored about 8:09 A.M. Already at anchor in the harbor was the flagship of Admiral Andrew Cunningham, First Sea Lord and chief of the British Naval Staff. What now would be the proper protocol? *Iowa* had on board a chief of state who outranked a First Sea Lord, but *Iowa* saluted with the crew mustered on deck and solved the protocol puzzle. Then the President was wheeled out on deck in his cape, wearing his floppy campaign hat and with his cigarette holder tilted at a rakish angle. After the Secret Service agents had lifted him into a motor whaleboat on the port side of *Iowa,* the boat was lowered into the water and then came around to the gangway where Hopkins and the Secret Service agents entered it. The President's wheelchair was placed in the motorboat, which then headed for the dock. Picket boats carried the other passengers from *Iowa* to the dock. As the passengers came ashore, Army personnel handed each person a slip of paper showing the car number and the number of the plane in which each passenger would fly from Oran to Tunis.

At the dock, a cavalcade formed with American military police on motorcycles and cars to carry the President and his party. Armed American soldiers were posted along the streets at intervals, at intersections, and at curves in the streets. Some faced outward and others faced the cavalcade as it passed. At the airport, Roosevelt and his party found Army Air Force planes lined up with signs designating the number of each plane. Roosevelt was placed in plane number one. The chiefs of staff boarded the second plane and the Secret Service detail the third. The fourth C-54 was a standby in case one of the first three C-54s broke down. The rest of the passengers, including six mess attendants, were loaded on the other C-54s and flown directly to Cairo.

From Oran, the three planes flew along the North African coast, protected by fighter planes much of the way. Head winds and cross winds made the flight bumpy. After three and a half hours, the planes landed at El Aouina airfield, twelve miles northeast of Tunis, where wrecked German aircraft still littered the ground. Awaiting his father was Colonel Elliott Roosevelt, commanding officer of a photo reconnaissance wing, who had flown in his own aircraft.

"A drive took us through the ruins of Carthage (but of a Roman date) to my villa—the Casa Blanca—most apt," Roosevelt wrote in his diary on November 20. The "White House" had been used by the Germans during their occupation of Tunis. Eisenhower, who had made it his headquarters, had turned it over to the President; shortly after being settled in his new "White House," he was at work on official mail.

Roosevelt's departure from Tunis, originally scheduled for 6 A.M., November 21, was delayed until 10:30 P.M. because a night flight was considered safer and would not require a fighter escort. The President used the afternoon to tour the nearby battlefield. Another convoy formed up with three trucks filled with armed military policemen, one truck going ahead of the President's car and two following behind. Eight military policemen on motorcycles roared off, leading the convoy and clearing the road of all traffic. Eisenhower, riding with the President, described the action, pointing out the places where the fighting had been bloodiest. Burned-out tanks still littered the battlefield; uncleared minefields were roped off and marked with signs on which a crude skull and crossbones had been drawn. The rains had not yet obliterated the foxholes left over from the fighting.

As the President and Eisenhower drove through the silent battlefield, they were aware of the war still in progress elsewhere. Overhead, flights of bombers were returning from missions on the European continent. Fields along the highway on which they rode were filled with ammunition dumps. They passed fresh military cemetaries, American as well as German. And even as the war continued, Tunisians were repairing damaged farms and buildings.

When the convoy stopped for a picnic lunch, a cordon of military policemen was immediately thrown around the picnic. The tour ended when the Secret Service agents advised Roosevelt that the convoy had rested long enough on an open, exposed plain. The convoy formed up again and returned to the Tunisian "White House." There Roosevelt dined that evening with his sons, Elliott and Franklin Jr., before leaving for the airport and the flight to Cairo.

In his diary, Roosevelt wrote: "Today we have motored to the battlefields west of Tunis where our troops broke through the German-Italian lines, and though not many buildings were destroyed, the fields still contain many tanks and trucks destroyed by gun-fire and much barbed wire—and there are many little cemetaries. France in 1918 was far more destroyed but this was open warfare over in a very short time in comparison."

The plane which the President boarded during the night was an Air Transport Command C-54 that had been remodeled for his use. It was outfitted with a galley, special leg rests, a work table, and two berths, one for Harry Hopkins whose physical condition required that he frequently rest. A knockdown ramp had been built into the plane in order to avoid the use of the usual thirty-foot ramp which when set up signaled the impending arrival of Franklin D. Roosevelt.

Roosevelt's plane landed at a Royal Air Force field west of Cairo on the morning of November 22, two and a half hours behind schedule. Two separate fighter plane groups had rendezvoused at the scheduled times but failed to make contact with the President's plane, which had detoured south at his order so that he might see the Nile and the Pyramids from the air: "We came in the 'back way' so as to avoid German planes and from the desert saw the Nile 100 miles So. of Cairo—an amazing scene and followed the narrow belt of fertile fields, with many villages, until we came to the big pyramids."

After his plane had landed. the ramp was broken out and the President was wheeled down to the ground. He went by automobile to the villa of the American ambassador, Alexander C. Kirk, seven miles west of Cairo and close to the pyramids. Here he stayed with Hopkins and Admiral Leahy.

H.M.S. *Renown*, with "Colonel Warden" aboard, docked at at Alexandria on the morning of November 21. Churchill flew to a Royal Air Force landing field near the Pyramids and then went to the villa of Richard Casey, the British minister, which had been placed at his disposal. A half mile away was the villa where Chiang Kai-shek and his wife were staying—they had already arrived.

It had been planned that everyone would land at a secret airfield which would not require driving through Cairo and risking recognition. The Chiangs, however, arrived two days earlier than expected at an airfield east of the Nile and then drove through the center of Cairo looking for their accommodations. Once they found them, Madame Chiang had to locate a hairdresser. Her search brought her once more into Cairo and produced a large crowd of curious Egyptians who gazed at the beautiful, exotic lady from China.

The area around the villas and the meeting place, the Mena House Hotel, was crammed with soldiers and antiaircraft guns for the protection of all the "very important people." After the guests at the Mena House Hotel had been obliged to depart for other accommodations, the troops had set up barbed wire around a three-mile area centering on the hotel. Within the area, thirty-four villas had been commandeered for the conference; they had been surrounded by guns, searchlights, pillboxes, gun emplacements, and fire watchtowers.

As for the afternoon's activities, the President reported:

"This p.m. the Prime Minister and his daughter Sara [sic] and the Chiangs came to call. Then we drove out to see the Pyramids and my old friend the Sphinx. We all dined (not the Sphinx) at my villa—also Elliott and Harry's boy, Robert. F.D.R., Jr. went back from Tunis to join his 'Mayrant' [sic] to start home for the U.S.—She is really badly damaged."

7
SEXTANT

THE GUNS WERE EMPLACED around the villas and the Mena House Hotel. Fighter planes of the RAF were ready to scramble if Luftwaffe intruders threatened the VIPs who had traveled thousands of miles for what should have been a conference of great significance for the future of much of the world. Central to this meeting was the slim Oriental whose face too often resembled an expressionless mask, Chiang Kai-shek. Instead of a tough brainstorming session in preparation for the meeting with Stalin, Roosevelt turned Chiang and his plans into the chief topic of the Cairo Conference.

On the morning of November 23, the Combined Chiefs of Staff assembled with Roosevelt and Churchill for a meeting with Chiang. To their surprise, when Chiang entered, Madame Chiang accompanied him; she was dressed in clinging black satin, her tight skirt slit up the side to reveal a very shapely leg. "She certainly has a good figure which she knew how to display at its best," observed Brooke.[1] As she entered, someone emitted a deep sigh. Madame Chiang had established a record that would remain unbroken throughout World War II: no other wife of the major Allied war leaders ever crashed a top-level meeting of the Combined Chiefs of Staff.

After Roosevelt had welcomed the Chiangs and the Chinese delegation, he called upon Lord Louis Mountbatten, the dashing supreme commander of the Southeast Asia Command, to describe the operations planned for Southeast

161

Asia. Mountbatten explained the plans aimed at clearing the Japanese from Burma. When Chiang demanded simultaneous naval operations to prevent the Japanese from reinforcing their troops, Churchill reminded the Generalissimo that Allied naval cooperation would be difficult because the base of the fleet would be thousands of miles away from the theater of operations. Naval actions along the Burmese coasts were not comparable to the Allied landings in Sicily. Chiang waved this aside, declaring that Burma was the key to the whole campaign in Asia. Churchill and Chiang debated the matter until Roosevelt changed the subject. There was no more time that morning for argument over Burma. Instead, Roosevelt hoped that Chiang would discuss this matter with the Combined Chiefs of Staff.

As it turned out, this was going to be the only meeting of Chiang with the Combined Chiefs of Staff. In the afternoon, the chiefs learned from General "Vinegar" Joe Stilwell, commanding general of the American forces in China, Burma, and India, that Chiang would not have any proposals for Chinese action to present to the Combined Chiefs until he had consulted further with Roosevelt and Marshall. As substitutes, he sent in his generals, whom Brooke welcomed to the meeting of the Combined Chiefs of Staff. He asked them for their views and criticisms of the plans which had been given them for their study. "There ensued the most ghastly silence." The Chinese officers whispered among themselves and finally their spokesman announced that they had not had time to study the Allied plans. "We wish to listen to your deliberations." When asked additional questions about their plans, another long silence followed. Stilwell tried as best he could to speak for them. In his diary he wrote, "Terrible performance. They couldn't ask a question. Brooke was insulting."[2] Brooke suggested they leave, study the plans, and return in twenty-four hours. In great relief, the Chinese slipped out of the room. Brooke wiped his brow and turned to Marshall. "That was a ghastly waste of time," he said.

"You're telling me!" replied Marshall.[3]

In the evening, when Roosevelt and Hopkins dined with Chiang and his wife, the President sought to soothe Chiang's ego by declaring that China must become one of the Big Four, share in decision making, and play "the leading role in the post-war military occupation of Japan." Chiang, however, did not eagerly accept the proferred role in the occupation forces. Roosevelt suggested that both countries would assist each other in case of foreign aggression, and to achieve this aim the United States would maintain impressive military forces in the Pacific area. Such a prospect pleased Chiang. Both the Generalissimo and Roosevelt agreed that Korea and Indochina ought to be independent. But Roosevelt vetoed Chiang's request that China and the United States form a joint council of their chiefs of staff or that Chiang should join the Combined Chiefs of Staff.

Roosevelt met again with the Chiangs in the afternoon of November 25 with Elliott Roosevelt present. Because Madame Chiang interpreted for her husband, there were no minutes of this meeting. Here Roosevelt probably promised Chiang that Operation BUCCANEER would be set in motion within a few months. This operation involved an Allied assault on the Andaman Islands in the Bay of Bengal to support the campaign in Burma. Roosevelt's casual promise to Chiang would cause future trouble among the Combined Chiefs of Staff because it would mean the allocation of landing craft, which were in very short supply.

The next afternoon, for the last time, Roosevelt met with Chiang and his wife; Churchill was also present. Their talk ranged over the impending Burma campaign, the Chinese economy, and postwar problems. Again Roosevelt massaged Chiang's ego in order to keep a loyal ally. He dared not antagonize him either because his conduct would quickly be reported in the American press. Loud repercussions would follow—many Americans regarded Chiang as a very great democratic ally.

Roosevelt catered to Chiang because he believed that in the postwar world, the United States would need a friend in Southeast Asia. After Japan had been defeated, the United States would face Russian and British demands in Asia. Then the support of China, weak though she might be, would be better than nothing. Roosevelt also courted Chiang because he believed everything must be done to keep the Chinese in the war so that China might provide an assault base for the final attack on Japan.

In fact, much of what had been discussed at the Cairo

Conference about China would have little impact on the conduct of the war because U.S. Marines had already begun to land on Makin and Tarawa in the Gilbert Islands. This was the first successful assault in a series of landings on Pacific islands that would ultimately cancel the need for China to serve as a base for the final attack on Japan. The Burmese campaign would also be unnecessary because the assault across the central Pacific, combined with the drive of American forces under General Douglas MacArthur north from Australia, would undercut the need for extensive Allied aid to Chiang's armies.

Roosevelt's trip to Cairo, had, however, set a precedent: he had conferred with the leader of China. (It would not happen again until Richard Nixon met Mao Tse-tung in 1972.) The meeting with Chiang had really been Roosevelt's goal: to show the Chinese people the importance of their leader and to indicate that China was now truly one of the great world powers.

In addition to meeting Chiang Kai-shek, Roosevelt used the location to make contacts with VIPs in the Middle East. Because of his physical condition, he could not travel about Cairo, and as a result, there was a constant stream of callers at the presidential villa. Roosevelt noted the callers on November 24:

> We have been hard at work—Plenary sessions, etc. but this p.m. I received the following!!
> 3 Egyptians including Nhas Pasha the Premier & the Crown Prince.
> The King of Greece, & his P.M.
> The King of Yugo Slavias & his P.M.
> Lord Killeam, Brit. Ambassador.
> 4 British Admirals & Generals.
> Ambass Steinhardt (Amb. to Turkey)
> Ambass Harriman (Amb. to Russia)
> Ambass Kirk (to Egypt—I am in his villa)
> Dinner party every night.

For Churchill, the Cairo Conference was a waste of time and a foretaste of what lay ahead. When other Allies were involved, Roosevelt ignored British interests. Churchill never got the heart-to-heart talk with Roosevelt which he wanted in preparation for the meeting with Stalin. He could do little other than stand by and "play the role of courtier and seize opportunities as and when they arose. I am amazed at the patience with which he does this," observed Eden. Both men agreed that Roosevelt was "a charming country gentleman" but his methods of doing business were almost nonexistent.[4]

Beneath the pleasantries, the British sensed the truth: they could no longer control the negotiations. The country squire from Hyde Park, New York, enjoying his role as world statesman, had no wish for discussions with Churchill. Roosevelt's behavior signaled the profound change in Anglo-American relations that was to come when he met Stalin in Teheran.

On the morning of November 24, Churchill and Roosevelt joined the Combined Chiefs of Staff for a preliminary survey of operations in the European theater. Roosevelt observed that "the final decisions would depend on the way things went at the conference shortly to be held with Premier Stalin," clearly indicating the importance he attached to that meeting.

The opinions expressed about Stalin and his thoughts and plans for the British and American forces were mixed. In Roosevelt's view, "Premier Stalin would be almost certain to demand both the continuation of action in the Mediterranean, and OVERLORD." As for the Mediterranean, Roosevelt believed that Allied action would depend on whether Turkey would enter the war—a topic he thought worth discussing with Stalin.

Churchill launched into a survey of the past year, which was "a year of unbroken success in North Africa and the Mediterranean, in Russia, and in the Pacific, but the last few months had produced a series of disappointments." In Italy, the lack of sufficient power prevented the Allies from driving the Germans northward, while across the Adriatic they had let slip an opportunity that developed after Mussolini's government had collapsed. In the Aegean, "the picture was equally bleak." There the loss of the Dodecanese Islands left the Germans in control. He was certain that if Rhodes could be seized, and if Allied planes could operate from Turkish bases, then the other islands could come under Allied control. He hoped that the Russians would "share our view of the importance of bringing Turkey into the war because the effect on the satellite states would be profound." In Italy, the prime minister preferred to concentrate on moving up to the Pisa-Rimini line and sending supplies and air support to the Yugoslavs; but he was cool to the proposal to launch an attack in the Pacific against the Dutch Netherlands.

As for OVERLORD, Churchill "had in no way relaxed his zeal for the operation." It "remained the top of the bill" for him, but he did not want all other operations ruled out in the Mediterranean because OVERLORD had become a tyrant. He argued that the "timing of the operation depended more on the state of the enemy than on the set perfection of our preparations."

In his comments, Churchill revealed the fear that ate at him over OVERLORD. Britain's sixteen divisions, earmarked for OVERLORD, would be the limit of her contribution. There could be no further call on Britain after that for more troops because British manpower had reached its limit. Churchill's confession that he lacked additional manpower to fill in the decimated ranks should German reinforcements wreck OVERLORD signaled his deep reluctance to go through with OVERLORD unless fully assured that the German armies had been so weakened that they could not drive the Allied armies into the Channel. Roosevelt did not let slip the opportunity to underline the difference between the American and British manpower resources by reading off the figures which the Joint Chiefs had handed him on board *Iowa*.

Both Roosevelt and Churchill then directed the Combined Chiefs to study the scope, the dates, the problems of the scope and timing of operations in Europe and in the Mediterranean in order to reach an agreed view before the meeting with the Russians.[5]

The Combined Chiefs did more than "study" the scope and timing of operations the next day, November 25. The argument became so heated that after sending the secretaries out of the room, the generals and admirals went into closed session where they did not keep records of their arguments. The British chiefs argued that it was madness to adhere to an invasion date which had been intended only as a general target date, and to refuse to inflict losses on the Germans in Italy and in the Mediterranean. In effect they wanted to delay the invasion date of OVERLORD in order somehow to exert more pressure on the Germans in the Mediterranean. The American chiefs of staff, under orders from Roosevelt, would make no concessions to the British about the timing of the invasion. The meeting ended without any decision.

November 25 was Thanksgiving Day for the Americans, who were guests of the British in Cairo. The hosts arranged for a Thanksgiving service in the Anglican cathedral in Cairo, and in the evening Roosevelt entertained guests, including Churchill, his daughter Sarah, Eden, three ambassadors, and others, at a Thanksgiving dinner complete with turkey and all of the fixings. Churchill, who had not been well, recovered enough to attend the dinner and enjoy the turkey. He was impressed by the President's masterly skill with the carving knife as he portioned out the turkey among the guests, asking each, "White or dark?"

In his toast, for the benefit of his British guests, Roosevelt told the history of Thanksgiving and explained how American soldiers were spreading the custom around the world, and how personally delighted he was to share this Thanksgiving Day with the prime minister. Before Churchill could respond, Roosevelt continued and said that large families were usually more closely united than small families. "This year, with the United Kingdom in our family, we are a large family and more united than ever."[6]

An American GI dance orchestra from Camp Huckstep, near Cairo, played popular songs while the guests enjoyed their turkey. When the orchestra began the Marine hymn "From the Halls of Montezuma to the Shores of Tripoli," Churchill jumped to his feet and stuck up his fingers in the "V" for Victory sign while Roosevelt sang the hymn with the orchestra. After the orchestra had left, someone found a record player and the floor was cleared for dancing. But there was only one lady there to dance with the gentlemen: Sarah Churchill. Because she had her work cut out for her, Churchill and "Pa" Watson, Roosevelt's tall and very fat military aide, did a cakewalk up and down the floor.

Roosevelt recorded in his diary on November 26: "Yesterday was a real Thanksgiving day. The Chiangs to tea—and the British to dinner. W.S.C.—Sara—etc. with 2 turkeys I brought from home—It is an enormous satisfaction to have my mess crew from the Potomac and Shangri La. Music by an army band, & later W.S.C. cakewalked with Pa Watson."

The Combined Chiefs of Staff celebrated Thanksgiving by themselves, calling a truce in their arguments over the date for the invasion of France. But the next day the truce ended when they took up the question of the link between OVERLORD and the campaign in the Mediterranean.

The British again objected to allowing the date fixed for OVERLORD to become the pivot of Allied strategy. By spring, the strength of the German forces in France might make the invasion impossible. The British chiefs did not see that the attempt to achieve a certain degree of military strength by a specific date would necessarily be the best policy to win the war as quickly as possible. Such a policy would paralyze action elsewhere. The British wanted to attack the Germans continuously everywhere that the Allies had superiority. They strongly opposed allowing the date of OVERLORD to become their master and so prevent them from taking advantage of any opportunity that might develop. When Admiral Leahy commented that the proposals for action in the Mediterranean ought not to interfere with Operation BUCCANEER, Brooke agreed provided that the date for OVERLORD was put back later. He went on to argue that BUCCANEER ought to be put off in order that the full weight of the Allied forces could be brought to bear on Germany. Marshall rejected postponing BUCCANEER. "It was not long before Marshall and I had the father and mother of a row," as Brooke put it.[7] Once more the secretaries were sent out of the room and the admirals and generals argued the matter out between themselves.

When it was over, the American chiefs would not accept the postponement of BUCCANEER; the matter would have to be taken up at a higher level between the prime minister and the President. But they had agreed on the questions about the Mediterranean which they would discuss with the Soviet staff. There was also an agenda, and at the top was the need to coordinate Soviet and Anglo-American operations, something that had not yet been achieved. Other topics included the Italian campaign, the entry of Turkey into the war, supplies for the Soviet Union, strategic bombing, and the entry of the Soviet Union into the war against Japan. And that was the best that the Combined Chiefs of Staff could accomplish on the eve of their meeting with the Soviet leaders.

Afterward, the Chiangs hosted a tea party. It was "a dismal show," wrote Brooke. "Very hot and stuffy room. He did not impress me much, but hard to tell at a meeting like that. Meanwhile Madame holding a court of admirers. The more I see of her, the less I like her."[8]

As the Cairo Conference drew to a close, there were the usual housekeeping chores: photographs and a press communiqué to be released after the meeting with the Russians.

Roosevelt had informed Stalin on November 22 that the Cairo Conference would soon take place between himself, Churchill, and Chiang Kai-shek. After the departure of Chiang, Roosevelt and Churchill, together with their staffs, would journey to Teheran, arriving in the afternoon of November 29. Roosevelt was prepared to stay for at least four days, depending on how long Stalin would be able to remain away from his work. Roosevelt asked Stalin to telegraph the date he wished set for the opening of the conference, as well as the length of his stay in Teheran.

The President understood that the Soviet and British embassies in Teheran were located close to each other but the American legation was some distance away. "I am advised that all three of us would be taking unnecessary risks by driving to and from our meeting if we were staying so far apart from each other. Where do you think we should live? I look forward to our talks with keen anticipation." In this message Roosevelt was hinting to Stalin about an invitation to live in the Soviet Embassy during the Teheran Conference.

The next day, Hull reported that Stalin would arrive in Teheran no later than November 28 or 29. Stalin's personal reply came on November 25. "I will be at your service in

Teheran the evening of November twenty-eighth."⁹ Preparations for the move to Teheran had to be speeded up.

Preparing for the President's journey from Cairo to Teheran, two men already had been directed to go to Teheran to examine the route and the security problems: Mike Reilly, chief of the Secret Service detail, and Patrick Hurley, the Oklahoma lawyer with the rank of ambassador and the temporary rank of major general.

Because there had been reports that the American minister in Teheran, Louis Dreyfus, was having trouble with the Russians, Admiral Leahy had urged that a "two-fisted general" be sent to Iran to coordinate the military, diplomatic, and economic missions, and late in October Hurley was ordered there on a special mission. He was to bring about better cooperation with the Russians, advise Roosevelt during the conference, and improve cooperation between Allied agencies in Teheran.

Dreyfus had left for the United States with Cordell Hull, when he returned from the Moscow Conference by way of Teheran. The news that Hurley would be "our man in Teheran" during the important conference did not suit Hull. At Marrakesh, Dreyfus left Hull and went back to the legation in Teheran in time to meet Hurley when he arrived on November 24 with Reilly.

Reilly and Hurley were deputed to check out the best route for the President to follow in traveling from Cairo to Teheran. They were also to inspect the accommodations in Teheran for the President and to evaluate the security problems. But their first concern was the route.

Admiral Ross McIntire, the President's personal physician, opposed flying the whole way from Cairo to Teheran. Instead, he wanted the President to fly to Basra, in Iraq, and then travel to Teheran by train, a distance of more than four hundred miles. McIntire feared that the President's health would not permit him to fly at a height of 16,000 feet (even Presidents did not yet have pressurized cabins in official planes).

Reilly reported that by air, the plane would not have to fly higher than 8,000 feet. As for train travel, Reilly found that the railroad line reached a height of 8,000 feet in some of the mountain passes. The only usable railroad cars suitable to carry the President belonged to the shah's personal train, four private cars with gold fittings. But railroad lines in Iran were periodically attacked by the tribes. Already American military policemen riding the trains as guards had been killed. If the trip were to be made by train, the President would have to fly to Abadan and then travel seven miles to the railroad terminal. En route, he would have to cross a stream in a small boat.

There was another route: Cairo to Basra by plane, and then by rail to Teheran. But that rail trip would involve passing through two hundred tunnels and across many bridges—all of which could be sabotaged. Reilly recommended that Roosevelt fly directly to Teheran from Cairo. He pointed out that if the choice was rail, it would mean two full days of travel.

When Hurley and Reilly inspected the American legation, Louis Dreyfus, the American minister, was lunching with the minister of the Iranian court. A telephone call from the legation interrupted the lunch—a group of American officers had entered the legation and had begun to examine the building. Dreyfus hurried to the legation where he found the inspection party, led by an old foe, General Donald H. Connolly, commander of the Persian Gulf Command, and Reilly with other officers standing around. "They curtly informed me that they had looked at the residence and had decided to take it over for the President," Dreyfus wrote in a memorandum for the record. He of course replied that it would "be a pleasure for me to turn it over to the President for his use."[10]

Hurley had another task to perform in Teheran for the President. He was to inspect the Soviet Embassy and give Roosevelt a first-hand report. On November 23 in Cairo, Andrei Vyshinsky, who had gained notoriety for his vitriolic performance as the prosecutor in the staged Moscow purge Trials of the 1930s, had called on Roosevelt and invited him to stay at the Soviet Embassy in Teheran. Churchill had also extended an invitation for the President to stay in the British Embassy during the Teheran Conference. Roosevelt declined both invitations because he wished to be independent, so it was stated.

Normally the President would have been expected to stay

in his own nation's embassy or legation. Teheran, however, posed a problem. Diplomatic protocol at such a conference, where all three leaders were away from home and no one could function as host, required that the meetings be rotated between the American legation and the British and Soviet embassies. The Soviet and the British embassies were located side by side, but the American legation was on the opposite side of the city. As a result, during the conference it would be necessary for the leaders to drive back and forth through a city which lacked broad highways for swift travel by motorcade.

In Teheran, the Soviet chargé d'affaires called on Hurley on November 26 to invite Roosevelt, on behalf of the Soviet government, to be the guest of the Soviet government during his visit. Hurley explained that Roosevelt had already decided to stay at the American legation.

Then, Hurley, General Connolly, and James J. Rowley of the Secret Service drove across the city to inspect the quarters which the Soviet government had offered Roosevelt. In the embassy building, there was a suite of six rooms—one large reception room, four smaller rooms, which could be used as bedrooms, and a bedroom with an adjoining bath. There was a dining room and below the main bedroom, a kitchen. The suite also had a private entrance. The bathtubs and toilets had been removed but they could easily be reinstalled if the rooms were to be used by the President. Based on "your convenience and comfort, from the standpoint of conference communications and security, these quarters are far more desirable than your own legation," Hurley informed the President.[11]

But the question of where the President would stay while in Teheran was to become more complex. Before Reilly left Teheran to return to Cairo and report to "the Boss," a general in the NKVD informed him that German parachutists had landed in the Soviet zone only a day earlier. The Germans were in Iran, the general reported, either to assassinate the leaders or to wreck the railroad line from Basra to Teheran. None of the parachutists had been caught by the Soviet troops.

Back in Cairo, Reilly recommended that the President fly directly from Cairo to Teheran. His recommendation stemmed from fears for the President's safety on the train, the threat of parachutists, and the dangers accompanying an outbreak of typhus in Iran. Roosevelt and McIntire concurred with Reilly's recommendation.[12]

The British, however, had hoped that the President would stay at their legation, and had made the necessary plans.[13] But Roosevelt declined Churchill's invitation because he feared that if he lived in the same residence as Churchill, Stalin's suspicions would be aroused. He would imagine the pair were hatching some scheme with which to confound him. Roosevelt would go to any lengths to avoid manufacturing suspicions that might undermine the conference he had worked so long to achieve and from which he expected so much.

After his final meeting with the Chiangs, Roosevelt dined early and went to bed in preparation for the flight the next day to Teheran. In his diary he wrote:

Today I wound up all that can be accomplished—a really successful meeting & a good announcement to be given out in four days. Meanwhile we are off to Teheran in the morning.

8
On to Teheran

In Cairo on November 27 with the dawn came fog. Roosevelt and his party had been up early preparing for their departure from Cairo West Airport at 5 A.M., but they had to sit in the plane until the fog lifted sufficiently for takeoff at 7:07 A.M. Roosevelt's plane passed over the Suez Canal near Ismailia, then north over Jerusalem, where the pilot circled to give the passengers a view of the city. The plane then flew east to the Euphrates River, turning northeast and passing north of Bagdad. After crossing the Tigris River, the pilot picked up the highway from Abadan to Teheran until reaching Hamadan, and from there directly to Teheran.

The city, located in a valley, is surrounded by mountains which reach 18,000 feet on the north and 16,000 feet on the south. If the pilot did not wish to fly over the mountains, he had to go through the passes. Major Otis F. Bryan, who was piloting the President's plane, had instructions from McIntire not to exceed 8,000 feet because of the President's sinus condition and "Pa" Watson's high blood pressure. Bryan obeyed the doctor's orders and by 3 P.M. he had landed the plane at a Soviet airfield five miles south of Teheran. Roosevelt wrote his impression of the flight:

On Saturday we passed over Bethlehem and Jerusalem—everything very bare looking—and *I don't want* Palestine as my homeland. Then hundreds of miles of Arabian desert, then a green ribbon and Bagdad and

175

the Tigris, with another green ribbon, the Euphrates—bare mountains and we followed the highway over which so much lend lease goes to Russia.
Then a vast plain or saucer with Tehran and its snow
peaks to the north. I went to the Am legation which
is 1 mile from the Brit. and Russians. I am glad we
did not go in by train for we saved much time—No
bandits in the air. But I still don't like flying. This is
a very dirty place—great poverty.

The President had his geography slightly confused: the Euphrates was crossed before the Tigris. His reference to dis-
liking flying referred to his inability to balance himself in a
plane of that era whenever the weather became rough.

Louis Dreyfus heard the news of the President's arrival
in the evening of November 26 when he returned from a trip
outside the city and found tents already set up on the legation grounds. Hundreds of American soldiers were at work
laying wires and preparing for the arrival of their commander-in-chief. At that time Dreyfus and his wife learned
that they had to vacate the legation before noon the next day.

The next morning Hurley appeared to announce that
Roosevelt would arrive that afternoon. Dreyfus and his wife
would receive the President at the legation, turn it over to
him, and then "quickly disappear." Dreyfus asked if he might
welcome the President at the airport as he had done for visitors who were not so important. But according to Hurley,
security needs forbade Dreyfus, a civilian, going to the airfield. Dreyfus argued that he was an official, not a civilian.
Hurley claimed that the military authorities responsible for
the President's safety would not allow him to welcome the
President at the airfield. Dreyfus gave up the fight. His wife
had volunteered to assist in the arrangements at the legation, but she was told that she would not be needed. So
Dreyfus and his wife packed up and left the legation.[1]

Already the legation was under twenty-four-hour guard by
American soldiers now living in the tents on the legation
grounds. Only the Iranians whose duties were the most essential were permitted within the compound.

When Roosevelt's plane touched down at the Russian-controlled airfield, only General Connolly met him. Guarded by the ever-present Secret Service and American troops, Roosevelt was driven to the legation where Dreyfus, his wife, and Hurley welcomed him. After Roosevelt had been placed in his wheelchair, he was pushed up on a specially constructed wooden ramp into the building.

Quartered in the legation with Roosevelt were Admiral Leahy, Admiral Brown, Major John Boettiger (Roosevelt's son-in-law), and Harry Hopkins. The remainder of those who had traveled with Roosevelt were given quarters at Camp Amirabad just outside Teheran, the headquarters of the United States Persian Gulf Command.

The Americans at the legation wanted some liquid refreshment, preferably alcoholic. The host, to his embarrassment, could not meet their request because the ramp constructed by the Army carpenters for the President's wheelchair blocked the only entrance to the cellar in which the legation kept its liquor supply. It was the ultimate humiliation for Dreyfus: not only had he been forbidden to meet the President at the airfield, but now he could not even offer him a drink! Dreyfus had to ask his British colleague for eight cases of whiskey for the President's use. The British officials, who had felt snubbed when Roosevelt refused to accept Churchill's invitation to stay at the British legation lest Stalin think the capitalists were ganging up on him, now had their own joke about the American whiskey shortage.

Churchill had flown into the same Russian airfield. Unlike his American colleague, the British minister in Teheran, Reader Bullard, met Churchill at the airfield and drove with him to the British legation, taking what had been thought to be an offbeat route across fields that had been searched for mines. As their car approached the city, the "road was lined with Persian cavalrymen every fifty yards for at least three miles," wrote Churchill. "It was clearly shown to any evil people that somebody of consequence was coming, and which way." The cavalry advertised the route but offered the prime minister little protection if an assassin had been lurking close by. Security was further lessened by the police car which drove ahead of Churchill's car warning passers-by that someone very important was approaching. Gradually the speed of the automobile became slower as the people standing between the mounted horsemen crowded toward the road. Churchill grew more uneasy because he could not see a policeman on foot.

When they drew nearer to the center of Teheran, the crowds had swelled until they were standing four and five deep along the road. The people seemed friendly enough as they pressed round the car which carried His Majesty's First Minister. "There was no kind of defense at all against two or three determined men with pistols or a bomb." Near the British legation they ran into a traffic block—"We remained for three or four minutes amid the crowded throngs of gaping Persians." To Churchill it appeared that someone had planned "to run the greatest risk, and have neither security of quiet surprise arrival nor an effective escort." His car was now at a standstill. "I grinned at the crowd and on the whole they grinned at me."[2]

Anthony Eden had been driven away from the airfield in state without waiting for Churchill. A cavalcade of cavalry trotted alongside Eden's car and he realized that he was the "decoy duck." Everything went smoothly until his car reached the gates of the British legation compound. There an Iranian citizen and his donkey blocked all traffic until they could be moved after concerted shouting, curses, and appropriate obscene gestures. Eden had enough time to reflect "that if anyone wanted to toss a bomb into the car, I was a sitting target." At the legation he found an irate prime minister.

"Where have you been?" asked Eden.

"They brought me the back way," grumped Churchill.[3] In contrast to Churchill's ride through the city, when Stalin arrived, heavily armed Russian soldiers were posted along the route leading to the embassy as his car sped swiftly past.

Stalin had been the first to arrive, traveling by train from Moscow by way of Stalingrad, to Baku on the Caspian Sea. Because there was no direct rail connection between Baku and Teheran, Stalin was forced to fly, a method of transportation that he dreaded. The commander-in-chief of the Soviet Air Force arranged for Stalin's plane to be piloted by a Soviet lieutenant general. Another plane carrying the more subordinate Soviet personnel would have a colonel as pilot. However, because Soviet lieutenant generals did not get much practice flying, Stalin had to settle for a colonel, too, as his pilot. Escorted by three squadrons of Soviet fighter planes, Stalin flew into Teheran and there he was driven to the Soviet Embassy through streets heavily guarded by Russian troops.

Both Roosevelt and Churchill, surprised to learn that Stalin had already arrived, wanted to start the conference immediately. Stalin, however, declined Roosevelt's invitation to come to the U.S. legation for a dinner meeting. Then the President invited Churchill to dinner, but his daughter, Sarah, who had accompanied him to Teheran, and his personal physician, Lord Moran, concerned over his exhaustion and his loss of voice, had made him eat his dinner in bed and get a good night's sleep.

By nightfall on November 27, 1943, the leaders of three most powerful of the United Nations had gathered within the city limits of Teheran. Not since ancient Persia had been the center of the known world in the sixth century B.C. had the city played so important a role in international affairs. Then Cyrus the Great established the Persian Empire as the premier power of the known world. His grandson Darius pushed the frontiers to the Indus River, only to die while preparing an expedition against the Athenians, who had defeated his army in the Battle of Marathon in 490 B.C. Darius's son, Xerxes, suffered defeat at the hands of the Athenians in the naval Battle of Salamis in 480 B.C. which ended the expansion of the Persian Empire. Alexander the Great destroyed the Persian armies and added their empire to his new realm. After his sudden death, Persia became a part first of the Seleucid Empire and then of the Parthian Empire. By A.D. 226 the new Persian dynasty of the Sassanians had been founded, but it was wiped out by the Arabs in the seventh century. During the succeeding eight centuries, Persia endured domination by the Seljuks, the Mongols, and the Turkomans. A form of Persian independence maintained in the eighteenth century ended when the country became a pawn in the struggle between Britain and czarist Russia in the nineteenth and twentieth centuries over domination of the Middle East.

Among the Persians, who craved to be free of foreign influence, was a tough commander of the Persian Cossacks, Reza Khan Pahlavi, who ordered the Cossacks to march on Teheran in 1921. In the resulting *coup d'état*, Reza Khan overthrew the inept prime minister and established a new government which made him chief of the army. His appointment as minister of war soon followed, and using this office as a power base, he expanded his political influence until he could engineer an appointment as prime minister in 1923. His manipulation of the Majlis (Parliament) brought the deposition of the last shah of the Qajar dynasty in 1925 and the establishment of the Pahlavi dynasty with Reza Khan as the shah, entrusted with all the powers of government. His eldest son would become the heir apparent to the throne.

Shah Reza Khan was one of thirty-two children born in 1878 to one of the seven wives of Colonel Abbas Ali Khan, an officer in the regular Persian army stationed in a village northeast of Teheran. At the age of fifteen, Reza Khan enlisted in the Persian Cossacks—a force commanded by Russian officers loaned to the Persian government—and worked his way up through the ranks until he replaced the last Russian commander in 1920. Tall, broad-shouldered, a quick-tempered, hardworking officer, Reza Khan's soldiers respected him for the bravery he had often displayed in campaigns against the unruly tribes.

Nothing enraged Reza Khan more than the cynical intervention of Britain and Russia in the internal affairs of his helpless country. As shah, he became resolved to throw off foreign influences that had made Iranian independence a farce and to reform Iran along western lines. He created a centralized monarchy backed by the army, which served him by overcoming the nomadic tribes and breaking their resistance to his authority. Tribal chieftains were exiled to Teheran, and the tribes, forced to cease migrating, had to settle on the land.

His government erected cement mills, expanded the port facilities, and built miles of needed roads. Reza Khan concentrated much of his energy on expanding the railroad system with the aid of experts from the United States, Germany, and Scandinavia. He personally walked over much of the route, checking on the progress of construction and upbraiding the engineers when it fell behind schedule. The Trans-Iranian Railway was probably his greatest material innovation and one that gave him great delight.

Reza Khan also sought to modernize Iranian cities. The greatest changes came in Teheran, where electric street lighting was introduced in 1925, and electricity became available for private homes in the same year. The shah approved plans for a new city, with wide, paved streets flanked by imposing government buildings sporting fountains and a variety of statues of the shah. The city that Churchill, Roosevelt, and Stalin saw in November 1943 was a mixture of old and new: an old quarter with narrow alleys, and the new city, partly finished, with wide avenues that intersected at right angles. As so many of the streets were still unpaved, they became dusty in summer and muddy in winter. Camels still wandered the streets, and beggars lay in wait at the entrances of mosques and bazaars to importune the wary passer-by. The shah had failed to modernize the water system. In 1943 foreigners were warned to beware of "Teheran tummy," because not every building had running water. The water, brought down from the mountains, flowed through much of the city in a network of uncemented open-air canals. But those who remembered the city before Reza Shah regarded his changes as miraculous if not revolutionary.

More than modernizing Teheran, the shah's overriding ambition was to make Iran truly independent. By the eve of World War II, he had succeeded in winning independence from political and economic dominance by Russia and Britain. But in his zeal to break out of the Anglo-Russian control which had prevailed before he seized power, Reza Shah had sought friendship and support from other powers. His search had led him ultimately to Germany. The Junkers Company helped expand airlines in Iran; German motorcycles, automobiles, and airplanes were all exported to Iran. In 1937, Lufthansa received extensive rights to link Teheran and Berlin by air. German architects and builders carried out the construction program for Teheran. In Iran, German companies dominated the electrical and the armaments industries; by 1939, Germany was the most important trading nation as far as Iran was concerned. In addition to trade, there were close cultural ties between Berlin and Teheran. Specialized schools in Iran were staffed by German faculty, and young Iranians studied at German universities under the Hitler regime. A special decree of the Reich in 1936 exempted Iranians from the provisions of the Nüremberg Racial Laws by designating them "pure Aryans."

When German armies invaded Poland in September 1939, the shah chose a policy of neutrality because of the traditional dislike of Britain and his concern over the apparent friendship of Nazi Germany and Soviet Russia. The situation changed when the Wehrmacht swept across the Soviet borders on June 22, 1941. With Britain and Soviet Russia now forced to become Allies, once more Iran faced her two old antagonists. The shah issued another declaration of neutrality that did little to satisfy either Moscow or London because it did not deal with the presence of a significant number of German citizens who were living in Iran. Almost seven hundred German nationals were employed by the Iranian government in 1941, and with their wives and children totaled nearly two thousand potential members of a "fifth column." The new Allies demanded that Reza Shah's government expel the Germans living in Iran. His ministers, acting of course under his orders, replied that to expel the Germans would violate neutrality; moreover, they claimed, the Germans were being kept under careful watch. But the shah and his ministers failed to gauge the determination of the British and Soviet governments.

To the Iranian leaders, Germany appeared on the verge of another victory by the summer of 1941. Wherever Hitler's armies had gone, they had overwhelmed their adversaries. It was another repeat performance of an old script. Germany would win the war by a victorious drive through the Caucasus region which bordered on Iran. After Germany had defeated Soviet Russia, then areas taken from Iran by the czars early in the nineteenth century would be returned. But those lands would not revert to Iran if she acceded to Anglo-Soviet demands.

Reza Shah was not alone in his belief that the Red Army would not survive the German attack. American and British officers had much the same opinion. From the Iranian viewpoint, it appeared shortsighted to surrender to Britain and Russia, who were bound to lose the war. Iran had to resist because when Nazi Germany finally overcame her enemies, Iran, even if occupied, would be on the winning side.

At last the Allies' patience was exhausted. At 4 A.M. on August 25, 1941, the Soviet ambassador and the British minister presented notes to the shah's government expressing their government's regrets that they must take action and occupy Iran. When Reza Shah was told that British and Russian forces were about to enter Iran, he found the news unbelievable. "Our friends, England and Russia, are giving us exactly the same treatment which Hitler gave to Belgium and Mussolini gave to Greece," he said to his prime minister.[4]

At dawn on August 25, British units from the Indian army landed at the head of the Persian Gulf at Bandar Shapur and pushed on north into the oil fields. Other British columns struck from Iraq. Soviet planes dropped leaflets on Teheran announcing that the Soviet forces were entering Iran because the government had been reluctant to expel German spies and terrorists. Soviet bombing of some Iranian cities helped to frighten the shah's confused soldiers, many of whom had been caught sleeping in their barracks. The army of Reza Shah, capable of putting down tribal revolts, could not resist a sudden attack by modern forces. Officers deserted their units, which quickly melted away. The army on which he had lavished so much care and attention was breaking up, leaving him defenseless.

The cabinet resigned, and a new prime minister announced that orders had been given to the army to cease all resistance on August 28. The Iranian government at last had to accept the Allies' demands that the Germans would be expelled. But the authority of Reza Shah had been destroyed; his army had ceased to exist. Worst of all, the Soviet armies were marching on Teheran. He faced an uncertain fate: either remain a puppet under rule of the occupying forces or risk assassination by the Russians. To save the throne for his son, Reza Shah abdicated on September 16 and left Teheran. A British ship took him and his family to Bombay but he was not permitted to land. Instead, he was taken to the island of Mauritius in the Indian Ocean. When the climate proved unhealthy for him, he was allowed to travel to South Africa where he died in Johannesburg in 1944.

The abdication of Reza Shah brought his eldest son to the throne, the young, inexperienced Prince Mohammed Reza. Prince Mohammed had often been ill during his childhood and his father had been uncertain whether he would survive to inherit the throne. The prince had studied in a military elementary school established especially for him. In 1932, his father sent him to a preparatory school in Switzerland where his classmates were unawed by the heir to the Iranian throne. On his return to Iran in 1936, on his father's orders the prince attended the Iranian military college where he had to undergo forced marches and study tactics and strategy. He was graduated as a second lieutenant in the Iranian army. Soon he gained a reputation as a lover of fast women and faster cars. His father decided that the prince would marry the daughter of the king of Egypt, a family that was more royal than the Pahlavis. And so it was done.

Reza Shah tried to introduce his heir to the procedures of governing Iran personally, but the father was not the best of teachers. Suddenly, in mid-September 1941, following his father's abdication, Mohammed Reza Pahlavi became the shah of Iran, a country occupied by the armies of two foreign powers. Soon a third nation's army would join them.

The British and Soviet governments created three zones of occupation in Iran: Soviet in the north; a neutral zone around Teheran; and the British in the south and southwest. In a tripartite treaty with the Iranian government signed on January 29, 1942, Britain and the Soviet Union promised to protect Iran from German aggression and to respect Iranian territorial integrity and sovereignty. They pledged to withdraw their forces from Iran no later than six months after the end of hostilities. Iran pledged cooperation with the occupying powers.

Originally, the British and Soviet armies had invaded Iran in order to deny the area to Hitler's forces, which seemed on the verge of overrunning the Middle East. But events soon made Iran a major supply corridor for sending aid to the Soviet armies and at the same time brought U.S. military forces into Iran. Late in 1941, an American military mission had been dispatched to Iran and Iraq to implement Lend-Lease aid to British forces in the Middle East. The role of the United States in Iran changed because of the crisis that took place during 1942.

By the summer of that year the Afrika Korps, under Field Marshal Erwin Rommel, had swept to the Egyptian frontiers. The fall of Alexandria and Cairo appeared imminent. Soon the swastika might be waving over the Suez Canal and units of the Afrika Korps poised to strike into Saudi Arabia. In Russia, the German summer offensive had driven deep into the Caucasus Mountains. Nazi forces seemed about to overrun the Middle East. Using a gigantic pincers movement through Egypt, Saudi Arabia, and through Russia, they would seize the oil fields in Saudi Arabia, Iran, and Iraq, and at the same time cut off all aid to Russia. There was also a crisis in American aid to Britain and Russia.

After the Japanese attack on Pearl Harbor on December 7, 1941, and Hitler's declaration of war on the United States, U.S. naval forces were unable to carry out the duty suddenly thrust on them of protecting American positions in the Pacific theater. Nor could the American Navy protect Arctic convoys around Norway carrying supplies for Russia via the port of Murmansk. This burden had to be carried by the Royal Navy. But the destruction of Convoy PQ 17 in July 1942, when only eleven ships from a thirty-three-ship convoy reached Murmansk, halted the shipment of supplies to Russia by the Arctic route. A safer alternative was to increase the shipment of supplies to Russia via the Persian Gulf and Iran, which had a common border with the Soviet Union. Already supplies were piling up on the Iranian docks as more ships sailed from American ports bound for the Persian Gulf. Churchill admitted to Roosevelt that Britain lacked the manpower resources to expand the flow of supplies to the Soviet Union. By the end of August 1942, plans were under way to give the United States Army a greater role in supplying aid to Russia through what became known as "the Persian Corridor."

To ensure not only that the flow of war supplies to the Soviet Union through the Persian Corridor was uninterrupted but also that it increased, on September 22, 1942, the Combined Chiefs of Staff approved an American plan to create the Persian Gulf Command under Major General Donald H. Connolly, a graduate of West Point who had engineered rivers and harbor projects, administered programs of the Works Progress Administration, and overseen the construction of airports for the Department of Commerce. The task given Connolly and the thirty thousand troops under his command was to develop and operate port facilities in the Persian Gulf, maintain roads leading from the Iranian ports to Teheran, operate truck convoys over these roads, and develop and operate the Iranian State Railway from the ports on the Persian Gulf to Teheran. Beyond that city, the supply lines became the responsibility of the Soviet troops. Ultimately, the Persian Gulf Command would deliver five million tons of supplies to Soviet Russia. More important, it marked an official American involvement in Iranian affairs that would continue until the fall of the shah's government in 1979.

In the presence of so many foreign troops, how could the young shah, Mohammed Reza, be master of his own kingdom? Every day his government moved closer to complete breakdown. Tribal chieftains, released from detention after the abdication of Mohammed Reza's father, returned to their tribes where they incited their men to rebel against the national government, arming them with weapons seized or purchased from the discredited Iranian army. In the north, Kurdish tribes raided villages, defying the central government to bring a halt to their forays. The powerful Qashqai rebelled in 1943 and demanded the restoration of lands taken from them by the shah's father. The government tried negotiation, and when that failed dispatched an army which the Qashqai routed in June 1943. More negotiations brought relative peace in August 1943.

The government's efforts to maintain a crude form of law and order were not helped by a severe shortage of food. The Allied monopoly of transportation left little available for the shipment of foodstuffs for the Iranian people. The Soviet sector was the chief grain-producing area, but the Soviet forces shipped this grain to Russia, which had lost food because of the German invasion. As a result, in much of Iran there was famine. Late in 1942 when Teheran endured food riots, it became necessary for Britain and the United States to allot precious shipping space to transport food to Iran.

More important for the three occupying powers, the anarchy in the countryside endangered their efforts to ship supplies to Russia. Truck convoys were often ambushed along the highways, and British and American troops were killed and wounded. Trucks carrying ammunition were favorite targets of the tribal raiders. Trains were derailed, telephone lines were cut, and army paymasters robbed. All of these events made Iran an insecure site for the meeting of the three Allied leaders. In August 1943, British military intelligence reported that the Qashqai were a virtually antonomous "nation." As to the general condition of the country:

> Events seem to be leading to a gradual, but ultimately complete breakdown of government and of the administration, or to a violent change in the regime. Insecurity, indiscipline and disorder are spreading.
>
> Hooliganism and wounding by stabbing have become so common in Teheran that the Majlis passed a law with double urgency authorizing the police to arrest or expel from Teheran persons guilty of, or from their past record known to be likely to commit such offences.[5]

The American government was also concerned for the safety of its foreign service personnel in Teheran. The American legation had been repeatedly robbed, but General Connolly had refused to detach troops to protect the legation because he considered that his task related only to transporting supplies through Iran to the Soviet Union. This was the situation facing Roosevelt, Churchill, and Stalin on November 27, 1943. The conditions in the city led to an invitation from Stalin that Roosevelt should move across to the Soviet Embassy.

Early in the evening of November 27, Averell Harriman, whom Roosevelt had directed to come to Teheran, went to

the Soviet Embassy to discuss the arrangements for the conference. There Harriman expressed the President's regrets
at being unable to accept the invitation to stay in the Soviet
Embassy because he feared that it might create bad feelings
among the British. Molotov, however, assured Harriman that
the rooms would be available if the President changed his
mind or if some difficulty should develop.

After obtaining Stalin's approval, Molotov accepted the
arrangements for the next day, which Harriman proposed on
behalf of Roosevelt. All of the meetings would take place in
the American legation. (Consequently, Stalin and Churchill
would have to drive through the crowded streets of Teheran.) At three in the afternoon Stalin would pay a call on
the President, and an hour later they would meet with Churchill and the military staffs. Dinner would follow at seven-
thirty.

Then Molotov asked for an agenda, but Harriman refused, explaining that the President had none because he
considered this to be a personal meeting with Stalin, Churchill, and their advisers. Later when Harriman went to the
British legation, he discovered that Molotov had fared better
with the British who were scrambling to put together an
agenda. At Harriman's urging, they dropped any idea of an
agenda.

After Harriman had returned to his quarters, about midnight he received a call that Molotov wished to see him. Returning to the Soviet Embassy, he found Archibald Clark-Kerr,
his British colleague in Moscow, already there. To their surprise, Molotov announced that he had information that German agents were already in Iran and they knew about
Roosevelt's presence in Teheran. These German agents were
now planning to assassinate the three leaders. Speaking for
Stalin, Molotov urged that Roosevelt move either to the British legation or the Soviet Embassy, where a house within the
embassy compound had already been prepared for him, including a newly installed bathtub for his convenience.

The following morning, Roosevelt's advisers conferred
over the question of moving him to the Soviet embassy compound. For political reasons, he would never go to the British legation. Moreover, the small British legation was already

crowded with British diplomats and military personnel. His advisers agreed that he ought to move to the Soviet compound to avoid the need for the three leaders traveling back and forth through the streets of Teheran to the American legation, which was about a mile from the British legation. Otherwise, during these trips, Nazi assassins would be offered three excellent targets.

Harriman doubted that Molotov's story was true, but he pointed out to Roosevelt that he would be held responsible if either Churchill or Stalin were assassinated while crossing the city for a meeting with him at the American legation. If he moved to the compound, there would be no need to travel through a city infested with enemy agents.

Mike Reilly agreed fully with the proposal to move the President to the Soviet Embassy because the NKVD had informed him that thirty-eight German parachutists had been dropped over Iran and six German agents were in the vicinity of Teheran. The NKVD agents were fearful, not only that Roosevelt might lose his life, but that they might pay the ultimate penalty if he was assassinated. Even Churchill, who had been unnerved by his journey from the airport to the British legation, was not averse to the move. Among those who conferred in the American legation, only Admiral Brown was negative. He raised the question: Why did Stalin now fear the security of Teheran after demanding that the three leaders meet in this very city?

"Do you care which embassy I move to?" Roosevelt asked Reilly.

"Not much difference, sir," replied Reilly.

"All right. It's the Russian, then," Roosevelt announced. "When do we move?"[6]

That same afternoon the standard cavalcade was prepared, with gun-laden jeeps traveling slowly through the streets guarded by American soldiers. A Secret Service agent played the role of the President in the dummy caravan. Shortly after the dummy caravan had left the American legation, Roosevelt, Hopkins, Admiral Leahy, and Major Boettiger, with a Secret Service agent as the driver, left the American legation in an Army staff car without any armed escort. Driving swiftly through the back streets of Teheran, the staff car arrived at the Soviet compound before the dummy caravan finished the trip. The air of mystery, the fast ride through narrow streets spiced with the danger of assassins, delighted Roosevelt—to him it was a great lark.

Of the move from the American legation to the Soviet Embassy, the President wrote in his diary:

> Yesterday morning the Russians discovered a plot to get him [Stalin] & W.S.C. and me as we drove to each other's legations so at Stalin's plea I moved down to the Russian compound where there is an extra house—and the danger of driving thro' the streets is eliminated as W.S.C. lives next door & there are flocks of guards.

The Soviet Embassy was a square building of light-brown stone set in a small park. On the front was an imposing portico with white Doric columns, which proved to be an excellent setting for taking pictures of the assembled VIPs. The park was surrounded on all sides by a high stone wall, and within the park were fountains, a small lake, apartments for the Soviet diplomatic personnel, a club, and a canteen. Strollers in the Soviet grounds swore that Russian guards armed with submachine guns peered out from behind every tree.

The British legation was a ramshackle building that had been constructed by the Indian Public Works Department when the British minister required a small escort of Indian cavalry for his personal protection. The legation stood within a walled compound, which had stables and outhouses at one end, now housing British troops to guard the legation. The legation grounds, dotted with trees and bushes, may have been a pleasant area for a stroll after a good dinner, but they were a security officer's nightmare. An assassin could have easily scaled the legation wall and found ample cover to await his target.

The Soviet Embassy and the British legation were separated by a narrow street which had now been closed off to all traffic with screens of barbed wire. Heavily armed guards, 2nd Battalion the Buffs and NKVD troops, patrolled the area.

At night the Russian Embassy grounds were lit by flood-lights, and by day armored cars patrolled the nearby streets. All of these activities signaled to the citizens of Teheran that something very important was occurring behind the armed barricades. Any Nazi agent plotting an assassination would have known where the three leaders were staying because of the elaborate precautions. But were there in fact Nazi agents hurrying through the alleyways of Teheran intent on assassinating Roosevelt, Churchill, and Stalin?

Throughout the summer of 1943, Allied intelligence officers received numerous reports about mysterious airplanes flying over Iran and occasionally dropping German parachutists along with equipment and explosives, but search parties failed to reveal either parachutes or Nazi agents. Probably all of the mystery flights were Allied planes on their wartime missions. Rumors of German agents inside the city of Teheran as late as November 22, 1943, remained only rumors as far as British and American intelligence was concerned. The Soviet ambassador in London had informed the Foreign Office on November 18, 1943, that the Soviet authorities had reliable information that during the next few days a number of Iranian subjects and subjects of other countries would be arriving in Iran from Germany. The majority were agents from German intelligence services entering to carry out acts of sabotage and intelligence gathering. Later only the NKVD claimed to have captured any German agents, but they never released any information to their allies about the interrogation of these "agents."

On August 14, 1943, near the Teheran railway station, the British had arrested one important German agent, Franz Mayer. He had held a secretarial position in the *Reichsgruppe* Industries before the war. In 1940 he was transferred from a signals unit to the Sicherheitdienst or SD, the Nazi party intelligence organization. Although lacking any experience in the Middle East, Mayer volunteered to serve there, and in October 1940 he reached Iran. When the British and Soviet forces occupied Iran in August 1941, he was as surprised as Reza Shah.

Mayer was totally unprepared for the situation in which he found himself. He was trained neither for espionage nor sabotage, he could not operate a radio, and he had no specific assignment. No arrangements had been made to supply him with courier service to Germany. He could only do the best possible and make contacts with the Iranians, hoping to organize them into a fifth-column movement. But that proved difficult because the Iranian tribesmen often preferred to fight among themselves rather than unite against the Allied troops and the Iranian government. When the German armies drove into the Caucasus Mountains in 1942, Mayer laid plans to instigate a revolt of the Iranian army and the tribes against the occupation forces. After the German armies had broken through the Russian forces in the Caucasus and driven southward toward the Persian Gulf, Iranians led by a few German agents would seize airfields, block roads, and set up a military government. But the campaign failed. By the fall of 1942, the German armies had to pull back from the Caucasus because they were in danger of being cut off thanks to the Soviet counterattack at Stalingrad.

Mayer was hiding out in Isfahan. After a quarrel with an Armenian confederate who went over to the British, British security forces raided his hideout in November, but he had fled, leaving behind his diary and other papers which enabled the British to identify the Iranians who were conspiring with Mayer. With the capture of Stalingrad early in 1943, Mayer had to make fresh plans.

He wanted Berlin to send him a radio operator and additional funds; on March 30, 1943, he received six agents, two of them radio operators. With them came money, weapons, and equipment to blow up bridges. Berlin intended that the group blow up railroad bridges, but only one member had any training in sabotage, and he was not an expert. Mayer was uninterested in sabotage, fearing that it would bring on a clash with the central government which he wished to avoid. He preferred political activities—stimulating and organizing tribal revolts.

In July three more German agents were dropped by parachute, along with radio sets and explosives in the Qashqai region near Fars. They made contact with two other German agents who had been in Iran since the Allied occupation. The five men lived with the tribes, quarreling among themselves and drinking too much arak. British security forces knew about them but did not consider them a menace because they were practically prisoners of the Qashqai. They were captured in March 1944. Mayer and the six agents dropped in March were all arrested in August 1943.[7]

Before Mayer's arrest, the British had begun to prepare a list of Iranians whose names had been found among the papers seized at his hideout in November 1942. Reader Bullard, the British minister, wanted his American colleague, Dreyfus, to join in pressing the Iranian government to take action against the Iranians who had been linked to Mayer. But Dreyfus had not wished to interfere in what he regarded as internal affairs of Iran, preferring to leave the matter of the arrests up to the British. Bullard thought that Dreyfus was continuing the traditional American hostility to British imperialism in Persia, oblivious to the fact that since American troops were also in Persia (without permission) his policy was out of date. The State Department, according to Bullard, "ought to have pulled him up, but instead they seem to have encouraged him."[8]

Dreyfus for his part thought the Iranians were playing at espionage rather than working seriously in Germany's interests. The information sent him by Bullard, Dreyfus claimed, "while containing always a germ of fact and truth, has been built up and exaggerated." But in view of the arrest of Mayer and the other agents, plus the additional information found in his papers, Dreyfus could not see how the arrests that were about to be made could be opposed.[9]

By November 1943, British intelligence agencies believed that any potential Iranian fifth-column movement under German direction had been broken. The approach of winter and the advance of the Soviet armies would make parachute landings impracticable. Agents would have to be infiltrated by overland routes.

The only major roundup of suspected agents had taken place late in August, when sixty-eight employees of the Iranian State Railway and twenty-seven army officers were arrested as the result of Allied pressure on the Iranian government. In addition, the government announced that a German organization had been discovered planning an insurrection against the government and plotting to wreck bridges and tunnels in order to cut supplies to the Allied armies and to interrupt the transport of goods needed by the Iranian people.

The Mayer network was never as widespread or as strong as had been imagined—and it was the only one that the British had uncovered by the time the Teheran Conference opened. The interrogation of Mayer and the examination of his papers demonstrated the inadequacy of German espionage inside Iran. The German High Command had been so confident of victory that there had seemed no reason to waste manpower in organizing an effective espionage organization or a fifth-column movement inside Iran. To Hitler and his associates, Iran was a minor sideshow. The main action was in Russia, where it had been expected that the Wehrmacht would destroy the Red Army and open up Iran to German domination.

At the time of the Teheran Conference, the reports that parachutists had been dropped in Iran helped create the illusion that they were intent on assassinating the three leaders. These were the reports which led to Roosevelt's move from the American legation to the Soviet Embassy. None of the occupying authorities in Iran ever produced one German agent who had been dropped by parachute with the intention of attacking the three leaders.

Despite the secrecy, the presence of the three leaders was generally known throughout Teheran even though every measure had been taken to prevent this. The city had been sealed off from the outside world—trains were halted, telegrams held up, bank transfers blocked lest they contain a coded message. Air travel came to a standstill. The Teheran radio station went off the air; daily newspapers were void of all news about the conference. Nevertheless, the Allies gave it all away by the massive military precautions which could not be hidden from the public. American soldiers surrounded the American legation even after Roosevelt had moved into the Soviet Embassy. The heavy detachment of Soviet and British troops surrounding the two compounds became an armed camp within the city of Teheran. Secret agents plotting an assassination would certainly have known where their three targets were living.

Was there really a plot against Roosevelt, Churchill, and Stalin? Harriman believed that the Russians had thought up this device to get Roosevelt inside the Soviet compound. After his return to Moscow, he tried to get the truth out of Molotov. "I said that I had a question to ask him, which he could feel free not to answer if he didn't wish to: namely, whether the plot in Teheran had been a German plot or a Molotov-Harriman plot? Molotov said that they knew there were German agents in Teheran but they had no information about a specific plot to attempt the life of any of the three men in Teheran; Marshal Stalin thought it would be safer if the President stayed at the Soviet Embassy." [10]

In his memoirs, Mike Reilly inferred that because of any possible danger to the President, the Soviet Embassy would be the safest place for the man whose life he had to protect at all costs. The files of the Secret Service do not contain any report from Reilly about the plot to assassinate the President. Reilly probably thought such a report unnecessary because there was no plot. The only Secret Service report on the trip omits all mention of a plot.

The British authorities in Teheran received no information other than Molotov's statement. Those intelligence files in the Public Record Office which are open to the public (1980) are devoid of comments about the existence of a plot. "After the Conference," wrote Bullard, "our security officers ragged their Soviet opposite numbers about it. The poor Russians put on a look of helplessness mixed with an appeal for sympathy, as though to say: 'You know what it is: if Molotov says there's a plot there is a plot.' " [11]

In 1968, Victor Yegorov published a book in Moscow purporting to describe the Soviet infiltration of the German secret service which Yegorov claimed helped destroy the plot to assassinate the three leaders. The book is not only difficult to read and understand, but impossible to believe because it is unsubstantiated by documentary evidence. [12]

In London when the Joint Intelligence Committee of the War Cabinet considered the matter, they agreed that the alleged plot was "complete baloney." Soviet security authorities determined that Stalin should not have to go to the American legation because that required a journey through the crowded part of the city. Then the Russians decided that

Roosevelt had to stay at the Soviet Embassy. "With this end in view they produced a hair-raising story of an imaginary plot on his life." As the British legation and the Soviet Embassy were side by side, security for the conference would be an easy matter.[13]

Since no hard evidence has ever been found indicating that a plot really existed, the only conclusion must be that it was dreamed up by Soviet plotters. Stalin had left the Soviet Union for the second time in his life, the first time since he had become dictator. He would certainly fear traveling through the streets of a foreign city in time of war even though surrounded by his own troops. His travels in the Moscow streets were elaborately guarded and never revealed, and the idea of moving back and forth between the American legation and the Soviet Embassy must have frightened Stalin even more. In Teheran he would be in a country where German agents were still thought to be at large. If such agents were there, Stalinist logic would have concluded that they would attempt an assassination.

Stalin was still suspicious of his capitalist allies. If the most powerful ally lived within the Soviet compound and the other stayed across a narrow street, then close check could be kept on their movements and discussions. Probably Soviet security technicians had installed listening devices in the building before Roosevelt moved in so that his private comments could be heard.[14] In addition, all of the servants waiting on Roosevelt and his party were probably members of the NKVD. Telltale bulges underneath the uniforms of the maids and butlers revealed that they were carrying weapons while waiting on the President. Their true professions became known after the conference had ended. Roosevelt had instructed Lieutenant (jg) William Rigdon, his secretary, to obtain the names of all those servants to whom letters should be sent thanking them for their services. The information was never provided because after Roosevelt and his party had left the compound, to Rigdon's surprise, the "servants" appeared in uniforms of officers in the NKVD, including colonels and a general. They certainly served as human microphones overhearing Roosevelt's talks with his advisers.[15]

Roosevelt would probably not have been unduly concerned if Soviet agents had overheard his conversations because then perhaps Stalin would have been more willing to trust him. Indeed, the President would have perhaps preferred that Stalin have knowledge of his conversations during the Teheran Conference. He had agreed to the need to move to the Soviet Embassy because it would be another step in his plan to get to Stalin and to prove to him that he had no reason to suspect Roosevelt. He believed that Stalin was "get-atable"—that he could break through the barrier of suspicion and convince him that he could be trusted. There could be no better way to "get at" Stalin than by moving within the Soviet compound and living there during the Allied conference in Teheran. If Roosevelt's plans for a better world after the war had ended could be helped by living inside the Soviet Embassy and risking having conversations overheard by whatever means, he would probably welcome the opportunity.

In fact, Roosevelt was put so close to Stalin that the Soviet ruler was able at will to enter Roosevelt's quarters to inquire if there was anything his guest desired and to chat with the President. It was the very situation Roosevelt wanted in order to reach Stalin—and good reason for him to travel from Washington to Teheran during a world war.

9
Churchill, Stalin, and Roosevelt

THREE MEN FROM DIFFERENT countries and with contrasting careers traveled toward Teheran where as allies in a world war they would discuss strategy and begin working on plans for the postwar world. Each brought his intelligence, his personal experiences, his weaknesses and prejudices. Through his own life each had prepared for this meeting. Except that two men shared the same language, the trio had little in common. Stalin had been a professional revolutionary, Churchill a cavalry officer, and Roosevelt had the only university degree. Churchill had been a newspaper correspondent, and Roosevelt the governor of New York State. Stalin had sent millions of his fellow countrymen to their deaths. Roosevelt was a cripple; Stalin drove his wife to suicide. All three men had spent most of their careers in some form of political activity. Nothing, however, could be more different than their personal histories up to that moment when they would meet in Teheran.

Winston Leonard Spencer-Churchill arrived in the world two months ahead of schedule at Blenheim Palace in Oxfordshire on November 30, 1874. A fall while out walking with the shooters and a rough drive in a pony carriage helped bring on his mother's labor pains. As all the preparations had been made for Winston's birth to occur at his parents' home in London, there were no baby clothes in Blenheim. His first clothes were borrowed from the wife of the local solicitor who was expecting her first child in January.

Winston's parents represented British aristocracy and American wealth. His father, Randolph, brilliant and erratic, had recently become the Conservative Member of Parliament for Woodstock. He was the second son of the seventh Duke of Marlborough and a descendant of the Spencer family, which had been prominent in British political life in the seventeenth and eighteenth centuries. The first Duke of Marlborough, John Churchill, had commanded the English armies during the War of the Spanish Succession. Blenheim Palace, Winston Churchill's birthplace, had been given by Queen Anne to the first duke in gratitude for his military service to England. Winston's mother, the beautiful and vivacious Jennie Jerome, born in Brooklyn, the daughter of Leonard and Clarissa Jerome, grew up amid wealth and ease. Her father, who had made and lost fortunes, became best known as the founder of the American Jockey Club. Jennie so enjoyed London's fashionable society that she left the rearing of her son to his nannie, Mrs. Everest, to whom he remained devoted all his life.

Packed off to school at the age of seven, young Winston came to hate the schoolmasters' efforts to force him to learn Latin. At Harrow, young Churchill found himself placed at the bottom of his class. Because of his inability to master Latin, he was considered fit only to learn English. His teachers proceeded to drill him in the basic English grammar. "Thus," he wrote, "I got into my bones the essential structure of the ordinary British sentence—which is a noble thing."[1]

Winston's erratic academic record convinced Randolph Churchill that his son lacked talent for the bar, the usual path to a career in British politics. Watching his son play with his extensive collection of toy soldiers led Randolph Churchill to decide on a military career for Winston. After three attempts, young Churchill passed the entrance examinations to the Royal Military College at Sandhurst. Here he was in a world that he enjoyed, a world without Latin or schoolmasters, a world dominated by horses, military tactics, and formations. Churchill completed Sandhurst near the top of his class, receiving the Queen's Commission in February 1895 in the Fourth Hussars.

At that time, the British army allowed officers two and a half months of leave during the year. Churchill, wishing to learn more about his profession, looked around for an available war and found it in Cuba where Spain was struggling to suppress a rebellion. After pulling the right strings, he received permission to join the Spanish army. There in Cuba, on his twenty-first birthday, the young subaltern came under fire: "for the first time I heard shots fired in anger and heard bullets strike flesh or whistle through the air."[2] Churchill's experiences in Cuba gave him the opportunity to write articles for the *Daily Graphic* and begin his writing career.

On his return from Cuba, Churchill joined his regiment for the long journey to India. There, when not playing polo, he educated himself through a stiff regime of reading Gibbon, Macaulay, Darwin, and even Adam Smith. Yet he was always eager to find action and again he pulled strings to get himself attached to a brigade fighting on the northwest frontier of India. In September 1897 he became a combatant once more and at the same time wrote dispatches for newspapers. Drawing on these experiences later, he wrote his first book, *The Story of the Malakand Field Force.*

By 1898 a more important war attracted Churchill to Egypt, where the British army under Sir Herbert Kitchener sought to recapture the Sudan from the Dervishes. In order to join Kitchener, Churchill used a meeting with the prime minister, Lord Salisbury, to wangle permission to be attached to the Twenty-first Lancers for the campaign in the Sudan. He rode with them at the Battle of Omdurman, the last great cavalry charge of the British army, and nearly became a casualty. From these experiences came another more successful book, *The River War,* which provided Churchill with enough profit for him to resign his commission.

Army life proved very expensive for a young officer who lacked a substantial fortune. Randolph Churchill had died in 1895 after a long illness and a disappointing political career. His widow had only enough for herself and little for Winston, who had to earn his own living now through writing.

Through his articles and books, Churchill had aimed at keeping his name before the public in order that he might eventually launch himself on a political career. To this end, he returned to Britain after the victory in the Sudan and stood for Parliament in his first election in 1899, which he lost. A new war erupted in South Africa and offered him another opportunity to advance his career.

The war in South Africa stemmed from quarrels between the Boers and their British overlords which ended in hostilities. Even before the fighting had begun, Churchill, appointed a special correspondent for the *Morning Post,* was on his way to the scene of the fighting. Soon after arriving in South Africa, he was traveling on an armored train out on a reconnaissance mission when the Boers ambushed the train and derailed some of the cars. Churchill volunteered to help clear the line, but he became cut off from the main body of troops and a lone Boer captured him. His captor was a future prime minister of South Africa, Louis Botha. After Churchill made a daring escape from the prisoner of war camp, news of his exploit brought him fame. For six more months, however, he remained in South Africa serving as a lieutenant in the South African Horse, returning for the general election in 1900. This time he won a seat in the House of Commons and was launched on his political career.

Churchill had stood as a Conservative, his father's party; but in 1904 he took the unthinkable step of crossing the floor of the House to take his seat with the opposing Liberal party. Before the year ended, he had his first post, undersecretary for colonies, which became a springboard to a seat in the cabinet in 1908, as president of the Board of Trade. Two years later, Churchill became Home Secretary. In these years at the Board of Trade and the Home Office, he carried out a legislative program of social reform which seemed quite radical to conservative Englishmen. His program encompassed establishing a standing court of arbitration for industrial conciliation, setting up minimum rates for timework, instituting compulsory unemployment insurance, creating labor exchanges to provide information on jobs, setting standards to improve mine safety, and correcting prison conditions. Next, as First Lord of the Admiralty, from 1911 to 1915, he enjoyed four of the happiest years of his career. Administering the fleet found him in his element, particularly after the outbreak of World War I.

In 1915, Churchill became the driving force behind the effort to have British warships force the Straits of the Dardanelles and bring aid to Russia. When the ships failed to silence the Turkish forts, British and Commonwealth troops were set down on the Gallipoli peninsula in a vain and bloody attempt to take the forts by land. Much of the blame for the ultimate failure and the withdrawal of Allied forces from Gallipoli was thrust on Churchill. Obliged to resign his cabinet position, he took up his commission, went to France, and there commanded the 6th Royal Scots Fusiliers. When he lost his command because the regiment was combined with another, he requested his release from the army. Lord Kitchener, Secretary of State for War, released Churchill on condition that he not apply for war service again.

Churchill, however, had not given up his seat in the House of Commons and he returned eagerly to the political wars. Back in London by 1917, he became minister of munitions in the Lloyd George cabinet. Other important posts followed. As Secretary for War and Air, 1919–21, Churchill stirred up controversy by his efforts to further the Allied intervention in the Russian civil war, which had now become an anti-Bolshevik crusade, but his bold policy found little support among his cabinet colleagues. When the intervention failed and all the troops had been withdrawn, Churchill had to bear much of the blame.

He was also responsible for helping the Lloyd George government dismember the armed forces through severe reductions in military and naval expenditures. Churchill cut the funds for the Royal Air Force so drastically that an air force which had been ranked among the greatest in the world in 1918, by 1921 possessed only three squadrons in Britain. He also took the initiative in persuading the cabinet to agree that military budgets ought to be based on the assumption that "the British Empire will not be engaged in any great war during the next ten years and that no Expeditionary Force will be required."[3] The "Ten Year" rule would have a lasting effect on Britain's preparedness for war.

As colonial secretary in 1921–22, Churchill fought off every effort to undo the Balfour Declaration, issued in November 1917, which declared that the British government looked with favor on the establishment of a national home for the Jewish people in Palestine. In speeches and in talks with Arab leaders, he urged them to accept the Balfour Declaration, to develop amicable relations with the Jews, and to work with them in improving the resources of Palestine.

While Churchill served as colonial secretary, he became a central figure in the struggle to end the Irish troubles. He played a major role in negotiating the Irish treaty of 1921 and in piloting it through the House of Commons. But he found himself moving more toward the right politically. He failed to win a seat in Commons in the general elections in 1922 and 1923. Another defeat came in a by-election in 1924, but in the general election in the fall of 1924 Churchill won as a Conservative candidate. In the new government formed by Stanley Baldwin, Churchill became Chancellor of the Exchequer because Baldwin preferred to have him inside the cabinet rather than outside where he could not be controlled. For Churchill it was a wonderful moment: at last he had reached the cabinet position once held by his father.

As chancellor, he presided over the return to the gold standard which ultimately resulted in the pound becoming so expensive that British goods were priced out of the world market. Orthodox financial opinion held that this was the proper course. Churchill, knowing his own lack of expertise on this question, had sought out the best financial experts for their opinions, which he followed. More far-reaching was his continued slashing of the British military budget. But in the House of Commons he had to endure attacks from the Labour party because his cuts had not been deep enough. To justify further budget cuts, Churchill had the "Ten Year" rule made a formal part of British policy. It would now be a "standing assumption that at any given date there will be no major war for ten years from that date."[4] Such would be the rule unless changed by the Foreign Office or one of the military services.

Churchill survived the election of 1929 when many of the leading Tories were defeated, but he was out of office and would remain so until war broke out in 1939 because his attacks on the bill to reform the government of India made him only more hated by Tory leaders. In the affair of Edward VIII and Mrs. Simpson, they turned on him when the romantic streak in Churchill led him to seek to prevent the king's abdication. When he asked for a delay in the abdication, he was shouted down in the House of Commons on December 7, 1936, and forced to withdraw.

By 1938, the British political establishment had written off Churchill as a rash, overly ambitious adventurer. His speeches in a half-empty House of Commons brought little change in government defense policies. His constant harping on the German menace and the need for additional defense expenditures soon bored the members of Parliament. Many of his hearers thought that his speeches only proved that he had enjoyed war too much. Churchill did not rule out negotiations with the Nazi government, but he urged negotiating from strength—a condition that could be attained only by rearming to a greater degree than the Chamberlain government wished to achieve.

After the Munich Agreement had been signed, Churchill seemed almost alone in the Conservative party, so great was the widespread relief at the avoidance of war. Because he abstained in the vote in the House of Commons on the government's handling of the Munich crisis, a movement developed within his constituency organization to disown him. Although he survived the attempt by a narrow margin, his career appeared to be finished.

Despite this blow to his ambitions, Churchill still retained enormous vitality and drive. His extraordinary constitution allowed him to eat, drink, and smoke as he wished. Throughout his political career, he drove himself; he seemed always in a hurry, determined to dominate, and to be the aggressor. Yet he often suffered from a deep depression, the "black dog," as he called these periods. His driving ambition, his impatience, and his desire for action and fame provoked his colleagues to question his judgment and stability. But Churchill was not an actor; he behaved in the public eye just as he did in private life.

During the 1930s while out of office, he lived at the family home, Chartwell, where he built brick walls, created lakes, and enjoyed the most productive period of his writing. At Chartwell he assembled assistants to carry on the research for his books. He would use the research to dictate the narrative and then rewrite the dictation after it had been typed out. Even after the books were in page proof, he continued to rewrite.

His masterpiece was probably *World Crisis,* his account of the World War I era. Another important work was his biography of his ancestor, the first Duke of Marlborough. Although lacking professional training as a historian, his well-researched books were distinguished by magnificent narration. Nevertheless, while he wrote, he yearned to return to a major role in British political life.

The fall of Czechoslovakia in March 1939 helped turn opinion in favor of Churchill's views. Newspapers began to campaign for his return to the government. However, such pressure would not sway Neville Chamberlain to admit him to the cabinet until after Hitler's armies invaded Poland. When Churchill returned to the cabinet as First Lord of the Admiralty on September 2, 1939, the signal went out to the fleet: "Winston is back."

Always ready with fresh ideas, he bombarded Chamberlain with proposals for carrying the war to the enemy, but always he remained a loyal colleague. The Allied defeat in Norway in 1940 ended the Chamberlain government. Although Churchill bore much of the blame for the British losses in Norway, in the end all political parties had to turn to him to lead the nation in its hour of gravest peril even though he was not the heir apparent to Chamberlain. The political outcast had become the prime minister who would lead the nation through the Battle of Britain, the Blitz, and on to final victory. But in 1940 most of the Conservative party accepted him without enthusiasm. The very thought of Churchill as prime minister chilled the civil servants. To them he was an adventurer, a brilliant, inspired orator who could not be entrusted with the affairs of state at this terrible moment in the history of the British Empire. But within days the tone of the British government had changed now that Winston Churchill was at No. 10 Downing Street. He created a sense of urgency in the government. Civil servants almost seemed to be running through the corridors of Whitehall. The English weekend was no longer sacrosanct. "Business as usual" had ended.

In a period of great national crisis, Churchill's speeches in Parliament and on the radio helped inspire the British people. Lively, often humorous, his speeches may not have sounded as well on the radio of the era as they do now from recordings. He dictated these carefully prepared speeches to secretaries, often working in relays. Then he rewrote and corrected the typed manuscript up to the final moment of delivery. The radio speeches had to be written out for him because he could not deliver them impromptu and also because he had difficulty pronouncing the letter "S," which could make his speech sound slurred. Most political speeches make dull reading but with Churchill that was never the case.

Of the three men who would confer at Teheran, Churchill was the only one who had commanded troops in battle. He had also administered the senior British military service, the Royal Navy. His experience paid off in the new method of administration which he created after he became prime minister. Under Chamberlain, administration of the war had been loose and often responsibilities were undefined. Churchill set up a small War Cabinet, limited to five ministers, which had the overall task of running the war. Then he created the post of minister of defense for himself. Through this office he could preside over the meetings of the chiefs of staff committee where military problems could be thrashed out in debate with the admirals and generals. This arrangement combined in one man the political and military authority to run the war.

Churchill constantly spurred on the generals, admirals, and ministers to greater efforts, firing off to them memoranda tagged "Action this day." But unlike Stalin, who had his generals shot when he became dissatisfied with them, Churchill could only fire them from their commands if he found them hesitant or failing to get on with the job. Admirals suffered also. Someone estimated that at one time or another Churchill attempted to relieve every admiral who had an important sea command.

When he reached Teheran, the major question facing him would be the second front, which the Americans wanted as the chief operation scheduled for 1944. Such concentration on one campaign frightened him because he had been driven from office in 1915 by the Gallipoli disaster. Britain's losses in Norway had brought down Chamberlain's government, and Churchill had been prime minister when the British Expeditionary Force had been driven from the European continent in 1940. For him there was always the nightmare of another British army being once more driven into the sea or suffering casualties as heavy as those endured on the Somme in 1916 or in Flanders in 1917. This nightmare had become more frightening after the series of defeats His Majesty's forces had suffered since 1940. British armies had been driven out of Norway, France, Belgium, Greece, Crete, Malaysia, and Hong Kong. There had been only one major British victory amid all of those catastrophes: El Alamein. Despite this victory, the fear of another British defeat gnawed at Churchill. "We must take care," he often repeated, "that the tides do not run red with the blood of American and British youth, or the beaches be choked with their bodies." Such fear could be overcome only if the Soviet and American Allies joined fully in the great battle to invade Europe. The need of these Allies meant a change in power relationships. Until now Churchill had operated on a basis of equality with Roosevelt and Stalin. He had enjoyed the visits to the White House and the informal meals with Hopkins and Roosevelt, which went on far into the night and which gradually came to bore Roosevelt. But in the Teheran meetings, a third party would join their select circle.

Winston Churchill was five years old when Josef Djugashvili, known to history as Joseph Stalin, was born to peasant parents in Gori in the area of czarist Russia known as Georgia. Both of his parents had at one time been serfs; his father, a cobbler with a reputation as a drunkard, died when Joseph was eleven years of age. The rearing of the boy became the sole responsibility of his mother, who had born three other children, all of whom had died at birth.[5]

Ambitious for her son, she obtained a place for him in the local church school where he learned Russian, sang in the choir, and made a high academic record. In the autumn of 1894, to the delight of his mother, Joseph matriculated at the theological seminary in Tiflis. Although a poor boy could obtain a good education in the seminary, Joseph soon found the atmosphere repressive. The monks spied on the students, denouncing them to the principal for the slightest infraction of a multitude of rules, and they took pains to prevent their charges from reading radical books. In his third year, the monks caught Joseph reading some of the forbidden books. By this time he also had joined a secret socialist organization in Tiflis. Because his actions were becoming more rebellious, on May 29, 1899, he was expelled from the seminary, ostensibly for failing to take an examination.

By the time Stalin left, he had become converted to Marxism and could now devote his entire life to being an organizer, propagandist, journalist, and strike leader in the cause of socialism. By 1902 he had been arrested in Batum, where he had gone to organize a strike among the oil workers. Although he was exiled to Siberia for three years, escape was so easy that in 1904 he reappeared in Tiflis. He had become a Bolshevik, joining the faction of the Social Democratic party which Lenin dominated. A year later he came to Lenin's attention, and before the year ended, they met in Finland for the first time.

The Bolshevik party in 1907 had fallen on hard times as the police rounded up activists and sent them into exile in Siberia. To Lenin, Stalin appeared to be working wholeheartedly for the cause of Bolshevism, struggling on despite arrests and exile to Siberia in 1908 and again in 1910. His persistence so impressed Lenin that he co-opted Stalin into the Central Committee of the Bolshevik party while he was in exile in Siberia. After the outbreak of World War I, exiles became eligible for military service, but the military authorities rejected Stalin because of his physical condition. During his childhood he had contracted blood poisoning from an ulcer on his left hand which brought him close to death. After his recovery, he was unable to bend his elbow and would have found it difficult to fire a rifle because his left arm was shorter than the right. The February–March revolution brought him freedom from Siberia and a trip back to St. Petersburg in time to greet Lenin after the Germans allowed him to return from exile in Switzerland in April 1917.

When the Bolsheviks seized power in November, Stalin belonged to the inner circle of the Bolshevik party. Gradually he made a reputation as an administrator who worked hard at jobs which other party members found unglamorous and dull. Lenin used him as a troubleshooter, dispatching him on a variety of missions which helped him to develop political contacts. On these missions Stalin displayed a capacity for hard work and a ruthlessness pleasing to Lenin. Since Stalin came from Georgia, Lenin regarded him as a specialist on nationalities (minorities) within Soviet Russia, and so appointed him Commissar for Nationalities to deal with the minorities, which made up 40 percent of the population.

Stalin continued to accumulate other important appointments, becoming Commissar for the Workers and Peasants Inspectorate which had been created to root out inefficiency and corruption from within the civil service. He also sat on the Politburo, the small, vital committee of the Central Committee of the Communist party charged with handling urgent political matters. In addition to this job, he served on the Orgburo (Organization Bureau), which oversaw Communist party personnel records and assignments. His collection of offices multiplied with his appointment as general secretary of the Central Committee in 1922.

Stalin's new office afforded him a powerful operating base in a government whose only political party formed an elite to lead the masses. At the time of his appointment, few party members regarded his new job as a political plum but rather as bureaucratic drudgery; however, for Stalin it became a source of power. As general secretary, he drafted the agenda and supplied the relevant documents from the files for the meetings of the Politburo. As general secretary, he had daily contact with the lower ranks of party officials in all areas of the Soviet Union. His office handled appointments, dismissals, and promotions of all party officials. Through the opportunity to interpret the decisions of the Politburo and to administer the party machinery, an enormous source of political power was thrust into his hands. By its nature, the Soviet government was overcentralized, and now the administration of the party had been centralized in the hands of one man whose ambitions grew daily.

Using his office as general secretary of the Communist party, Stalin built a power base within the government, the party, and throughout the nation. He developed a form of personal chancery with aides chosen for their talent and loyalty who kept him informed about every aspect of Soviet affairs, and who acted as his agents and spies throughout the Soviet bureaucracy and government. Out in the countryside, he built up a network of clients among party officials, rewarding their loyalty by promoting them to higher party offices. He tightened his grip on the Soviet government by filling the slate of nominees for party conferences and congresses with his supporters. As there was no opposing slate, his nominees always won the election. Through all of these practices, he turned the office of general secretary into the most powerful political office in the nation.

Even as Stalin established the base from which he would exert such immense power, his mentor, Lenin, worried about his ambitious protégé. He muttered in a private meeting: "This cook will concoct nothing but peppery dishes."[6] By 1922, when Lenin became ill, he had begun to understand just how much power Stalin had concentrated in his hands. He may have been contemplating removing Stalin from office, but death prevented him from taking action other than to draft a postscript to his "Political Testament" warning that Stalin ought to be removed from the post of general secretary.

Because Stalin had already begun politicking when Lenin became ill, he survived Lenin's posthumous attack. His labors paid off. In the power struggle within the party, Gregory Zinoviev and Lev Kamenev, members of the Politburo, recruited Stalin into a triumvirate aimed at defeating the brilliant orator and writer Leon Trotsky, who seemed to be the heir to Lenin's power and position. At the Thirteenth Party Congress in 1924, Zinoviev and Kamenev defended Stalin when Lenin's accusations were read to the Central Committee, and helped save his career. After they realized the extent of Stalin's power and ambition, they joined Trotsky in a triumvirate against the general secretary, but they were too late. Stalin had them expelled from the party in 1927 and they lost their political clout. By 1929 Stalin became supreme in the Soviet Union, having defeated another faction headed by Nikolai Bukharin.

Stalin's opponents consistently underrated his abilities because they could not imagine that this bureaucrat could so deftly manipulate the powers of the office of general secretary that his opponents would first be isolated, then defeated. They learned too late how Stalin could exploit the centralized bureaucracy to pack conferences and congresses with his adherents, who voted through resolutions and decrees which he had dictated. In addition, Stalin had another advantage: factionalism was a heinous sin against the party. Since the party was always correct, anyone who differed from the party line could not be a loyal party member and risked expulsion. Once outside the only legal political party in the Soviet Union, the ex-party member lost all influence. Stalin used this weapon to destroy his enemies because any political activity not approved by the party smelled of treason.

As he achieved the defeat of his enemies, he also made himself into a preeminent Marxist thinker by contributing to Communist theory with his concept of "Socialism in One Country," which he stumbled on in his power struggle with Trotsky, who had argued in favor of a permanent revolution. According to this theory, socialism in Russia could never succeed unless revolution became international, with western nations undergoing their own revolution. Consequently, the success of socialism in the Soviet Union depended on outside events. Realizing that the masses would lose heart waiting for a world revolution, Stalin appealed to the Russian spirit of nationalism by proclaiming that socialism could be constructed in one country (Soviet Russia) without waiting for the revolution elsewhere and without outside help. However, the construction of socialism in the Soviet Union would require vigilance against the capitalist powers bent on waging war against the only socialist nation. For the protection of socialism against the warmongering capitalists, a strong system of national defense had to be established. In order to defeat the capitalists and to provide for the military needs, Russia must be industrialized as swiftly as possible. Moreover, the security of the Soviet state demanded that all Soviet citizens be ever alert against enemies, foreign and domestic, and to that end a powerful police force would be required. All spies and saboteurs had to be rooted out before they undermined the security of the only socialist state.

To achieve the goal of "Socialism in One Country," Stalin had no intention of moving gradually over a long period of time, using persuasion. Instead of gradualism, he resolved on another great revolution in which the leading role would be his. Soviet Russia would go through another heroic period in which he would become an even greater figure than Lenin.

If Stalin's goals were to be achieved, the Soviet Union had to be industrialized quickly in order to provide the necessary industrial base which would supply consumer goods for everyone and raise the standard of living. More vital to the security of the socialist state was the need to industrialize in order to supply the necessary armaments for defense against the attacks by western capitalist powers. In 1928, Stalin launched a Five Year Plan to industrialize Russia, but no one realized what Russia was about to undergo: a second revolution as Stalin rushed to transform Soviet Russia into an industrialized state as quickly as possible regardless of the cost in lives, standard of living, or in personal liberties. For Stalin intended to have Soviet Russia pass through the stages of industrialization at a much faster pace than that experienced by the western nations. Consequently, a great nation whose population was comprised largely of illiterate, uneducated peasants would now have to learn the techniques of industrial production immediately. Stalin could not wait for generations to be gradually educated to industrial methods: there would be a crash industrialization, and damn the human consequences.

The Five Year Plan aimed at increasing the quantity of heavy industry products, not consumer goods. The goals were numerical quotas, which once attained had to be surpassed. On December 31, 1932, the first Five Year Plan was judged completed ahead of schedule. In many industries, the goals were pronounced achieved, in others not attained. The figures had little meaning because the goal was rapid industrialization. Stalin declared: "We are fifty or a hundred years behind the advanced countries. Either we do it, or we shall be crushed."[7]

His greatest battle came with the peasants, whom he

feared as class enemies because by withholding crops from the market, they could raise prices and wreck his drive for industrialization. The peasants, particularly those dubbed "*kulaks*"—the name for the wealthier peasants—must be forced to produce more food for the workers at lower prices. This goal would be achieved through the collective farms— *kolkhoz*. In theory, these would be large farms where the peasants had consolidated their holdings and where they worked the land cooperatively, utilizing modern farm machinery. For Stalin, the collective farms became a means to help pay for industrialization. Appointed party managers would oversee the operation of these farms in which peasant holdings had been consolidated by force. The government would set the prices paid the peasants for their produce as low as possible, and the agricultural produce would then be sold to the public at prices again set by the government. In this way the peasants would be unable to hold back their produce from the market in order to get higher prices.

Stalin knew that forceful collectivization would mean violence, which he welcomed because it would be class war. As collectivization expanded, it became open warfare with peasants resisting and suffering death and imprisonment. Peasants either joined the *kolkhoz* voluntarily or they were compelled to do so. However, before entering the collective farms, they slaughtered their cattle, horses, and pigs, destroyed farm implements, and allowed their crops to rot in the fields. But Stalin triumphed in the end. By 1938 the peasants had been collectivized and made to live on the collective farms. But in the process of forcing the peasants to join the collectives, a great famine broke out with a loss of life estimated as high as ten million Soviet citizens.

Although Stalin won the battle to control the peasants, he lost the battle for greater agricultural production. But that had never been the goal in the war with the peasants: he wanted to control agricultural production so that the Soviet government could take agricultural products from the peasants as cheaply as possible. Then the government could process the food and sell it to the city workers at the government's own price. The government would use its profits to finance industrialization.

Stalin's greatest revolution came in the terrible purges of the 1930s when millions of Soviet citizens were executed or condemned to work and die in slave-labor camps. Known as a "purge," the concept had been invented by Stalin's mentor, Lenin, who had used the device on the Communist party, relying on public show trials for propaganda purposes. Stalin's collectivization had led to the establishment of a string of slave-labor camps in which peasants were forced to work on projects in areas of Siberia where the conditions and the climate were very harsh. In addition, through the years, Lenin and Stalin had developed an efficient secret police. Together, all these elements—show trials, labor camps, and secret police—produced the purge of the Soviet people.

Stalin's revolutions in industry and agriculture could not avoid arousing opposition even among the elite of the Communist party. With his network of personal agents and police, Stalin could not miss the mutterings and complaints, chiefly about the speed of industrialization with its resulting errors, and the widespread suffering of the peasants as the result of collectivization. To someone as suspicious as Stalin, these people who muttered and complained must be crushed because they constituted a potential threat to his drive for power.

By 1932 even members of the Politburo elite were calling for a relaxation of the drive for industrialization and collectivization, and an end to the strife that was tearing the country apart. Stalin considered such talk counterrevolutionary, threatening his position and his power. At the Seventeenth Party Congress early in 1934 there was loud applause for a new member of the party secretariat and Politburo, the party chief in Leningrad, Sergei Kirov, who had been credited as a moderate. He was now marked for execution.

A young Communist, Leonid Nikolaev, fatally shot Kirov on December 1, 1934, at the party headquarters in Leningrad. Stalin's role in the assassination is unclear, but Nikita S. Khrushchev hinted in 1956 that Stalin had figured prominently in organizing the death of Kirov. Most certainly Stalin exploited the death of a potential rival for power. Secret directives, immediately issued, speeded up cases of people accused of terrorism. Investigations would be accelerated and followed by executions without appeals for mercy. At once batches of prisoners were executed, charged with being "White Guards." Those blamed for Kirov's murder were hastily tried in secret and executed; even police investigators were later executed mysteriously.

Using the shock provided by the assassination, Stalin moved against Communist party members, who were tried for maintaining secret centers of opposition in Moscow. Old Bolsheviks, including Kamenev and Zinoviev, received prison sentences after a secret trial. During 1935, Stalin placed his henchmen in key positions in the party and police to achieve a more efficient purge. Preparations were made for a massive assault on members of the Communist party, which Stalin launched in 1936 with the first of three great show trials. This public trial shocked and fascinated the world as men once prominent in the Communist party apparatus openly confessed to a variety of criminal acts against the security of the very government they had fought to establish. A second show trial astonished the world in 1937, and during that summer, the purge engulfed the high command of the Red Army. The last of the show trials took place in 1938. In only one instance did an accused repudiate a confession in open court, but after a night with the NKVD he returned to confess as his accusers required. All of the defendants confessed to the crimes with which they had been charged. No valid evidence was introduced to substantiate the charges other than the confessions.

The purge spread into all levels of the Communist party and Soviet society. People were tortured into implicating others by guilt through association. Friends and relatives implicated each other; children were urged to inform on their parents. Soviet men and women who had traveled abroad, read foreign books and newspapers, knew foreigners personally, or studied foreign languages were all suspect. The secret police received quotas and they had to make arrests and force confessions from enough people to fulfill their quotas. As a result of their actions, the Great Purge tore Soviet society apart, leading to a condition in which hundreds of badly needed engineers and scientists were shipped to the slave-labor camps, the GULAG. Stalin's purge finally struck at the Soviet armed forces, with 90 percent of the generals and 80 percent of the colonels being arrested. All ranks of the armed forces suffered, but no valid evidence has ever been produced to prove the existence of a plot among the Soviet military services aimed at overthrowing Stalin's regime.

In the prisons the word "Why?" could often be found scrawled on the walls. Throughout the purge Stalin made the reason for this agony appear to be solely a question of defense against the enemies of the Soviet Union, internal and external, who were bent on wrecking the Soviet economic system and sowing political dissension. The arch villain, the leader of a gigantic conspiracy, according to the Soviet persecutors, was Leon Trotsky, whom Stalin had murdered in Mexico in 1940. Through the device of a plot and conspirators bent on destroying the Five Year Plans, Stalin sought to thrust all of the blame for the industrial failures and economic hardship on someone other than himself.

Stalin's true goals in unleashing the purge were not so obvious. He intended to remake the Communist party into an organization of doers, not Marxist theoreticians, who had no value in his system and who remembered when he was subordinate to Lenin and Trotsky. Stalin wanted to eliminate all future rivals for power in Soviet Russia. Through the device of the purge, he aimed at breaking up groups or cliques who might have enough cohesion to rely on each other in building a rival political organization. To destroy this cohesion and trust, Stalin sowed mistrust and suspicion in order that Soviet citizens would denounce their friends, relatives, and neighbors. Finally, he sought to restock Soviet society with a new generation of men and women educated for the new technical era in Soviet Russia. They would know that they were all replaceable, and they would also understand that the ultimate Soviet authority, Stalin, had placed them in their new position, and to the same authority belonged final allegiance. Personal relations, family, career, nothing could protect any Soviet citizen. Stalin had also renewed the Communist party with citizens who were bound to him, whom he could manipulate as he chose.

A Soviet source places the number of those sent into exile or sentenced to the labor camps at between four and five million, but that figure may be too low. The same source estimates the number of those executed at 400,000 to 500,000. Robert Conquest estimates that twice that number were executed.[8] No matter how many Soviet citizens were executed or sentenced to the GULAG, everyone understood Stalin's message. No one was safe from arrest and possible execution, not even those who had enjoyed the high status of belonging to the elite, the Communist party. Moreover, fleeing abroad would not save them from execution. Soviet men and women knew that to deviate from the party line, to question orders from superiors, to doubt, to hesitate, invited a terrible retribution. Truly no czar had ever been able to exert the power now in the hands of Joseph Stalin.

Stalin, as well as Hitler, hated the 1919 peace settlement. He sought an arrangement between them which would return the Baltic States to Russia as well as the Russian areas of Poland. But such an arrangement would be impossible to achieve, given Hitler's public statements about the sins of Bolshevism. Consequently, Stalin had to resort to furtive probings in an effort to convince Hitler that a deal could be made. Stalin made one agreement hinting how difficult the Soviet Union could become if German armies became aggressive—the Franco-Russian Mutual Assistance Pact, in 1935. Although it might have appeared to be a bulwark against German expansion, neither France nor the Soviet Union actually meant to carry out the pact. Stalin hoped that it would provide him with the leverage necessary for an agreement with Hitler. But he wrecked the pact when he began to purge the armed forces in 1937, alleging that they had been plotting with the Nazis. No foreign military staff now dared plan with Soviet officers for a war against Germany when these same officers were being denounced by their own government as traitors who had been conspiring with Nazi officers.

Stalin feared a European war because any war involving Soviet Russia might endanger his power within the Soviet Union. To avoid being dragged into a war to defend Czechoslovakia, Stalin had a clause inserted in the Soviet pact with Czechoslovakia promising to help that nation provided France came to her aid first. He was betting that the French would not fight on behalf of Czechoslovakia. When the Sudeten

German question developed into a full-blown international crisis in the summer of 1938, the Soviet government informed Berlin that the entire matter was a question of internal concern. At that moment, war was unthinkable for the Soviet Union because so many of the Soviet military leaders were either dead, in prison, or woefully inexperienced.

When the Polish question finally erupted in 1939, Stalin made the first overture to Hitler which culminated in the notorious Nazi-Soviet Pact of August 23, 1939. Here, in a non-aggression pact, Stalin promised Hitler that the Soviet Union would remain at peace whenever Hitler attacked Poland. Hitler had Stalin's permission to begin a war. After Poland had been defeated, they agreed to divide up that country between themselves.

In agreeing to this pact, actually drafted in the Kremlin, Stalin has been excused on the grounds that he thought he was protecting himself from becoming involved in a war over Poland. But Stalin opened up Soviet Russia to attack because after the disappearance of an independent Poland, Soviet Russia and Nazi Germany now shared a common frontier. As a result of this deal, Stalin had surrendered the Soviet buffer against a German invasion. For Stalin's mistake, millions of Russian men, women, and children would pay with their lives.

In making his pact with Hitler, Stalin had gambled that when the war began, it would be long-drawn-out, providing him with an opportunity to wheel and deal with both sides. But the swift defeat of Poland and the sudden German attack on western Europe meant that he had to seize whatever he could while Hitler's armies were occupied elsewhere. Following quickly on the Polish defeat, Stalin dispatched an ultimatum to Finland, bringing on a war which revealed the damage done to the Soviet military leadership by his purges. Finland made the Soviet armies pay heavily for the victory that came in March 1940. Next, after the Wehrmacht had become engaged in western Europe, Stalin annexed the Baltic States, recovering territory lost after World War I, and compelled Rumania to surrender not only Bessarabia but also Bukovina. These actions served to move Hitler toward war against the Soviet Union.

By the summer of 1940, Hitler had resolved on attacking

Soviet Russia as soon as preparations could be completed for a campaign in 1941. Once German war preparations were under way, they could not be hidden from American and British intelligence sources. Both governments warned Stalin, but to the suspicious Soviet ruler these were provocative acts on the part of capitalists who wanted to see Germany and the Soviet Union fight each other. Any Soviet war preparations would needlessly antagonize Hitler. Better to continue trading with Germany and assure Hitler that Soviet Russia was his friend. For Stalin, however, an attack on the Soviet Union would mean that his policy toward Hitler had failed—he had been tricked and his image damaged. But to admit error was out of the question, so he could only continue to profess allegiance to the pact with Hitler to the very end.

During the night of June 21–22, 1941, with information pouring into the Kremlin that an attack was imminent, Stalin held to his provocation theory and left the city for his suburban villa. There in the early hours he awoke to learn the news of war, news which he at first rejected—the attack was only a German provocation, a probing movement that would be broken off when the Russians fought back. So he had orders issued to repel attacks but not to pursue the invaders back across the frontiers. The news of the attack and reports of its strength—within forty-eight hours some German units had driven over one hundred miles into Soviet Russia—panicked Stalin. He went back to his villa, remaining there until July 3. The government of Soviet Russia was headless; the war had no direction. At that point a Russian Bonaparte could have overthrown Stalin and taken command, but he had ensured that all potential Russian Bonapartes were either dead or in labor camps. He had made himself so indispensable that in 1941 no one dared imagine moving against him. In this crisis, Stalin was the only man it seemed who could save the very nation that was now being ravaged by war because of his mistakes. On July 3, the Soviet people heard Stalin on the radio calling on them to unite in a relentless battle against the invaders.

By August he had made himself the commander-in-chief of the Soviet armed forces and began an on-the-job training for military command. Eventually he learned his new trade, but while his education continued, the Russian people had to pay the costs with their lives.

At the beginning of the war, Stalin would not appoint and support competent commanders, preferring to choose those whom he knew to be politically safe. Most of the commanders were those who had toadied to him and survived the purges. Stalin could not trust generals when they reported losses; he found it difficult to judge military strategies separate from some devious political goal. His orders to fight for every foot of Soviet soil, instead of retreating to a more defensible position, cost the armies countless lives. Not until 1942–43 did Stalin at last begin to understand the art of war, but not before he had panicked again in mid-October 1941 and fled from Moscow. Anarchy reigned in the streets of Moscow until Stalin returned on October 19, when a state of siege was proclaimed. By early November the Stalin of old was in command, secure enough to order the annual parade on the anniversary of the November Revolution with the Soviet leaders reviewing the marchers atop the Lenin Mausoleum. In his speech to the nation, Stalin proclaimed a national war, and recalled the names of czarist generals who had led the armies of pre-revolutionary Russia to victory.

Stalin did more than make speeches to arouse the nation. He remained at the supreme headquarters in the Kremlin, directing the war and never visiting the troops in the front lines. From his headquarters, he kept tight control over every aspect of the war. His general staff had to report twice daily by telephone and in the evening in person. The evening sessions often lasted far into the night, and because of the loss of sleep and the nervous tension, physical and mental breakdowns were common among his staff. Generals were summoned from their troops to report to Stalin in person, a prospect that unnerved the toughest officers. Because of their fear of Stalin, officers dared never suggest innovations lest they fail and be blamed for the failure.

Unlike Roosevelt and Churchill, Stalin could order commanders who had failed to complete assignments to a penal battalion which would be sent immediately into enemy fire. He had no hesitation in ordering generals to be shot. But in contrast to the democratic leaders, Stalin had to be constantly on guard against the appearance of a communist Napoleon. To that end, he kept tight rein on operations, and only when the need became overpowering did he appoint Gregory Zhukov as deputy supreme commander. Stalin came to rely on Zhukov's opinions; but soon after the war had ended, he relegated Zhukov to an obscure military post and had his role in winning the victory downgraded.

The man who frightened generals was below medium height—Stalin wore built-up heels to make himself appear taller. His face was pockmarked, his teeth poor. At one time he wore the worker's cap and blouse, but when he promoted himself to marshal during World War II, he began to wear carefully tailored uniforms. Stalin was always careful to stage his appearance according to the occasion, for he had become a consummate actor. With military men he would be the man of steel, to workers he appeared in the role of the father of his people, and to journalists he acted the part of a business-like politician. In interviews with foreigners, he assumed the appearance of a perfectly reasonable statesman, a devout believer in Marxism-Leninism but not a bloodthirsty tyrant. H. W. Wells observed, "I have never met a man more candid, fair and honest."[9] Stalin impressed Anthony Eden with his good manners and his appearance, "well laundered and neatly dressed." In their meetings, Eden "always found the encounter stimulating, grey and stern though the agenda often had to be." He never knew anyone better able to handle himself in a conference.[10]

Another side of Stalin never seen by foreigners was his fear. He was so frightened of assassination by his fellow countrymen that he took elaborate precautions for his personal safety, becoming a prisoner of his own system. Within the Kremlin walls, his life went on as if under siege. Thousands of NKVD troops stationed in the vicinity of the Kremlin guarded him around the clock. These troops, after undergoing an elaborate screening process to prevent infiltrators bent on killing him from penetrating the guard, were constantly rotated in their stations. They searched visitors to the Kremlin continually and provided Stalin with protection whenever he moved from his quarters to the Kremlin palace. NKVD agents sat among the deputies at the meetings of the Supreme Soviet and the party congresses.

As a result of his dread of assassination, Stalin never visited art galleries, museums, or any public places where he might encounter his embittered subjects. He faced the Soviet public only at parades, state funerals, and occasionally the theater with visiting guests such as Churchill.

He had to appear in public on the two Bolshevik days of celebration, May 1 and November 1. On these anniversaries, when the troops paraded past Stalin standing atop the Lenin Mausoleum, the soldiers were forbidden to carry live ammunition and a file of trusted security agents paraded in the right-hand line of every column closest to Stalin. Armed NKVD agents also were scattered about the reviewing stands, and close by, heavily armed security detachments awaited the call to protect their leader from Russian assassination attempts.

In order for Stalin to travel to one of his many dachas outside Moscow, which meant leaving the security of the Kremlin, specially constructed broad avenues enabled him to travel at high speeds unimpeded. He sped through Moscow in an armor-plated, bullet-proof Packard. Hundreds of NKVD agents in a fleet of Lincolns, sirens screaming, accompanied the Packard. All traffic was barred from the route, and Soviet citizens avoided the area when Stalin's motorcade raced past. Along the way, thousands of NKVD troops searched buildings and homes and guarded their leader from his people. The route was decided by Stalin at the last possible moment. When he had to travel by train to his dacha on the Black Sea, before and ahead of the train were armored trains filled with NKVD troops and provisioned to withstand a siege.

One method of travel was especially dangerous: flying. The opportunities for assassination were too many for Stalin to risk this method of travel. However, because no rail line connected Baku and Teheran, Stalin was obliged to fly to the conference—the only time in his life that he ever dared entrust himself to a pilot and an airplane. Only the opportunity and the importance of a meeting with the President of the United States could have persuaded Stalin to endure the terror of flying to Teheran.[11]

* * *

In contrast to Stalin's early years, Franklin Delano Roosevelt had enjoyed a life of affluence and leisure, thanks to a father whose business sense left his wife and son with a comfortable income. Born in 1882 in a mansion in Hyde Park, New York, young Franklin, an only child, enjoyed a happy childhood, protected and secure, with ponies to ride, fields to roam, and boats to sail on the Hudson River. A succession of nurses and governesses attended to his needs, and private tutors taught him until his mother, Sara, decided that he was old enough to be sent away to a private school, Groton, in 1896.[12]

Franklin's four years at Groton were not the happiest because to his classmates he seemed a trifle odd—they soon nicknamed him "Uncle Frank." Insecure and uncertain of himself after the protective years at Hyde Park, young Franklin did his best to enter into the vigorous athletic life at Groton, where the founder, Endicott Peabody, sought to instill into every student the elements of Christian character that would be needed in a carrer of public service.

After Groton, Franklin entered Harvard in 1900, spending four years in Cambridge which were more pleasant than those at Groton. His grades were barely C level because he enjoyed the Boston-Cambridge social life, worked on the staff of the *Crimson,* and tried to make the football team—at which he failed. Roosevelt also failed at campus politics, and he was passed over in his attempt to join a Harvard club, Porcellion. For Roosevelt, however, Harvard was not an exciting intellectual experience, and the education he received did little to prepare him for a strenuous political career.

After his father died during his freshman year, his mother moved to Boston to be near her son. She always tried to exert her influence in his life even after he had married and begun a political career. She even sought to block his marriage to a fifth cousin, Eleanor Roosevelt, the daughter of a younger brother of President Theodore Roosevelt. Finally Sara Roosevelt relented, and the happy couple were married in 1905, with Uncle Teddy giving the bride away and Endicott Peabody performing the marriage ceremony. After their honeymoon in Europe, the young couple settled down in a house on West 36th Street in New York City.

Roosevelt had enrolled in Columbia Law School in 1904, but he never finished law school, perhaps because his record was not outstanding. As soon as he had passed the bar examinations, he dropped out to enter the firm of Carter, Ledyard, & Milburn. But finding law practice boring, he turned to politics. A career in politics seemed more exciting to Roosevelt particularly after he and Eleanor had visited Uncle Teddy in the White House. Already Roosevelt had been speculating on a career modeled after Uncle Teddy's. To a fellow law clerk, he had outlined the blueprint of his political ambitions: election to the New York State legislature, then a job in Washington, perhaps Assistant Secretary of the Navy, next governor of New York, and from there to the White House. Few politicians have predicted their future career so accurately.

In 1910 he ran as a Democrat for state senator in the heavily Republican district in which he lived at Hyde Park. In his speeches, he favored good government and progressivism, and opposed political bosses. Roosevelt won the election by a majority of 1,140, running ahead of the Democratic ticket in his district. In Albany, he gained a statewide reputation by leading the battle to block the election of a typical Tammany Hall politician, "Blue-Eyed Billy" Sheehan, for U.S. senator when senators were still elected by the state legislators. The fight gained national attention, which helped the career of the handsome young state senator from Hyde Park.

Roosevelt became an early supporter of Woodrow Wilson's presidential candidacy, laboring for the New Jersey governor at the nominating convention in Baltimore during the hot summer of 1912. In November, Roosevelt won re-election to the state senate even though he had been ill with typhoid fever during much of the campaign. For his battle on behalf of Wilson, he was rewarded with the position of Assistant Secretary of the Navy.

In 1912 the office carried a distinction of its own because the administrators and assistants had not yet proliferated. Roosevelt exploited the opportunity given him to make his name and face known, not only in Washington but nationally. His enthusiasm for naval power, his efficiency and good administration, and his excellent seamanship, which he yearned to display, all won him supporters among professional naval officers. For the first time Roosevelt had to deal with organized labor in naval shipyards and depots.

In 1914, Roosevelt suffered his only election defeat during his entire career when he lost the primary election for the Democratic nomination for the Senate. The defeat could be attributed partly to weak support from Wilson, who had no wish to tangle with Tammany Hall—the power and influence of which young Roosevelt underestimated when he challenged the regular party nominee. His defeat taught him a lesson in state politics: a Washington job did not mean a statewide victory without the support of the Democratic party regular organization, Tammany Hall.

With the outbreak of war in Europe in 1914, Roosevelt became a vigorous advocate of a strong navy and began to agitate for American entrance into the war. After the United States became a belligerent in 1917, he immersed himself in war administration, wrestling with the problems involved in the expansion of a peacetime navy, and enjoying the work, the conferences, quick decisions, and long hours. Disappointed because he could not be in uniform, he made one trip overseas which gave him the opportunity to see combat areas. In London, he met Winston Churchill, but neither made a significant impression on the other, and Churchill soon forgot the meeting.

The years in Washington helped Roosevelt gain the nomination for the vice presidency in 1920, only to go down to defeat with James Cox, the presidential candidate. But their unsuccessful campaign gave Roosevelt the experience of barnstorming across the country and meeting politicians who could be valuable contacts in the future. With few political prospects in sight, Roosevelt turned to a business career; this soon proved to be the wrong choice for him because he was a speculator who invested in schemes that brought little profit.

Roosevelt's life changed suddenly in August 1921 when he was stricken with poliomyelitis while on vacation at Campobello, the family summer home on the Bay of Fundy. Following agonizing weeks in a hospital, he was discharged with the notation on his medical chart: "Not improving." The disease had left his legs paralyzed for the remainder of his life. Nevertheless, for years he underwent treatment in the hope that some day he would be able to walk without crutches or heavy braces, and not have to depend on others to help him move about. Given his physical condition, his expectation of continuing in politics would have appeared nil, but his will drove him to battle a physical handicap that would have destroyed the resolution of a weaker man.

Neither Churchill nor Stalin would ever endure the physical pain which had engulfed Roosevelt during the illness and subsequent months of treatment. He bore the pain with grim determination, always trying to smile gallantly, resolved to overcome the disease and its effects as best he could. For the rest of his life, however, he would have to use crutches to move about and wear heavy, steel braces to enable him to stand before an audience. Getting into an automobile became a physical ordeal for him. This tall, handsome man now had to be pushed about in a wheelchair or carried by grown men as if he were a helpless infant.

Roosevelt's illness halted his political career while he searched vainly for a cure. Campaigning for political office had to be postponed for years until he could recover as fully as possible. In the long run, however, his absence from active politics helped him, because the 1920s were lean years for the Democratic party. Ultimately, when the Democrats could return to power, Roosevelt would be there ready to run for office. Had Roosevelt been physically able to pursue an active political career in the 1920s, he could well have worn himself out in losing campaigns and built a record as a loser. Instead, his illness forced him to remain free of the political battles until the Republican tide had run out.

Roosevelt took the first step on the road to the White House by accepting the nomination to run for governor of New York at the urging of Alfred E. Smith, who had been governor for eight years and who was running for President in 1928 at the head of the Democratic ticket against Herbert C. Hoover. In the November election when Hoover overwhelmed Smith, Roosevelt squeaked into office, but he had attained another of the goals outlined to that law clerk years ago.

Although his achievements were modest in his first term as governor, he projected the image of an executive who did not fear to seek change. Roosevelt's next victory came in November 1930 when he won reelection easily, even carrying upstate New York against his opponent. By this time he had to deal with the growing economic depression. He created a Temporary Emergency Relief Administration to help people suffering the effects of unemployment. To head the agency he found a social worker, Harry Hopkins.

In January 1932, Roosevelt announced his candidacy for the presidency. The battle for convention votes continued throughout the spring and on to the convention in Chicago in hot July. Not until the fourth ballot was Roosevelt victorious. Back in Albany, as soon as he heard the welcome news, Roosevelt announced that he would fly to Chicago to accept the nomination in person—beginning the first of many precedents he would set during his many years in the White House. In November, Roosevelt carried forty-two states because of his broad appeal to farmers and labor, and because of the solid Democratic South. For the future, this became the coalition that Roosevelt would have to maintain.

In Washington, he gathered around him a wide spectrum of advisers ranging from eastern college professors to financiers, labor leaders, newspaper editors, and state politicians. From these people and others, Roosevelt absorbed ideas, listening intently, talking endlessly. He depended on no single person in his search for a solution to the American economic depression, nor did he have any single great idea or overall blueprint for economic salvation. He was a pragmatic politician who dared try anything to extract the nation from the depression. Already, before he became President, the unemployed were living in shacks called "Hoovervilles," banks were closing, and men and women were pawing through garbage cans in search of scraps of food. Throughout the United States, despair prevailed.

Through his speeches as President of the nation, through his "fireside chats" on the radio, Roosevelt tried to arouse people and to end the deep feeling of despair. His optimism, enthusiasm, fervor, and sense of humanity appealed to the American people, who sought a leader to bring them out of the depths of economic depression.

In the first hundred days of his administration, Roosevelt, moving swiftly to put measures on the law books that would save American capitalism, called Congress into special session and declared a bank holiday to gain time to devise new measures for the banking industry. In the series of laws that emerged from Congress, Roosevelt began to change the relationship of the federal government to the nation: increasingly, Washington would have a greater role in managing the nation's business. Banks became more closely regulated, as were the stock markets. New legislation guaranteed the rights of labor and established maximum hours and minimum wages for workers in interstate industries. Farmers, in need of help to avoid bankruptcy, were aided by government-backed loans. To help the unemployed, Congress created the Federal Emergency Relief Administration to distribute aid to the needy, established the Public Works Administration to provide federally funded work projects for the unemployed, and in an innovative law created the Civilian Conservation Corps which enabled young men to work on reforestration and fire prevention projects, bridges, and woodland trails. One of the most revolutionary measures for the time was the Social Security Act to provide help to retired workers, widows, children, and the unemployed.

Roosevelt's policies made him hated and loved as much as any President since Abraham Lincoln. Large segments of the population fervently adored him. He successfully appealed to black Americans, winning their fervent loyalty even though he never dared sponsor civil rights legislation because of the bitter opposition of southern Democrats who had become a significant part of his coalition. New Deal labor legislation meant that Roosevelt would have the support of the unions, which had gained enormous strength thanks to this legislation. But because Roosevelt aroused such passionate adoration, he also created deep hatred. Vested interests in corporations and banks damned "that man in the White House" for what they regarded as radical, socialist legislation.

Roosevelt jokes were common, many vicious and bitter. But he loved to tell jokes about himself. One of his favorites was about the commuter from Westchester County, a Republican stronghold north of New York City, who walked into the railroad station every morning and handed the newsboy a quarter for the *New York Herald Tribune,* a newspaper with a conservative viewpoint. The commuter glanced at the front page, then handed the paper back to the newsboy as he raced to catch his train. The curious newsboy at last had to ask the commuter why he glanced only at the front page.

"I'm interested in the obituary notices," replied the commuter.

"But they're way over on page twenty-four, and you never look at them," said the puzzled boy.

"Boy," replied the commuter, "the son-of-a-bitch I'm interested in will be on page one!"[13]

Roosevelt antagonized many Americans, like the fictitious Westchester commuter, because of his break with presidential traditions and practices. He made the first appointment of a woman as a cabinet officer in an age when the issue of equal rights for women aroused little interest. He became the first President to make extensive use of radio as a means of appealing to the voters over the heads of his congressional opposition. Roosevelt developed the press conference as a major tool of presidential politics. He shattered the tradition of a two-term presidency and drove the Republicans to amend the Constitution in order to prevent another President, Republican or Democrat, from ever running for a third or fourth term. Probably Roosevelt's greatest break with tradition was involving the national government in the daily business of the American people. His changes and innovations were often deliberate choices on his part; but others, such as foreign policy, were forced on him.

Roosevelt did not begin his presidency advocating a bold, internationalist policy; rather, he adhered to the isolationist policies of his predecessors, Calvin Coolidge and Herbert Hoover. Even had he not been so inclined, there was no political gain to be won by calling for a vigorous foreign policy. In Europe, Adolf Hitler seemed only a funny-looking politician who resembled Charlie Chaplin; it was unthinkable that he would ever be so crazy as to start another world war. Actually, Roosevelt was fully occupied in the job of finding a way out of the grinding depression which had spread so much suffering and unhappiness among the American people. He left the running of the State Department to Cordell Hull, whom he had appointed Secretary of State not for his knowledge of foreign affairs, but for his congressional experience and his connections with southern Democrats. Hull's chief interest lay in tariff reform because he believed that the lowering of tariffs would be a major step toward disarmament, improved trade, and world peace. As the international crisis worsened, Roosevelt superseded Hull, becoming his own Secretary of State.

When Germany, Italy, and Japan commenced their aggressions in the 1930s, Roosevelt's statements followed the isolationist line. He insisted that the United States follow a path of neutrality to avoid being drawn into war and that the nation should set an example for others. Certainly Roosevelt was sincere in his statements that an isolationist policy was best for the United States. His aversion to war was best symbolized by the phrase from his speech in August 1936, which has been so often quoted, "I have seen war. . . . I hate war." Given the economic distress, the isolationist feeling of the country, and the power of Congress, there was little that Roosevelt could have done even had he been so inclined. It would take aggression and war for him to express other views.

The Japanese invasion of China in 1937 led him to his famous speech in Chicago implying that aggressors ought to be placed in quarantine. However, he never indicated how that could be accomplished because he simply did not know. His speech revealed a moral concept, certainly accepted by many people, and showed a desire to find a way out of the maze: how to halt aggression without resorting to war.

But Hitler's aggressive moves so alarmed Roosevelt that in January 1938 he toyed with the idea of calling a meeting of the Washington diplomatic corps to consider an agreement on the main principles of international conduct. These would include the reduction of armaments, methods to promote economic security, and the protection of neutrals in wartime. Once agreement had been reached, then a smaller group would develop specific recommendations—all without any commitment from the United States to accept any responsibility. Hull opposed the idea, partly because his rival, Under Secretary of State Sumner Welles, had originated it. Roosevelt broached the idea to Chamberlain, who declined to participate because he preferred to follow a policy of appeasement and feared that Roosevelt's proposal might antagonize Hitler and Mussolini. Consequently, Roosevelt's scheme was stillborn.

When the Czechoslovak crisis drove Europe to the brink of war, Roosevelt could do little save propose a resumption of negotiations after they had broken down following the Godesberg meeting. Later he appealed for an international conference of nations directly involved in the crisis but the United States would have nothing to do with the negotiations. At the height of the crisis, Roosevelt made a bizarre proposal to Chamberlain through the British ambassador. If the heads of state, including Hitler, would call a world conference to rearrange all frontiers along national lines, Roosevelt would attend, provided the conference were held in the Azores or on some Atlantic island. In this same discussion, Roosevelt implied that the United States might again become involved in a European war if the Germans were to invade Britain, an event that would arouse enough emotion to permit the dispatch of American troops in Europe. The British government, intent on finding an escape from the Czechoslovak crisis, paid no attention to Roosevelt's scheme. But when he learned that Chamberlain would go to Munich for the famous conference, Roosevelt cabled only: "Good man." There was little more that he could say; however, the crisis had shown him how much the peace depended on one man, Adolf Hitler.

As war approached in 1939, Roosevelt was reduced to issuing a public message to Hitler and to Mussolini asking them to promise neither to attack nor to invade thirty-one nations for a ten-year period. Apparently Roosevelt hoped that this message would put them on the spot, but Hitler held Roosevelt up to ridicule before the Reichstag when he sarcastically read the list of names to gales of laughter from the deputies.

At the outbreak of war, Roosevelt followed the law and proclaimed neutrality while putting an arms embargo into effect. The swift fall of Poland, Norway, Denmark, France, and the Low Countries before the Nazi onslaught educated the American people and Roosevelt to the power of the German armed forces. The German victories helped Roosevelt in his proposals to the Congress for an increase in the military budget. By June 1940 he began to denounce the neutrality policy as a delusion and to promise aid to Britain and to France. Already, late in 1939, he had convinced Congress to repeal the arms embargo, enabling Britain and France to purchase arms and munitions in the United States on a "cash and carry" basis. But Churchill had been asking that the United States send destroyers to replace those lost in action. Here was a step that Roosevelt approached carefully. Not until September 1940 could the deal be struck: fifty over-age American destroyers in exchange for eight bases on British islands in the Caribbean and in the Atlantic. Once again Roosevelt had hesitated until he sensed that he had enough public support for a move without congressional legislation.

In his unprecedented campaign for a third term, Roosevelt pledged to keep the United States out of a foreign war unless attacked. In Boston he delivered a speech with the famous words: "And while I am talking to you brothers and fathers, I give you one more assurance. I have said this before, but I shall say it again and again and again: Your boys are not going to be sent into any foreign war."[14] Probably at that time Roosevelt still believed that through all-out aid to Britain he could help Churchill achieve victory while keeping the United States out of the war.

After his reelection, Roosevelt proposed Lend-Lease aid because Churchill had reported that Britain was running out of money and would soon be unable to pay for the supplies purchased in the United States. By March 1941 Congress had approved Lend-Lease, a measure that resembled an act of war. Once more, public opinion supported Roosevelt.

Nevertheless, Britain's resources were strained to protect convoys carrying Lend-Lease materials across the Atlantic Ocean. In April 1941, Roosevelt extended American naval patrols halfway across the Atlantic and ordered American naval vessels to search for German submarines and to alert British ships to their presence. When a U-boat fired a torpedo at the U.S.S. *Greer*, Roosevelt went on radio to announce that United States naval vessels would escort all merchant ships engaged in commerce in American defensive waters. Following on this announcement, and buoyed up by public support, Roosevelt convinced Congress to repeal the neutrality laws and to permit American merchant ships to carry supplies to Britain.

By this time Roosevelt had probably convinced himself that the United States would have to enter the war. During 1941 the outlook for those nations fighting Hitler's armies appeared grim because after the invasion of Russia, Soviet armies had been driven back with grievous losses. At their meeting at Argentia in August 1941, Churchill pressed Roosevelt about a declaration of war. The President explained that if the issue of peace or war were to be put to the Congress, it would be debated for three months. Roosevelt said that he could wage war but that he could not declare it. He would become more provocative in the Atlantic and he "made it clear that he would look for an incident which would justify him in opening hostilities."[15] An incident must precipitate war and force Hitler to take the final step of declaring war. But while Roosevelt concentrated on Hitler, he failed to fully anticipate the threat from Japan.

He wanted to avoid war with Japan in order to concentrate on helping Britain defeat Hitler's armies, which appeared more menacing than the Japanese forces. Revisionist historians have alleged that Roosevelt plotted to conceal knowledge of the impending attack on Pearl Harbor in order to bring on war with Japan. He had been reading the MAGIC intercepts of the Japanese diplomatic messages, which seemed to intimate that Japan was moving toward war, but which did not point to an attack on Pearl Harbor. Like most Americans, Roosevelt probably never imagined that the Japanese High Command would be so foolish as to deliberately attack Pearl Harbor.

The December 7 attack by the Imperial Japanese forces and Hitler's declaration of war on December 11 together made the United States an ally of Great Britain as well as the Soviet Union. Without these events, Roosevelt would not have sought a meeting with Stalin. In the past, no American President would have dared suggest such an encounter, but now there seemed to be sufficient reason for this meeting and for such a long, arduous trip.

Personal diplomacy between heads of government brought face to face cannot but be influenced by the opinions of each of the men involved. Yet nothing is more difficult than determining what was in a politician's mind as he approached an important meeting. Here the historian flirts with guesswork since there is little to rely on unless the statesman put his thoughts into writing or talked at length with an associate who left a written record. Franklin Roosevelt left no memoirs and his notes and memoranda tell little about his innermost thoughts. Contemporary accounts of the opinions of Roosevelt about Russia and Stalin are both varied and confusing.

As to his knowledge of Soviet Russia, Roosevelt never studied the sources of Marxist thought nor had he immersed himself in books about the Soviet Union. Roosevelt was not inclined to read scholarly works, preferring to learn through conversation with his associates. Of those who had personal contact with him, only two men had first-hand knowledge of Soviet Russia: Joseph E. Davies and William Bullitt. Davies did not know the language and his view of things Soviet was anything but critical. Bullitt, because of his gossip regarding Sumner Welles, had been cut off forever from Roosevelt, but in his communications with the President before the separation he had been consistently anti-Soviet in his views.

In a long memorandum to Roosevelt in January 1943, Bullitt, now only Assistant to the Secretary of the Navy, discounted reports that Stalin had become a changed man as a result of Hitler's attack on the Soviet Union and would now cooperate with the United States and Britain in establishing peace. He rejected the argument that if Stalin's distrust could be overcome then his full cooperation would be available. Moreover, the United States and Britain must not allow a war to prevent Nazi domination of Europe to be converted into a war aimed at establishing Soviet domination of Europe. He urged Roosevelt to invite Stalin to Washington, or if that failed to meet him in Alaska. In that meeting the President should use economic help for the Soviet Union as the stick to change Stalin's policies in Europe. Bullitt prophesied that after the defeat of Germany when Britain and the United States were fighting Japan, no power would be left in Europe to block Soviet forces from overrunning that continent. To avoid this disaster, Bullitt begged Roosevelt to get Stalin to agree to make war against Japan. He also proposed an invasion of Europe through Greece, Turkey, Bulgaria, and Rumania in order to place Anglo-American forces in central Europe.[16] Bullitt's memorandum amounted to a severe critique of Stalin's policies, in sharp distinction to those policies advocated by Davies. However, Roosevelt preferred to talk privately with Davies, leaving Bullitt fuming in the Department of the Navy.

After the Teheran Conference, Roosevelt confessed to Frances Perkins, Secretary of Labor, "I wish someone would tell me about the Russians. I don't know a good Russian from a bad Russian. I can tell a good Frenchman from a bad Frenchman. I can tell a good Italian from a bad Italian. I know a good Greek when I see one. But I don't understand the Russians. I just don't know what makes them tick. I wish I could study them. Frances, see if you can find out what makes them tick."[17] Realizing that he was in earnest, Frances Perkins read what she could about Russia and periodically gave Roosevelt a digest of her reading. Her digests came, however, after Roosevelt's first meeting with Stalin, and they may have made him realize how vast was his ignorance of Russia and the Russians.

As for works on Stalin, in 1943 there was only one critical biography, written by Boris Souveraine. Trotsky had also written about Stalin, but there is no record that Roosevelt had read either work. His reading encompassed chiefly newspapers, and for relaxation he read detective novels. Yet on the voyage to North Africa, Roosevelt would have had time to read serious studies on the Soviet Union and Stalin, few though they might have been. All the evidence indicates that he did not read such works on board ship, probably because none had been brought for him.

Not only did Roosevelt avoid reading scholarly studies of the Soviet Union, he ignored the State Department as well.

The President had little use for Foreign Service officers, preferring to rely on his own handpicked emissaries to handle important foreign policy missions and to supply him with the confidential information he needed without going through the State Department channels. He characterized professional American diplomats as reactionaries, dilettantes, and "fossilized bureaucrats." [18]

Apparently Roosevelt made only one specific request for information about the Soviet Union that has been recorded. In October 1943 he told anthropologist Henry Field that he feared Stalin might throw irrelevant questions at him in order to throw him off guard and provoke an argument. Because he anticipated questions from Stalin about the "Negro problem" and lynchings, he asked Field for information about Soviet minority questions. In addition, the President requested data on Soviet conservation efforts so that he could congratulate Stalin on this work. Although Field prepared the materials for Roosevelt to study on the trip to Teheran, there is no indication that they were even included in the files taken to Teheran by the President's secretary.

As the plane carried Roosevelt closer to Teheran and the meeting with Stalin for which he had labored so long, he felt supremely confident that he alone could iron out the differences existing between the Soviet Union and the United States. He would achieve this goal through his ability to sway people if he could only talk with them. By the sheer force of his personality, Roosevelt believed that he could smooth over all ideological differences and ultimately bring Stalin to cooperate in the postwar world.

Roosevelt's conviction bordered on arrogance. His enormous self-confidence about his political judgment stemmed from his successful political career, with the unprecedented election to three terms in office. His political victories had made him supremely confident of his ability to deal with other politicians, including Stalin, whom he had never met. Through this personal meeting, Roosevelt believed that he could convince Stalin that the American offers of cooperation were genuine and that the American people wanted to be friends with the Soviet people instead of enemies. Because he had been able so often to convince people about his own ideas, Roosevelt believed that he could succeed with Stalin. "What helps a lot is that Stalin is the only man I have to convince," Roosevelt exclaimed in a conversation on board *Iowa*. "Joe doesn't worry about a Congress or a President. He's the whole works." [19]

Roosevelt explained away Stalin's distrust as a product of a lifetime that from his early manhood had involved robbery and murder, justified by the Marxian theory that the ends justifies the means. According to Roosevelt, Stalin had been forced into dictatorship by the struggle for power, and consequently he distrusted everyone. Roosevelt felt assured that he could personally overcome Stalin's distrust and bridge the gap between democracy and communism. He would make Stalin feel that Americans trusted the Russians implicitly and valued Soviet-American cooperation in the war and in the peace above every other possible alliance.

In the preparation for his meeting with Stalin, only one man had shared Roosevelt's confidences: Harry Hopkins. He had visited the Soviet Union only once and had been one of the few foreigners permitted a private meeting of any length with Stalin. Hopkins had returned from his trip elated by his meetings, at which the Soviet ruler had played the role of the wise, world statesman. "No man could forget the picture of the dictator of Russia as he stood watching me leave—an austere, rugged, determined figure in boots that shone like mirrors, stout baggy trousers, and snug fitting blouse," wrote Hopkins. "He wore no ornament, military or civilian. He's built close to the ground like a football coach's dream of a tackle." Stalin impressed Hopkins by his efficiency in speaking. "It was like talking to a perfectly co-ordinated machine, an intelligent machine. Joseph Stalin knew what he wanted, knew what Russia wanted, and he assumed that you knew." [20]

Through his intimate contact with Roosevelt, Hopkins pressed on him his ideas about the way to deal with Soviet Russia—ideas which Roosevelt made his own. Hopkins believed that Soviet aid was needed to help defeat Germany and ultimately Japan. He knew that after the war Soviet Russia would become one of the most powerful nations in the world. In order to create a postwar world, the United

States and Soviet Russia must be friendly so that both could help shape world events in a way that would provide security and prosperity. The United States must be so friendly and so helpful to Russia that she would not only fight on until Germany had been defeated but would also join in defeating Japan. Then, after the war, the Soviet Union would gladly join the United States in establishing peace and maintaining mutually beneficial relations. Now while the war raged, a Roosevelt-Stalin meeting was vital to improve Soviet-American relations.

In addition, every department of the American government must treat Soviet Russia as one of the three greatest powers in the world and regard her as a genuine friend. Everyone who had contacts with Russians must believe deeply in this concept. Finally, Hopkins urged that everything should be done to establish a peace that would meet the legitimate aspirations of the Soviet Union.[21] These theories of Hopkins certainly influenced Roosevelt's thinking as he journeyed to Teheran.

Hopkins's ideas are important because they replaced any briefings from State Department experts. In his preparations for this conference, his first with the Soviet leader, Roosevelt received no briefing from the State Department. Nor did he receive any briefing books in which experts might have attempted to set out basic positions of the U.S. government and presented background information about the problems that would probably be discussed. Since he did not have such briefings, Roosevelt would carry on the discussions based on his instincts and whatever knowledge he had, his "feel" of the talks, and whatever he might learn from those who traveled with him to Teheran. His closest adviser would be Hopkins. But throughout, Roosevelt would rely on his own resources, without any support or advice from professional experts on the Soviet Union. Such a condition was Roosevelt's desire because he distrusted expert opinion. Any errors he might make would be his and not those of anyone else. The errors would be his and the triumphs his also. The lack of briefing books and the absence of State Department advisers made the Teheran Conference unique. Here the President of the United States would be conferring and negotiating without expert knowledge and advice. He would be alone at the summit.

But how did Stalin regard a meeting with the leaders of his two capitalist allies? Certainly he was not looking forward to it as eagerly as Roosevelt. For the great leader of the Soviet people to condescend to a journey, even to Iran, and there to negotiate with imperialist leaders was somewhat unseemly, if not dangerous. Far better to have them come to Moscow as Churchill had done in August 1942, signaling the prominent position of Stalin. He may have resented the need to meet with imperialists because it implied a form of equality which Stalin did not relish.

Of the imperialist pair, Stalin regarded Churchill as the deep-dyed, old-fashioned type who had tried once before to strangle Bolshevism at its birth. There had been no sign of friendship for the Soviet Union from Churchill until Hitler's attack in June 1941 had transformed Britain into an ally. Churchill to Stalin was an old enemy. "We like a downright enemy better than a pretending friend," Stalin told Churchill in 1942.[22]

In the context of this statement, Stalin probably regarded Roosevelt as a "pretending friend," one of those reformers who gave the working classes small concessions in order to save capitalism and avoid a revolution. Roosevelt's expressions of friendship and cooperation probably appeared to Stalin as the expected conduct of a capitalist power whose cordiality masked a greedy imperialism. Stalin's entire political philosophy rejected Roosevelt's protestations, which were aimed at breaking down the barriers of suspicion and distrust through private talks filled with expressions of friendship for Stalin and the Soviet people. He regarded Roosevelt's overtures, aimed at disarming Stalin's hostility, in the exact opposite sense intended by Roosevelt. Although Roosevelt would try to show himself as more democratic and less imperialistic than Churchill, it made no difference to Stalin. In 1944, Stalin would observe that Churchill would pick your pocket for a kopeck. "Roosevelt is not like that. He dips in his hand only for bigger coins."[23]

Stalin had been deeply suspicious of the Allies because

of the delay in establishing the second front in France—a delay that appeared to him to be a plot to allow Nazi Germany and the Soviet Union to battle each other to exhaustion so that Churchill and Roosevelt could then save their resources. It was this suspicion that Roosevelt was determined to overcome through the power of personal persuasion in his face-to-face meetings with Stalin in Teheran.

10
Face to Face

MINUTES AFTER ROOSEVELT had moved into the chancellery building within the Soviet compound after the fast drive through the back streets of Teheran on November 28, a message came that Stalin was on his way to meet the President in his quarters, where he was resting after the exciting ride. At the same time a call went out for the official American interpreter, Charles E. Bohlen.

He had been tested as an interpreter at the foreign ministers' conference in Moscow. Hull, satisfied with his work, had recommended Bohlen to Roosevelt as qualified to interpret at the Teheran Conference. As a young Foreign Service officer, Bohlen had decided to specialize in Russian language and Soviet politics. He had served in Moscow from 1934 to 1940, and had then been transferred to Tokyo because a specialist on Soviet policy was needed to watch Soviet-Japanese relations. After his internment following the attack on Pearl Harbor, he returned to Washington and an appointment as assistant chief of the Russian section. In this position he had gone to Moscow with Hull in October. Now at Teheran he would act as Roosevelt's interpreter, but he would not advise him on Soviet policies because he was "State Department" and from the Russian section, which was considered anti-Soviet. Nevertheless the appointment to interpret at the Teheran Conference changed Bohlen from a desk officer to "a participant in the most critical diplomatic negotiations the United States had ever engaged in."[1]

Bohlen's job at Teheran became the "hardest sustained period of work I ever did." He had to interpret, take notes, and then dictate his notes of the talks to an Army stenographer. At dinner meetings he had to interpret while others feasted. After interpreting at the evening session, he again had to dictate his notes to the stenographer and correct the typescript until the early morning hours. If there were to be a breakfast meeting requiring interpretation, he had to be awake and ready for it.

In the few minutes before Stalin arrived, Bohlen explained to Roosevelt how he preferred him to speak. He asked the President to break up his comments into short periods because if he talked for too long a time, his Russian hearers would lose interest in what he was saying. Short periods of speech, two or three minutes, would hold their attention and ease Bohlen's job. As it worked out, Roosevelt spoke and Bohlen interpreted into Russian. A similar practice was followed by Stalin and Churchill with each speaker's interpreter translating the comments.

Dressed in a blue suit, Roosevelt was sitting in his wheelchair when Stalin walked into the room, accompanied by V. N. Pavlov, his interpreter, and escorted by a young American Army officer. When the door was closed, the young officer remained within the room. Bohlen had to explain that there was no need for him to do so, and he then left. Roosevelt's confidants—Hopkins, Harriman, and others standing outside—had become excited because they imagined that the escorting officer intended to stay inside for the entire meeting.

Roosevelt saw a short, stocky man, about five feet four inches in height, with gray hair and dark brown eyes. A mustache covered much of his mouth; his face was pockmarked, the teeth broken and stained, and his left arm was slightly deformed. He wore a khaki tunic. On his chest was the Order of Lenin.

It was an historic moment: the crippled patrician from Dutchess County and the revolutionary from Georgian Russia represented the greatest military powers in the world and two diametrically opposed political and social systems. For the first time in the history of the United States, a President had personally met the leader of the Soviet government. This meeting in Teheran marked the first in a series of conferences that subsequent American Presidents would have with Soviet rulers.

"Hello, Marshal Stalin," the President said as he held out his hand. "I am glad to see you. I have tried for a long time to bring this about." Stalin apologized for coming so soon after the President's arrival, but he was only doing his duty as host because Roosevelt was his guest.

"Tell me, Mr. President, are you comfortable here? Perhaps there is something you would like?"

"No thank you, everything's fine. I feel quite at home."

"You like it here then."

"I'm very grateful to you for giving me the use of this house."

Stalin offered Roosevelt a cigarette, but the President declined in favor of his own brand of American cigarettes.

"Have you any suggestions as to the topics we should cover in this talk?" asked Stalin.

"I don't think we should rigidly define the range of topics. We might simply have a general exchange of views about the situation and the prospects. I would also be interested to hear from you about the position on the Soviet-German front."

"I am willing to fall in with that," Stalin replied. He admitted that the Soviet forces had lost Zhitomar and expected to lose Korosten, an important rail center. The Soviet armies still retained the initiative but could mount offensive operations only in the Ukraine.

"I would like to divert some thirty or forty German divisions from the Soviet-German front," declared Roosevelt.

"If that could be done, it would be good."

"This is one of the questions on which I intend to give my explanations here in Teheran in these next few days. The difficulty is that the Americans are faced with the problem of supplying a force of two million at a distance of 3,000 miles from the American continent."

Roosevelt turned next to the question of the American and British merchant fleets, which he said would be in surplus after the war had come to an end. He wished to discuss with

Stalin the possibility that the surplus ships would be made available to the Soviet Union. Stalin thought that an adequate merchant fleet would help in the development of relations between Soviet Russia and the United States after the war had ended. If these ships were sent to the Soviet Union, the Marshal declared, "a plentiful supply of raw materials from that country would be made available to the United States."

The conversation switched to the Far East. Roosevelt commented that he had had "an interesting conversation" in Cairo with Chiang Kai-shek on China. He reported to Stalin that the United States was supplying and training thirty Chinese divisions for operations in South China and planned to do the same with an additional thirty divisions. Stalin observed that the Chinese had fought very badly and that was the fault of their leaders.

Stalin then turned the conversation to the problem of Lebanon. There, the Chamber of Deputies had voted to end French control and to proclaim independence. In response to this vote, the French Committee of National Liberation (headed by General Charles de Gaulle) had suspended the Lebanese constitution as well as the government. The usual riots had followed. After the U.S. government had expressed dissatisfaction, the decrees suspending the constitution were abrogated. Roosevelt blamed the trouble on the Committee of National Liberation and de Gaulle.

Stalin said that he did not know de Gaulle personally, but he regarded the general as "very unreal in his political activities." He described de Gaulle as representing the soul of France, but the physical France under Pétain was helping the common enemy, Germany, through the facilities that were made available to the German forces. The de Gaulle movement, observed Stalin, lacked communications with "physical France," which ought to be punished after the war. "De Gaulle acts as though he were the head of a great state, whereas in fact, it comands little power," said Stalin.

Roosevelt agreed with Stalin. No Frenchman over forty years of age and no Frenchman who had held a position in the present Vichy government should be allowed to return to the government in the future. Stalin approved of Roosevelt's observation that General Henri Giraud, whom the President had tried to get to make peace with de Gaulle at Casablanca, was "a good old military type, but with no administrative or political sense, whatsoever." Stalin also did not want the French ruling classes to share in the benefits of peace in view of their past collaboration with the Germans. According to Roosevelt, Churchill wanted France to be quickly reconstructed as a great nation. But Roosevelt did not share this view because he believed that it would take "many years of honest labor" before France would once more become a great, strong nation. First, the government and the people must "become honest citizens."

The conversation turned to the French Empire. Stalin opposed shedding Allied blood to restore Indochina to French colonial rule. France must not regain Indochina and the French must pay for their "criminal collaboration with Germany." Roosevelt agreed fully with Stalin on the question of Indochina—"After 100 years of French rule in Indochina, the inhabitants were worse off than they had been before." The President wanted a form of trusteeship for the people of Indochina which would work to prepare them for independence within perhaps twenty to thirty years. He had even had Hull take a document to the Moscow Conference containing a proposal for a committee to visit the colonies of all nations and through public opinion correct any abuses. Stalin found merit in the idea.

Turning to India, which was then the current colonial area American liberals wanted to reform, Roosevelt admitted that "it would be better not to discuss the question of India with Mr. Churchill." He believed that Churchill had no solution to the question and proposed to defer the problem until the end of the war. However, at some future time, Roosevelt wanted to talk with Stalin about India. The best solution, the President believed, "would be reform from the bottom, somewhat on the Soviet line."

Roosevelt's comment reflected either immense ignorance of the real nature of the Bolshevik Revolution or an intention to flatter Stalin and to intimate that he admired the system Stalin had created. Stalin, however, would not be caught on this matter. He found the Indian question "a complicated one, with different levels of culture and the absence of relationship in the castes." He warned: "Reform from the bottom would mean revolution."

It was now time for the first plenary session of the Teheran Conference. As they left the room together, Roosevelt declared his happiness at being in a house in the Russian compound because it afforded him the "opportunity of meeting Marshal Stalin more frequently in completely informal and different circumstances."[2]

The next day, the President told his son, Elliott, about the meeting with Stalin.

"What'd you talk about?" asked Elliott. "Or was it state secrets?"

"Not a bit of it," said the President. "Mostly it was 'How did I like my quarters?' and 'Thank you very much for turning over the main house to me' and 'What is the news from the eastern front?' (It's very good, by the way; Stalin's most pleased; he hopes the Red Army will have crossed the Polish border before we leave.) That sort of thing. Polite chitchat. I didn't especially want to start in on business right straight off the bat."

"Measuring each other, eh?" asked Elliott.

"I wouldn't say that."

"I was kidding."

"We were getting to know each other. We were finding out what kind of people we are."

"What kind of people is he?"

"Oh . . . he's got a kind of massive rumble, talks deliberately, seems very confident, very sure of himself, moves slowly—altogether quite impressive, I'd say."

"You like him?"

To his son, the President appeared emphatic in his liking of Stalin after their first meeting.[3]

It had been the type of talk that Roosevelt had wanted to have with the Soviet ruler: private, man-to-man. He hoped that it would be the beginning of a close relationship and would help to break down the barrier of suspicion which, if allowed to endure, might endanger postwar collaboration on keeping the peace. Moreover, to show his intense desire to get on friendly terms with Stalin, Roosevelt had insisted that only interpreters would be present at their first meeting. Not even Harry Hopkins had been allowed into the room. It was the type of meeting that Roosevelt had sent Davies to Moscow to arrange.

Roosevelt had carefully skirted any question that could have aroused Stalin's ire. According to the record of their conversation, Stalin left the initiative in the discussion to the President. Both men avoided the topic of Soviet frontiers because it was not the time to bring this up. Stalin, for his part, avoided demanding a second front as soon as possible.

As an indication of American generosity, Roosevelt had suggested giving surplus ships to the Soviet government which would be taken from the Allied merchant fleets after the war had ended. Stalin's hint of raw materials that would become available to the United States was the answer that a Bolshevik would expect a capitalist would like to hear.

Probably Roosevelt's eagerness to cut France off from American support must have surprised Stalin. His comments about Charles de Gaulle revealed a fear that this tall, hard-nosed Frenchman aimed at reviving France and making her a potential rallying point for western Europe. In de Gaulle, Stalin sensed a tough-minded opponent. Roosevelt's anti-French attitude must have pleased him.

Roosevelt's opposition to colonialism was the standard liberal belief of the era. His views on Indochina were sincere; he had often expressed them in other places to different audiences. His belief in trusteeship of colonies was his method of solving the question of colonial independence. It was a topic on which Roosevelt knew that he and Stalin would stand united against Churchill.

Now they were to meet with Churchill in the first plenary session of the conference. Roosevelt hoped that this short conversation with Stalin would lay the groundwork for productive negotiations that would ultimately lead to a peaceful world.

11

The Battle over OVERLORD

IT HAD BEEN A beautiful Sunday afternoon in Teheran. At
the Soviet Embassy, surrounded by British and Soviet troops,
a group of foreign politicians and military officers were now
gathering for the first plenary session of the conference to
which they had traveled from their distant capitals.

In preparation for this session, Roosevelt and his chiefs
of staff had met that morning in the American legation. Their
discussion rambled from one topic to the other without any
conclusions; questions thrown out by Roosevelt were unre-
lated to the conversation. The discussion was unplanned because the group sought to anticipate questions which the
British, and particularly the Russians, would raise at the first
plenary session.

No one seemed certain about exactly what the Russians
might demand. According to George Marshall, the Russians
wanted an operation more immediate than OVERLORD, which
was planned for the spring of 1944. "The main problem as
regards collaboration with the Soviets," he said, "is that they
desire pressure exerted within the next two months." But if
the Russians did not want an immediate operation, then it
would be possible to push further north beyond Rome, to
undertake the Rhodes campaign, and even to delay OVER-
LORD. Such a delay would be necessary if there were to be
an additional operation in the Mediterranean—taking Rhodes,
for example.

As for the British, he said, they wanted the Rhodes op-

eration and Turkish entry into the war, and they were opposed to the Andaman Islands operation, BUCCANEER. But at
Cairo, Roosevelt had promised Chiang that BUCCANEER would
be mounted, and now he told his chiefs, "We are obligated
to the Chinese to carry out the amphibious operation BUC-
CANEER." As far as Rhodes was concerned, after it had been
taken, then the British would say, " 'Now we will have to
take Greece.' " As for the Turks, he lacked the conscience to
urge them to come into the war. And as for the question of
the British and their goals in the Mediterranean, Roosevelt
reminded his audience that the British looked on the Mediterranean as an area under their domination.

He asked Marshall what should be said if the Soviets announced that they would soon be in Rumania and wanted to
know what the United States and Britain could do to help
them. Marshall suggested helping them by operations along
the Adriatic coast, opening ports, and getting supplies to Tito's forces. Roosevelt favored operations in the Adriatic rather
than in the vicinity of the Dodecanese Islands; small groups
of commandoes could penetrate north from Trieste and
Fiume. These operations could be under way by January
1944. But Marshall questioned their value because they would
require landing craft, thus delaying operations in Italy. Roosevelt could not understand how two thousand commandoes
would require many landing craft.

Finally, Marshall summed up the problem facing them:
"The real issue is what do the Soviets mean by 'immediate
help'? The U.S.S.R. evidently wants Turkey into the war as
a cold blooded proposition. The Soviets definitely want
something, and we should find out what it is." But Roosevelt feared that Stalin would ask how many German divisions could be withdrawn from the Soviet western front
immediately.[1] It was the best that Roosevelt and his chiefs
of staff would do in preparing for the first plenary session of
the Teheran Conference.

The British chiefs of staff, who had also met that morning, were as badly prepared as their American counterparts.
"We were worried with the whole situation," Brooke wrote
in his diary. "We had not got any agreement with the Americans on the main points for discussion and it was evident
that we were heading for chaos."[2]

Churchill, still battling a head cold, by now had developed a sore throat and could scarcely speak. The British chiefs tried to get him to agree to Operation BUCCANEER in order to get the Americans to consent to expanding operations in the Mediterranean, but he rejected the compromise.

On the subject of Churchill's view of Allied strategy at the opening of the Teheran plenary session, much nonsense has been written. His views can be found in a minute for the chiefs of staff which he drafted in Cairo before leaving for Teheran. He saw the war in the Mediterranean as taking an unsatisfactory course. Troops had been in action too long; landing craft had been withdrawn to the United Kingdom for OVERLORD and could not be used in amphibious operations along the Italian peninsula. The buildup of the air force in Italy had hampered the reinforcement of the armies. The entire Italian campaign had flagged. The Germans were even able to withdraw divisions from Italy to meet their needs on the Russian front. "We have therefore failed to take the weight off the attack of the Soviets." Moreover, insufficient support had been given to the guerrilla forces in Yugoslavia and Albania which were containing many German divisions. Now the Germans were systematically mopping up the guerrillas. "We shall certainly be rightly accused of short-sightedness or even worse in all this affair."

The cause of the trouble Churchill found in the imaginary line drawn north and south through the Mediterranean theater of war, with the western portion commanded by Eisenhower and the eastern by General Sir Henry Maitland Wilson, who lacked the necessary forces (none could be spared from Eisenhower's command). As the result of insufficient strength in the eastern Mediterranean, the Allied forces could not stop the Germans from becoming the masters of the Aegean.

The causes of the poor Allied progress in the Mediterranean, he claimed, could be found in this artificial line and in OVERLORD. At the Quebec Conference the decision on OVERLORD had been made before the successful landing on the Italian peninsula. "We are now faced with the prospect that a fixed target date for OVERLORD will continue to wreck and ruin the Mediterranean campaign; that our affairs will deteriorate in the Balkans and that the Aegean will remain firmly in German hands. All this is to be accepted for the sake of an operation fixed for May upon hypothesis that in all probability will not be realized at that date and certainly not if the Mediterranean pressure is relaxed."

Churchill argued that of the more than two million Allied forces in North Africa, Sicily, and Italy, only 170,000 were in the line. Here was the place where Allied forces were in contact with the enemy and where superior numbers could be brought to bear. "It is certainly an odd way of helping the Russians, to slow down the fight in the only theater where anything can be done for some months." Consequently he wanted to stop further movement of troops from the Mediterranean, to take Rome, to bring Turkey into the war, to seize ports on the Dalmatian coast, and to use airborne and commando units to bring all possible aid to the guerrilla forces.[3]

At the moment of their meeting with the Russians, there was a basic difference between the strategies propounded by the British and the American military leaders. Admiral Ernest J. King explained it best in an off-the-record talk with newspaper correspondents held two months earlier. "The British seem to favor what might be called 'an opportunist war,' that is, striking where and when the circumstances seem to dictate at a given moment. Americans, on the other hand, like to plan and fight by that plan and not run a hit or miss war." King had to admit that the British were "virtually out of manpower" and their inhibition against a cross-Channel operation could be attributed to the memory of Dunkirk.[4]

It was time for the plenary session. Roosevelt and Churchill had not conferred in preparation for the session, and their military staffs had argued bitterly in Cairo without reaching a consensus about the strategy to be followed. There was no agreed agenda and now they were to face Stalin and his advisers.

For the plenary session, the generals, admirals, and the politicians with their assistants and interpreters assembled in a large Empire-style hall next to Roosevelt's quarters. In the center of the hall stood a round oak table with a green baize cover; it had been specially constructed for the conference. Around the table were ranged ornate mahogany chairs upholstered in striped silk. A stand with the three flags of the conference powers was in the center of the table. There were places for twelve delegates, four from each country, and before each place lay pads and pencils. The remaining officials and observers sat in rows of chairs ranged behind the table and around the room. At the windows, curtains let in the November afternoon light. Soviet secret policemen guarded the room. For most of the conference, American Secret Service agents and their British counterparts would be barred from the room.

Roosevelt was wheeled up to the table. Harriman sat on his right, Bohlen to his left, and Hopkins next to Bohlen. Churchill entered with Eden, Lord Ismay, the deputy secretary to the War Cabinet, and Major A. H. Birse, the British interpreter. Stalin brought with him his shadow, Molotov; Pavlov, the interpreter; and as his military adviser, Marshal Klimenti E. Voroshilov. Seated around the room were members of the Combined Chiefs of Staff, with only General Marshall and General Arnold missing. After Roosevelt had told them nothing was planned for the afternoon, they had taken an automobile and driven north to see the country and learn the extent of the Soviet zone of occupation. By the time they discovered the foul-up, it was too late for them to return and join the meeting.

While Roosevelt and Churchill had come with their chiefs of staff, Stalin, lacking a similar staff, had brought only Voroshilov. A coal miner by age seven who could not read or write until he was twelve, a strike leader who became a Bolshevik, Voroshilov had fought in the November Revolution, enlisted in the Red Army in 1918, and commanded troops in the civil war. His Stalin connection dated from service under him in the defense of Tsaritsyn (later changed to Stalingrad) in the summer of 1918. A brave man on the battlefield, Voroshilov's military expertise was greatly overblown. Appointed to the Central Committee of the Communist party in 1921, he became one of Stalin's faithful henchmen. War minister by 1925, he later assisted Stalin in purging the Soviet armed forces and undermining the strength of the Red Army. After the Russo-Finnish War had revealed the weaknesses of the Red Army, he lost his post as war minister.

Following the German invasion in 1941, he commanded the northern front for a few weeks until incompetence led to his removal from command. Nevertheless, he still remained on the powerful Politburo, serving his master's wishes.

Along with Voroshilov, Stalin had brought the ever faithful Molotov, and no one else. He had chosen this pair of Bolsheviks to accompany him on his first trip outside the Soviet Union since attaining supreme power because he knew that they could be depended upon to follow his instructions faithfully while in Teheran. They would take no initiative, but only do and say whatever he required of them. Upon return to Moscow, Stalin knew that their reports would flatter his image. Their inclusion in his official party may have indicated his uncertainty in meeting with two leaders of the capitalist world. What better form of security than to have two old Bolshevik comrades with him whose loyalty had been thoroughly tested.

Churchill and Stalin had earlier agreed that Roosevelt, as the only head of state present, should preside at the first formal plenary session. As the chairman of a meeting for which he had worked so long to convene, Roosevelt gave the appearance of a tall, strong man; only the wheelchair bore witness to his infirmity. He beamed "on all around the table and looked very much like the kind, rich uncle paying a visit to his poorer relations."[5] As he spoke, he often took off his pince-nez, using it to make a point.

It was about 4 P.M. when the President opened the meeting by welcoming the "new members to the family circle," referring to the Soviet officials who had joined a very select group that had already met in Washington, Casablanca, Quebec, and Cairo. "We are sitting around this table for the first time as a family, with the one object of winning the war." As chairman, he proposed the guidelines for the conference. In the past meetings, he explained, "it has been our habit, between the British and the United States, to publish nothing but to speak our minds very freely." In so large a family circle, he hoped that "we will be very successful and achieve constructive accord in order that we may maintain close touch throughout the war and after the war." The military staffs would consider matters military. "Marshal Stalin, the Prime

Minister and I have many things to discuss regarding matters pertaining to conditions after the war. If anyone of us does not want to talk about any particular subject brought up we do not have to."[6] He urged everyone to speak as freely as they wished to do on the basis of friendship.

Churchill commented that they represented "the greatest concentration of worldly power that had ever been seen in the history of mankind." They had the potential to shorten the war; victory lay in their hands.

Stalin then welcomed everyone to the conference. He observed that they had all been "pampered by history." They had great forces and great opportunities. He hoped that "we shall do everything at this conference to make due use, within the framework of our co-operation, of the power and authority that our peoples have vested in us." He urged them to get down to work.

Roosevelt started by giving his audience a survey of the war from the American point of view. First he spoke of the war in the Pacific, which concerned the United States more than the other two Allies. Here a war of attrition was being waged against Japan with the sinking of more Japanese ships than could be replaced. American forces were moving toward Japan from the south and through the islands on the east. On the west, China had to be kept in the war, aided by operations through North Burma and into Yunan Province. By opening the Burma Road, it would be possible to transport supplies to China and thereby place American forces in a position from which to bomb Tokyo.

Then the President turned to "the most important theater of the war—Europe." In the past year and a half, he said, during conferences with Churchill, the military discussions had revolved around plans to cross the English Channel. Owing to transportation difficulties, until the Quebec Conference they had been unable to set a definite date. Because the English Channel was such a "disagreeable body of water," the cross-Channel operation could not be started before May 1. The bottleneck in the matter, said Roosevelt, was the landing craft. For that reason, it would be necessary to give up the cross-Channel operation completely if a large expedition were to be mounted in the Mediterranean. "Consequently, both he and the Prime Minister felt that in this military conference it was essential that they should have the advice and experience of Marshal Stalin and Marshal Voroshilov as to what action would be of the greatest service to the Soviet."

Roosevelt felt that even if OVERLORD were to be delayed, "we can draw more German divisions from the Soviet front by means of that operation than any other." There were other operations that could be mounted in the Mediterranean: a drive up through Italy, a move from the northeast Adriatic, an operation in the Aegean Sea, and operations from Turkey. The conference would have to decide which of these to adopt, because "we want to create a withdrawal of German divisions from the Western Front."

It was Churchill's turn to speak next, but he chose to reserve his remarks until after Stalin had spoken. The Marshal at once confirmed the report from Hull at the Moscow Conference regarding the entry of the Soviet forces into the war against Japan. At the present time, he declared, the Soviet forces could not join in the struggle against Japan because all forces had to be deployed against Germany. "Once Germany was finally defeated, it would then be possible to send the necessary reinforcements to Siberia and then we shall be able by our common front to beat Japan." (This statement was omitted from the published Soviet version of this meeting.)

Stalin reviewed the developments on the Soviet-German front, where the Germans had attacked first that year only to fail. The Soviet armies, which had gone on the offensive during the summer and the autumn, had achieved unexpected successes. These armies had been victorious, Stalin explained, because of numerical superiority—330 Soviet divisions opposing 260 Axis divisions. But that numerical superiority, he warned, was gradually decreasing because the Soviet advance was hampered by supply problems. In some areas the Germans had already taken the initiative and the Soviet forces expected to lose some major points.

Stalin turned next to the question of where the Anglo-American forces could best help the Soviet armies. The Italian campaign was of value only in opening the Mediterranean to Allied shipping—a campaign of no great importance as far as the defeat of Germany was concerned. Stalin reminded his audience that in 1799, Russian armies under Field Marshal Alexander Suvorov had discovered that the Alps were an insuperable barrier to invading Germany from Italy. Soviet generals believed that Hitler sought to retain as many Allied divisions as possible in Italy where no decision could be reached.

"We Russians believe that the best result would be yielded by a blow at the enemy in northern or north-western France." It would be nice if Turkey would open the way for an Allied invasion of the Balkans; even then, the Allied armies would be far from the heart of Germany yet this would still be better than an invasion of Germany attempted from Italy. "But Germany's weakest spot is France," he concluded. "The Germans will fight like devils to prevent such an attack."

There it was: Stalin had thrown in his support for the attack across the English Channel and through France.

Churchill hastened to rebut the Marshal's arguments, launching into a long speech on his views about the future course of operations. Time would not permit him to explain why OVERLORD could not be launched in 1943, but how they were determined to carry it out in the late spring or early summer of 1944. Both he and the President recognized that the operations in North Africa and Italy were secondary in character, but that was the best possible that could be done. According to Churchill, the forces that would be involved in OVERLORD comprised sixteen British and nineteen American divisions. Each of these divisions, however, was stronger than a German division. After the sixteen British divisions had landed in France, no additional British divisions could be dispatched to Europe because of other commitments in the Middle East and in India. The reinforcement of the Allied invading force would have to come from the United States.

Turning to the campaign in Italy, Churchill stated that after Rome had been captured by January 1944, only six months would remain before the beginning of OVERLORD. What could be done with the Allied forces available in the Mediterranean to take the weight off Russia without delaying OVERLORD more than a month or two? The British and American governments had kept their minds open on this subject until they could learn the Soviet government's views. After Rome had fallen, Churchill conjectured, the Allied forces would halt north of Rome along a line between the cities of Pisa and Rimini. Then it would be possible to establish a third front, which might involve moving into southern France or moving from the head of the Adriatic toward the Danube. "There was much to be said for supporting Tito, who was holding a number of German divisions and doing much more for the Allied cause than the Chetniks under Mihailovic."

That brought Churchill to what he called "the biggest problem" which needed consideration by the military staffs: "namely to force Turkey into the war and open communications through the Aegean to the Dardanelles and thence to the Black Sea." At this point Churchill wandered off into a long discussion of the benefits to be derived from bringing Turkey into the war. With the use of Turkish air bases, the Allied forces could capture islands in the Aegean Sea with comparative ease. Then, with access to the Black Sea ports, convoys could sail to these ports continuously, affording a ceaseless flow of supplies. There were other questions: How to persuade Turkey to enter the war, what would they be asked to do, should they merely provide bases or declare war on Germany? What would be the effect on Bulgaria, Rumania, and Hungary if Turkey were to enter the war? There might be "a political landslide among the satellite states which would enable the Greeks to revolt and hustle the Germans out of Greece." But nothing could be decided about these operations in the eastern Mediterranean until more was known about the Soviet viewpoint. Churchill asked if the objectives he had outlined made the Soviet government wish to go ahead even if it would mean a one- to two-month delay in launching OVERLORD.

Stalin in return aimed a series of questions at the prime minister, seeking to pin him down to the exact number of divisions that would be committed to battle.

"I understand that there are thirty-five divisions for invasion operations in the north of France."

"Yes, that is correct," Churchill replied.

"Before the operations to invade the north of France it is

planned to carry out the operation in the Italian theater to take Rome after which it is planned to go on the defensive in Italy," said Stalin.

"Yes. We are already withdrawing seven divisions from Italy." These would be used to complete the thirty-five needed for the invasion of France. Thereafter, as Churchill explained, it would be impossible to transfer any more because of the limited shipping capacity.

"Another question," said Stalin. "Did I understand correctly that apart from the operations to take Rome it is planned to carry out another operation in the Adriatic, and also an operation in southern France?"

"The plan is to carry out an attack in southern France at the moment Operation OVERLORD is launched," Churchill replied. "Troops that can be released from Italy will be used for this. But this operation has not yet been worked out in detail."

"Another question: if Turkey enters the war, what is to be done in that case?" asked Stalin.

"I can say that it would take no more than two or three divisions to take the islands along the west coast of Turkey so as to allow the supply ships to go to Turkey, and also to open the route to the Black Sea. But the first thing we shall do is send the Turks twenty air squadrons and several air defence regiments, which can be done without detriment to other operations."

But Stalin had had enough of this discussion. "It would be a mistake to disperse forces by sending part to Turkey and elsewhere and part to southern France," he argued. "The best course would be to make OVERLORD the basic operation for 1944 and, once Rome had been captured, to send all available forces in Italy to southern France. These forces could then join hands with the OVERLORD forces when the invasion was launched. France was the weakest spot on the German front." Stalin did not expect that Turkey would enter the war.

Churchill said he had thought that the Soviet government wanted Turkey in the war. Although he agreed with Stalin's view about dispersion being undesirable, a "handful of divisions—say two or three" could be used in making contact with Turkey. Churchill dreaded six months inactivity between the fall of Rome and OVERLORD. The Allies ought to be fighting Germany the entire time.

Stalin replied that the Allies ought to remain on the defensive in Italy, dispense with the capture of Rome, and release ten divisions for use in invading southern France two months before OVERLORD. The diversion of German troops from northern France would assure the success of OVERLORD. But Churchill would not hear of giving up the drive to take Rome. The airfields north of Rome were needed for the bombing of Germany, and to give up the capture of Rome would "be regarded on all sides as a crashing defeat and the British Parliament would not tolerate the idea for a moment."

Roosevelt, who had been silent throughout this debate, spoke at last. Stalin's proposal about the timing of the invasion of southern France interested him greatly. He found the question of the relative timing of operations, particularly that of the eastern Mediterranean in relation to OVERLORD, most important. Personally, Roosevelt felt that "nothing should be done to delay the carrying out of OVERLORD which might be necessary if any operations in the eastern Mediterranean were undertaken." The President proposed that the staff commence to work on a plan of operation for an invasion of southern France based on the timing suggested by Stalin.

Stalin claimed that Soviet experience during two years of fighting had shown that an attack from one direction was not as effective as an offensive from two directions at once. Offensives from two directions forced the enemy to disperse his forces and, as the two offensives converged, enabled them to support each other and increase their strength. This principle should be applied to France.

But Churchill was not finished. Although he did not disagree on principle with Stalin, he "could not in any circumstances agree to sacrifice the activities of the armies in the Mediterranean, which included twenty British and British controlled divisions, merely in order to keep the exact date of the 1st May for OVERLORD." Churchill asked that they meditate on these discussions and continue them the next day. Roosevelt was agreeable and proposed that the staffs set

Nov. 13 '43

This will be another Odyssey — much further afield & afloat than the hardy Trojan whose name I used to take at Groton when I was competing for school prizes — But it too will be filled with sur- prises — # We are off shore — escorted by destroyers & planes — very luxurious on the Iowa which with her sister-ship the N.J. are the largest battleships in the world — They are officially

Page 1 of Roosevelt's personal diary of the trip to Cairo and Teheran, November 13, 1943

Roosevelt viewing
the pyramids with
Churchill near
Cairo, November
1943

The Combined
Chiefs of Staff in
Cairo

Generalissimo
Chiang Kai-shek,
Roosevelt, Chur-
chill, and Madame
Chiang

Roosevelt and General Dwight Eisenhower touring a U.S. troop-carrier airport en route from the Cairo-Teheran conferences, Castelvetrano, Sicily, December 8, 1943

Roosevelt visiting
the U.S. Army
troops at the Te-
heran Conference,
December 2, 1943

Roosevelt at Te-
heran with Stalin
and Churchill, No-
vember 29, 1943

Roosevelt greets Sara Churchill. *Left to right, standing:* Harry Hopkins, Molotov, Averell Harriman, and Anthony Eden (to Sara Churchill's left)

Roosevelt with Stalin at Teheran, November 29, 1943

Stalin well pleased by the Teheran Conference

Roosevelt, President Inönü of Turkey, and Churchill

Outside the Russian Embassy, November 29, 1943. *Left to right:* George Marshall, Archibald Clark-Kerr, Harry Hopkins, Pavlov (Stalin's interpreter), Stalin, Molotov, and Voroshilov.

Churchill and his
birthday cake

After handing over the Stalingrad sword, Churchill conducts Stalin down the conference room.

Presentation of the Stalingrad sword to Stalin by Churchill, Teheran, November 29, 1943

U.S. Office of War Information, No. 208-N-19942, National Archives

Roosevelt viewing
the Stalingrad
sword, Teheran,
November 29, 1943

Celebrating Chur-
chill's birthday.
Harry Hopkins is in
the foreground.

U.S. Office of War Information, No. 208-N-19943, National Archives

Roosevelt visiting
with the Shah Mo-
hammed Riza Pah-
lavi in Teheran,
November 30, 1943

to work the next morning on the matter of operations against southern France.

Stalin was agreeable also, but he commented: "We did not expect a discussion of purely military matters, that is why we did not invite representatives of the General Staff to come along, but I think that Marshal Voroshilov and I can arrange something." It was agreed that Brooke, Portal, Leahy, Marshall, and Voroshilov would comprise the military conference, to be held in the Soviet Embassy the next morning.

Churchill was still not finished. He wanted the conference also to consider what to do with Turkey, what they were prepared to offer Turkey in order to get her into the war, and what would be the consequences of their offer. Stalin reminded the conference that Turkey was an ally of Britain and on friendly terms with the United States. It would be up to them to persuade Turkey to enter the war. But "all neutral states, including Turkey look upon belligerents as fools." Roosevelt promised to do his best to persuade the president of Turkey to enter the war, but he expected that the president would demand such a high price in planes, guns, tanks, and equipment that OVERLORD would have to be postponed. Stalin thought the Turkish government would reject the suggestion that they enter World War II. Churchill replied that "in his opinion the Turks were crazy." Stalin ended the meeting with the observation that "there were some people who apparently preferred to remain crazy." The Soviet hosts then served their guests tea and cookies.

For the British, it had been a disastrous afternoon. When asked by his personal physician, Lord Moran, how the first session had gone, Churchill growled: "A bloody lot has gone wrong."[7] For Churchill the disaster had commenced earlier in the day when Roosevelt refused his request to see him either in the morning or at luncheon to agree on the military matters that would be discussed with Stalin. Roosevelt had been adamant; he would not see Churchill privately because he knew that Churchill would press him to approve the eastern Mediterranean strategy even if it meant a delay in OVERLORD. More important, Stalin would soon learn about the meeting and suspect that they were plotting against him.

Now Churchill and those closest to him had to face a most unpleasant truth: Roosevelt was siding with Stalin in the discussions about strategy. As Brooke commented: "This conference is over when it has only just begun. Stalin has got the President in his pocket."[8]

Moreover, the two stronger powers were joining sides against the weaker power in concurring on strategy that frightened the weaker member. Britain had suddenly been thrust into the role of the junior partner in the Great Alliance. It was at the Teheran Conference, Churchill later remarked, that he realized how small Britain was. "There I sat with the great Russian bear on one side of me, with paws outstretched, and on the other side the great American buffalo, and between the two sat the poor little English donkey, who was the only one . . . who knew the right way home."[9]

Brooke as British chief of staff thought the politicians were getting it very muddled. Roosevelt made "a poor and not very helpful speech. From then onwards the conference went from bad to worse. Stalin replied by advocating cross-Channel operations at the expense of all else. Winston replied and was not at his best. President chipped in and made matters worse. . . . We sat for three-and-a-half hours and finished up the conference by confusing plans more than they have been before."[10]

Certainly the British believed that Roosevelt had given too much away by announcing early in the meeting the expected date of OVERLORD. Such exactness was not desired by the British, who did not believe that strategy ought to pivot around a date. They remembered the war of 1914–18, when the date of an offensive leaked to the enemy but the high command refused to alter the decision to "go over the top" and thousands of British soldiers were slaughtered in order to keep a date.

Stalin increased the pressure to keep this date when early in the meeting he confirmed the report of Hull, during the Moscow Conference, that Soviet Russia would join in the war against Japan after Germany had been defeated. Now Britain and the United States must reciprocate by speeding up the invasion of France. By supporting the American concern about the war against Japan, Stalin had acquired the admiration and support of the American Joint Chiefs of Staff. They were delighted that he had come down hard in favor of OVERLORD and had opposed operations in the eastern Mediterranean that could become protracted, leading to a delay in launching the invasion of France.

But it was the delay that the British really desired, although Churchill dared not defend the British position with the open confession that he and his advisers dreaded OVERLORD because of the anticipated casualties. Churchill hinted at the fear when he declared that once Britain had committed sixteen divisions to OVERLORD, no more reinforcements would be forthcoming.

Operations in the eastern Mediterranean appeared to the British more promising because they believed the Germans were sitting on a volcano and the Allies could start the eruption with less cost in lives than in an assault on Fortress Europe through France.[11] When that came, OVERLORD might not be necessary. For although the British had agreed on a date for OVERLORD at Quebec in August, and although they had agreed that it would be the main effort for 1944, their hearts were really not in it. They preferred the indirect approach through the eastern Mediterranean, hoping that it would mean fewer casualties.

Perhaps this argument would not have consumed so much time in Teheran if the Anglo-American differences had been thrashed out fully before encountering Stalin. Two more days would be wasted in wrangling over OVERLORD, when political questions requiring extensive discussions had to be pushed off to the final hours. Much of the responsibility for the lack of planning belonged with Roosevelt. He contributed a good deal to the confusion by his refusal to be tied to a formal agenda, by his rejection of any pre-conference discussion with the British, and by bringing Chiang Kai-shek to Cairo to prevent joint planning for Teheran.

There may have been another reason for Roosevelt's seeming confusion and inadequate planning: his desire for better relations with Stalin. If the Allied planners had come to Teheran with every position thoroughly prepared in advance, it could have appeared to Stalin that his allies were ganging up on him. Roosevelt's lack of preparation may have been deliberate in order to give Stalin the opportunity to appear to play the role of the deciding voice in the alliance. In that way there would not be any chance that Stalin could imagine others were plotting at his expense. By this tactic, Roosevelt hoped to gain the friendship of Stalin in the difficult years that lay ahead.

Stalin, however, had been surprised at the disunity of the British and Americans and their lack of agreement on OVERLORD. Every account of this session indicates his astonishment that the session had become a strategic conference— he had come to Teheran expecting to negotiate political questions, not to debate OVERLORD. None of his staff officers was present. He had only Voroshilov, who would have to substitute for a more qualified officer.

The launching of OVERLORD had great political meaning for Stalin. If British and American armies landed in France, instead of continuing the protracted Mediterranean campaign, Stalin's allies would require Soviet help in the form of an attack by the Red Army from the east. Anglo-American need would hand him enormous political leverage with the capitalist Allies. Unless the Soviet armies attacked, Hitler would be able to shift divisions from the east to the French coast in order to repel the Anglo-American invaders. However, Stalin did not intend to squander this advantage by allowing the Allies to tie OVERLORD to political negotiations and to insist on some political quid pro quo before promising to launch OVERLORD on time.

To Stalin, a decision on OVERLORD was vital. Once it had been launched, the British and the Americans would be fully committed against Germany, with little chance of attempting a deal with Hitler in order to concentrate their forces on defeating Japan. With Anglo-American armies fighting the Germans in western Europe, Stalin would no longer have to risk making an agreement with Hitler. Moreover, he could expect the weakening of Germany to strengthen the Soviet position in eastern Europe.

As a result of the OVERLORD debate, Stalin had to reconsider his tactics. A change was necessary because he regarded the opening of the second front as a pledge of good faith required in advance of any serious political negotia-

tion. The Moscow Conference had convinced him that the
OVERLORD question would be settled quickly by the start of
the Teheran Conference; he would only have to approve the
date agreed on at Quebec. But on the afternoon of November 28, his expectations disappeared in the face of strong
British opposition to OVERLORD. A change of tactics was required.

Until there was a decision on OVERLORD, Stalin would
focus on undermining the British opposition. To that end, he
would refuse any negotiation on all other political questions
of interest to Roosevelt and Churchill. At the same time, he
would make Churchill the target of his anger and frustration.

Earlier in the day, Roosevelt had informed his staff that he
wished to host a dinner that evening. William Rigdon passed
the presidential request to the chief steward. Back came the
report that a dinner could not be cooked in the building that
had been turned over to Roosevelt because the kitchen had
been stripped of everything—cooking utensils as well as
stoves of any type. An emergency call went out to General
Connolly at Camp Amirabad for help in equipping the kitchen.
Within less than an hour, an Army truck appeared carrying
an Army field range, coal, cooking utensils, and even additional food. The equipment was set up and the Filipino mess
crew prepared steak and potatoes for the guests. The next
day when Roosevelt learned about the missing stoves and
cooking utensils, and the hurried call to Camp Amirabad, he
expressed only mild concern because he took it for granted
that the cooks and stewards could carry on and provide him
and his guests with a banquet.

Before the dinner, Roosevelt himself mixed the cocktails.
He was proud of his talent with a cocktail shaker, but those
who drank his concoctions may have had a different view of
his talent. When he made martinis, according to Bohlen, "he
put a large quantity of vermouth, both sweet and dry, into a
pitcher of ice, added a smaller amount of gin, stirred the
concoction rapidly, and poured it out." After Stalin had tasted
one of the President's martinis, Roosevelt asked him if he
liked it. "Well, all right, but it is cold on the stomach," replied Stalin, who preferred vodka neat.[12]

In the course of dinner, Stalin and Roosevelt discussed possible sites for future meetings. Both men found Fairbanks, Alaska, to be a suitable location.

Stalin spent much of the evening elaborating his views on the future treatment of France and Germany. He would not give France any consideration; she had no right to have her empire returned. Nor should France be left with any important strategic points after the war because the "entire French ruling class was rotten to the core and had delivered over France to the Germans and . . . in fact, France was now actively helping our enemies."[13] But Churchill could not conceive of "a civilized world without a flourishing and lively France." Stalin sneered at his concern, saying, "France could be a charming and pleasant country but could not be allowed to play any important role in the immediate post war world."

Roosevelt agreed in part with Stalin, for that afternoon he had told him that everyone over forty years of age had to be eliminated from the French government. The President stressed the threat of New Caledonia to Australia and to New Zealand and the threat of Dakar to the Americas. Churchill suggested that certain strategic points should be placed under the control of the four victorious nations, the United States, Soviet Russia, Great Britain, and China.

When their talk turned to Nazi Germany, Stalin took the lead in condemning Germany, seeking to draw out Roosevelt and Churchill in order to learn their views. Stalin wanted the Reich made so impotent that it would never be able to make war again. To this end, he would have the victors keep control of strategic positions to block the revival of German military power. But he seemed to find all of the proposed measures for controlling Germany inadequate. He did favor dismemberment. He had no faith in the German people or the prospect that they would ever reform. He mentioned an incident which he claimed to have seen in Leipzig in 1907 when two hundred German workers failed to attend a mass meeting because there was no railroad employee to punch their tickets so they could leave the railroad station.

When Roosevelt commented that Hitler was mentally unstable, Stalin dissented—"Only a very able man could accomplish what Hitler had done in solidifying the German people whatever we thought of the methods."

On one feature of dismemberment of Germany, Stalin was resolved: "Poland should extend to the Oder . . . and the Russians would help the Poles to obtain a frontier on the Oder."

Changing the subject, Roosevelt explained that he favored a form of trusteeship for the approaches to the Baltic Sea and an international state in the vicinity of the Kiel Canal to maintain free navigation through the approaches to the canal. But as a result of an error in translation, Stalin thought that the President was advocating an international state for the Baltic States which Stalin coveted. He retorted, "The Baltic States had by an expression of the will of the people voted to join the Soviet Union and . . . this question was not therefore one for discussion."

Nobody replied to Stalin's distortion of history because Roosevelt suddenly broke out in a sweat and "turned green." He said nothing but seemed about to faint. The President's sudden illness frightened Hopkins, who had him wheeled out of the room and taken to his bedroom where his physician examined him. Everyone in the room was unnerved. Perhaps the President had been poisoned. Could it be that the assassins were genuine and not an invention of Stalin and Molotov? Or had the President suffered a heart attack brought on by the travel and excitement? Later, Admiral McIntire reported that it was only indigestion. Roosevelt did not return to the dining room that evening.

Stalin and Churchill, together with Eden and Molotov, adjourned to another room in the embassy. There Churchill and Stalin, seated on a sofa with cigars and coffee, began to talk about what might happen after the war had been won. Churchill reminded Stalin that "this was an historical meeting and that so much depended upon the friendship of the three heads of government and the decisions reached at this conference." But Stalin wanted to consider the worst that might happen. He feared that within fifteen to twenty years, Germany would recover her might. Consequently, they must establish a strong body to prevent Germany from starting a new war. Churchill felt that they had to keep the world safe for at least fifty years or else they would have betrayed their soldiers.

Stalin wondered about the economics of keeping the peace. Would Churchill forbid factories making watches and furniture that could easily be converted into armament factories? After all, the Germans had used toy rifles to teach thousands of men how to shoot. Churchill disagreed. "We have now learned something. Our duty was to make the world safe for at least fifty years by disarmament, by preventing rearmament, by supervision of German factories, by forbidding all aviation, and by territorial changes of a far-reaching character." But Stalin reminded him that the Germans (as they had done after World War I) might work through other countries. Churchill rolled on. "It all came back to a question of whether Great Britain, the United States and the U.S.S.R. kept a close friendship and supervised Germany in their mutual interest."

Again Stalin reminded the prime minister that control had been tried after World War I but it had failed. Churchill discovered a difference this time: Russia. In the last war, Russia had not been a party at the Paris Peace Conference. Moreover, Prussia would be dealt with so severely this time that the other German states would not want to rejoin her. But Stalin found it all "good but insufficient."

Churchill reminded him that Russia would have her army, Britain and the United States their navies and air forces. The three powers must never disarm their forces—"They were the trustees for the peace of the world. If they failed, there would be, perhaps, 100 years of chaos." It was more than mere peacekeeping. "The three powers should guide the future of the world. . . . They must keep friends in order to insure happy homes in all countries."

And what about Germany, asked Stalin. Churchill was "not against toilers in Germany, but only against the leaders and against dangerous combinations." Stalin for his part was not so considerate of the toilers because many of them fought in the German army under orders. When he asked German prisoners who came from the labor classes why they fought for Hitler, they answered that they were executing orders. He had such prisoners shot.

Churchill then suggested that they turn to the Polish question, and Stalin invited him to begin the discussion. To the British, said Churchill, Poland was important because they had declared war on her account. He wanted heart-to-heart talks with the Russians about the security of the Russian western frontier. When Stalin was ready to discuss the matter, it should be discussed, and they would reach an agreement. Stalin asked for a more precise explanation.

Churchill acknowledged that after the end of the war, Soviet Russia would be an "overwhelmingly strong power and would have a great responsibility for hundreds of years in any decisions she took with regard to Poland." Churchill personally thought Poland might move westward "like soldiers taking two steps left close." If Poland trod on some German toes, it could not be helped, but there must be a strong Poland. "This instrument was needed in the orchestra of Europe."

"Are we to try to draw frontier lines?" asked Churchill.

"Yes," replied Stalin.

Churchill explained that he lacked power from Parliament to draw frontier lines, and he did not think that Roosevelt had such power, but at Teheran they ought to attempt to work out a policy that could be pressed upon the Poles and which they could recommend to the Poles, advising them to accept.

"We could have a look," replied Stalin.

Both men agreed that an arrangement on frontier lines would be worked out without Polish participation. Afterward they would take the matter to the Poles. Then Eden raised the point made earlier by Stalin that Poland should be moved as far west as the Oder River. Jokingly, Stalin asked "whether we thought he was going to swallow Poland up." Eden did not know how much the Russians would eat—"How much would they leave undigested?" Stalin replied, "The Russians did not want anything belonging to other people, although they might have a bite at Germany."

Before their talks had ended, Churchill, using three matches, showed how Poland could be moved toward the west and at the same time give Russia the frontier which Stalin demanded.

As their talk came to an end, Churchill commented: "I believe that God is on our side. At least I have done my best to make Him a faithful ally." Stalin grinned at the translation.

"And the Devil is on my side," he replied. "Because of course everyone knows that the Devil is a Communist and God, no doubt, is a good Conservative." [14]

In the chat without Roosevelt, Stalin had left the initiative up to Churchill; he had acted as a straight man feeding the lines to the prime minister. Perhaps it was the hour combined with the food, drink, and the long day, but Churchill seemed at times to have forgotten the real world in talking about the role of the Soviet Union in the postwar period. With Hitler destroyed, how could three armies keep the peace? Was friendship alone to make the difference? Churchill may have imagined that he had to reassure Stalin that the Soviet Union would be trusted to play a major role in maintaining peace and not be left out of the international affairs as had happened after the Bolsheviks seized power in 1917.

By taking the initiative on the question of Poland, Churchill brought out into the open the question that had troubled Roosevelt and Hopkins because of political repercussions in the United States. But Churchill and Eden knew how much Stalin wished this matter to be settled. They knew how very important it was to him. And yet Stalin had volunteered little except the remark about the Oder River—which would prove prophetic.

12
The Battle Renewed

In Washington on the morning of November 29, the Senate Military Affairs Committee prepared to learn if any other incidents had taken place similar to that notorious incident when General George S. Patton had slapped a soldier's face in an Army hospital in Sicily. The committee was considering Patton's nomination to the rank of permanent major general.

But the war news was grim that day. In Italy, the Fifth Army had made its first gain in two weeks—all of two miles. The Allied armies were still seventy-seven miles from Rome. Out in the Pacific, Marines were securing Tarawa atoll even as the American public learned of the heavy casualties suffered in the operation.

In Berlin, Dr. Paul Joseph Goebbels, Hitler's propaganda minister, had notified the German people that for the moment Allied air attacks constituted the most acute problem for the Third Reich. But the German morale, he declared, would never crack under such blows. He threatened the Allies with reprisals for their attacks on peaceful towns.

During the night, President Roosevelt had recovered from his attack of indigestion and so it had not been necessary to cancel the conference. In Teheran that morning, a small group of Allied officers assembled in the conference room in the Soviet Embassy. There were the usual military secretaries and interpreters to assist selected members of the Combined Chiefs of Staff, who were detailed to meet with Klementi Voroshilov. It had been agreed that members of the military staffs would meet to consider the timing of operations in the Mediterranean with the proposed invasion of southern France, but there was neither agenda nor directives.

Leading the Americans was the tall, bush-browed Admiral William D. Leahy, a Naval Academy graduate who had first seen action in the Spanish American War. A former governor of Puerto Rico, a former chief of naval operations, and the ex-ambassador to the Vichy government of France, he carried the imposing title of "Chief of Staff to the Commander-in-Chief of the United States Army and Navy."

With Leahy came General George C. Marshall, Army Chief of Staff, graduate of Virginia Military Institute, a brilliant staff officer in World War I who caught the eye of "Blackjack" Pershing and became his personal aide during his term as chief of staff. Thoroughly professional, disciplined, and so aloof and reserved that Roosevelt, who always addressed everyone by first name, only called Marshall "George" once. Congressional respect for Marshall was legendary.

For the British there was the French-born chief of the Imperial Staff, Sir Alan Brooke, veteran of the 1914–18 war and commander of the II Corps in 1940 during the battle of France. An artillery specialist, a brilliant teacher who learned to enjoy pig sticking during his service in India, and a student of ornithology, he often had to handle some of the wilder Churchill plans for carrying on the war. Cool toward the Americans at first, he became friendly with them. The charm and dignity of George Marshall appealed to him.

With Brooke came beak-nosed Air Chief Marshal Sir Charles Portal, chief of the RAF, who had begun his career in World War I as a dispatch rider in the Royal Engineers. In 1915 he obtained a commission as an observer in the Royal Flying Corps, and by war's end he had become a squadron leader in the newly organized Royal Air Force. During most of the Battle of Britain he led Bomber Command, becoming chief of Air Staff in October 1940.

For the Russians there was only Voroshilov, whose military training was decidedly inferior to that of the men meeting with him.

Brooke presented the British view of the war in relation to OVERLORD. He argued that because OVERLORD could not be mounted until May 1, during the intervening five to six months some means must be found to engage the German divisions by taking advantage of the Allied forces that were in the Mediterranean area. Operations in Italy were intended to keep German divisions there and to wear them down. The present plan was to drive the Germans north of Rome and to use amphibious forces to strike around the flanks. The German troubles in Yugoslavia should be increased by sending assistance to the Partisan forces under Tito. Brooke repeated Churchill's arguments in favor of the entrance of Turkey into the war and described the resulting benefits to the Allied cause. But in order to open communications through the Dardanelles, Brooke observed, it would be necessary to capture some of the Dodecanese Islands, beginning with Rhodes. Landing craft for all of these operations would have to be retained in the Mediterranean, which meant delaying OVERLORD. These operations which Brooke had described, combined with other amphibious operations in Italy, would help to hold German forces in the Mediterranean while preparations were under way for OVERLORD.

Brooke did not agree with Stalin's view that the invasion of southern France should be launched two months before OVERLORD because if that were attempted, the Allied forces would be driven into the sea. Both operations ought to be carried out about the same time. To Brooke, the dangerous period in OVERLORD would occur during the buildup of the forces after the initial landings. "It was essential," he concluded, "that the Germans should not be in a position during that build-up period to concentrate in too great numbers against the landing."[1] Now came Marshall's turn.

He reminded Voroshilov that the United States was carrying on a war on two fronts, Pacific and Atlantic. But he found the United States in a dilemma because although there was neither a lack of troops nor a lack of supplies, there was a lack of shipping and landing craft. The United States had fifty divisions which it wanted to deploy as soon as possible. Air forces were being sent overseas as soon as they had been trained. Consequently, a reason for favoring OVERLORD from the start had been that it was the shortest overseas transport route. Once landings had been made in France, transports could be sent directly from U.S. ports to France.

The question to be decided: What would be done in the next three to six months? Marshall argued with Brooke over the question of the timing of the invasion of southern France with OVERLORD, but he warned that if operations were undertaken in the Mediterranean, OVERLORD would be delayed because of the shortage of shipping and landing craft, not to mention fighter aircraft which would be needed to give protection in all of these landing operations. He reminded Voroshilov that the United States was engaged in landing operations in five different places in the Pacific and four were planned for January. All would require landing craft.

Marshall was followed by Air Chief Marshal Sir Charles Portal, who commented briefly on the air war in Europe which was forcing the Germans to concentrate between 1,650 and 1,700 fighters on the defense of Germany and leaving only about 750 planes for other fronts. He hoped the time would come when Russian air forces could be spared from the land battle to join in attacking German industrial targets.

It was Voroshilov's turn. He had a few questions for Marshall and Brooke. First, what was being done to solve the problem of shipping and landing craft in order that OVERLORD would be launched on time? His next question was aimed at the British qualms about OVERLORD. Did Brooke consider OVERLORD "to be an operation of the first importance?" Did he think the operation to be necessary? Should it be replaced by another operation if Turkey entered the war?

Marshall replied that the United States was preparing for OVERLORD with a target date of May 1, 1944. Already one million tons of supplies were in England ahead of the troops. Now they had to bring the number of troops up to the supplies. Marshall repeated that the problem was landing craft. Should landing craft be taken away from OVERLORD and thus delay the operation? It had to be done if operations were to be launched elsewhere.

Brooke, forced to wait his turn to retort, announced that the "British had always attached the greatest importance to this operation and considered it an essential part of the war. The stipulation that had been laid down was that the operation must be undertaken at a moment when it offered chances of success." The entire British army in the United Kingdom had been reorganized for OVERLORD. But as Marshall had already stated, landing craft was the essential problem. If the May 1 date must be kept, then landing craft would have to be withdrawn from the Mediterranean and operations in Italy would come to a standstill. To the British, this was most undesirable because such operations were necessary not only to hold the maximum number of divisions from proceeding to the Russian front but also to make OVERLORD possible in 1944. During the preparations for OVERLORD it was essential to keep on fighting the Germans to the maximum possible extent.

Voroshilov was not yet satisfied. Did General Brooke as the chief of the Imperial General Staff consider OVERLORD to be as important an operation as General Marshall had indicated that he did? Voroshilov wanted Brooke's personal opinion.

Brooke's patience was indeed being tested. As chief of the Imperial General Staff he considered Operation OVERLORD to be of vital importance. But he had one stipulation. Because he knew the strength of the defenses in northern France, he did not want to see the operation fail. And if the circumstances were not right, OVERLORD was bound to fail.

Voroshilov proceeded to express the Russian point of view. Stalin and the Soviet General Staff regarded the operation in northern France as very serious and difficult; but the experience of the British and American forces, the action of their air forces over Germany, their extensive preparations, their naval strength, and the Allied superiority in the Mediterranean, added to the will and desire of the British and American staffs, would all combine to make OVERLORD a success. "It would go down in history as one of our greatest victories."

He agreed with Brooke that smaller operations in the Mediterranean would be necessary to divert the Germans and to draw troops from the Russian front and from northern France. But OVERLORD must be considered as the most important operation; other auxiliary operations must not be allowed to interfere. Operations in Italy and elsewhere in the

Mediterranean must be considered of secondary importance because, from these areas, Germany could not be attacked directly with the Alps in the way. Stalin insisted that the operation against northern France should take place in the manner and on the date already agreed.

As for the Channel crossing, in Voroshilov's view it was "more difficult than the crossing of the big river, but somewhat similar." In their recent operations, the Russian forces had crossed several large rivers even though the Germans had defended them from reinforced concrete fortifications on higher western banks. Concentrated fire from machine guns, mortars, and artillery had overcome the German defenses. He advised Brooke and Marshall that with similar tactics the difficulties in the cross-Channel operation could be easily overcome.

Brooke fought to keep his temper under control. It was not a question of whether or not OVERLORD would be launched in 1944—that had definitely been decided. But the operations in the Mediterranean—which were secondary in nature—had been coordinated in the overall war plan and laid out with their eventual influence on the eastern front and OVERLORD clearly in mind. The Channel crossing had been studied for years, but there were technical difficulties such as long shelving beaches that made landing operations difficult: Calais was one of the worst. Exercises had even been carried out in the Channel in hopes of luring the German Luftwaffe out for battle, but the Germans refused the bait.

Marshall pointed out that failure to cross a river was a reverse, but the failure of an attempted landing by sea would be a catastrophe because of the heavier losses of men and equipment. To which Voroshilov announced that he frankly disagreed. Marshall, too, would be frank. His military education had been based on roads, rivers, and railroads, but during the last two years he had had to acquire an education in oceans. Before the war the only landing craft that he had known about was a rubber boat. Now he thought of nothing else.

The last word belonged to Voroshilov, who finished his lecture on how to achieve a successful landing on the beaches of northern France. The landing should be conducted just like a land battle: Destroy the enemy, then land small parties of troops and follow up with the main force. The result would not be a catastrophe but a brilliant success. It was then agreed that they would meet again the next morning at ten-thirty.

Voroshilov's tactlessness had been exceeded only by his conceited ignorance of what the crossing of the Channel and the invasion of France involved. But he was really there to probe, to learn how committed were the Combined Chiefs to OVERLORD. His questions revealed particular interest in British intentions. His report to Stalin could certainly have contained no surprises. Later Stalin decided that there was really no need for this group to meet again.

By now Churchill had reason for being displeased because Roosevelt and Stalin seemed to be lining up against him. Already they had conferred together privately. To shore up his position with Roosevelt, Churchill asked for a luncheon meeting before the second plenary session. Roosevelt refused since he did not want any report to reach Stalin that he and Churchill were conferring privately and hatching up some scheme aimed at him. When he heard of Roosevelt's refusal, Churchill muttered, "It is not like him." [2]

Roosevelt may have already realized that the Soviet servants who waited on him were actually NKVD agents. Their reports of any conversations between the President and the prime minister would only fuel Stalin's suspicions. Moreover, Roosevelt knew how far he could go with Churchill but he was uncertain about how far he dared go with Stalin without creating distrust, which he wanted to avoid at all costs. To appease Stalin's suspicions, Churchill would have to forgo private meetings with Roosevelt. Averell Harriman had the task of informing Churchill that the President had refused a luncheon meeting with him.

"I shall insist on one thing: that I be host at dinner tomorrow evening," Churchill told Harriman. "I think I have one or two claims to precedence. To begin with, I come first both in seniority and alphabetically. In the second place, I represent the longest established of the three governments. And in the third place, tomorrow happens to be my birthday." [3]

* * *

After luncheon, Roosevelt sent Harriman to the Soviet Embassy office, probably with his request for another meeting with Stalin. Then he held a short meeting with the Joint Chiefs of Staff in which they reported to him on their views about the invasion of southern France. They also gave him their memoranda on steps to be taken in advance of the Soviet entry into the war against Japan.

At 2:45 P.M. Stalin arrived for his second private meeting with the President. Again to maintain the atmosphere of intimacy, each man brought only his interpreter. Roosevelt handed Stalin a report from an American officer who had spent six months in Yugoslavia living with Tito and observing his forces, the Partisans, in action. The author, Major Linn M. Farish, was ecstatic in his praise for the qualities of the Yugoslav fighters, and called for improved methods of supplying the Partisans, chiefly by air. He explained that the Yugoslavs were sympathetic to the United States and believed steadfastly that they would come to their aid. Farish made no reference to aid from the Soviet Union.[4]

Stalin thanked Roosevelt for the report and promised to return it after he had read it. Although he probably read the report, he never returned it, and he never commented on it for the rest of the conference. Certainly Stalin preferred as little Allied intervention as possible in this area. He would let others bring up this subject.

Next, Roosevelt handed Stalin a memorandum dealing with a subject that had been proposed at the Moscow Conference: making air bases available in the Soviet Union where American bombers could be refueled, repaired if necessary, and rearmed in order to shuttle back and forth across Germany bombing selected targets. The foreign ministers had also proposed a more effective interchange of weather information and an improvement in air and signal communications between the United States and the Soviet Union. Roosevelt understood that the Soviet government had agreed in principle to these proposals and that the appropriate Soviet authorities would be instructed to meet with the American military mission in Moscow to consider the measures necessary for carrying out the proposals.

Then Roosevelt expressed his happiness in hearing Stalin's words about the Soviet Union joining in the defeat of Japan after the victory over Germany. As they must prepare for that eventuality by advance planning, he was giving Stalin two papers on planning for air and naval operations in the northwestern Pacific. In the first paper, Roosevelt requested that after the Soviet Union had commenced hostilities with Japan, U.S. bombers should attack Japan from bases in the maritime provinces of Russia. To that end, he and the Joint Chiefs wished that the American military mission in Moscow receive information about airports, housing, supplies, communications, and weather in these provinces, where it was hoped to base four-engine bombers and their crews. Planning ought to begin immediately.

In his second paper, Roosevelt requested that arrangements be made for the exchange of information and for appropriate preliminary planning for Soviet operations against Japan after the defeat of Germany. He also requested combat intelligence information about Japan; he asked about the possibility of basing Soviet Far Eastern submarine and destroyer forces at U.S. bases and about the extent of aid that might be forthcoming if the U.S. forces attacked the Kurile Islands. Finally, he asked for information about Soviet ports that American naval forces might use. All of these questions could be discussed with the American military mission in Moscow whenever Stalin found it appropriate.

Roosevelt had asked Stalin directly about these technical matters because in Moscow American officials had learned that such information could never be elicited from cautious Soviet bureaucrats. It could only come from the very top. But Stalin never discussed these matters with Roosevelt at Teheran because the information could not be given lightly, even to the President of the United States. Later, however, Stalin agreed to take up these questions in Moscow with Harriman.

(In 1944, Stalin granted permission to the U.S. Army Air Corps to use three bases in the Soviet Union for shuttle bombing of Germany from June to September 1944. But after Soviet forces had advanced into eastern Europe, shuttle bombing from bases within the Soviet Union was forbidden. Stalin never permitted American bombers to be based in the

Soviet Maritime Province, and when the Soviet Union finally entered the war against Japan, such bases were unnecessary. In spite of the efforts of Harriman and the American military mission in Moscow, Soviet officers evaded all meaningful discussions about joint planning for the Soviet entry into the war against Japan.)

Changing the subject, Roosevelt said that there were many matters relating to the future of the world which he wished to talk over informally with the Marshal and to obtain his views on. He was willing to discuss any military or political subject Stalin wished. Here Roosevelt hoped that Stalin would at last divulge his suspicions of the capitalist Americans or confess his unhappiness with Soviet-American relations. It was for an opportunity like this that Roosevelt had traveled so far in wartime. He waited for Stalin to voice his suspicions and to list his complaints. But Stalin replied only that "there was nothing to prevent them from discussing anything they wished." It was up to Roosevelt to propose the next topic.

So Roosevelt launched into a description of a postwar organization to preserve peace. His plan involved first a general organization, composed of thirty-five members of the United Nations that would meet periodically to discuss problems and to make recommendations to a smaller body. He also proposed an Executive Committee composed of Soviet Russia, the United States, the United Kingdom, and China, along with two additional European states, a state in South America, one in the Mideast, one in the Far East, and one British dominion. Churchill objected to this proposal, Roosevelt added, because the British Empire had only two votes. The Executive Committee would deal with nonmilitary questions, involving agriculture, food, health, and the economy.

Stalin asked if this committee would have the right to make decisions binding on the nations of the world. Roosevelt answered, "Yes and no." The committee could make recommendations for the settlement of disputes and hope that the nations involved would accept the recommendations. But he doubted that Congress would accept the decisions of this committee as binding on the United States.

Roosevelt proposed a third organization, "The Four Policemen," composed of the Soviet Union, United States, Great Britain, and China. This body would have the power to deal immediately with any threat to the peace and any sudden emergency that required action. He envisioned using it in a crisis such as the Italo-Ethiopian War, when he had begged the French to close the Suez Canal but they did nothing except refer the matter to the League of Nations, "which disputed the question and in the end did nothing." With his "Four Policemen," Roosevelt believed that it would have been possible to have closed the Suez Canal.

Stalin thought the small nations of Europe would object to the "Four Policemen," and in particular to China. He doubted that China would be a very powerful state after the war. Stalin suggested that there should be a Far Eastern committee and a European committee with Britain, Russia, and the United States as members.

Roosevelt pointed out that Churchill had proposed a similar arrangement of regional committees—one for Europe, one for the Far East, and one for the Americas—with the United States being a member of the European committee. He doubted if Congress would agree to membership in a European committee that might order the dispatch of U.S. forces to Europe. It would take a war, he thought, before Congress would agree to such a step.

Stalin argued that the proposed world organization and the concept of the "Four Policemen" would require the dispatch of American troops to Europe. Roosevelt backtracked. He was thinking only of sending American planes and ships to Europe; Britain and Russia would have to supply the troops to keep the peace. He admitted that it would have been impossible to send American troops to Europe without the Japanese attack on Pearl Harbor.

To deal with threats to the peace of the world, Roosevelt suggested two methods. In case of a revolution or a crisis in a small country, the quarantine method: closing frontiers and imposing embargoes. In a more serious crisis, the "Four Policemen" would have to send an ultimatum and upon refusal, bombard the defiant nation, and, if necessary, invade it.

Stalin brought up his discussion with Churchill about protection against Germany, which had occurred the previous evening after Roosevelt had gone to bed. He had found Churchill much too optimistic about the threat of a revival of German strength, believing that Germany would not rise again. Unless prevented, Stalin declared, Germany would recover within fifteen to twenty years. Consequently, "we must have something more serious than the type of organization proposed by the President." He reminded Roosevelt that the first German aggression had come in 1870, and forty-four years later in World War I, but only twenty-one years had elapsed between the close of the last war and the opening of the present one. Stalin did not believe that in the future the revival of German strength would take a longer period, and as a result, the organizations the President had outlined were inadequate.

Stalin stressed the need to occupy certain strongpoints either within Germany, along the German borders, or at some more distant point in order to ensure that Germany could not once more embark on the path of aggression. He suggested Dakar as a possible area to be occupied. It would also be necessary to occupy strategic positions in the Far East as well, in order to prevent Japan from starting another war. The commission created to preserve peace ought to have the right to occupy strongpoints near Germany and Japan. Here Roosevelt was in one hundred percent agreement with the Marshal. Stalin was dubious about China participating, but Roosevelt explained that he was thinking of the future because it would be better to have China friendly than a "potential source of trouble."

Roosevelt next turned to Stalin's statement, made at the first plenary meeting, that furniture factories could be transformed into airplane factories and watch factories could manufacture fuses for shells. The President felt that a strong organization of the four powers would react quickly to any sign that factories were being converted to the manufacture of weapons. Stalin replied that the Germans were very able at concealing the beginnings of converting factories to military purposes. Roosevelt had to agree with him and also with his idea of placing strategic positions at the disposal of a world organization to halt the revival of German and Japanese aggression.

Their talk at an end, both men now left for an important ceremony in the conference room.

Once more Stalin had revealed little of his suspicions or his distrust of the western powers. He still had not opened up to Roosevelt about his plans and hopes for the future. Again he had left the initiative to Roosevelt. Throughout their talk, the Marshal had been reserved except on the question of Germany whose revival he certainly feared. His idea of occupying specific points within or close to Germany implied Soviet military units stationed in central Europe, a prospect which did not seem to trouble Roosevelt. Instead, the President had labored to show his eagerness for Soviet Russia to be a force in the postwar world. Soviet Russia would be welcomed, not kept in isolation. Soviet Russia would enter into the inner circle of the great powers, the "Four Policemen," charged with keeping peace in the world. Stalin certainly had knowledge of Roosevelt's concept of the "Four Policemen" because the President had broached the idea to Molotov when he visited Washington in 1942. By using this device, Roosevelt hoped to avoid the clumsy machinery of the League of Nations, which required unanimous agreement before any action could be taken. And by making Soviet Russia one of the policemen, Roosevelt wanted to involve Stalin in the founding of the postwar peacekeeping organization.

His comments, however, were not always accurate or logical. There was no record that he had ever begged France to close the Suez Canal, which had been operated by Britain. Could the United States act as one of the "Four Policemen" without sending troops to Europe? If only British and Soviet armies could be used as peacekeeping forces, then the larger army would dominate Europe. But accuracy and logic were not important to Roosevelt that afternoon. He was bent on enlisting Stalin in his crusade for a postwar organization that would preserve peace. With this talk, he hoped that he had recruited the Marshal.

Before the day's plenary session, Churchill, under instructions from King George VI, was to present a sword to Stalin which the king had ordered specially designed and constructed to commemorate the defense of the city of Stalingrad. It was four feet long, with a blade of tempered steel, and a hilt of silver with leopard heads at the end. The scabbard was covered with crimson Persian lambskin with mounts of wrought silver. On the blade was inscribed in English and in Russian: "To the steelhearted citizens of Stalingrad, the gift of King George VI, in token of the homage of the British people."

Originally it had been planned that the ceremony of presenting the sword would take place outside where the better lighting would permit the event to be recorded on motion pictures. But Stalin vetoed the plan for security reasons, and also perhaps because he did not wish to appear on camera with his capitalist allies.

For the presentation ceremony inside the Soviet embassy, a British guard of honor composed of noncommissioned officers from the Buffs, chosen for their height, stood in line with fixed bayonets on their rifles. On the opposite side of the room was a Soviet guard of honor, all over six feet in height, dressed in black boots, dark blue trousers, khaki tunics, and with tommy guns slung across their chests. Between the two lines of soldiers was a round table on which lay the sword.

Churchill entered dressed in the uniform of an air commodore, followed by Anthony Eden and the British chiefs of staff. Churchill stopped beside the table. Everyone awaited the entrance of Stalin. Dressed in a marshal's uniform with a single star on the breast, he entered, his face impassive, his movements slow and solemn. Stalin was followed by Voroshilov, Molotov, and Pavlov, one of the Soviet interpreters. Roosevelt was wheeled into the room, and sat at one end watching the ceremony. The American chiefs of staff stood quietly along the wall behind Roosevelt.

A Soviet army band struck up the "Internationale," followed by "God Save the King," as Churchill and Stalin saluted. A British lieutenant handed the sword to Churchill, who presented it to Stalin. Churchill said that he had been commanded by King George VI, who had chosen and approved the design of the sword, to present the sword to Stalin for transmission to the city of Stalingrad. Churchill then read the inscription. Stalin expressed his deep appreciation for the gift, and he asked Churchill to convey the thanks of the people of Stalingrad to King George VI. Looking deeply moved, Stalin accepted the sword, kissed the hilt, then handed it to Voroshilov and as he did so, lowered the hilt of the sword toward the floor. The heavy sword, carefully forged by English craftsmen, slid smoothly out of its jeweled scabbard. Voroshilov (other observers reported that he was drunk) caught the weapon inches from the floor and clasped it to his chest. He handed it to a Russian officer, who marched smartly out of the room bearing the sword shoulder high accompanied by four Russian soldiers.

With the ceremony ended, the "Big Three," their generals, admirals, and diplomats, trooped out onto the front portico of the Soviet Embassy. There they posed with Stalin, ironically, seated on Roosevelt's right and Churchill on his left, while American, British, and Russian military photographers recorded the event for history. The picture-taking session so moved Admiral Leahy that he wrote: "I felt this meeting at Teheran might be recorded in history as being comparable to the Field of the Cloth of Gold, with this difference—the surroundings offered little pageant but, instead, much suffering and squalor."[5]

After everyone had returned to the conference room and was once more seated about the round table, the second plenary session began. Roosevelt and Stalin both asked for a report on the military discussions. Brooke reported that the committee had not finished its work but that it had surveyed various operations and examined OVERLORD. Marshall added little except to underline the problems that concerned the United States: ships, landing craft, and sufficient airfields close to the scene of operations. Voroshilov explained that his questions had been answered but that no date had been specified for OVERLORD. The details of that operation would be considered at the next meeting of the military committee.

Stalin suddenly changed the subject. "Who was going to command OVERLORD?"[6]

"The matter has not yet been decided," Roosevelt replied.

"In that case," Stalin answered, "nothing will come of Operation OVERLORD. Who bears the moral and military responsibility for the preparation and execution of Operation OVERLORD? If that is unknown, then Operation OVERLORD is just so much talk."

Roosevelt explained that General Frederick Morgan had been made responsible for preparing the plans for OVERLORD. But Stalin was not satisfied.

"Who is responsible for carrying out Operation OVERLORD?"

"We know the men who will take part in carrying out Operation OVERLORD, with the exception of the commander-in-chief of the operation," answered the President. He sat next to Admiral Leahy, and leaning over whispered to him, "That old Bolshevik is trying to force me to give him the name of our Supreme Commander. I just can't tell him because I have not yet made up my mind."[7] Stalin remained dissatisfied. General Morgan, he argued, might consider that he had completed the task of preparing the operation, but the commander-in-chief could consider that the operation was not prepared. There had to be someone responsible both for preparing and executing the operation. Churchill explained that he and Roosevelt had agreed on the appointment of Morgan. The British government had expressed willingness to place their forces under an American commander for Operation OVERLORD because the United States would be responsible for the buildup of the invasion forces and would have a preponderance in numbers of troops. The command in the Mediterranean would go to a British officer because most of the naval forces were British and there was a predominance of British troops there. The choice of the supreme commander was a matter for decision by the three heads of government, and not by such a large conference. Churchill was hinting at the presence in the room of General George C. Marshall, who was still thought to be in line for the appointment as Supreme Allied Commander of Operation OVERLORD.

But neither Roosevelt nor Churchill would please Stalin. "I should like it to be understood that the Russians do not claim participation in the appointment of the commander-in-chief, but the Russians would like to know who is going to be the commander. The Russians would like him to be appointed soon, and would like to see him responsible for the preparations as well as for the carrying out of Operation OVERLORD." Churchill, agreeing quickly with Stalin's blunt declaration, promised a decision would be reached within a fortnight.

Then the prime minister embarked on a lengthy defense of the case which he had been pleading. He and his chiefs of staff were concerned about the prospect of the British army in the Mediterranean lying passive for six months. What help could then be given to OVERLORD by these forces? He wanted landing craft for two divisions to be kept in the Mediterranean—a landing force that would help the advance up the leg of Italy through flanking movements. These landing craft could help in the capture of Rhodes and would open up the Aegean Sea when Turkey entered the war. Such a force would also aid the invasion of southern France in conjunction with Operation OVERLORD. However, the landing craft for the two divisions could not be retained in the Mediterranean without setting back the date of OVERLORD for six to eight weeks or recalling the assault craft that had already been sent to the Far East to be used against the Japanese. Churchill wanted the advice of Stalin and Voroshilov on this question.

Turning to the topic of Yugoslavia, Churchill moved to an area dearer to Stalin. The prime minister told Stalin that "we had no interest in the Balkans of an exceptional or ambitious kind." He only wanted to nail down the thirty divisions, German and Bulgarian, that were in Greece and Yugoslavia; on this matter, the British wanted to work harmoniously with the Russians. Therefore, why should not Eden and Molotov meet with a representative or Roosevelt on the question?

As for Turkey, Churchill wanted Eden, Molotov, and the presidential representative to meet and to advise the conference on the best way to bring Turkey into the war. Such a development would be a "terrible blow to Germany" because it would weaken Bulgaria. Already Rumania wanted to surrender and Hungary would be severely punished by such a development.

Churchill declared that the object of the operation in the Mediterranean, which he had been discussing, was to take the weight off Russia and to give the best possible chance to OVERLORD.

It was once more Stalin's turn. As for Turkey entering the war, Yugoslavia being helped, and Rome being captured, these were "relatively unimportant matters," he declared. "If we are prevailed upon here to discuss military questions, we regard Operation OVERLORD as the main and decisive question."

Stalin insisted that the military committee, which had been formed earlier, should be given specific directives. Operation OVERLORD should be carried out; it must not be postponed beyond the limiting date, May 1. Secondly, the attack in southern France should, if possible, precede OVERLORD by two months. If that was impossible, then the landing should be made simultaneously with OVERLORD or later. Thirdly, he urged that the committee take up the appointment of the commander-in-chief of OVERLORD as soon as possible. This was a matter belonging to the President and Churchill, but Stalin wanted it decided while they were at Teheran. "The USSR does not enter into the matter of this selection but the Soviets definitely want to know who he will be."

Roosevelt finally voiced support for Stalin's view. The question was "whether to carry out OVERLORD at the appointed time or possibly postpone it for the sake of other operations in the Mediterranean." He warned that if two or three divisions were to be used in the eastern Mediterranean, they could evolve into larger operations, requiring the landing craft which could not then be withdrawn in time for Operation OVERLORD. Once committed to the eastern Mediterranean, it would not be easy to pull out of the commitment. But aid could be dispatched to Tito without interfering with OVERLORD. He would send commando raids into the Balkans and send supplies to Tito in order to force the Germans to keep divisions in the Balkans. Nothing should be done on such a scale that it would prevent the launching of OVERLORD on the time agreed at Quebec, May 1.

Stalin reinforced Roosevelt's statement about the timing.

He thought it a good idea to carry out Operation OVERLORD in May, May 10, or the 15th, or the 20th, but he wanted a definite date. As for the operations in the Mediterranean, "they were really only diversions."

Desperately, Churchill tried to rebut the arguments that were being mounted against him. The possibilities in the Mediterranean must not be sacrificed "as if valueless merely on the issue of a month or so for the launching of Operation OVERLORD."

Churchill came to the heart of his case. As agreed at the Moscow Conference, the success of OVERLORD depended on three conditions: (1) a reduction in German fighter strength must be achieved in northwestern Europe before the assault; (2) German reserves in the area should not amount to more than twelve divisions on the day of the assault; (3) during the first sixty days of the operation, the Germans must not be able to transfer more than fifteen divisions from other fronts. In order to achieve these conditions, as many Germans as possible must be held in Italy and in Yugoslavia. If Turkey entered the war, that would help. If the Allies slacked off in Italy, the Germans would return the troops to France from whence they had come. "If we engaged them as fiercely as possible during the winter months in the Mediterranean this would make the best possible contribution towards creating the conditions desired, which would enable OVERLORD to be successfully carried out." Churchill rehearsed the argument about involving Turkey in the war and taking the island of Rhodes. After taking Rhodes, it would be possible to push the Germans out of the other Aegean Islands and move British troops northward from Egypt. He warned that if landing craft could not be retained in the Mediterranean for these operations or found elsewhere, operations on any scale in the Mediterranean would be impossible, including the assault on southern France. Churchill proposed that the two foreign secretaries meet with Hopkins to discuss political problems, and that the three leaders draft directives for the military committee to consider.

Stalin asked: "How long do we intend to stay at Teheran?"

"I am prepared to stop eating until these directives are

worked out," replied Churchill, according to the Russian version of the minutes.

"What I mean," replied Stalin, "is when shall we end our conference?"

Roosevelt declared: "I am prepared to stay at Teheran as long as Marshal Stalin remains at Teheran."

"If it is necessary," Churchill announced, "I am prepared to stay in Teheran for good."

But Stalin was not prepared to stay that long. He had reconsidered his position. The issues were: "The date of OVERLORD, the appointment of the commander-in-chief and whether any supporting operations could be carried out in the south of France." The three leaders could decide these questions. There was no need for a commission of foreign secretaries. Nor would he stay there forever. "We Russians are limited in our time of stay at Teheran. We could stay on until December 1, but we have to leave on the 2nd. The President will recall that we agreed on three or four days." Stalin had been outside the Soviet Union long enough and wanted to return to the safety of the Kremlin.

Roosevelt proposed a directive for the military committee composed of the chiefs of staff and Voroshilov. The committee should assume that OVERLORD would be the dominating operation in 1944; it should make recommendations about any subsidiary operations in the Mediterranean, taking into consideration that any delay should not affect OVERLORD. He needed to know the date in order for the Soviet forces to prepare for an attack against the Germans. Roosevelt insisted that the date for OVERLORD had been fixed at Quebec and only some other extremely important matter should change that date.

Once more Churchill plunged into battle. Both committees should meet. He wanted time to consider the proposed directive presented by Roosevelt. Churchill had his own directive for the military committee. It should consider the timing of OVERLORD with regard to any subsidiary operations which might be undertaken to create the conditions that would be necessary for the success of OVERLORD and that would help to keep as much weight off Russia as possible during the period before the assault. The committee should recommend subsidiary operations.

Stalin had had enough. He saw no need for a military committee to reach decisions on matters that would have to be dealt with by the three heads of government, who had more power than the committee. He had an indiscreet question to ask Churchill. "I should like to know whether the British believe in Operation OVERLORD or simply speak of it to reassure the Russians?"

Now it was out in the open. He had challenged Churchill to say publicly if the British were really willing to follow through with OVERLORD. Churchill glowered at Stalin as he heard the translation, chomped on his cigar, then replied: "If the conditions set forth at Moscow were present it was the duty of the British government to hurl every scrap of strength across the Channel."

Sensing the sudden tension in the room, Roosevelt interrupted. "We are very hungry now, and I propose that we adjourn to attend the dinner given us today by Marshal Stalin." He wanted the military committee to meet the next day, but Stalin vetoed the idea—"superfluous." But he would concede that the British and American staffs could meet to seek an agreed recommendation for the conference.

Churchill inquired about the foreign secretaries meeting with Hopkins. Stalin shot back: "This committee is not required either. But if Mr. Churchill insists, we do not object to its formation." It was agreed that the next plenary session would take place at four o'clock the following afternoon, November 30. Roosevelt, Churchill, and Stalin would lunch together while the foreign secretaries and Hopkins lunched separately. The session ended at last. The British provided tea and cream for everyone.

In his diary, Brooke recorded his view of the afternoon's work:

> Bad from beginning to end. Winston was not good and Roosevelt was even worse! Stalin meticulous with only two arguments—Cross Channel operations on 1st May, also offensive in southern France!
>
> Americans supported this view quite unaware of the fact that it is already an impossibility. . . .
>
> I have little hope of any form of agreement in discussion. After listening to the arguments put forward

during the last two days I feel more like entering a lunatic asylum, or nursing home, than continuing my present job.

I am absolutely disgusted with the politicians' methods of waging war. Why will they imagine they are experts at a job they know nothing about! It is lamentable to listen to them!

May God help us in the future prosecution of this war, we have every hope of making an unholy mess of it and of being defeated yet![8]

Clearly, Stalin had dominated the meeting that afternoon, forcing Churchill on the defensive and compelling Roosevelt to forsake Churchill lest he antagonize Stalin. It was a stellar performance as Stalin played the role of the resolute leader who knew what he wanted and intended to get it, even from Allies. Most of his audience was impressed by his performance. In his journal, General Arnold revealed the effect on him:

Stalin, the man of steel, fearless, brilliant mind, quick of thought and repartee, ruthless—a great leader, courage of his convictions as indicated by his bold humorous, half scathing remarks about the British— the P.M. and Brooke. I doubt if either was ever talked to like that before.[9]

Ismay saw another facet of Stalin:

His expression was inscrutable as the Sphinx and it was impossible to know what he was thinking about. He did not speak much, but his interventions, made in a quiet voice and without any gestures, were direct and decided. Sometimes they were so abrupt as to be rude. He left no doubt in anyone's mind that he was master in his own house.[10]

To Brooke, Stalin had a "military brain of the very highest caliber." In none of his statements "did he make any strategic error nor did he ever fail to appreciate all the implications of a situation with a quick and unerring eye."[11] George Marshall's opinions of Stalin mirrored those of Brooke—"I found the Generalissimo a very astute negotiator. He had a dry wit. . . . When it came to the exact discussion of the military phases, Stalin was reasonably precise. . . ." In negotiations, Marshall thought Stalin ought not to be treated as if he were a product of the diplomatic service. "He was a rough SOB who made his way by murder and everything else and should be talked to that way."[12] Admiral Cunningham tended to agree: "I was impressed; but conceived an instinctive dislike . . . he gave me a feeling of unease and distrust."[13] And Stalin impressed the irascible Admiral King. "Stalin," he said later, "knew just what it was he wanted when he came to Teheran—and he got it." According to King, "Our people came out of these meetings much impressed with Stalin, who was appraised as a cool, calm, extremely realistic man who had no time for non-essentials."[14]

Stalin's performance had been masterful. He had played the role of the decisive, cool-headed statesman and strategist. There had been no indication of the stubborn bungler whose refusal to permit troops to withdraw from hopeless positions had caused the needless slaughter of Russian soldiers. No sign either of the sadist who made wives and children of his opponents suffer or of the tyrant who had unleashed a reign of terror that liquidated the leadership of the Soviet armed forces and in so doing gave immeasurable aid to Adolf Hitler.

Throughout the afternoon, Stalin's tone had been generally matter of fact even though the OVERLORD operation was of intense interest to him. He seldom gestured and never displayed any agitation. Rarely consulting Molotov or Voroshilov, he sat quietly, speaking softly, doodling wolf heads on a pad with a red pencil and smoking black Russian cigarettes in two-inch cardboard tubes. His doodlings became the most sought-after souvenirs of the conference.

Stalin's demand that a commander be named for OVERLORD was on target. A commander with the necessary authority to organize the invasion force would have speeded up the process and perhaps have been able to launch the invasion at an earlier date. Much of the delay in getting OVER-

LORD under way had hinged on the choice of commander. Part of the reason had been Anglo-American politics: Would the commander be British or American? At one time Brooke had been Churchill's candidate for the post. But Roosevelt, sensing opposition from congressional quarters to the prospect of an Englishman commanding a force in which American troops predominated, got Churchill to accept the idea of an American general. George Marshall was the obvious candidate, but Roosevelt was loath to lose him as chief of staff. To solve that problem, an American proposal had been drafted for Marshall to command OVERLORD but still continue as the chief of staff. In the second capacity he would also continue as a member of the Combined Chiefs of Staff—an arrangement that would mean he would issue orders to himself! Not only was Marshall to command OVERLORD but he would have overall command of all Allied operations in Europe, including the Mediterranean. By giving Marshall such command, he would be able to block the launching of any British "sideshows" in the Mediterranean such as Rhodes.

Churchill was willing to have an American officer commanding OVERLORD but he insisted that a British officer command in the Mediterranean. Roosevelt was still loath to lose Marshall. To have him step down as chief of staff in order to command OVERLORD would be considered as a demotion in the halls of Congress. Roosevelt the politician was waiting until circumstances forced him to name a commander. Now Stalin was doing his best to force that decision on the President.

For Churchill, it had been another bad afternoon. Both Stalin and Roosevelt were lined up against him. During the meeting, the President had not once supported him but remained silent while Stalin demolished Churchill's case, which he had not argued well. Perhaps part of the fault was his health. Churchill was having difficulty talking because he was fighting a cold that would ultimately turn into pneumonia. In his long speech he had mentioned almost everything but OVERLORD: Turkey, Bulgaria, Yugoslavia, and Rhodes. But he dared not mention the fear that lay on his mind: casualties and another Dunkirk, which would have immense political repercussions in Britain. By continuing operations in the

Mediterranean there would perhaps be less potential for heavy British losses. Churchill did not want to commit Britain irrevocably to OVERLORD until there was no alternative.

Roosevelt had sat silent for most of the session, listening, choosing not to intervene on Churchill's side. Roosevelt did not even mediate. His silence was more potent than any comment he could have made. He preferred that Stalin wear down Churchill. Any intervention on Churchill's side could lead Stalin to suspect that the pair were ganging up on him. By his silence Roosevelt tried to signal Stalin that he had no reason to quarrel with the President but that his real opponent was that old British imperialist.

The conference had reached a crisis. Stalin sensed that Roosevelt would not support Churchill on OVERLORD. His threat to end the conference forthwith unless Churchill relented on the date was aimed at shocking Roosevelt into pressuring the prime minister to give way before Stalin's demands. One ally sought to use another ally against Churchill, who was stalling, unwilling to settle on a fixed date for OVERLORD because that would mean no turning aside for "sideshows." The commander would be appointed, the plans would be made, the troops would be trained, and one day they would embark on schedule for a landing on the coasts of France. The casualties would follow—and Churchill's political future could be in jeopardy.

Much of the responsibility for the afternoon's argument was Roosevelt's. His desire not to offend Stalin by making an agreement beforehand with Churchill had helped produce this farce. Roosevelt and Churchill should have agreed on the commander of OVERLORD long before they traveled to Teheran. They had come a long way to endure an argument between Stalin and the prime minister which Churchill had not won. Worse was to follow later that evening.

It was Stalin's turn to be the host at the dinner for the other two leaders. Even though it was wartime and people in Leningrad were starving to death, the quantity and quality of the food provided by the Soviet hosts were awesome. "There were cold hors d'oeuvres to start with, then hot borscht, fish, meat of various kinds, salads, compotes, fruits, vodka, and wines," reported Charles Bohlen.[15] During the entire dinner, a Russian waiter approximately six feet four inches tall stood behind Stalin's chair, dressed in a white jacket. Later, when Roosevelt sent Bohlen with a carton of cigarettes as a gift for the "head waiter," Bohlen found him wearing the uniform of a major general in the NKVD.

During the dinner conversation, Stalin never let slip any opportunity to get in a dig at Churchill. Although outwardly friendly, all of his remarks aimed at Churchill had a nasty bite to them. Stalin wanted to put the prime minister on the defensive. He insinuated that Churchill secretly nursed an affection for Germany and preferred a soft peace. Already Stalin feared a revived Germany, armed and eager once more to plunge Europe into another world conflict. Unless German military revival was prevented, Stalin foresaw a repeat of history. After the debacle of June 1941, he feared and respected German military organization, planning, and production. To Stalin's suspicious mind, Churchill's attitude in the plenary session masked a plot to use revived German militarism as a weapon against the Soviet Union.

During the dinner, Stalin confessed that the Soviet army had been poorly organized for the war against Finland and that it had been necessary for the entire army to be reorganized. He acknowledged that even when Hitler's armies attacked in 1941, the Soviet army was not yet a first-class fighting force. But since the invasion of Russia, the Red Army had improved until it had become a "genuinely good army."

Then the conversation turned to a recurring problem for the three leaders, particularly Stalin: the future treatment of Germany. He repeated his fear that unless the Germans were effectively controlled, they would rise again within fifteen or twenty years and plunge the world into another conflict. To prevent this catastrophe, two conditions must be met. From 50,000 to 100,000 German officers must be liquidated, and the Allies must retain control of strategic points around the world in order to stop German operations. Was Stalin joking about shooting 100,000 German officers? During the Great Purge he had ordered more than 50,000 officers imprisoned or shot without a trial. Would he have any qualms about German officers? Churchill took Stalin seriously.

"The British Parliament and public will never tolerate

mass executions. Even if in war passion they allowed them to begin, they would turn violently against those responsible after the first butchery had taken place. The Soviets must be under delusion on this point," Churchill burst out.

"Fifty thousand," said Stalin in a joking tone, "must be shot."

"I would rather be taken out into the garden here and now and be shot myself than sully my own and my country's honor by such infamy," exclaimed an angry Churchill.[16]

Roosevelt, thinking that he could smooth matters over with a joke of his own, proposed that instead of 50,000 officers being shot, they should shoot only 49,000. By now, Eden, sensing that in his anger Churchill might make remarks he would later regret, tried to signal that it was just a joke.

Stalin, looking around at his guests, asked for estimates on how many should be shot. There were embarrassed mumbles until his question reached Elliott Roosevelt. The President's son had arrived earlier in the day. Although he had not been invited, when he passed by the open door of the dining room, one of the NKVD men pointed him out to Stalin who asked Elliott to come in to dinner. The younger Roosevelt, who had been drinking Russian champagne continually during the numerous toasts, rose unsteadily to his feet.

"Isn't the whole thing pretty academic? Look: when our armies start rolling in from the west, and your armies are still coming on from the east, we'll be solving the whole thing, won't we? Russian, American, and British soldiers will settle the issue for most of those fifty thousand, in battle, and I hope that not only those fifty thousand war criminals will be taken care of, but many hundreds of thousands more Nazis as well." As he started to sit down, a grinning Stalin came around the table, flung his arm round Elliott's shoulders, and congratulated him on his statement.

"Are you interested in damaging relations between the Allies?" cried Churchill in his fury. "Do you know what you are saying? How can you dare say such a thing?" Young Elliott, shocked that he had so aroused Churchill, sat very quietly for the remainder of the evening, worried about the consequences of his drunken remarks.[17]

Those remarks were too much for Churchill. He rose, left

the table, and walked out into the garden even as Eden and Roosevelt once more signaled that it was all a joke. Churchill had not been standing there long when he felt a pair of hands clamped on his shoulders. He turned around and there stood a grinning Stalin with Molotov, who was also grinning, trying to make amends. It was only a joke, they said. It all ended in a convivial embrace with Churchill and Stalin standing with their hands on each other's shoulders looking into one another's eyes while Molotov continued to grin.

Stalin's wish to massacre fifty thousand German officers could be easily passed off as a joke after an evening of drinking. But history would indicate that he was deadly serious. Millions of Soviet citizens had already been put to death; eventually, more than fifty thousand German officers would indeed perish in Soviet Russia.

The men returned to the dining room, Stalin still trying to reassure Churchill.

"You are pro-German," Stalin announced. "The devil is communist, and my friend God a conservative."

"I'd like to go to your front. I'm in my seventieth year," declared Churchill to show that he was not pro-German.

"You need not boast about that," answered Stalin. "I'm in my seventieth year."

Their talk ended in another convivial embrace while Molotov continued his best grin. In remembering this scene, the British ambassador in Moscow, Clark Kerr, observed: "I wish we had a record of what was said, that people might know what piffle great men sometimes talk."[18]

The talk wandered back to the question of strongpoints near Germany and Japan which the President wanted held. Churchill, still agitated over Stalin's remarks, told the President pointedly that Britain had no desire to acquire new bases or territory and intended to hold all that she already had. Nothing would be taken from Britain without war, and he included specifically Singapore and Hong Kong. Churchill conceded that some areas in the British Empire might eventually be granted independence, "entirely by Great Britain herself, in accordance with her own moral precepts." Britain would occupy some bases under trusteeship arrangements but others would have to help pay the cost. His remarks were aimed at Roosevelt, who had listened to Stalin's snide comments and said nothing lest Stalin believe that he was taking sides against him.

Stalin confessed that Britain had fought well and that he would favor an increase in the British Empire. What territories interested the Soviet Union, asked Churchill, to which Stalin replied coldly: "There is no need to speak at the present time about any Soviet desires, but when the time comes, we will speak."[19]

During the evening the conversation turned to the Munich Agreement and the crisis over Czechoslovakia in 1938. Stalin said that he had never believed the Czechoslovaks would fight. This opinion had been reported to him by officers from the Red Air Force who had been sent to Czechoslovakia to consider using Czech bases in the event of war.

When Churchill admitted that after World War I he had done everything possible to prevent the spread of Bolshevism in Europe and the creation of Communist regimes, Stalin commented ironically that Churchill "need not have worried quite so much as the Russians had discovered that it was not so easy to set up Communist regimes."[20]

Filled with food and drink, the diners went their separate ways. Elliott Roosevelt hurried to his father's apartment to apologize for damaging Allied relations. The President roared with laughter. "Don't think a second about it," he said. "What you said was perfectly all right. It was fine. Winston just lost his head when everybody refused to take the subject seriously. Uncle Joe . . . the way he was needling him, he was going to take offense at what anybody said, especially if what was said pleased Uncle Joe. Don't worry, Elliott."

"Because you know . . ." stammered Elliott, "the last thing I'd—"

"Forget it," interrupted his father, laughing again. "Why, Winston will have forgotten all about it when he wakes up."[21]

But Elliott Roosevelt felt that Churchill did not forget the incident. For the remainder of his tour of duty in Britain, he was never again invited to spend a night a Chequers, the prime minister's country home.

Back at the British Embassy in Teheran, the guard of the

Buffs waited to turn out to salute the prime minister when his car passed through the embassy gates. After hours in the cold night air, the signal came: the prime minister's car was approaching down the street. With its usual clash and clatter, the guard turned out, fell in, and presented arms as a large car flying the badge of the Warden of the Cinque Ports drove through the embassy gates. As it was well past midnight, there would be no further need for the guard to salute anyone else coming through the gates, so the guard turned in.

In one of the walls surrounding the British Embassy there was a small wicker gate. A sentry was posted there with others to allow no one through at night. Soon the sentry heard sounds of merriment in the street outside. There were snatches of song, laughter, and oaths when someone stumbled. It sounded as though a couple of drunks were passing by. But then he heard someone banging at the gate. Pointing his rifle he called out: "Halt! Who goes there?"

The reply came: "It's the Prime Minister and Mr. Eden. Let us in!"

The voice sounded like a passable imitation of the famous guttural tone with the well-known lisp. But the sentry had been told that the prime minister had come back to the embassy and passed through the main gate.

"Go on," yelled the guard. "Bug off!"

The voice at the gate became louder and more demanding. A tour of guard duty on a chilly night in Teheran was not the time for practical jokes. "Bug off," the guard shouted. "Who the bloody hell d'you think you're fooling? You heard me—bug off!"

But the voice only became more imperious. The sentry, influenced at last by the tone, lowered his rifle and slowly opened a spy hole in the gate. There in the lamplight he saw two figures supporting each other. One was short and broad and very angry; the other was tall and mustached. The private was extremely frightened.

Apparently Churchill had decided that he needed a breath of fresh air and some exercise before going to bed. He sent his car back to the embassy and together with Eden walked back through the dark streets of Teheran. No disciplinary action was taken against the soldier who had sworn at Winston Churchill and gotten away with it.[22]

Later within the embassy, Lord Moran, Churchill's physician, found the dispirited prime minister slumped in a chair musing on the future of the world.

"There might be a more bloody war. I shall not be there. I shall be asleep. I want to sleep for billions of years. But you will be there. . . . I realize how inadequate we are."

"You mean a war with Russia?" asked Moran.

"Stalin said we ought to take Turkey by the scruff of the neck," Churchill continued his monologue. "I said: 'I think we ought to say to them: you are missing the chance of a lifetime if you do not accept Russia's invitation to be one of the victorious powers at the peace conference. If you don't Russia has several things to settle with you. And we shall take no further interest in Turkey. If Russia has views about the Straits, that will not affect us.' "

For a moment Churchill was silent. "But Russia has not worked out a role for Turkey if she does declare war. That is obvious." Churchill relit his cigar. "The President said to me: 'You may go at the election, but I shan't.' I said, 'Anthony will have to wait.' "

Churchill rambled on. "Stalin was ready to talk about the frontiers of Poland, but I said I had no mandate from the Cabinet nor the President's agreement. So it was left. If present ideas go, there will be a stronger Poland than before the war."

Moran asked if Roosevelt had taken an active part in the conversation.

"Harry Hopkins said the President was inept. He was asked a lot of questions and gave the wrong answers."

Back in his bedroom, Churchill could not shake off his fear of an impending catastrophe. He stopped and looked at Moran. "I believe man might destroy man and wipe out civilization. Europe would be desolate and I may be held responsible."

Then he asked: "Why do I plague my mind with these things? I never used to worry about anything."

His face grave and solemn, he went on: "Stupendous issues are unfolding before our eyes, and we are only specks of dust that have settled in the night on the map of the world. Do you think," he asked Moran, "my strength will last out the war? I fancy sometimes that I am nearly spent." Then he undressed, got into bed, and was soon asleep.[23]

The day's events must have confirmed what Churchill had long predicted. In the presence of Stalin, the two leaders of the democracies were divided. Churchill could not rely on the President to support him against Stalin. What frightened Churchill was that Stalin realized this, too. By playing off one against the other, Stalin could do as he wished and Churchill was impotent to stop him.

Churchill's depression was also deepened by a message Hopkins had brought him after dinner: The prime minister was fighting a losing battle in his campaign to delay the invasion of France. Hopkins advised Churchill to yield gracefully because there was very little that he could do.[24] The Americans had been agreed on the importance of OVERLORD for some time. The Russians were just as obstinate. It was time for Churchill to surrender.

13
The Battle Decided

IN LONDON AND IN WASHINGTON on the morning of November 30, rumors were spreading that a meeting between Roosevelt, Churchill, and Stalin would be held shortly either in Cairo or in Teheran. In Washington, the White House and the State Department said nothing. From London came reports that a declaration of "epochal importance" would be announced shortly, involving demands for Germany's surrender, and it would be signed by Roosevelt, Churchill, and Stalin in their first meeting. From Berlin came word that a conference of the three leaders had opened somewhere in the Middle East. Travelers arriving in Lisbon reported that Roosevelt and Churchill had been together for several days. Stalin was reported on the way to join them at Teheran.

In Teheran, another fine day. Churchill awakened none the worse for his night at the Soviet Embassy, his physician noted. The prime minister now knew that Roosevelt would not support him in his efforts to push for operations in the Mediterranean which might delay OVERLORD. Through his questioning and prodding, Stalin had forced a decision on Churchill. Apparently he had informed the British chiefs of staff about Roosevelt's position, which had been conveyed to Churchill by Hopkins.

A meeting of the Combined Chiefs of Staff was scheduled for that morning. Before joining their American counterparts, however, the British chiefs held an early discussion and drafted proposals to be placed before their colleagues later in the morning.

When the Combined Chiefs assembled in the British legation at about nine-thirty that morning, Brooke opened the meeting by laying out the operations in the Mediterranean. There should be an Allied operation in southern France, and the Allied forces should advance farther up the Italian peninsula, probably as far as the Pisa-Rimini line. Landing craft would be needed; Eisenhower had asked for them to be held until January 15, 1944, for use in Italy. Help should also be given to the Yugoslav Partisans. If Turkey could be brought into the war, then the Dardanelles should be opened and there would have to be operations in the Aegean area, including of course Rhodes, but only, Brooke stressed, if Turkey came into the war.

Admiral Leahy saw the problem from another angle. It was a "straightforward one of the date of OVERLORD." The Russians wanted OVERLORD on a fixed date in May. They also wanted an expedition against the south of France at the same time, perhaps a little earlier or later. As far as Leahy could see, only the date of OVERLORD confused the issue. If that matter could be decided, everything would be settled. The Americans calculated that if the landing craft were held in Italy until January 15, 1944, then they would be back in the United Kingdom in time for OVERLORD. The argument about the landing craft revolved around the length of time that they could be retained in the Mediterranean for operations in Italy. What was the latest date that the landing craft—some sixty-eight of them—could be kept in the Mediterranean and still be returned in time for the assault on France? Both sides had differing estimates which they batted back and forth.

A solution came first on the timing of the invasion of southern France and OVERLORD. Marshall opposed attacking the south of France before OVERLORD; they ought to be simultaneous operations. To this there was agreement. (Stalin had urged putting the operation in southern France before OVERLORD, which could have been disastrous.)

The generals and admirals also agreed that a tighter control ought to be kept on the use of the landing craft. They ought not to be diverted to other uses and thus become lost to OVERLORD, a reference to some of Churchill's schemes.

But there still had to be an agreement on the actual date

of OVERLORD. Brooke reminded the admirals and generals that OVERLORD had to be coordinated with Russian plans for an offensive from the east. Stalin would want the British and American forces to draw as many German troops as possible away from the eastern front before the Soviet offensive had opened. No Russian offensive had ever begun before the end of May; however, there would be no point in proceeding with the conference if they did not give the Russians a firm date for OVERLORD. (Here Brooke must have been following instructions from Churchill.) Sufficient landing craft would be available for a June 1, 1944, invasion date if Operation BUC-CANEER were to be canceled, Brooke declared. But the generals and admirals knew that Roosevelt had made this operation a political question by his promise to Chiang Kai-shek. The American brass would not dare consider canceling OVERLORD after the President's promise to the Generalissimo.

When Admiral Cunningham, the First Sea Lord, commented that June 1 was the earliest date for OVERLORD, the American admirals, King and Leahy, retorted that they knew only of a May 1 date for the assault. Brooke countered that May 1 had been decided on at the conference in Washington in May 1943 by "splitting the difference between the U.S. suggestion of 1 April and the British suggestion of 1 June." There had been no strategical basis for this date. Ismay, deputy secretary to the War Cabinet, reminded the group that the Russians had never been told May 1 but only "some time in May." Brooke proposed they tell the Russians that OVER-LORD could be undertaken no later than June 1, but in that case they would expect the Russian offensive to take place also no later than June 1.

Out of the wandering discussion between the admirals and generals a consensus developed. They would inform their superiors that the advance would continue to the Pisa-Ri-mini line in northern Italy, with the sixty-eight landing craft for OVERLORD remaining in the Mediterranean until January 15, 1944. They agreed that an operation would be launched against southern France; its strength would depend upon the number of available landing craft. And at last they agreed "to recommend to the President and Prime Minister respectively that we should inform Marshal Stalin that we will launch OVERLORD during May, in conjunction with a supporting operation against the south of France on the largest scale that is permitted by the landing craft available at that time." The Combined Chiefs would do nothing about operations in the Aegean (which could use those precious landing craft) until instructed by the President and the prime minister.[1]

In his memoirs, Brooke claimed that he, together with Churchill, had saved the British and the American armies from the "worst disaster . . . in military history." He was reluctant to admit that both he and Churchill would have preferred that some other method be found to bring about a German collapse without a landing on the beaches of Normandy. He rationalized the chosen date as necessary because by that time the Russian armies would have launched an offensive that would tie down German troops in eastern Europe. Because of the weather, the Soviet armies had not attacked before June 1. The promise, made by Stalin in person, of a Russian offensive at the same time as the invasion would be the best insurance that the Combined Chiefs could obtain. Brooke really preferred, however, more operations to draw the Germans farther away from Normandy. At the same time, the American chiefs feared these operations might become ends in themselves, tying down troops and landing craft, and forcing a postponement of OVERLORD. Now both had a proposition to present to Stalin.

But the landing craft argument ignored the experience of the recent past. The amount of landing craft available for OVERLORD would be smaller than that used in the landing in Sicily. Much of the landing craft problem had developed when these vessels had been drawn away from the Mediterranean to the Pacific theater after OVERLORD had been postponed. If there were to be another delay, more landing craft would disappear.

While the Combined Chiefs were debating landing dates and numbers of landing craft, Roosevelt visited the Post Exchange which had been set up in the Russian Embassy for his convenience. The exchange was stocked with items that would interest the American tourists—Persian knives, daggers, and rugs. There Roosevelt selected a kashan bowl as a present for Churchill, whose birthday would be celebrated that evening. On his return to his quarters, Roosevelt received a visit from Shah Mohammed Reza Pahlavi.

Their meeting was one in a series of gaffes which upset the already nervous American minister, Louis Dreyfus. It all began when Dreyfus was forbidden to inform the Iranian government of the impending visit of the President to Iran, but his British and Russian colleagues were instructed to advise the government of the upcoming visit of Churchill and Stalin for the purpose of a conference with Roosevelt. To smooth over this discourtesy, Dreyfus excused the omission on the basis of the military nature of the conference and the need for extreme secrecy.

On November 26, the shah had sent Hussein Ala, the minister of the court, to the American legation, where he made an impassioned plea to Richard Ford, the chargé, for "the party" to use one of the royal palaces or if needed, all of them. Ala reminded Ford that it was customary for a visiting sovereign to be the personal guest of the host sovereign. "What if someone went to visit Ankara, for example, would he not live in a palace rather than in his country's embassy?" asked Ala. Ford, pleading ignorance, claimed that the American legation would probably be chosen for the President's residence because of reasons of security. "I stressed this security angle for about five minutes, became slightly dewy eyed in my protestations of gratefulness for his and HM's generous offer—so typical of fine old Persian customs—and feel that I convinced him that if and when the 'party' did arrive, and did not stay at a palace, no repeat offense would be intended, implied or otherwise anywhere near anyone's mind," Ford reported to Dreyfus.

Hussein Ala had apparently just left the British Embassy, where "he had been assured confidentially that our big cousin was expected 'any minute.' " Ford told Ala that "our information to date consisted of rumors of things to come."[2]

To add to the gaffes, the shah was forbidden to go to the airport in his own capital to welcome the President of the United States. The Americans also rejected his offer of a guard of honor for the President.

Hussein Ala came to the American legation on November 28 with another invitation for the President to avail himself of one of the royal palaces as a residence and conference hall. Again the offer was refused. Ala announced that the shah requested an opportunity to meet President Roosevelt. Moreover, the shah would be happy to make the first visit, protocol notwithstanding. Would Dreyfus make the necessary arrangements?

Dreyfus hurried to find General Edwin "Pa" Watson, the President's portly military aide. Watson made the appointment for the meeting for the next day, November 29. But when Dreyfus informed Ala of the appointment, the minister of the court asked about the hour of the President's return visit to the shah, insisting that this appointment be fixed before the shah called on the President. Dreyfus went back to "Pa" Watson, who replied that because of the President's physical disability, a return visit was totally out of the question.

When the shah learned of the American position on return visits, he was reported deeply grieved, but he failed to understand how the President could travel from the American legation to the Soviet Embassy twice a day but could not pay a single call on him. Dreyfus explained to Ala that Stalin, because of the President's physical handicap and wishing to spare him hardship, had invited him to be his guest at the Soviet Embassy. This news irritated Ala. He had been informed that the President often greeted distinguished visitors at the Pennsylvania Railroad Station in Washington; he had even gone to Annapolis to greet Lord Halifax, the British ambassador. Dreyfus said he knew nothing about that. The shah, Ala declared, would not consent to visit the President unless there was an agreement about a return visit. "The Iranians might expect treatment of this kind from the British but were surprised and shocked to encounter it from the Americans who had always been held in such high esteem in Iran."

Dreyfus, fearing that American-Iranian relations were in jeopardy, hurried to the Soviet Embassy to confer with the President. He got only as far as "Pa" Watson. "The matter was too trivial to bother the President about," said Watson. "The President had never made a visit such as that contemplated and never would." But after listening to the pleas of Dreyfus, Watson went to Roosevelt and returned with his decision: There would be no visit.

By this time the matter had been turned over to the Iranian foreign minister. Dreyfus begged him not to let the shah insist any further on a return visit, stressing the President's physical condition as the reason for the refusal to call upon the shah. At last the shah, unwilling to let protocol stand in the way of a meeting, decided to call on the President lest relations between Iran and the United States be marred by this incident. Certainly at this time the Iranian monarch had no wish to antagonize the United States, whom he wanted to play off against Britain and the Soviet Union.

But the shah, unwilling to be humiliated by calling on Roosevelt at the Soviet Embassy, asked if his call could be made at the American legation. Once more the Squire from Hyde Park denied the request of His Imperial Majesty, the Shah of the Shahs. The President would see the shah at the Soviet Embassy on November 30 either at noon or at 2 P.M. The shah then asked that arrangements be made so that he could be admitted without being challenged by the sentries and being humiliated when someone had to vouch for him, as was the case whenever anyone entered the Soviet compound.

Dreyfus called for the shah at eleven-thirty on the 30th, and, together with the prime minister, the foreign minister, and Ala, went to the Soviet Embassy where they passed unchallenged. They arrived promptly at noon. Hurley and Watson met the Iranians and ushered them into a waiting room. All stood and waited for the President. As the moments passed, the foreign minister and Ala became fidgety. Turning on poor Dreyfus, they asked if the appointment had not been arranged for noon. Dreyfus did not know what to do, but at that moment Watson returned to usher them into the room where Roosevelt sat ready to receive them. The foreign minister and Ala hung back, angry at the delay, but Hurley shoved them into the room.

After Dreyfus made the introductions, the interview was under way. Elliott Roosevelt was also present, eager to watch because he had heard lurid tales about the shah's reputation as a playboy. To Elliott, the young shah appeared earnest, serious, and very intent on making a favorable impression on the President of the powerful and wealthy United States. Roosevelt, turning on his famous charm, talked about the barren deserts that made up much of Iran. He brought up the possibility of a gigantic reforestration program. Then the talk turned to those villains, the British, who had a tight grip on Iran's oil and mineral deposits. Nodding in sympathy, Roosevelt agreed that something ought to be done to protect Iran's natural resources. The interview ended after about twenty minutes. "Roosevelt gave me the impression of being in the long tradition of distinguished westerners who have become enraptured with my country and culture," the shah wrote years later.[3] The same day, the shah sent Roosevelt a gift of a large Isfahan carpet, worth about $20,000 at the time.

Before the shah left the Soviet Embassy, he had a short visit with Churchill, who had come to the embassy expressly for that purpose.

Eden, Molotov, and Hopkins, as instructed by their chiefs, met for luncheon at the British legation on November 30. Just as their chiefs, they too had no agenda, and consequently their discussion wandered from one topic to the next. The luncheon was unique because Harry Hopkins, the ex-social worker, was discussing world affairs with two foreign ministers. In effect, he had become the Acting American Secretary of State for this luncheon conference.

The trio began talking about "strong points" which would be garrisoned by the victors in the postwar world. Molotov expressed interest in Bizerta and Dakar which, he suggested, might be controlled by the United States or Britain or by both nations.

Talk of Dakar—then the property of the Free French— sent the trio off on a discussion about the inequities of the French. Molotov denounced them for supporting German strategy, refusing to aid the Allies, and collaborating with Germany. As to the future treatment of France, Eden swore that "nothing was too bad for the Lavals and Pétains." Hopkins pointed out that it would be easier to arrange for bases in former enemy countries than in those which had been friendly because of complications arising from the question of sovereignty rights.

Eden suggested that, in the arrangements for leasing bases, an example that could be followed was the leasing of bases in the West Indies to the United States by Britain in return for destroyers. It had really been done, Eden said, because "we like the United States to be there." But when asked to agree with Eden's conclusion, Hopkins objected because it could make the United States appear to be more friendly to Britain than to the Soviet Union.

Molotov, voicing Stalin's views, declared that in order to maintain peace after the war, the states responsible for keeping the peace must have the main strategic bases under their control. Britain and the United States ought to control strongpoints taken from Germany and Japan. Molotov assumed that the United States would control the Atlantic. Eden did not correct this assumption but said that Britain did not want any more territory. As for the bases taken from Japan and Germany, these ought either to be under joint Anglo-American control or United Nations control. Taking over strategic points from France, Eden believed, would be difficult for Britain, owing to former close relations with the French and a desire to see France strong again. French pride could be saved if the French turned their bases over to United Nations control.

Hopkins voiced Roosevelt's view that Russia, Britain, and the United States had to work out the control question among themselves and ensure that no nation would arm against another. Even after Japan and Germany had been defeated, the public would consider them as potential enemies. He saw no difficulties in deciding on bases in the Pacific to guard against Japanese aggression. Even after the Philippine Islands had received their independence, the U.S. government would still consider it advisable to have naval and air bases in the islands.

According to Hopkins, two questions troubled President Roosevelt. The United States did not want to take control of the mandated islands that would be freed from Japanese control. The United Nations ought to decide the type of bases and the strength that would be required in these islands. The other question related to the type of bases in the Pacific and who would operate them. Roosevelt wanted the three powers to decide the basic questions about the strongpoints, including who would control them. Hopkins admitted that it would be easier for the United States to discuss strongpoints in Europe because the United States had no territory in Europe which Germany could threaten. It would be up to Britain and Russia to enforce peace upon Germany from their strongpoints. He foresaw difficulties arising over points essential for the maintenance of peace but which were located in friendly territory.

"This whole question of strong points is one of the most important postwar problems," said Hopkins. "It would be fully worthwhile," he believed, "if the President, Prime Minister, and Marshal Stalin could further discuss this problem." But time was growing short. Perhaps the trio could discuss the problem some more. Molotov was agreeable, but Eden abruptly changed the subject.

He wanted a joint summons to Turkey to enter the war. In addition, he wanted President Inönü of Turkey to be invited to come to Cairo to meet with the prime minister and the President. If possible, he would like to have Russian participation in that meeting. Hopkins added that the President wanted to know more about the Soviet attitude toward Turkish entrance into the war. Molotov said nothing about the invitation to Inönü until pressed for an answer. Then he replied that it seemed to him a good idea but he would have to ask Stalin for his view.

Hopkins surprised Molotov by indicating that Turkey's entrance into the war would compel a change in Allied strategy because a commitment would have to be made involving the occupation of Rhodes and the other Dodecanese Islands. According to the Combined Chiefs of Staff, it would mean a delay in OVERLORD. To Molotov, this was "highly undesirable." Thinking he may have misunderstood Hopkins, Molotov asked if "Mr. Hopkins connected the entry of Turkey into the war with delaying operation OVERLORD?"

"The Chiefs of Staff considered that Turkey would not declare war unless we seized the Dodecanese," said Hopkins. But if bringing Turkey into the war would delay OVERLORD, Marshal Stalin would be opposed, Molotov warned.

Hopkins hoped that some formula might be found that would enable the action to take place in the eastern Mediterranean without delaying OVERLORD.

When the discussion turned to aiding Yugoslavia and Tito, Eden offered an air base in North Africa to the Russians. Molotov thanked him. Where would Mr. Molotov like to have the base located? Molotov left that to the discretion of Mr. Eden, but since the British had their base at Cairo for supplying the Yugoslavs, that would be a good location for the Russians. Eden promised to make the necessary arrangements for a Russian air base at Cairo.

Then the talk turned to Poland. Already, Eden complained, there had been "indiscreet conversations" about the question between Churchill and Stalin. "He did not want this question to be a source of friction between the three countries, if it could be avoided." Hopkins commented, "President Roosevelt would say all that was on his mind about Poland to Marshal Stalin."[4] They agreed to meet the next day for lunch at the Russian Embassy. (The meeting never occurred because of other decisions.)

The committee of the two foreign ministers plus Hopkins, the substitute, had been supposed to confer on political issues which had been raised during the conference. Although they followed instructions, little had been achieved. Hopkins's comments on the "strong points," as they related to Europe indicated that already, because of anticipated congressional opposition, Roosevelt expected that American forces would ultimately be withdrawn from Europe and that the task of maintaining guard over Germany would be left to Britain and Soviet Russia. But Hopkins did not rule out American forces holding such points in the Pacific area.

Of the trio, Hopkins was concerned most with the question of "strong points." Eden worried more about Turkey entering the war. Molotov feared only that the entry of Turkey into the war would delay OVERLORD. On Poland—the subject requiring intense discussion—they desired only that everyone should be in agreement.

Early in the afternoon, Churchill had a private meeting with Stalin. Roosevelt, because he was living in the Russian Embassy compound, had met privately with Stalin, but he had rejected all meetings with Churchill. Undoubtedly Churchill had been riled by Roosevelt's tactics in lining up with Stalin and by Stalin's cutting remarks the previous evening. Consequently, Churchill feared that Stalin might be under the impression that he and the British chiefs of staff meant to stop OVERLORD if they could because they wanted to invade the Balkans instead. So it was that Churchill sought to explain his case to Stalin.

At the outset, he pointed out that he was half-American on his mother's side. To Stalin, that was not new information. But it was important for Stalin to understand this, Churchill explained, because he did not wish the Marshal to think that he was trying to disparage the Americans. He would be loyal to them, "but there were things which it was better to say between two persons."

In the Mediterranean the British had the preponderance of troops, and he wanted them to be used all the time. An argument had been made that there was a choice between keeping the date of OVERLORD or pressing on with operations in the Mediterranean. "But that was not the whole story." The Americans (he should have said Roosevelt) wanted a landing in the Bay of Bengal (BUCCANEER) but he himself "was not keen about it." If the landing craft for the Bay of Bengal were retained in the Mediterranean, then "we would have enough to do all we wanted in the Mediterranean and still be able to keep to an early date for OVERLORD." To Churchill, it was a choice between the Bay of Bengal and the date of OVERLORD. As it was, the Americans had pinned the British down to a definite date for OVERLORD and operations had been suffering because divisions were being withdrawn for OVERLORD.

As for the appointment of the commander-in-chief, Churchill too thought it a vital matter. At the Quebec Conference, Roosevelt had talked him into agreeing to an American commander-in-chief for OVERLORD. He had accepted the proposal, and it was now up to Roosevelt to make the nomination. Churchill attributed the delay to "domestic reasons connected with high personages."

The real bottleneck to OVERLORD, Churchill insisted, was landing craft. After Stalin's announcement about coming into the war following Hitler's surrender, he had suggested to the Americans that they should find the necessary landing craft for the Bay of Bengal operation or else transfer landing craft from the Pacific to be used in OVERLORD. "But the Americans are touchy about the Pacific."

Churchill begged Stalin to understand that he was not lukewarm about OVERLORD but that he was trying to obtain everything he could for the Mediterranean while still keeping the OVERLORD date. He had wanted to have the entire matter hammered out at Cairo before coming to Teheran, but unfortunately Chiang had been there and Chinese questions had taken up nearly all their time.

He promised Stalin: "The British will be ready for the date that is fixed." Britain would have sixteen divisions—over half a million men. "These would consist of some of our best troops including battle worthy men from the Mediterranean." The Royal Navy would handle the transportation and protect the army. American troops were arriving daily in greater numbers, thanks to the defeat of the U-boat.

"A great battle is impending in Italy," exclaimed Churchill. An offensive was planned to start in December. A large landing would be carried out on the west coast of Italy, north of the present front line, roughly in the estuary of the Tiber. These operations would culminate in the encirclement of all the German troops in that area. "It will be a miniature Stalingrad." (He was referring to the upcoming landing at Anzio on January 22, 1944, which in fact immediately became bogged down because of the timidity of the American commander.)

Coming to the end of his defense, Churchill asked if Stalin had any questions. Stalin replied with a warning: The Russian army depended on the successes of OVERLORD. If no operation came in May, then the Russian army would believe that no operation would be launched that year. He did not want the Red Army disappointed because disappointment would only create bad feelings and he did not want that to happen. "If there was no big change in the European war in 1944 it would be very difficult for the Russians to carry on. They were war weary." He feared that if OVERLORD did not take place, a feeling of isolation might develop in the Red

Army. For that reason he wanted to know if OVERLORD would take place on time as promised. "If not, he would have to take steps to prevent a bad feeling in the Red Army."

OVERLORD would most certainly take place, Churchill assured him, "provided the enemy did not bring into France larger forces than the Americans and the British could gather there." If the Germans assembled thirty to forty divisions in France, he doubted that the Anglo-American forces could hold their positions. What might happen then in the succeeding days—the 30th, 40th, 50th? "But if the Red Army engaged the enemy and we held them in Italy perhaps the Yugoslavs and possibly the Turks came into the war, then [Churchill] was hopeful that we could win and that Germany would not have enough troops."

Stalin promised to prepare an offensive against the Germans that would be in time to coincide with OVERLORD. "The Germans were afraid of their eastern front because it had no Channel which had to be crossed and there was no France to be entered," declared Stalin. "The Germans were afraid of the Red Army advance. The Red Army will advance if it sees that help is coming from the Allies.

"When will OVERLORD begin?"

Churchill would not answer without Roosevelt being present. "The answer [would] be given at lunch-time, and [Churchill] thought that the Marshal would be satisfied." It was time for them to join Roosevelt for lunch.[5]

In this pre-luncheon chat, Churchill had tried to pay Roosevelt back for attempting to curry favor with Stalin at his expense. He had implied that any delay in launching OVERLORD was the fault of the Americans (Roosevelt), who had diverted landing craft and who wanted to launch an operation in the Bay of Bengal. It was Roosevelt's fault that no commander-in-chief had been appointed. Britain would send sixteen divisions when OVERLORD began. When Churchill hinted at his misgiving over being compelled to undertake OVERLORD on a scheduled date, he disclosed his fear of another Dunkirk, Somme, or Gallipoli. He wanted a sure guarantee that enough German forces would be drawn away from northern France to enable the British forces to get ashore and to remain there without being pushed back into the sea. Once more Stalin had threatened, although very subtly, to reach a separate peace with Germany. Certainly that was the meaning of his statement that "if there was no big change in the European war in 1944 it would be very difficult for the Russians to carry on." If there were no OVERLORD, then he had a valid reason for seeking peace.

When the three leaders and their interpreters met in Roosevelt's quarters on November 30, the President read out the recommendations of the Combined Chiefs of Staff which had been approved by him and by the prime minister. Stalin promised that the Red Army would undertake the offensive at the same time as OVERLORD. Once more he asked when the commander-in-chief of OVERLORD would be named, but Roosevelt would only promise an answer within three or four days, certainly after he and Churchill had returned from Teheran to Cairo.

During the luncheon that followed, their conversation rambled from Korean independence, on which all were agreed, to the return of Manchuria, Formosa, and the Pescadores Islands to China—again they were all in agreement. The talk turned to the Soviet Union and its size. Churchill observed that because Russia had such a large land mass, she deserved access to warm water ports. Stalin exclaimed that he would like to discuss that question at the proper time. But since the prime minister had raised the question, Stalin was interested in the problem of the Straits of the Dardanelles. He wanted the restrictions relaxed—if Britain had no objection. Of course, Britain had no objection to Russian access to warm water ports now, although, Churchill confessed, in the past she had had strong objections. He advised that nothing be done about the matter at the present because they all hoped to bring Turkey into the war.

Roosevelt returned to the question of the approaches to the Baltic Sea. For that area he favored the formation of a free zone created from the old Hanseatic cities, Bremen, Hamburg, and Lübeck, and including the Kiel Canal, which would be placed under international control. The Straits of the Dardanelles ought to be free to the world's commerce. When Stalin asked if that would apply to Russian commerce,

Roosevelt and Churchill agreed that it would.

"What could be done for Russia in the Far East?" asked Stalin. Churchill expressed interest in hearing the views of the Soviet government about the Far East and the question of warm water ports in that area. But Stalin backed off, saying that "The Russians had their views but . . . it would perhaps be better to await the time when the Russians would be taking an active representation in the Far Eastern war." Yet, he mused, Russia had no port in the Far East that was not closed off. Vladivostok was free from ice only part of the year and it was covered by the Straits of Tsushima, which the Japanese controlled. Roosevelt, who liked the idea of a free port, mentioned Dairen as a possibility. But Stalin was not certain that the Chinese would like such a proposal. Roosevelt thought they would like the idea of a free port which was under an international guaranty. Petropavlosk, according to Stalin, was available as an ice-free port but it lacked a rail connection. Russia had only one ice-free port, Stalin reminded his audience, and that was Murmansk.

With the matter of OVERLORD decided and their thoughts turning to the allotment of territory, Churchill waxed philosophical. "The government of the world must be entrusted to satisfied nations, who wished nothing more for themselves than what they had," he said. "If the government were in the hands of hungry nations, there would always be danger. But none of us had any reason to seek for anything more. Peace would be kept by people who live in their own way and who were not ambitious. Our power placed above the rest. We were like rich men in their habitations." Both Roosevelt and Stalin solemnly agreed.

The trio decided to have one more full session that afternoon and to meet the following day with their foreign ministers, plus Hopkins, for a discussion of political matters. Mentioned as possible topics for discussion were: Finland, Sweden, and most important of all, Poland.[6] The Americans then served tea with lemon.

The full conference—Roosevelt, Churchill, Stalin, the generals, admirals, foreign ministers, Hopkins, interpreters, secretaries—twenty-eight people in all, assembled in the conference room for the final plenary session on the afternoon of November 30. The tension was gone because the great decision had been made.

Roosevelt expressed his delight that they had at last come to a decision and asked Brooke to report on the results. After a meeting of the Combined Chiefs of Staff, Brooke said, they had recommended to the President and to the prime minister: "Inform Marshal Stalin that we will launch OVERLORD in May, in conjunction with a supporting operation against the south of France on the largest scale that is permitted by the landing craft available at that time." Now it was time for general rejoicing, good wishes, and promises of future cooperation.

Churchill urged that they seek to maintain close and intimate contact with Stalin and his staff so that operations on the eastern, as well as the western and Mediterranean fronts could all be concerted together. "By this means the three Great Powers would close in on the wild beast so that he is engaged on all sides at the same moment." He called for coordination with Turkey if she entered the war, as well as with the resistance forces in Yugoslavia.

Stalin declared that he was aware of the importance of the decisions adopted by Russia's allies. There could be a danger as OVERLORD unfurled that the Germans would attempt to transfer troops from the eastern front to hamper OVERLORD. To prevent the Germans from moving their reserves and transferring any large forces from the eastern front to the west, Stalin promised a great Russian offensive against the Germans in several places by May, in order to pin down the German divisions on the eastern front and to prevent them from creating difficulties for OVERLORD.

Roosevelt, too, wanted to have the closest cooperation between the three staffs. "Now that they had gotten together, he hoped that they would stay together." He repeated his promise of appointing a commander-in-chief for OVERLORD within three or four days after he and Churchill had returned to Cairo. Roosevelt proposed that the British and American staffs return to Cairo on December 1 and commence their work on the remaining decisions. Churchill and Stalin assented.

Churchill reverted once again to the question of landing craft. "The main question now was to find enough landing craft for all our needs," he declared. "With five months still to go before the launching of OVERLORD, it should be possible to do this with all the resources of America and Great Britain at our disposal. If OVERLORD was to be done it must be done with smashing force." Churchill wanted "to place that man in a position where there was no way out for him." He reminded the meeting that political questions remained to be discussed. He hoped that the President and Marshal Stalin would be willing to discuss these matters on December 1 and 2, leaving Teheran on December 3. To this schedule, Roosevelt and Stalin agreed. Roosevelt's suggestion was approved for the military staffs to commence drafting a short communiqué as well as military conclusions for the consideration of the three leaders.

After Churchill had reminded everyone that the preparations for OVERLORD would become known to the enemy, he asked if arrangements had been made for a combined cover plan for OVERLORD. Stalin gave a short lecture on the Soviet experience in misleading the enemy by constructing dummy tanks, airplanes, and airfields. These were moved to sectors where they did not plan any action and the movements were soon picked up by German intelligence. "Meanwhile there is absolute quiet where the offensive is really being staged. All transportation takes place at night." In addition, radio traffic was used to confuse the enemy. "In areas where no offensive is planned, radio stations exchange messages. These stations are monitored by the enemy, and he receives the impression that a great force is deployed there. Enemy planes often bomb these places night and day although they are absolutely empty."

"Truth," declared Churchill, "deserves a bodyguard of lies."

"This is what we call military cunning," replied Stalin.

Churchill thought it "rather military diplomacy." He recommended that arrangements be made between the three military staffs concerning methods of deception and propaganda. From Churchill's cogent sentence would come the code name for the deception cover plan for OVERLORD— "Bodyguard."[7]

In his diary, Roosevelt wrote: "The conferences had been going well—tho I found I had to go along with the Russians on military plans. This morning the British came along too, to my great relief."

At last the protracted argument between the Allies over OVERLORD had ended. Anglo-American forces would come from the west, Soviet armies would mount an attack from the east. No one knew then where the armies would meet, not even Stalin. Certainly the British and the Americans hoped that the Soviet armies would fight on until final victory because there had been fears that these armies might halt at the 1941 frontiers. But wherever they stopped, the political orientation of the people involved would be affected. No one realized this more clearly than Stalin, who later told Tito, "This war is not as in the past; whoever occupies a territory also imposes on it his own social system. Everyone imposes his own system as far as his army can reach. It cannot be otherwise."[8]

By finally agreeing to the Russo-American position on OVERLORD, Churchill had accepted a policy not to his liking. His chiefs of staff too were not fully in agreement, and had the conduct of the war been wholly in their control, strategy might have been very different. The landing on the French beaches would be aimed at German forces who would be aware of the attack and fully prepared. Consequently the British wanted to mount the attack only under the best of conditions, and to that end they wanted to draw as many German divisions as far as possible from the French beaches. The Italian campaign ought to be exploited for that purpose, and if circumstances offered new opportunities to punish the Germans, even at the price of postponing OVERLORD, such should be done.[9]

Churchill's fixation on the eastern Mediterranean masked the fear that keeping to a rigid timetable, regardless of other developments in the war, could lead to a determination to press on with the invasion disregarding losses, as happened so often in World War I. Flexible timing seemed best if lives could be saved and success assured. But to the Americans it seemed that he was only interested in backing out of OVER-LORD. Now that question had been settled.

However, there is no genuine proof that Churchill had

argued over OVERLORD because he was bent on satisfying the interests of British imperialism in the Mediterranean and the Balkans, as both the Americans and Russians tended to believe. Nor did he aim at establishing a base in eastern Europe from which to oppose Stalin's future empire. All of Churchill's thoughts then were on the prosecution of the war. In time he would become fearful of the growing Soviet empire in eastern Europe. For the present, he comprehended that Britain was fast becoming the junior partner in the Great Alliance.

For the moment, he and Roosevelt had made a pledge to Stalin, who thus gained the advantage. By pledging to invade France, the British and the American leaders became dependent on a Soviet attack from the east to prevent the Germans from transferring their forces away from the eastern front. Because they were now under an obligation to Stalin, they dared do nothing that would arouse his suspicions so much that he would be led to withhold his attack. In the coming months he held an advantage which he would not hesitate to exploit. Nevertheless he was not wholly convinced of the sincerity of the Roosevelt-Churchill pledge to mount OVERLORD at the agreed time. On his return to Moscow, he told Marshal Zhukov, "Roosevelt has given his word that large scale action will be mounted in France in 1944. I believe he will keep his word. But even if he doesn't we have enough of our own forces to complete the rout of Nazi Germany." When Eduard Beneš, the president of the Czechoslovak Government-in-Exile, traveled to Moscow in December 1943 to sign a treaty with Stalin, the suspicions of the Allies slipped out. Stalin asked Beneš if Britain and the United States intended to pursue the war "to the end with all its consequences and what were their intentions concerning the invasion of the European continent." Evidently he still mistrusted his capitalist allies.[10]

At last the three-day debate over OVERLORD had ended. It never should have taken place. Roosevelt, Churchill, and the Combined Chiefs of Staff should have achieved agreement before leaving Cairo. Roosevelt should have decided on the commander-in-chief of OVERLORD much earlier. Instead, they wasted three days debating military decisions

when there was mounting need for discussions about important future political problems. These problems would now
have to be squeezed into the final day of the conference.

All of the meetings of the conference so far had been held
in the Soviet Embassy. Finally, Churchill announced that he
would be host at the third dinner, to be held in the British
legation. He claimed this right on the basis that Great Britain and Churchill came first alphabetically; in seniority, he
was four or five years older than Roosevelt and Stalin; and
of the three governments, Britain's was the eldest by centuries. He did not add that Britain had been the longest in the
war. But most important of all, November 30 was Churchill's
birthday. Because the prime minister won the argument, Sir
Reader Bullard, the British minister, had to make the preparations for a dinner for nearly forty persons in the British
legation.

The guest list included the Combined Chiefs of Staff,
Voroshilov, Churchill's daughter Sarah, his son Randolph, all
of the diplomats, Harry Hopkins and his son Sergeant Rob
ert Hopkins, as well as the interpreters. Conspicuously absent was the American minister, Louis Dreyfus, to his
embarrassment. He assumed, probably quite correctly, that
his name had been struck off the guest list by Harry Hopkins. The list of prominent guests meant hectic preparations.

The only way of entering the British Embassy was up a
steep flight of steps. A wooden ramp was hastily constructed
so that Roosevelt's wheelchair could be pushed into the embassy. Before the dinner, the legation received two thorough
searches for possible bombs or assassins. First came the crew-
cut U.S. Secret Service detail, with the usual ominous bulges
under their armpits. They combed rooms, went through the
legation gardens looking under bushes and shrubs, then
peered behind doors, draperies, and curtains, and under the
tables and chairs. After they had completed their search, the
NKVD came to repeat the same procedure with the same result. Both units were fearful that the electricity might fail
during the evening as it often did in Teheran for one or two
hours at night. As a precaution, hurricane lamps were prepared for a possible blackout.

During the security searches, Churchill, dressed in a dinner jacket and smoking a large cigar, wandered about the legation like a good host trying to superintend the preparations for the dinner. Occasionally he wandered into the path of the Secret Service detail or the NKVD squad, who simply shouldered him aside. At last, finding nothing to do but wait, Churchill paced up and down until his guests arrived. Three nervous British stenographers stood by in hopes of catching a glimpse of the VIPs. Churchill asked if they were going to wish him a happy birthday. They could only giggle.

By that time the Secret Service detail was lined up for Roosevelt's arrival. Churchill asked if they were preparing to sing a chorus. They neither spoke nor sang. Then, accompanied by his son Elliott, the President was wheeled up the ramp and into the legation. Roosevelt had a shawl over his shoulders to ward off the cool night air. The President and Elliott both wished Churchill a happy birthday. Roosevelt gave Churchill his birthday present, the Persian bowl purchased at the Post Exchange. "May we be together for many years," the President declared to his host.

Meanwhile a Soviet bodyguard, dressed in yellowish, blouselike tops and baggy trousers, each man with his right hand thrust under the waist of his blouse apparently holding some type of weapon, lined up in the lobby of the embassy awaiting Stalin's arrival. When a Persian servant tried to pass through their ranks, they quickly shoved him back. Outside the legation, a picked guard of honor from the Buffs stood rigidly to attention in the cold night air awaiting Stalin's arrival.

At last, a long black, bullet-proof limousine rolled up the driveway and crunched to a halt. Out stepped Molotov, Voroshilov, and Stalin, all of whom ignored the Buffs' guard of honor, which stood at "Present arms." "The two subordinates walked side by side up the steps, Voroshilov with his pale Slav face looking like a retired boxer and Molotov, plump, pink-cheeked, toothbrush mustache and gold rimmed glasses, for all the world like a reasonably successful tradesman who might take the collection plate around the congregation at morning service."

Stalin walked slowly up the steps of the legation. At the top of the stairs he paused, stood rigid, staring straight ahead.

He was dressed in a saffron-colored uniform of silky material with red piping down the seams of his trousers. On his head was a peaked cap, "a cross between a kepi and a postman's cap," and on his shoulders a saffron cape with a brilliant scarlet lining. His face impressed all who saw him for the first time in that legation. "He looked like a farmer, but a shrewd and cunning one," observed one of the British stenographers, Joan Astley. An officer in the British Army remembered, "But, most of all, it is his eyes that I remember most vividly after nearly a quarter of a century. They were small, dark brown, unswerving. It would be impossible to read this man's thoughts from his eyes."

The Soviet trio waited. For the moment nothing happened. Then a servant, slipping past the Soviet bodyguard, started to take Stalin's cape. Instantly, the Soviet guards reacted. One man grabbed the servant and another drew an automatic pistol from beneath his blouse and thrust it into the servant's ribs. He was quickly rushed away. Throughout the hubbub, Stalin stood still, unmoving, unruffled.

The embarrassed host came rushing up. "Good evening, Marshal. Welcome to my party." Stalin ignored Churchill's greeting, as well as his outthrust hand, and slowly walked past him. Now, with all of the important guests assembled, everyone moved into the drawing room for cocktails.[11]

A. H. Birse, the British interpreter, had been instructed to stay close to Stalin and see that his wants were supplied. Stalin was suspicious of cocktails and asked Birse what they were. The interpreter's answer did not reassure the Marshal, who asked for something simple. Birse suggested whiskey which Stalin drank neat. He pronounced it good but he thought ordinary vodka better and decided to stay with that.

After cocktails, the guests moved into the legation dining room which had been built by the Royal Engineers in what some engineer had imagined to be a Persian style. "One might almost have been inside a Persian temple," observed Brooke. "The whole of the walls were covered with a mosaic of small pieces of looking glass set at every conceivable angle, the windows with heavy deep-red curtains, and the walls had on them the pictures of the royal family which one expects in an embassy or legation."[12]

The guests were served by Persian waiters dressed in red

and blue with white cotton gloves which did not quite fit their hands. The fingertips of the gloves hung limply and flapped about as they served the guests. Churchill sat with Roosevelt on his right and Stalin on his left. At the opposite side of the table were Eden, Molotov, and Pavlov, the Soviet interpreter. In front of Churchill was the birthday cake with sixty-nine candles and some of his birthday presents.

That evening, the distinguished guests dined on boiled salmon trout from the Caspian Sea, soup, turkey, cheese soufflé, all accompanied by French and Iranian wines.

Stalin at first seemed uncomfortable as he looked anxiously at the assortment of knives, forks, and spoons that surrounded him. Turning to Birse, he said, "This is a fine collection of cutlery! It is a problem which to use. You will have to tell me and also when I can begin to eat. I am unused to your customs." Taking Birse's advice to eat and drink when it pleased him, he soon began to enjoy the dinner on foreign soil, as it were.[13]

"This was a memorable occasion in my life," Churchill later wrote. There he was seated with his allies on both sides. The trio controlled armies of nearly twenty million men, vast navies, and much of the world's air forces. "I could not help rejoicing at the long way we had come to victory since the summer of 1940."

During the dinner, Stalin again asked Churchill: "Who will command OVERLORD?" Churchill could only say that Roosevelt had not yet made up his mind, though by that time he was certain that General George C. Marshall, sitting not too far away from them, would be appointed.

The speeches made during the dinner took the form of toasts. Estimates of the number varied. Roosevelt opened the proceedings with a toast to King George VI. Churchill in an official toast praised the President as "a man who had devoted his entire life to the cause of defending the weak and helpless." Then the prime minister toasted Stalin, acclaiming him a figure of Russian history who merited the title of "Stalin the Great."

In a personal toast to Roosevelt, Churchill declared that through his courage and foresight, he had prevented revolution in the United States in 1933. Churchill expressed admiration for the manner in which Roosevelt had guided the United States along the "tumultuous stream of party friction and internal politics amidst the violent freedoms of democracy."

Harry Hopkins then rose and announced that he had made "a very long and thorough study of the British constitution, which is unwritten, and of the War Cabinet, whose authority and composition are not specifically defined." As a result of his study, he had learned that "The provisions of the British Constitution and the powers of the War Cabinet are just whatever Winston Churchill wants them to be at any given moment." The Hopkins pronouncement was greeted with much laughter, particularly from Churchill.

The disaster of the evening occurred during one of Stalin's toasts. When he stood, Pavlov, the Soviet interpreter, stood also. The waiters had begun serving the dessert, for which the chef had produced a masterpiece: at the base was a slab of ice about a foot square and four inches deep. In the center was a lighted candle, above which was a large plate of ice cream held up by a perforated tube. When the candle was lit and carried aloft by the waiters, the effect was beautiful. As the waiters proceeded around the table with two such creations, serving the guests, the heat of the candle began to melt the ice and the tube supporting one plate of ice cream began to tilt. The plate on top had assumed a rakish angle. Brooke, seated next to General Brehon Somervell, commander of the U.S. Army Service Forces, saw the ice cream start to slide and yelled to Somervell to duck. Both generals buried their faces in their empty plates as the ice cream flew over their heads, missing Stalin. Like an avalanche, ice cream struck Pavlov on the head and cascaded down. His smart gray diplomatic corps uniform was covered with ice cream, which oozed out of his ears and hair, swamped his shoes. Brooke called for towels and the waiters hurried to clean up Pavlov, who never stopped translating his master's words. "Mr. Stalin says . . ."

In the course of the toasting, Roosevelt toasted General Alan Brooke, chief of staff of the British army. After the others, who were standing, had drunk their toast to Brooke and sat down, Stalin remained standing with his glass in his hand.

He wished to join in the toast to Brooke but he wanted to make a few observations. Although he acknowledged the general's greatness, he declared that Brooke had failed to show sincere feelings of friendship toward the Red Army. In the future, Stalin hoped that Brooke would "come to know us better and would find that we are not so bad after all."

The British were shocked. Brooke, who had already drunk too much vodka, realized that this was an insult that could not be allowed to pass. After getting his wits together, he rose, thanked Roosevelt for his toast, and faced the Marshal.

> Now Marshal, may I feal with your toast. I am surprised that you should have found it necessary to raise accusations against me that are entirely unfounded. You will remember that this morning while we were discussing cover plans Mr. Churchill said that "in war Truth must have an escort of lies." You will also remember that you yourself told us that in all your great offensives your real intentions were always kept concealed from the outer world. You told us that all your dummy tanks and dummy aeroplanes were always massed on those fronts that were of an immediate interest, while your true intentions were covered by a cloak of complete secrecy.
>
> Well, Marshal, you have been misled by dummy tanks and dummy aeroplanes, and you have failed to observe those feelings of true friendship which I have for the Red Army, nor have you seen the feelings of genuine comradeship which I bear towards all its members.

As Pavlov translated the toast to Stalin, the expression on his face never changed. When the interpreter finished, Stalin turned to Churchill. "I like that man. He rings true. I must have a talk with him afterwards."

Churchill later told Brooke that he had been quite nervous when Brooke referred to "truth" and "lies" in reference to Stalin's comments. But he felt that Brooke's toast had had the right effect. Brooke returned to Stalin and told him point-blank that he had been surprised and grieved that he had even found it necessary to make such accusations against him in the toast. Stalin replied: "The best friendships are those founded on misunderstandings." According to Brooke, "We finished the best of friends with a long hand-shake, and almost with our arms around each other's necks! He said that he liked the bold and soldier-like way in which I had spoken and the military strength of my voice."

In another toast, Churchill, commenting on the change in political conditions, observed that he could not speak authoritatively about the political views of the American people nor the changing political philosophy of the Russians. But as far as the British people were concerned, very definitely "their complexions are becoming a trifle pinker."

"That is a sign of good health!" Stalin called out. Churchill agreed with him, provided that it did not lead to congestion.

But Stalin could not resist again getting in a dig at Churchill's expense. He referred to both Roosevelt and Churchill as his "fighting friends," or "comrades-in-arms," adding in Churchill's case, "if it is possible for me to consider Mr. Churchill my friend."

As host, Churchill announced that he would make the concluding toast of the evening. In his toast, Churchill referred to the great progress that they had made at the Teheran Conference toward solving world affairs, and he then proposed a toast to the President and to Stalin. But the Marshal asked the host for the privilege of making one more toast before they all left the legation. Churchill consented.

Stalin praised the productive capacity of the United States which, as he had been informed, would soon be producing 10,000 airplanes a month. He contrasted this production goal with the 2,500–3,000 planes which the Soviet factories were able to produce in a month. Without these American planes, "the war would have been lost."

> I want to tell you, from the Russian point of view what the President and the United States have done to win the war. The most important things in this war are machines. The United States has proven that it can turn out from 8,000 to 10,000 airplanes per month.

Russia can only turn out, at most, 3,000 airplanes a month. England turns out 3,000 to 3,500, which are principally bombers. The United States, therefore, is a country of machines. Without the use of those machines, through Lend-Lease, we would lose this war.

Roosevelt asked for the last word. Although there had been talk about the various colors of their political complexions, "I like to think of this in terms of the rainbow," he said. In the United States the rainbow was the symbol of good fortune and hope. Its many colors blended into "one glorious whole.

"Thus with our nations," he said. "We have differing customs and philosophies and ways of life. Each of us works out our scheme of things according to the desires and ideas of our own people.

"But we have proved here at Teheran that the varying ideals of our nations can come together in a harmonious whole moving unitedly for the common good of ourselves and of the world.

"So as we leave this historic gathering, we can see in the sky, for the first time, that traditional symbol of hope, the rainbow."

It was after two o'clock before the birthday party broke up. Roosevelt's words in the light of what was to come in subsequent decades now seem naïve. But he expressed the longing of millions of people that the alliance of the three nations would create a brave new, peaceful world.

Churchill wrote: "I went to bed tired out but content, feeling sure that nothing but good had been done. It certainly was a happy birthday for me."[14]

14
Affairs of State

DURING THE NIGHT OF Churchill's birthday party, bombers from the U.S. 12th Air Force attacked twenty-three railroad lines, and repair shops, at Sarajevo, the site of the assassination of the Archduke Franz Ferdinand which had precipitated World War I. The morning newspapers on December 1 in London and Washington had begun to report the Cairo meeting with banner headlines. A Swedish newspaper reported that Roosevelt, Churchill, and Stalin would meet that week with Eduard Beneš. In Berlin, diplomatic sources reported that a meeting of the three Allied leaders would take place in Teheran.

At last on the final day of the Teheran Conference the three leaders would consider political questions hanging fire because of the three-day argument over OVERLORD. The delay in discussing political affairs had been caused, not only by the OVERLORD argument, but also by the lack of an agenda. All three men shared the responsibility for this omission, but chiefly Roosevelt, who refused to be tied to an agenda because he yearned to develop a close relationship with Stalin.

That last morning, December 1, according to the story Roosevelt told Frances Perkins, he made a final effort to break down the reserve that seemed to surround Stalin. For three days he had made no progress in establishing any kind of personal relationship, although he had done everything he had been asked to do:

349

I had stayed at his embassy, gone to his dinners, been introduced to his ministers and generals. He was correct, stiff, solemn, not smiling, nothing human to get hold of. I felt pretty discouraged. If it was all going to be official paper work, there was no sense in my having made this long journey which the Russians had wanted. They couldn't come to America or any place in Europe for it. I had come there to accommodate Stalin. I felt pretty discouraged because I thought I was making no personal headway. What we were doing could have been done by the foreign ministers.

Roosevelt thought it over and decided that he had to do something desperate because he could not stay in Teheran forever. He must break through that "icy surface" so that he could talk with Stalin some day on the telephone or write him in a personal way. Roosevelt had deliberately avoided seeing Churchill alone during the conference because he thought the Russians would resent the two men conversing privately in English.

After Roosevelt had signed the official mail that morning, he went to the branch Post Exchange in the Soviet Embassy and purchased some souvenirs and articles as gifts. Then he was wheeled toward the conference room for the first session. On the way Roosevelt met Churchill and said, "Winston, I hope that you won't be sore at me for what I am going to do."

"Winston just shifted his cigar and grunted. I must say he behaved decently afterward," Roosevelt observed to Miss Perkins.

I began almost as soon as we got into the conference room. I talked privately with Stalin. I didn't say anything that I hadn't said before, but it appeared quite chummy and confidential, enough so that the other Russians joined us to listen. Still no smile.

Then I said, lifting my hand to cover a whisper (which of course had to be interpreted), "Winston is cranky this morning, he got up on the wrong side of the bed."

A vague smile passed over Stalin's eyes, and I decided I was on the right track. As soon as I sat down at the conference table, I began to tease Churchill about his Britishness, about John Bull, about his cigars, about his habits. It began to register with Stalin. Winston got red and scowled, and the more he did so, the more Stalin smiled. Finally Stalin broke out into a deep hearty guffaw, and for the first time in three days I saw light. I kept it up until Stalin was laughing with me, and it was then I called him "Uncle Joe." He would have thought me fresh the day before, but that day he laughed and came over and shook my hand.

From that time on our relations were personal, and Stalin himself indulged in occasional witticism. The ice was broken and we talked like men and brothers.[1]

No other source has corroborated Roosevelt's account of this conversation, which he certainly embroidered. If his tale is true, Roosevelt had insulted Churchill, who admired him, and demeaned himself before Stalin, who trusted neither man. In his craving for Stalin's approval and friendship, Roosevelt imagined that the joke had been on Churchill and that Stalin had laughed with him. More probably Stalin had laughed at the President of the United States belittling an ally to find favor with a tyrant. Such conduct only reinforced Stalin's convictions regarding the imperialist Allies. Why should he trust them if they would turn on each other to curry favor with him? But in defense of Roosevelt, he had been driven to this ploy because of Stalin's tactic of refusing to unbend and discuss any question other than the launching of OVERLORD. Since the OVERLORD promise had been given, and since its success would be dependent on a Soviet offensive at the same time, Stalin would smile at one of his allies attempting to make the other play the fool.

At last the three-nation meeting dealing with political questions began, about noon, without the Combined Chiefs of Staff being present. The group was limited to the three leaders plus Eden, Harriman, Clark Kerr, Hopkins, Molotov, and

three interpreters.[2] In a rambling discussion, the three principals mulled over a possible scenario for bringing Turkey
into the war. Their only specific decision was to draft telegrams to be dispatched to the American and British ambassadors in Ankara, instructing them to inform President Inönü
that Churchill and Roosevelt had concluded their meeting
with Stalin and would be in Cairo on December 4–5, accompanied by a representative of the Soviet government.
They wished very much to meet the Turkish president in
Cairo.

Harry Hopkins, acting the role of an American Secretary
of State, fretted over the lack of an agreement about the type
of military assistance that would be given to Turkey if she
entered the war. Such an understanding ought to be developed before the meeting with Inönü. Roosevelt confessed that
his military staff had not yet worked out anything in detail
about such an agreement, but he would not volunteer any
military assistance to Turkey. Churchill would offer only
twenty squadrons of fighter aircraft plus three antiaircraft
regiments, but no other land forces. He thought only about
the usefulness of Turkish air bases from which Allied planes
could bomb the Ploesti oil fields in Rumania. When Churchill mentioned landing craft being needed to take the island of Rhodes in March 1944, Roosevelt doubted if sufficient
vessels would be available for such an operation. He wanted
military advice on this question, but he was unsure as to
whether the Rhodes operation could be sandwiched in between an Italian operation (the landing at Anzio) and OVER
LORD. Churchill foresaw no difficulty but he was unsure if
the Turkish president would come to Cairo. Stalin muttered:
"He might fall ill." But if that happened, Churchill proposed to go personally to Adana and there warn Inönü about
the consequences of Turkey's failure to accept the Allied invitation to enter the war and to paint the not very pleasing
picture of what Inönü would get if Turkey did not enter the
conflict.

Hopkins, disturbed by Churchill's assumption that an
abundance of landing craft would be available for the Rhodes
operation, pointed out that the American chiefs of staff had
not considered the requirements for a Turkish operation. The

whole matter of the Mediterranean would soon be reviewed by the Combined Chiefs of Staff. He reminded the meeting that the Americans believed no landing craft would be available for an attack on Rhodes, and if such landing craft were available, there had been no decision yet as to whether they might be used to better advantage in another operation. When Churchill suggested diverting landing craft from operations in the Pacific, Roosevelt vetoed the suggestion. Landing craft were needed in the Pacific, he declared, because of the great distances and because American forces pushed northward daily into the Gilbert and Marshall Islands to attack Japanese supply lines.

Churchill, filled with optimism over the prospect of Turkey entering the war, thought it might not be necessary to take the island of Rhodes if the German garrisons were starved out by airpower. As winter was approaching, he did not expect a German invasion of Turkey. The Allies would supply Turkey with arms, and in return she would receive "the priceless opportunity of accepting the Soviet invitation for Turkey to sit beside them at the peace conference."

Churchill did not have a very high opinion of the Turkish armies. "We had established military schools, but they were not attended regularly. The Turks were not clever, and they were not quick to learn. The Turkish army was a brave army, but not modern."

If the Turkish army was so inept, how then did Churchill expect that these soldiers could withstand an attack by the Wehrmacht? Probably he had convinced himself that the fighting on the eastern front would limit the forces Hitler could spare to deal with Turkey.

Throughout the Churchillian rhapsody on the benefits of Turkey entering the war, Stalin had said little. Finally he inquired what Churchill expected the Soviet Union to do in case Turkey declared war on Germany and Bulgaria. No one suggested a Soviet invasion of Bulgaria. Only Churchill commented that the mere approach of the Soviet armies would frighten the Bulgarian people. Stalin asked about the position of the Allied powers should Germany occupy Bulgaria, whose people might then ask for help from the Allies. Churchill saw only a benefit because Germany would have to withdraw troops from the eastern front.

Because nothing had been spelled out regarding the vital interests of the Soviet Union, Molotov raised the issue. He asked the meaning of Churchill's comments two days earlier that if Turkey did not enter the war, then her rights to the Dardanelles and the Bosphorus could not remain unaffected. Churchill replied that the regime of the Straits of the Dardanelles deserved review because Japan was a party to the Treaty of Montreux, which regulated the military status of the Straits. Molotov did not press the matter, observing that, "as a Black Sea power, the Soviet Union had a special interest in the Dardanelles but he would not insist on discussing the question that day." But he had set a price on Soviet help to Turkey.

As the luncheon was being served, Roosevelt asked that the meeting take up the question of Finland. During the Winter War of 1939–40, the Finnish cause had been popular among the American public, who had regarded Finland as the underdog and the Soviet Union as an international bully. More recently, the Finnish government, frightened at the prospect of suffering total defeat and Soviet occupation, decided to seek a separate peace with the Soviet Union. The Helsinki government had asked the United States to give advice on how best to approach Moscow without incurring Hitler's wrath.

Roosevelt brought up Finland because in December 1941 in his meeting with Eden, Stalin had demanded the 1941 frontiers with Finland. Roosevelt now asked what the United States could do to help extract Finland from the war. Stalin replied that the Swedish Foreign Ministry had asked about the Soviet Union's intentions regarding Finland because the Finns feared that Moscow wished to turn their country into a Soviet province. His government, Stalin avowed, had no wish to make Finland into a province, unless the Finns forced it to do so. The Finns should state their views and conditions about dropping out of the war. While in Teheran, Stalin had received the Finnish reply through the Swedish Foreign Ministry. The Finns mentioned only the 1939 frontiers, which they proposed be adopted with changes favorable to the Soviet Union. There had been no mention of

Finland separating from Germany. Stalin thought the Finns were not anxious to conduct serious negotiations. Their conditions were unacceptable, and they still hoped for a German victory.

Roosevelt acknowledged the conditions to be interesting but very unsatisfactory. He suggested that the U.S. government recommend that the Finns send a delegation directly to Moscow. Stalin had no objection but said it would do little good if they came to Moscow with these proposals.

Churchill confessed that he had been sympathetic to Finland during the Russo-Finnish War but that he had turned against Finland when she entered the war against the Soviet Union. "That was disgraceful." He wanted Russia to have security for Leningrad and its approaches; Soviet air- and seapower in the Baltic had to be secure. But nothing should be done that might impair Finnish independence. Finland was too poor for an indemnity. "The Finns might cut down a few trees, but they would not do much good."

Stalin, insisting that he did not want money, argued that Finland would be able to make good the damage caused to the Soviet Union within five or eight years by supplying Russia with paper, wood, and other commodities. The Finns must be given a lesson and he was determined to get compensation. But the harm Finland did by attacking Russia, Churchill argued, far exceeded what a poor country like Finland could pay. "There was now ringing in his ears, the famous slogan, 'No annexations and no indemnities.'" He feared that Stalin might find his statements displeasing, but Stalin only grinned. "I have told you that I am becoming a Conservative."

Stalin claimed to be reluctant to have Finnish negotiators come to Moscow without assurances beforehand that an agreement would be concluded, otherwise the Germans could capitalize on the failure to reach an agreement. But Roosevelt and Churchill pressed him to allow the Finns to come to Moscow for negotiations without such assurances. "All right," said Stalin, "let them come if you insist." If Roosevelt felt it worthwhile, Stalin had no objections.

Roosevelt and Churchill continued to debate possible conditions for an agreement that would enable Finland to leave the war. They urged various possibilities on Stalin until he finally stated his absolute conditions. The treaty of 1940 which ended the Winter War had to be restored; Petsamo should be exchanged for Hangö; there had to be compensation for half of the damage done to the Soviet Union; Finland must break with Germany; the Germans must be expelled from Finland; and the Finnish army should be demobilized.

Churchill immediately set about trying to modify the conditions stated by Stalin, fearing that the Finns would not be able to meet the demands for compensation. "The Finns had only poor little muskrats and ermine and they had nothing to give."

Stalin grinned. "What about your slogan against indemnities?" Churchill was talking about reconstruction. Stalin reiterated that he would give the Finns five to eight years to pay for the damage done to Russia. Churchill argued that it ought not to be more than that because large indemnities simply did not work. If the Finns did not pay, Stalin proposed to occupy a region in Finland until they paid up and then withdraw within a year. Churchill replied that "he had not yet been elected a Soviet commissar, but that if he were he would advise against this. There were much bigger things to think about." He was referring to OVERLORD.

As the meeting ended, Roosevelt announced his readiness "to stand behind all that had been said." As for Churchill, he "liked this talk." Stalin may not have liked the conversation because the Soviet version of the minutes of this meeting has never been published. Churchill, and Roosevelt to a limited degree, had questioned Stalin's demands on Finland. Nevertheless, he insisted on the territory Finland had surrendered in 1940 and heavy reparations. Unlike Poland, he had not demanded a change in the government.

Knowing that it would soon be necessary to discuss Poland in a plenary meeting with Churchill, Roosevelt asked Stalin to meet him privately again on the final day of the Teheran Conference in the presidential quarters. At about 3:20 P.M., Harriman, Molotov, and the interpreters Bohlen and Pavlov joined Stalin and Roosevelt. Missing from the room was

Hopkins, who had been playing the role of Secretary of State.[3]

Roosevelt explained the reason for this private meeting: He wanted to discuss with Stalin, briefly and frankly, a matter relating to internal American politics. There would be a presidential election in 1944, and although he personally did not want to run for President again, if the war was still in progress, he might have to do so. In the United States there were six to seven million Polish Americans, and as a practical politician, he did not want to lose their votes in the presidential election. He personally agreed with Stalin's views about restoring a Polish state and moving the eastern border farther to the west and the western border to the Oder River. But because of the political reasons he had outlined, he hoped the Marshal would understand that "he could not participate in any decision here in Teheran or even next winter on this subject and that he could not publicly take part in any such arrangement at the present time." Stalin understood the President's position.

Roosevelt continued. There were people of Lithuanian, Latvian, and Estonian origins in the United States. He realized that both historically and recently the three Baltic republics had been part of Russia. When the Soviet armies eventually reoccupied these states, joked Roosevelt, "he did not intend to go to war with the Soviet Union on this point." But in the United States, the question of referendum and the right of self-determination were major issues. Roosevelt thought world opinion would want some expression of the will of the Baltic people at some time after the Soviet forces had reoccupied the area. "He personally was confident that the people would vote to join the Soviet Union."

There had been no autonomy for the three Baltic republics under the last czar, who, according to Stalin, had been an ally of Britain and the United States. No one had raised the question of public opinion then, and Stalin could not understand why it was being raised now. "The truth of the matter," responded Roosevelt, was "that the public neither knew nor understood." Stalin replied, "They should be informed and some propaganda work should be done." As for expressing the will of the people, there would be many opportunities to do that in accordance with the Soviet constitution. Stalin rejected any form of international control over the Baltic States. But it would help him personally explained Roosevelt, if Stalin would make a public declaration regarding the future elections in the Baltic States. Stalin made no concession, repeating only that there would be plenty of opportunities for the people to express their will. Roosevelt ceased to press the matter and changed the subject to the question of his departure time.

During the Teheran Conference, weather reports had been closely monitored. Early that morning a report had come in of a cold front passing through Cairo. Meteorologists in Teheran predicted that this cold wave might close off the mountain passes by December 3. The American delegation had agreed that the conference business would have to be completed by December 1 in order for Roosevelt to leave the next day, December 2. He now informed Stalin about the time of his departure.

As the meeting drew to a close, Roosevelt commented that he had outlined to Stalin his ideas about the three world organizations (an Assembly, an Executive Committee, and "The Four Policemen"). He suggested that it would be premature to discuss his ideas on world organizations in Teheran with Churchill. It was just an idea whose exact form required more study. Apparently he sensed that his two allies were lukewarm regarding his proposals; neither showed much enthusiasm. It would be necessary for him to convert them to his views but there was insufficient time to accomplish that at Teheran.

At the end of their meeting, Stalin delighted Roosevelt by saying that he had been thinking about the question of the world organization as sketched out by the President. He agreed now with Roosevelt that it should be a worldwide organization and not regional.

Before they parted for the next plenary session at 6 P.M., Stalin promised to take up with Ambassador Harriman in Moscow the three papers Roosevelt had given him on November 29 dealing with possible American air bases in the Soviet Union and advance planning for air and naval operations in the northwestern Pacific.

For such an important subject, it had been a short meeting. If Joseph E. Davies's account of his trip to Mexico to inform Oumansky, the Soviet ambassador, that Roosevelt would not object to Stalin's demand about the Polish frontier is true, it would explain the brevity of both the meeting and the discussion. In effect, all that Roosevelt had done was to confirm Davies's message. Most certainly Stalin wanted direct confirmation from Roosevelt on a matter so important to him. At last he had it.

Roosevelt had come to Teheran to improve relations with Stalin and to make him feel less of an outcast by conferring with him on a personal basis. As a result of this conference, he hoped Stalin would join with him in planning for a peaceful postwar world. An argument over Poland at this time would only wreck his hopes of a more intimate relationship. Roosevelt did not intend to permit mere frontiers to block him from his goal.

His story about the 1944 presidential campaign was only an excuse to avoid a thorny problem which he preferred to postpone to the future when circumstances could very well have changed. Roosevelt balked at wrestling with details long before events made such an ordeal necessary. As it was, German forces had yet to be driven out of Poland, the war was not over, and a second front had yet to be opened in France. He refused to plan for events so far in the future because conditions might then be totally different and he would be tied to an agreement reached in the past under quite a different set of circumstances. As a pragmatic politician, Roosevelt dreaded prophesying future political realities. As he later wrote to Churchill about detailed planning for events after the landing in France, "I have been worrying a good deal of late on account of the tendency of all of us to prepare for future events in such detail that we may be letting ourselves in for trouble when the time arrives." He regarded detailed planning as "prophecies by prophets who cannot be infallible."[4] To Roosevelt, such was also the case with Poland. So he tried to have it both ways: Agree with Stalin's demands on moving the Polish boundaries but avoid a specific decision which might hamstring him in the future when he would sit down at the peace conference table under entirely different circumstances.

Roosevelt's statement, however, that he favored moving the Polish frontier in the east would be interpreted differently later by Molotov and Stalin. Months afterward they would claim that he had agreed to the Curzon Line as the eastern frontier of Poland. In October 1944, Molotov declared: "I can quite well remember that President Roosevelt said that he fully agreed to the Curzon Line and that he considered it to be just frontier between Poland and the Soviet Union; he thought, however, that for the time being it would be advisable not to give publicity to his view."[5]

Unfortunately, there is only one published record of this meeting and it was made by Charles Bohlen. The Soviet record has never been published. Bohlen's notes on the other Teheran meetings are often at variance with those made by the British and Soviet interpreters. The publication of the Soviet record could help clarify Roosevelt's statements on the question of the Polish frontier. Meanwhile it is necessary to rely on statements he made at other times in order to understand his intentions.

To an English visitor to Hyde Park, Roosevelt had expressed his views on the frontier in early November. The visitor commented on Polish alarm over the Soviet armies advancing to their borders. The President replied: "I am sick and tired of these people. The Polish ambassador came to see me a while ago about this . . . I said, do you think they will just stop to please you, or us for that matter? Do you expect us and Great Britain to declare war on Joe Stalin if they cross your precious frontier? Even if we wanted, Russia can still field an army twice our combined strength, and we would just have no say in the matter at all. What is more . . . I'm not sure that a fair plebiscite if there ever was such a thing would not show that those eastern provinces would not prefer to go back to Russia. Yes I really think those 1941 frontiers are as just as any."[6]

When he had talked with Cardinal Spellman on September 3, Roosevelt did not conceal his thoughts about Stalin and eastern Europe. Stalin would receive Finland, the Baltic States, the eastern half of Poland, and Bessarabia. There was no point in opposing "these desires of Stalin, because he had the power to get them anyhow. So better give them gracefully." Moreover, the population of eastern Poland "wants to become Russian." He expected eastern Europe to come under some form of Russian protectorate. "Be it as it may," he added, "the U.S. and Britain cannot fight the Russians."[7] It would seem that his mind had been made up before he boarded the U.S.S. *Iowa*.

Roosevelt's excuse for avoiding public approval of the Curzon Line as the Polish-Soviet frontier—the upcoming presidential election—was a half truth. To him there was a greater issue at stake than a frontier: Soviet-American friendship. He would not have that thwarted by a mere frontier. As for the Polish-American vote, it was not large enough to decide the outcome of a presidential election. The politician Roosevelt would do all that he could to avoid manufacturing an issue which might aid his opponents. Had he returned to Washington and announced acceptance of the frontier change while the war was still in progress, his Republican opponents would have used the Atlantic Charter to prove that he was agreeing to territorial changes without consulting the wishes of the people most directly concerned, the people whom Hitler had attacked first. The opposition could have denounced him for joining in dividing up Europe before peace had come. He would have stirred up a political storm with this issue and benefited his political enemies. Moreover, the angry debate over the frontier would only injure Soviet-American relations, which he desired so much to promote.

By using the election as his excuse for not approving the frontier publicly, Roosevelt signaled to Stalin that he had no intention of bargaining over Poland as Stalin had certainly expected him to do. Roosevelt feared that tough bargaining would have wrecked all chances of removing Soviet suspicions of the western nations, had he even been inclined to bargain over Poland. Like Churchill, he wanted nothing to interfere with Stalin carrying out his promise of an offensive to hold German troops in the east.

As for the Baltic States, Roosevelt implied that if Stalin held a few plebiscites, he could con the American public. Roosevelt seemed to imply that the American public could be fooled by a referendum when he told Stalin, "The truth of the matter was that the public neither knew nor understood."

In this the final private meeting between the two leaders, in his zeal to please Stalin, Roosevelt missed an opportunity to spell out the limits of Soviet expansion that he would be willing to accept in the future since Soviet troops were already close to Poland. He had the condition he had craved, face to face with Stalin, for a session in which to lay out his position on future Soviet power in eastern Europe. At that moment he held the best bargaining position that he would ever have; but he chose to throw it away because of domestic political necessities. To Stalin it appeared to be an invitation to aggrandizement in eastern Europe if he avoided involving Polish-American voters.

Even before he came to Teheran, Roosevelt had told his advisers, including Hull and Leahy, that he intended to appeal to Stalin "on grounds of high morality." He would tell Stalin that neither Britain nor the United States would fight Russia over the Baltic States and that it would be in Soviet interests to hold another plebiscite there. The same would apply to Poland: Britain and the United States would not fight over that issue. The new frontier would be to the east of the Curzon Line and there ought to be another plebiscite.[8]

In his talk with Stalin, however, he had followed the script except that there had been no appeal on grounds of "high morality," but rather on the grounds of helping him win a victory in the next presidential election.

Roosevelt's attitude may well have been the product of a Washington consensus that the eastern front was the main front of the war and that the Allied second front would be secondary to the Russian one. Unless Soviet Russia remained in the war, the Axis armies could not be defeated in Europe. After the war was over, Soviet Russia would have the dominant position in Europe: Once Germany had been crushed, no power in Europe would be able to oppose Russia's military force. Since Russia was the decisive force in the war, all assistance had to be given to her and every effort made to obtain her friendship. Finally, Soviet friendship had to be maintained in order to gain Russia's help in the war against Japan, otherwise the cost in life and resources might be so great as to abort the operations.[9] Such an attitude colored Roosevelt's thinking in his talk with Stalin where Poland and the Baltic States were concerned. Too much was at stake to argue over these matters. The President would follow much the same scenario in the final discussion with Stalin and Churchill later in the day.

About six o'clock in the evening the final political meeting of the Teheran Conference opened in the conference room with Roosevelt announcing that there were two main questions for discussion: Poland and the treatment of Germany. But Molotov interrupted to ask for a discussion of the Soviet request for ships from the Italian naval and merchant fleets.[10]

At the Moscow Conference in October, Molotov had made a request for Italian ships, including one battleship, one cruiser, eight destroyers, and four submarines, to be immediately dispatched to the northern ports of the Soviet Union. In addition, he requested 40,000 tons of Italian merchant shipping. Molotov justified the request because in her war against the Soviet Union Italy had caused great damage, particularly to Soviet naval and merchant fleets. When Hull passed the request along to Roosevelt, the President evaded full agreement by asking that Italian shipping be used wherever it could give the best service to the Allied cause. He wanted the determination of final ownership to await the peace conference.

When Churchill learned of Molotov's request at the Moscow Conference, he had hesitated to agree, fearing possible damage to Italian cooperation with the British and American military forces because Italian ships were aiding the Allies in the Mediterranean by escorting convoys and transporting supplies. He had the matter postponed until the Teheran Conference. Now Molotov, still dissatisfied, had repeated his request for the Italian ships.

Roosevelt announced that his position on this question was clear. The Allies had many Italian merchant ships and some warships; the three nations should use them in the common cause until the end of the conflict, when a division would be made. Molotov had a different view: The Soviet government wanted to use these ships now, during the war, and the question of possession should be discussed after the war. These ships could be used in the interest of the United Nations.

"Where would the Soviet government like them delivered?" asked Churchill. Stalin wanted them delivered to the Black Sea, but if Turkey did not enter the war that would be impossible. In that case, the ships would have to be delivered to the northern Soviet ports where they would be put to good use.

"I am for it," declared Churchill.

"I am also for it," said Roosevelt.

Churchill preferred to see the Italian ships in the Black Sea where he might also at the same time send some British ships to help the Soviet navy.

"All right, please," replied Stalin.

But Churchill reminded Stalin that he and Roosevelt needed time to arrange this matter with the Italians, who were helping in patrol work and whose submarines were transporting supplies to Allied garrisons. The affair must be arranged to avoid a mutiny in the Italian fleet that could lead to the ships being scuttled by their crews. The Italians would have to be handled like a cat handling a mouse.

Stalin asked for the ships by the end of January 1944, and both Roosevelt and Churchill agreed to his request. But at no time did they agree on the number and type of ships to be transferred to the Soviet government.

The Italian shipping question was not over yet, and the failure to agree on the number and type of ships to be transferred to the Soviet government would lead to a protracted negotiation in 1944. By his request, Stalin was attempting to obtain reparations before the war had ended. No one had consulted the Combined Chiefs of Staff, whose views as it later turned out were completely opposite to those of Churchill and Roosevelt.

At last the discussion turned from shipping to Poland. Roosevelt began by expressing the hope that relations between the Polish and Soviet governments could be resumed in order that any decisions would be accepted by the Polish government. He realized the difficulties which lay in the path of resuming relations. But Stalin did not want relations with a Polish government whose friends in Poland were in contact with the Germans and were killing partisans. "You cannot imagine what they are doing there," he declared. Roosevelt made no reply.

Churchill then attempted to explain the British position on Poland. It was because of Poland that Britain had declared war on Germany. But he confessed astonishment that Neville Chamberlain, who would not fight for Czechoslovakia at Munich, had suddenly guaranteed Poland after throwing away a more favorable opportunity. Churchill was astonished and glad that Chamberlain "should go back to a policy of war and guarantee Poland." Although unprepared, Britain had declared war on Germany and "had played a great part in screwing the French up." Even though France had gone down to defeat, Britain had the luck to be an island and went on fighting Germany. He understood the difference in historical background but hoped that the Russian ally would see Britain's position and understand how important Poland was to Britain. "We had done what we done and we did not regret it." He appreciated Russian policy when war broke out. Britain had been weak and there had also been the Munich Agreement and the French betrayal of the guarantee to Czechoslovakia. He also understood the reluctance of the Soviet government to risk its existence in view of the uncertainties. Churchill hoped that Stalin realized that Britain had gone to war because "we had promised Poland that if she were attacked we would go to war."

Churchill switched to outlining again his idea of the "three matches": Germany, Poland, and the Soviet Union. He assured Stalin that one of the main objectives of the Allies was "to achieve the security of the Soviet western frontier and so to prevent an attack by Germany in the future." Churchill reminded Stalin, "All these three matches must be moved to the West in order to settle one of the main problems facing the allies: to assure the Soviet Union's western borders."

Stalin interrupted Churchill's lecture with a bitter denunciation of the Polish government in London. "Yesterday there was no mention of negotiations with the Polish government. Yesterday it was said that the Polish government must be directed to do this and that." Today the matter was being put quite differently. Russia as much as any power was interested in good relations with Poland because it was a question of the security of Russia's frontiers. Russia favored the reconstruction, the development, and the expansion of Poland at Germany's expense. But he drew the line between Poland and the émigré Polish government in London. "We broke off relations with that government not out of any whim on our part, but because the Polish government joined Hitler in slandering the Soviet Union. All that was published in the press." Was there any guarantee that it would not happen again? He wanted a guarantee that the agents of the Polish Government-in-Exile would not fight partisans and would urge the Poles to fight the Germans. "We shall maintain good relations with any government that calls for active struggle against the Germans," but he doubted that the Polish Government-in-Exile would ever become the government that it ought to be. "If it sides with the partisans and if we are given the guarantee that its agents will not have ties with the Germans in Poland, we shall be prepared to start talks with it." Now he wanted to ask Churchill what those three matches meant.

But Churchill asked for the Soviet ideas about the frontiers with Poland. He would like to place the entire matter before the Poles and be able to tell them that it was fair. The British government would like to be able to tell the Poles that the plan was not only good but the best that they would probably get, and that at the peace table His Majesty's Government would not argue against the Soviet government. Then they could get on with the President's idea of resuming relations. "What we wanted," declared Churchill, "was a strong and independent Poland, friendly to Russia." Roosevelt remained silent.

Although Stalin agreed with Churchill's statements, he thought it unfair if the Poles were permitted to seize the Ukraine and the White Russian territory—"According to the 1939 frontier, the soil of the Ukraine and White Russia was returned to the Ukraine and to White Russia. Soviet Russia adhered to the frontiers of 1939, for they appeared to be ethnologically the right ones."

Anthony Eden broke in to ask Stalin if he meant the

"Ribbentrop-Molotov Line." "Call it whatever you like," replied Stalin. Then Molotov, joining in the discussion, explained that the line was generally the Curzon Line. At that point, Molotov and Eden began an argument over the degree of difference between the two lines, with Eden holding that there were important variations but Molotov contending that there were no essential differences.

The Curzon Line had first been drawn by the Commission on Polish Affairs at the Paris Peace Conference in April 1919 in accordance with Woodrow Wilson's thirteenth point in his famous Fourteen Points to "include the territories inhabited by indisputably Polish populations." In 1920, when the Polish armies were retreating before the Russian forces, Lord Curzon, the British foreign secretary, proposed an armistice with the Polish forces withdrawing to the west of this line. From that time the line became known as the Curzon Line. But the Poles forced the Russian armies to the east, and in 1921 under the terms of the Treaty of Riga, a frontier line was agreed on which lay some 100 to 150 miles farther to the east of the Curzon Line.

After the invasion of Poland in 1939, Ribbentrop and Molotov agreed on a line of demarcation that followed the Curzon Line along the middle, but in the north and in the south the new line bulged westward and was consequently more favorable to the Russians. Now at Teheran in 1943 to settle the disagreement between Molotov and Eden, maps were produced, both British and American.

The meeting broke up into two groups as everyone crowded around trying to locate the Curzon Line. Stalin, peering at the British map, complained that it had been drawn incorrectly—the city of Lvov ought to be on the Russian side of the line. He would have Molotov find a correct map of the Curzon Line and a description of it. Stalin did not want any Polish population and if he found any district inhabited by Poles he would gladly give it up.

At last Roosevelt spoke, asking if the frontier of East Prussia and the land east of the Oder River made up territory which was approximately equal in size to that of the eastern provinces of Poland. Stalin did not know, claiming that the area had not been measured.

Churchill thought the land between the frontier of East Prussia and the Oder River was more valuable than the Pripet Marshes—a vast unreclaimed swamp with thick forests which armies avoided. "We should like to be able to say to the Poles that the Russians were right, and to tell the Poles that they must agree that they had had a fair deal. If the Poles did not accept, we could not help it." But he spoke only for Britain, whereas "the President had many Poles in the United States who were his fellow-citizens."

Stalin swore that if anyone could prove to him that any area was Polish, he would not claim it. Taking a red pencil, he bent over the map marking areas west of the Curzon Line and south of Vilna which he conceded to be Polish. His marking brought more discussion as the maps were subject to further scrutiny.

After studying the maps, Churchill said that he "liked the picture." If the Poles did not accept, they would be fools. "He would remind them that but for the Red Army they would have been utterly destroyed and he would point out to them that they had been given a fine place to live in, more than 300 miles each way."

"It would indeed be a large industrial state," remarked Stalin.

"It would be a state friendly to Russia," Churchill replied.

"Russia wanted a friendly Poland," Stalin added.

Turning to Eden, Churchill exclaimed that he would not break his heart about ceding parts of Germany to Poland or about Lvov.

If Stalin would take the Curzon Line and the Oder as the basis for discussion, Eden suggested, they might have a base from which to negotiate. Stalin did not answer because Molotov had produced a map with the Soviet version of the Curzon Line and a copy of a telegram from Lord Curzon listing place names. Again the gentlemen examined the maps. Churchill announced that the "Poles would be wise to take our advice" because they would have a country that was three hundred miles square. "He was not prepared to make a great squawk about Lvov, and (turning to Marshal Stalin) he added that he did not think that we were very far off in principle."

Roosevelt, who had been listening, asked Stalin if a voluntary transfer of population would be at all possible. Stalin agreed that it would. But Roosevelt said no more about Poland.

The meeting turned next to the German question. Roosevelt and Stalin immediately agreed on splitting up Germany. Stalin joked that Churchill might object. Churchill would not object, but he was more concerned with splitting up Prussia and separating Bavaria from Germany. Then Roosevelt asked that they consider a plan which he had drafted to divide Germany into five parts.

Once more a grinning Stalin got in a dig at Churchill—"Mr. Churchill was not listening because he was not inclined to see Germany split up." Churchill, ignoring Stalin's jibe, declared that the root of the evil lay in Prussia, in the Prussian army and the General Staff. Roosevelt insisted that they ought first to examine the whole picture before looking at the component parts. At last he had their attention. Under Roosevelt's plan, he proposed to weaken Prussia as much as possible and to reduce its size. The second part of the shattered Germany would include Hanover and northwestern Germany. Saxony and the Leipzig area would comprise the third. The fourth part would contain Hesse-Darmstadt, Hesse-Cassel, and the areas to the south of the Rhine, as well as the old towns of Westphalia. The fifth would include Bavaria, Baden, and Württemberg. Each section would be independent. Two other areas would be under the control of the United Nations: the Kiel Canal and Hamburg, and the Ruhr and the Saar.

"The President had said a mouthful," Churchill remarked, and then launched into a description of his own plan for Germany. It was important to him first to isolate Prussia from the remainder of Germany. Secondly, he would separate the southern provinces—Bavaria, Baden-Württemberg, the Palatinate, Saxony, and Baden—treat them less harshly than Prussia, and have them in the Danubian Confederation. These were people who would not cause war. He wanted to see them living under more tolerable conditions, and within a generation they would feel differently.

But Stalin preferred a plan similar to Roosevelt's because

it would be more likely to weaken Germany. He wanted Germany really dismembered; it did not matter whether there were five or six states and two other areas. To create a large confederation would offer the Germans an opportunity to revive a great state. "When one had to deal with large masses of German troops, one found them all fighting like devils, as the British and American armies would soon learn. Only the Austrians when surrendering, shout 'I'm Austrian.'" All the Germans fought like beasts. Stalin would allow Austria, Hungary, Bulgaria, and Rumania to exist again as independent states. But after breaking up Germany, he thought it unwise to create new combinations.

Roosevelt agreed with Stalin's position. "There was no difference between Germans, and Bavarians and Prussians were much the same." Churchill did not want to seem to be opposed to partitioning Germany but he felt that if Germany were to be divided, as Roosevelt desired, the parts would only seek to reunite once more. It was important to keep Germany divided, if only for fifty years.

Stalin returned to attacking Churchill's plan. The Germans would use the Danubian Confederation as a skeleton to create a new German state. "It was far better to break up and scatter the German tribes," Stalin argued. "Of course they would want to reunite." This danger would have to be neutralized, by force if necessary. It was the only way to keep the peace. "But if we were to make a large combination with Germans in it, trouble was bound to come . . . Germans would always want to reunite and to take their revenge. It would be necessary to keep ourselves strong enough to beat them if they ever let loose another war."

Did Stalin contemplate "a Europe of little states, all disjointed, with no larger units at all?" asked Churchill.

"Not Europe, but Germany," replied the Marshal.

Roosevelt observed that Germany had been safer when she had been divided into 107 small principalities. Churchill grumbled that he hoped for larger units but this was only a preliminary survey of a great historical problem. "It was certainly very preliminary," Stalin commented.

Churchill returned to the problem of Poland. He was seeking a written formula similar to that which he proceeded to read aloud: "It was thought in principle that the home of the Polish state and nation should be between the so-called Curzon Line and the line of the Oder, including for Poland East Prussia (as defined) and Oppeln: but the actual tracing of the frontier line required careful study and possibly disentanglement of population as some points."

Roosevelt, uneasy because a deal was about to be hammered out over Poland, went back to the German question. He proposed that a three-power committee be created to study the question. They agreed that the European Advisory Commission would take on this task.

Churchill protested that the Polish problem was much more urgent. "The Poles would make a clatter." Could he not say something like this to them: "I do not know if the Russians would approve, but I think that I might get it for you. You see you are being well looked after." He admitted that they could never get the Poles to say they were satisfied. "Nothing would satisfy the Poles."

Stalin grinned. "The Poles in London seem to be most reasonable people." The Russians, he declared, wanted the warm water port of Königsberg. Taking the red pencil again, he sketched another line on the map which ran along the Nieman River and included Tilsit and Königsberg. "This would put Russia on the neck of Germany." If he could get this line, he would accept the Curzon Line as the frontier between the Soviet Union and Poland. This area, he argued, would not only give the Soviet Union an ice-free port but would also give Russia a piece of German territory which Stalin believed was deserved.

"This is a very interesting proposal," said Churchill, "which I will make a point of studying." Roosevelt said nothing. The meeting was over, and when they next met for dinner, it would be for the final session of the Teheran Conference.

In discussing the fate of Germany, Stalin had revealed his thoughts about the future Europe. By agreeing to Roosevelt's plan to break up Germany into five separate states, there would be no German state large enough to serve as a buffer against Soviet domination of eastern and central Europe.

Stalin's condemnation of Churchill's Danubian Confederation underlined his dread of a state that might again endanger the Soviet Union. That Churchill sensed Stalin's intention
could be seen in his question whether Stalin contemplated
"a Europe of little states, all disjointed, with no larger units
at all." Stalin had replied, "Not Europe, but Germany." He
had staked out his position: Germany must be broken up as
much as possible, never to be reunited. For the Soviet Union,
a united Germany could never be tolerated; the risk was too
great. As a result of this same danger, Stalin would not tolerate the Polish Government-in-Exile. Soviet security demanded a "friendly" government, subservient enough to
follow Stalin's bidding.

A formula had been hammered out that would become the
frontier between Poland and the Soviet Union. This formula
did not result from any wish to appease Stalin, nor was it a
sudden bribe. It evolved from months of discussion in London and in Washington after Stalin's demands had become
known, for he had issued them in 1941 and never withdrawn them.[11] Roosevelt had known of the demands and accepted them before sailing for Teheran. Neither man could
plead ignorance or surprise. Both contributed to the outcome, whether through their discussion (Churchill) or their
silence (Roosevelt).

Before coming to Teheran, Eden had proposed that in return for imposing the Curzon Line on the Poles, concessions
should be obtained from Stalin as compensation. Diplomatic
relations should be restored immediately between the Polish and Soviet governments. Arrangements ought to be made
for the Polish Government-in-Exile to return to Poland as soon
as military conditions would permit. Finally, the Polish people should have the opportunity to choose their own government freely and without pressure.[12] Even Roosevelt at one
time considered concessions from the Russians to make the
Curzon Line palatable to the Poles.[13]

Such concessions were not mentioned except for Roosevelt's hope that negotiations would be started for reestablishing relations between the two governments. He lapsed
into silence when Stalin retorted that the Polish government
was closely connected with the Germans, and their agents

in Poland were killing partisans. Churchill and Eden did not even go that far. Churchill never hinted at concessions, and Eden did not raise his list of concessions. Consequently, Churchill and Roosevelt would leave Teheran without securing any compensation for the change in the Polish frontier other than the territory that would come from Germany.

Churchill and Roosevelt had been worn down by the three-day debate over OVERLORD, an operation whose timing and importance had been accepted by everyone concerned. For OVERLORD to succeed, they knew that Soviet help was vital. Faced with OVERLORD and the resulting casualties, well aware of Stalin's position on the Curzon Line and the Polish government, neither Roosevelt nor Churchill would debate the Polish question with Stalin at that time. The cause of Allied victory was greater than a mere frontier in eastern Europe far from the Normandy beaches. If Stalin wanted this frontier, and if it would help end his suspicions of the western powers, it would have to be moved. Poland would be restored and receive territory at Germany's expense.

In negotiating with Stalin at this time, both Roosevelt and Churchill labored at a disadvantage: there had been great Soviet victories at Stalingrad and at Kursk without equivalent victories on their side. The defeat of Rommel's Afrika Korps did not appear as decisive as the Soviet victories. In Italy, victory seemed far away for the Anglo-American armies. For OVERLORD to succeed, a Soviet offensive from the east was essential. Consequently, military necessity required that they agree with Stalin on the Polish question.

Roosevelt and Churchill had also chosen to ignore Stalin's complaints about the Polish Government-in-Exile. They may have assumed that his tirades were only intended to win his position on the Curzon Line. If the Poles could be made to accept the Curzon Line, Stalin's growls would cease. But Stalin's tirades masked his intention to have a Polish government subservient enough to voluntarily cede these lands to the Soviet Union. For Stalin had concluded that security against a revived Germany required a Poland which the Soviet Union could dominate.[14] The Curzon Line was the first step in achieving this goal.

15
The Iranian Matter

As THE COOL EVENING DARKNESS settled over Teheran on December 1, the three Allied leaders and their associates gathered for a final dinner, hosted by Stalin in the Soviet Embassy. The records of the discussions are scanty because no major diplomatic bargaining occurred. Instead it became a time for tidying up loose ends, agreeing on the final drafts of conference documents, and appending the necessary signatures.

Chief among the documents accepted and signed at the last dinner meeting was the "Declaration of the Three Powers Regarding Iran." This began as a statement on Iran and would eventually involve the United States in its first confrontation with the Soviet power in the Mideast in 1946.

Until the Allied armies had occupied Iran during the war, American policy toward Iran had been barely outlined. Early in the year, Hull and Sumner Welles had approved a statement of policy drafted in the Division of Near Eastern Affairs. According to the policy statement, Iran constituted a test case for the good faith of the United Nations and their ability to work out problems involving each nation's rights and interests. Russian policy toward Iran had been fundamentally aggressive and Britain's basically defensive; as a result, the combination produced interference in the internal affairs of Iran. Both nations had sent occupation troops into Iran and the governmental machinery had been weakened. Only the United States was in a position to build up

Iran to the point that she would need neither British nor Russian help to maintain order. The United States should work to make Iran "self-reliant and prosperous, open to the trade of all nations and a threat to none," and should support its disinterested American advisers so strongly that no peace conference would approve a Russian or British protectorate over Iran. If Iran needed special assistance, the United States would provide it. The United States ought to put forward suggestions to improve conditions while neither supporting nor opposing British and Russian policies—"We should regard ourselves as at least equally responsible with the British and Russians for the solution of Iranian problems."[1]

But State Department memoranda on foreign policy had had little impact on Roosevelt's thinking until his personal representative, Patrick Hurley, sent him a long telegram about Iran on May 13. Hurley pointed out that strong action on the President's part would assure Iran that the United States insisted on applying the principles of the Atlantic Charter to that country. He warned Roosevelt that rivalry between the Soviet Union and Britain over Iran could alienate them from the United States and create disunity among the three leaders of the United Nations.

By the time of the Moscow Conference in October, both London and Teheran wanted a three-power declaration to reassure Iran that the occupying powers would withdraw their troops six months after the war had ended. Such a declaration would involve the United States in a pronouncement about Iran. Indeed, the adherence of the United States to such a declaration was vital to the Iranian government because now that Germany could no longer prevent Soviet or British domination, the United States could assume that role.

At the Moscow Conference, a British proposal for common policy toward Iran went nowhere. To the delight of Molotov, Hull suggested referring the matter to a subcommittee. Molotov announced that the 1942 treaty between the Soviet Union, Britain, and Iran required the presence of an Iranian representative at all international conferences at which questions concerning Iran were to be considered. It so happened that the Iranian ambassador had recently brought this matter to Molotov's attention. Following Hull's suggestion, the British proposal went to a six-member subcommittee where the Soviet members stonewalled, completely rejecting it. They demanded that the Iranian government be consulted before any action was taken; moreover, they argued that it was impractical to consider such a complex question without careful and prolonged study. They rejected all efforts at compromise because any such declaration was neither necessary nor desirable. Eden and Hull could only accede to the Russian objections. Molotov even refused to agree to later discussions of the question in Moscow. He would only permit them in Teheran.

Molotov's actions reflected his master's objections to the proposed declaration. Peculiarly objectionable was the promise that the three governments support the work of foreign advisers in Iran to relieve the economic difficulties of the people and to strengthen the authority of the Iranian government. This provision sanctioned the work of American advisers, particularly the economic mission of Arthur C. Millspaugh and the work of Colonel H. Norman Schwarzkopf, formerly head of the New Jersey State Police, in organizing the Iranian rural police.

More infuriating to Stalin was the promise that the three governments would respect the territorial integrity, sovereignty, and political independence of Iran and that they withdraw all their armed forces from Iran six months after the end of the war with Germany. Leaving Iran did not loom large in Stalin's plans since his forces were already so strongly entrenched in Azerbaijan—in northern Iran—that Soviet authority had replaced Iranian authority, and the Soviet-backed Tudeh party tolerated no opposition.

The Teheran Conference presented the Iranian government with the best possible opportunity to present its case for a declaration dealing with political independence and political integrity, public support by the United States, and promises of economic assistance. When Hurley and Louis Dreyfus called on Iranian Premier Ali Soheily and Foreign Minister Muhammed Sa'id on November 25, both officials brought up the question of the proposed declaration on Iran which the Soviets had vetoed at the Moscow Conference.

After Roosevelt had arrived in Teheran, Hurley discussed with him the possibility of obtaining a declaration on the status of Iran from the three chiefs of government while they were in Teheran. Roosevelt authorized Hurley to work something out with Eden and Molotov. By November 29, Soheily had proposed to Eden that a joint communiqué be issued covering Allied recognition of the help Iran had given during the war, confirmation of the pledges in the treaty of alliance regarding Iranian independence and territorial integrity, and assurances that Iran's economic needs would be considered when the final peace treaty was being negotiated. Although Eden agreed in principle, he advised Soheily to approach the Soviet representatives and the American minister.

In their talk on November 30, Hurley and Eden agreed on a proposed declaration. Hurley wanted a reaffirmation of the Atlantic Charter included. After Eden consented, they both agreed to drop the reference to foreign advisers, and decided to let the Iranians suggest the declaration to Molotov. Later that same day, the Iranian foreign minister reported to Dreyfus that Stalin and Molotov had consented to the declaration. Hurley, still unsure, asked Roosevelt to discuss the question with Stalin. Exactly what Roosevelt said is unknown, but apparently he made a strong personal request and Stalin agreed to sign the declaration.

Stalin had consented because by the evening of December 1 he had concluded his discussion with Roosevelt over Poland, and now he knew that Roosevelt would not demand any quid pro quo in return. It would cost him nothing to offer Roosevelt something in return by merely agreeing to a declaration without any teeth which seemed to mean a great deal to the President. Stalin indeed could now afford to be generous.

Stalin also probably signed because Roosevelt had sweetened his proposal by the suggestion of constructing a free port at the head of the Persian Gulf, under the trusteeship of three or four powers (one most assuredly the Soviet Union) and with a railroad that would connect the port with the Soviet Union. This concept stemmed from Hurley's idea, expressed in his May 13 telegram, that the Soviet Union would insist on a corridor to the Persian Gulf at the peace table. According to Roosevelt, Stalin thought the idea interesting and voiced no objections.[2]

The Teheran Conference was now in its final hours, so no time remained for lengthy discussions among the three leaders about the text of the Declaration on Iran. Only the Americans had a draft ready, prepared by John D. Jernegan, third secretary in the American legation, who had anticipated that this question might be considered at the conference. The draft filled the need for a three-power declaration. After Hurley made some suggestions, Jernegan wrote out a new draft which became the final version. Harriman, detailed to obtain the necessary signatures, showed the copy in English to Stalin, and asked if he wished to have it translated into Russian in order that both Russian and English texts be available for signing. Pavlov translated the draft to Stalin, who approved it, and because of the shortness of time, no Russian text was ever prepared for signing.

Stalin, however, declined to sign first, insisting that Roosevelt do so. Only after the President had signed the declaration did Stalin follow. Even then he insisted that Churchill precede him in signing. Stalin had a loud argument with Churchill over whether the declaration should call the country "Persia" or "Iran," with Churchill insisting on "Persia." Roosevelt sided with Stalin and it became "Declaration of the Three Powers Regarding Iran."

The declaration was as innocuous and as vague as a declaration could possibly be. The three governments recognized the assistance which Iran had given to the prosecution of the war, particularly by helping with the transportation of supplies to the Soviet Union. The three leaders promised to make available to the Iranian government such economic assistance as might be possible in view of the needs of the United Nations in the world conflict. In the postwar era, Iranian economic problems would be considered fully in conferences and by agencies dealing with international economic questions. Finally, they declared themselves "at one with the government of Iran in their desire for the maintenance of the independence, sovereignty, and territorial integrity of Iran."[3]

Omitted were all of the points so troubling to Molotov and Stalin, including the promised withdrawal of troops within six months after the cessation of hostilities and the approval of foreign advisers working with the Iranian government. However, Molotov could not insist as he had done at the Moscow Conference that a declaration on Iran could not be discussed without the presence of an Iranian representative.

For the Iranian government, the declaration signaled a major change in foreign policy: The United States had been substituted for Germany as the third power to counterbalance the British and Soviet presence in Iran. Already the Iranian government had signed a trade agreement with the United States which was another substitute for the German trade lost because of the war. Through that agreement, the Iranian government could demonstrate to the world that it was important enough to warrant a trade treaty with the United States. The declaration topped off the diplomatic victory of the Iranian government with the public statement that the United States supported Iranian independence and territorial integrity.

Roosevelt never imagined that one of the first international crises to face the United Nations after World War II would be the Soviet refusal to withdraw troops from Iran and end their support of a separatist movement in Azerbaijan. He had been sold on the declaration by Patrick Hurley, whose ideas about American-Iranian relations fitted in with Roosevelt's postwar plans. Hurley contemplated a scheme in which the United States would assist Iran in creating a government based on the consent of the governed and on the free enterprise system. Through a program of self-help, Iran could achieve the "fulfillment of the principles of justice, freedom of conscience, freedom of the press, freedom of speech, freedom of want, equality of opportunity, and to a degree freedom from fear." All of these goals would be attained through the help of expert American advisers whose salaries would be paid by the Iranian government, and who would make periodic reports to the State Department about their work in Iran. Such work would involve building schools, hospitals, and sanitary systems, improving transportation, communication, and the general welfare system. Hurley convinced Roosevelt that through such a plan, the United States could help less favored nations and at the same time bestow on them the principles of the Atlantic Charter and the Four Freedoms. Roosevelt commented on Hurley's suggestion, "I was rather thrilled with the idea of using Iran as an example of what we could do by an unselfish American policy. We could not take on a more difficult nation than Iran."[4]

Stalin had another plan to help Iran. Some time on November 30, he visited the shah, spending an hour and a half with him. He had not compelled the shah to travel again to the Soviet Embassy. "Stalin was particularly polite and well mannered and he seemed intent upon making a good impression on me," wrote the shah. In the course of their talk, Stalin offered the shah twenty T-34 tanks and twenty fighter planes as an absolute gift; he would also establish a flying school in northern Iran to train the pilots. The prospect of receiving modern equipment so pleased the young ruler that he accepted the gifts at once. Stalin's offerings were probably intended to make the Soviet occupation more endurable for the shah and to appeal to his yearning for a modern army. The gifts would also help to strengthen Soviet ties with Iran. American military intelligence believed the shah had hopes that the British would match Stalin's generosity with an equally impressive gift of military equipment. London chose not to engage in such a contest.

Later, the shah had second thoughts about Stalin's proffered gifts. They would mean Soviet instructors for troops and pilots, and these could become an effective method of infiltration. The maintenance of new equipment could become expensive, necessitating more Soviet aid. But there was a major limitation on the gifts: The Russians alone would decide where the planes and tanks were to be stationed. The period of training was unspecified, and until that ended, the tanks and planes would be under the command of the Soviet General Staff. The shah ultimately had to decline Stalin's offer.[5]

During the final hours of the Teheran Conference, in addition to signing the Declaration on Iran, other documents had to be completed: the military conclusions of the conference and the communiqué for the press. The military conclusions had been prepared on November 30 and the document was signed late on December 1. The conference decided to support Yugoslav Partisans with supplies and equipment as well as by commando operations. They agreed on the desirability of Turkey entering the war on the Allied side before the end of 1943. If Turkey were to enter the war against Germany, and if Bulgaria declared war on Turkey or attacked her, the Soviet government would immediately make war on Bulgaria. Operation OVERLORD would be launched "during May 1944 in conjunction with an operation against southern France." The strength of the operation against southern France would be dependent upon the availability of landing craft. The conference had noted Stalin's announcement that the Soviet armies would launch an offensive at the same time as OVERLORD to prevent German forces being transferred from the eastern front to the west. The military staffs would remain in close touch and would develop a cover plan to "mystify and mislead the enemy as regards these operations."[6]

The cover plan referred to the fabled BODYGUARD plan to deceive the Germans into making faulty strategic dispositions prior to the launching of OVERLORD. These involved persuading the German High Command to dispose of its forces in areas where they would cause the least damage to operations OVERLORD and ANVIL (the invasion of southern France). BODYGUARD would play a vital role in the ultimate success of OVERLORD.

The military decisions marked a victory for the American chiefs of staff, who had argued for a definite date for the invasion of the continent of Europe by Anglo-American forces. The wrangling and debating concluded, a bargain had been struck and a contract set down in the military agreement. But the document signified a change in the balance of world power then and for the future. The British had been compelled to yield to the Americans, backed by the Russians, because of superiority in men, weapons, and machines.

After the military agreement, one final document had yet to be drafted, the communiqué for release to the world. The communiqué went through three drafts before being approved in the last minutes of the dinner meeting on December 1. The various drafts were apparently all corrected by

Roosevelt and Hopkins. There is no record of any discussion of the content. Bohlen does record that when Stalin was examining the Russian text of the communiqué, Roosevelt called Bohlen over to give him a message to translate to Stalin. When Stalin heard the interruption, he exclaimed, "For God's sake, allow us to finish this work." Then he turned and to his embarrassment realized that it was Roosevelt who had interrupted him. This was the first and only time during the conference that Stalin displayed any embarrassment. Roosevelt had only asked for Stalin's autograph. Bohlen did not translate the remark for Roosevelt.[7]

The three leaders, through the communiqué, announced that they had been meeting in Teheran and there they had shaped and confirmed their common policy. They had concerted their plans for the destruction of the German forces and agreed on operations to be undertaken from the east, west, and south. As to the future peace, they were certain that their concord would make it endure. Recognizing their responsibility to make a peace that would "command the good will of the overwhelming mass of the peoples of the world, and banish the scourge and terror of war for many generations," the three men promised to obtain the cooperation of all nations to eliminate "tyranny, slavery, oppression, and intolerance." No power on earth could prevent them from destroying the German armies, U-boats, and war plants. It would be a relentless and an increasing attack. They looked to that day when people could live free lives, untouched by tyranny, and according to their desires and their consciences.

"We came here with hope and determination. We leave here, friends in fact, in spirit and in purpose." This conclusion today sounds ironic and naïve; but to a world suffering through another winter of war, the words could only reassure millions of people.

One paragraph eliminated from the first draft held the only note of hope for the German people: "We do not seek to enslave you. We do mean to destroy not only your military forces, but also the false leaders who have led a generation of Germans into bitter excesses against common decencies, culminating with your being plunged, by this same leadership, into a useless war which has caused millions of your sons to die, and may sacrifice millions more." Instead, the final version stressed the inability of the German forces to escape ultimate destruction.[8]

With the communiqué completed, at about ten o'clock the conference broke up. Roosevelt immediately left the Soviet Embassy and was driven to the U.S. Army Camp Amirabad, where he and his party spent the night:

> Today we have signed several "accords" and a statement for later issues—and we have said goodbye to all—tonight we go to the Am. Camp which is near the airport. This trip has been worth every mile of travel.

The next morning, December 2, seated in a jeep, Roosevelt was driven around the camp for an inspection tour. When the jeep stopped in front of the hospital, Roosevelt made a short speech to a group of Army patients and hospital personnel. He was then brought to the front of General Connolly's headquarters where a low platform had been erected; the jeep drove up and Roosevelt spoke to the assembled troops.

After his speech, the President traveled in a staff car south to the airfield outside Teheran over dusty dirt roads. His plane left for Cairo about 9:46 A.M., and by 4 P.M. he was in Cairo reading his accumulated mail. That evening he dined with Churchill, who had arrived earlier. They compared their reactions to Stalin, who had left Teheran about the same time as they, rehashed the discussions that had just ended, and argued over Roosevelt's promise to Chiang before the Teheran Conference to launch Operation BUCCANEER. For all his eloquence, Churchill could not change the President's mind.

Back in Teheran, the President's departure had not pleased the shah. On December 1, the minister of the court complained to Dreyfus about the shah's regret that Roosevelt had not returned his visit. Stalin had visited him for over an hour, and Churchill was expected to call again. (He never did.) Could not the President call on him on the way to the airfield? He would not even have to leave his car. But when Dreyfus brought this request to General Watson, he refused to refer it to Roosevelt. As a substitute for a presidential return call, Hurley and Dreyfus hastily prepared a letter for Roosevelt's signature in which he expressed his pleasure at meeting the shah on November 30. He thanked the shah for the gift of the carpet and for his invitation to be a guest at the royal palace, though the circumstances of the visit had made it impossible for him to avail himself of the offer. The President regretted leaving Iran without having an opportunity to see more of the country and the people. As a postscript, Roosevelt added: "I greatly hope that we shall have the pleasure of a visit from you to Washington." With the letter to the shah went a signed photograph of the President in a silver frame.

Dreyfus returned the next day to the palace to inform the minister of the court that the conference was over and that he had been unable to arrange a return visit. He added that the three-power Declaration on Iran had been signed, stressing that it was done especially at the President's insistence.

When Dreyfus paid his last call on the shah on December 6 before leaving for the United States, he found the shah still unhappy over Roosevelt's attitude. The failure of the President to pay a return call deeply humiliated him. Stalin had called on him, but the President, though unable to return the shah's call, had attended the dinner given that evening at the British legation. And when the "Sword of Stalingrad" was presented to Stalin, the shah declared, the President had stood up with all the others who were present. This lapse in protocol particularly galled the shah because when he met the President at the Soviet Embassy, Roosevelt had received the shah seated and excused himself from rising to his feet. Again the shah complained at being kept waiting at the Soviet Embassy when he called on the President at his insistence. A sovereign, said the shah, should not be kept waiting and should be received at the door with a guard of honor. Dreyfus could only fall back on the excuse that the President rose to his feet only with great difficulty, and there was no American guard of honor because he was staying at the Soviet Embassy instead of the American legation.

The minister for foreign affairs had been inclined to recommend to the cabinet the desirability of terminating the services of all the American advisers in Iran as quickly as possible and then he would resign his post in protest over the disrespect shown his sovereign. He claimed that he had refrained from this action only because of the Declaration on Iran.

As Dreyfus prepared to leave, the shah informed him that he would be very pleased if the visit to the United States occurred. However, he warned Dreyfus, considering what had happened in Teheran, he would never accept the President's invitation to visit Washington until every detail of protocol had been carefully worked out in advance. Then he wished Dreyfus a successful trip to the United States and a speedy return to Iran.

Not only was the shah unhappy over presidential protocol, so was Dreyfus. He had been shoved aside by Hurley, who sported the rank of ambassador and personal representative for the President of the United States. His exclusion from the conference can probably be traced to Hopkins, who claimed that Dreyfus would only provoke trouble. "The man just won't get along with anyone," said Hopkins. Thanks also to Hopkins, he never received a briefing about the conference and consequently could not answer any of the Iranian officials' questions as to how the outcome affected Iran. To top it off, Dreyfus's name had been removed from the guest list for Churchill's birthday dinner on November 30, thanks again to Hopkins.[9]

At Churchill's birthday dinner, during the general conversation, someone remarked that this event was so important it ought to be memorialized by a plaque. Churchill deputized Reader Bullard, the British minister, to carry out this task.

On October 5, 1944, a silver plaque, costing £165 and paid for by Churchill from a special fund, was unveiled in the British Embassy in Teheran to commemorate the occasion. It read:

In this room was celebrated
  on November 30th 1943
  the 69th birthday of
The Rt. Hon. Winston Churchill
  C.H., F.R.S., M.P.,
Prime Minister and Minister of Defence
of H.M. government in the United Kingdom.
  Among his guests were
The Hon. Franklin D. Roosevelt
President of the United States of America
                    and
Marshal Joseph Stalin
President of the Council of People's Commissars
  of the Union of Soviet Socialist Republics.
These three representatives of Allied states
  were at that moment met in Teheran
  to concert further measures
  whereby Nazi tyranny might be
  most speedily overthrown
  and mankind set free
to enjoy in peace the fruits of its labours
and to develop mutual aid for the good of all.
  To the fulfillment of this purpose
  they here pledged themselves anew
  to devote their unceasing efforts
    trusting for success
  to the toil, endurance and valour of
  the Allied peoples.
CRESCIT SUB PONDERE VIRTUS

Not to be outdone by their allies, the Russians had a plaque of white marble from the Ural Mountains unveiled in their embassy on the first anniversary of the conference. The tone of the inscription was more modest:

In this building, from November 28th to December 1st, 1943, was held the conference of the leaders of the three Allied powers, the President of the Council of People's Commissars of the U.S.S.R., J. V.

Stalin, the President of the United States of America, F. D. Roosevelt, and the Prime Minister of Great Britain, W. Churchill.

The conference adopted a declaration about joint operations in the war against Germany and the postwar cooperation of the three powers and also a declaration about Persia.

The Iranians present at the unveiling ceremony wondered why Roosevelt, a head of state, had his name listed after Stalin's, who was only the president of a council of ministers. Although pleased by the reference to the declaration regarding Iran, they could not conceal their skepticism about its meaning for their country, one year after all the speeches had been made and the toasts drunk by J. V. Stalin, F. D. Roosevelt, and W. Churchill.[10]

Instead of erecting plaques, the Municipal Council of Teheran decided to commemorate the Teheran Conference in its own way. The street leading to the American Legation was changed to Avenue Roosevelt; the street to the north of the British legation was named after Churchill; the street to the north of the Soviet Embassy became Avenue Stalin. But these changes may not have entirely pleased the Russians. The street named after Churchill was an important one, passing in front of the Soviet Embassy, but Avenue Stalin was short, unimportant in the rear of the Soviet Embassy without any entrance to it from the Embassy grounds. After the revolution in 1979, all of these street names were changed.

16

Back to the Pyramids and Home Again

FROM TEHERAN, Roosevelt and Churchill returned to their villas and guards outside Cairo. They were joined by the Combined Chiefs of Staff, who had stopped over in Jerusalem for sightseeing on their return to Cairo.

Already the world had begun to learn about a conference in the Middle East. In a radio speech in Fort Worth, Texas, on December 2, Senator Tom Connally, chairman of the Senate Committee on Foreign Relations, had announced that "another great conference is taking place in the Middle East between President Roosevelt, Marshal Stalin, and Prime Minister Churchill." *The New York Times* printed the story the next day.

But in Cairo, Roosevelt and Churchill had to clean up important tasks left over from the Teheran Conference. With Stalin they had agreed on OVERLORD and ANVIL, operations that would be mounted as close together as possible. The dates for these invasions would require the best possible use of landing craft. At the same time, landing craft would be needed in the Indian Ocean for Operation BUCCANEER, which Roosevelt had promised Chiang at the first Cairo Conference. Where would the ships be found? In addition to this problem, the Turkish president and his foreign minister were to come to Cairo for discussions about Turkey, the Allies, and the war.

The British were shocked to learn that the Americans intended to leave either on December 5 or 6. In his diary, Brooke recorded his unhappiness:

We were dumbfounded by being informed that the meeting must finish on Sunday at the latest (in forty-eight hours) as the President was off. No apologies—nothing! They have completely upset the whole meeting by wasting all our time with Chiang Kai-shek and Stalin before we had settled any points with them. And now, with nothing settled, they propose to disappear into the blue and leave all the main points connected with this conference unsettled. It all looks like some of the worst sharp practice that I have seen for some time.[1]

This news had come at the meeting of the Combined Chiefs of Staff on December 3. The chiefs had been discussing the military conclusions of the Teheran Conference when Admiral Leahy surprised them by his announcement. They decided little then except to realize that they faced the problem of finding sufficient landing craft for all of the scheduled operations.

That evening Roosevelt and Churchill remained long at the table after dinner talking about the Andaman (BUCCANEER) operation, which Churchill pressed the President to drop. Churchill wanted to use the forces in seizing his prize, Rhodes, which he argued would aid the entry of Turkey into the war. Roosevelt, refusing to budge, insisted that the promises he had made to Chiang must be fulfilled.

Eden, who was also present along with Leahy, supported Churchill in arguing about the future occupation of Germany. They wished to have the British troops in the north, but Roosevelt contended that the Americans should take that area for occupation. Churchill and Eden argued that it would make better logistical sense for the British to be in that part of Germany which was nearest to Britain. And so the evening ended.

The next day, all present joined in a meeting of the Combined Chiefs in Roosevelt's villa. Roosevelt at once announced that he must leave on December 6 at the latest. Except for the question of Turkish participation in the war, the only important problem seemed to be "the comparatively small one of the provision of about twenty landing craft or their equipment. It was unthinkable to be beaten by a small item like that, and he felt bound to say that it *must* be done."

Roosevelt's eagerness to leave probably resulted from weariness caused by the long trip and the meetings in Teheran, as well as uneasiness at being out of the United States for so long. Only by setting a deadline would he be able to cut short Churchill's oratory. Later he would observe: "Winston has developed a tendency to make long speeches which are repetitions of long speeches which he has made before."[2] Roosevelt's deadline, however, did not quite have the desired effect because Churchill kept on talking.

According to him, the British looked on the early ending of the Cairo discussions with much apprehension. "There were still many questions of first-class importance to be settled." He stressed that in the last few days, two decisive events had taken place. First, Stalin's announcement that Russia would join in the war against Japan after Germany's defeat meant that Russia would provide better air bases than could be found in China. His announcement also made it more important to concentrate on making OVERLORD a success. The military staffs should consider how this change would affect the conduct of the war in the Pacific and Southeast Asia.

The second decisive event was the decision to launch OVERLORD in May. Churchill preferred a July date instead of May, but he would do all in his power to make OVERLORD in May a success. To attain that goal, Operation ANVIL must be a success. Then he confessed that because of the new situation, he was no longer as concerned as before about Rhodes. Churchill urged that the cost of operations in Southeast Asia be judged in relation to OVERLORD. The requirements for troops for BUCCANEER which he had just received from Admiral Mountbatten astounded him. Now that Stalin had promised to enter the war in Asia, operations in Southeast Asia had lost much of their value. They had become too expensive. Churchill insisted that the large differences of opinion between the British and the American delegations should be cleared up.

Brooke complained about the course of the conference.

In previous conferences, he insisted, after meetings among the military men they had submitted their reports to the President and the prime minister and then discussed the ways and means to achieve their goals. All that had been altered by meetings at Cairo with the Generalissimo. Afterward the principal members of the delegations had flown to Teheran for plenary conferences, with the result that the Combined Chiefs now had little opportunity for discussion at Cairo. He presented his list of problems requiring decisions: the availability of landing craft; the long-term plan for the defeat of Japan; Stalin's promise to make war on Japan; the Mediterranean; and the question of ANVIL. Admiral Cunningham and Air Chief Marshal Portal joined in criticizing BUCCANEER. General Marshall agreed with Brooke's complaints that much yet remained to be decided. Churchill wanted the staffs to stay behind and reach the decisions. Admiral Leahy thought it would take them two or three weeks. Churchill returned to hammering at BUCCANEER.

But Roosevelt would not concede. Mountbatten would have to get along with the resources already allotted to his command; the military staffs could settle their problems in principle and leave the details to be worked out later. Brooke disagreed because there were too many questions yet to be settled. Admiral King offered to give newly constructed landing craft, destined for the Pacific, to OVERLORD in order that BUCCANEER could be launched. He reminded the meeting that a definite commitment had been made to Chiang for an amphibious operation in the spring of 1944. To Churchill, King's offer was a "fruitful contribution," but it did not change his opinion.

Roosevelt failed twice to get an agreement that OVERLORD and ANVIL were paramount and nothing should hinder their success, that the landing craft would have to be found for use in the eastern Mediterranean, and that Mountbatten should be told to get along with what he already had. Churchill argued that it might be necessary to reduce BUCCANEER in order to strengthen OVERLORD and ANVIL. Roosevelt could not agree. "We had a moral obligation to do something for China and he would not be prepared to forego the amphibious operation, except for some very great and readily apparent reason."

Churchill and Roosevelt ended the meeting with a request that the Combined Chiefs of Staff find some way out of the impasse, but the chiefs met twice without reaching agreement on this issue. On December 5, Roosevelt and Churchill met again with the chiefs to argue about BUCCANEER. Roosevelt said little, leaving most of the argument to Hopkins. The British were on the attack, forcing the Americans to realize that it would be impossible to mount all three operations, given the available landing craft and the need to ensure that the invasions of France would be successful.

The British wanted to drop BUCCANEER, the amphibious attack on the Andaman Islands, dominating the Bay of Bengal, which would launch the campaign to open the Burma Road and get supplies to Chiang Kai-shek's armies. They based their opposition to this operation on a low opinion of Chiang and his forces; moreover, they did not wish to expend their forces in opening the Burma Road. The American view involved not only the pledge to Chiang made by Roosevelt, but also the fear that without Chiang and his Nationalist armies continuing to fight, the Japanese forces, no longer tied down in mainland China, would be free to attack American forces moving through the Pacific. If they went back on the pledge to Chiang and China dropped out of the war, everything would depend on Stalin keeping his word to attack Japan. Could they run such a risk? "Suppose," commented Roosevelt, "Marshal Stalin was unable to be as good as his word; we might find that we had forfeited Chinese support without obtaining commensurate help from the Russians."

Late in the afternoon of December 5, Roosevelt called in the American chiefs of staff to tell them that he would cease arguing for BUCCANEER. He was the commander-in-chief, so that ended the argument as far as the chiefs were concerned. Soon Churchill received a message from the President: "BUCCANEER is off." If China left the war because of lack of supplies, the only other threat to Japanese forces would be Russian forces in the Far East.[3] At Teheran, Stalin had promised that after the defeat of the Germans, Soviet armies would enter the war against Japan. Now Roosevelt and Churchill could only trust him.

Roosevelt made only one comment on this decision that

has been recorded—"I've been stubborn as a mule for four days but we can't get anywhere, and it won't do for a conference to end that way. The British just won't do the operation, and I can't get them to agree to it."[4] The President may also have changed his mind because at Teheran, with Stalin as his ally in the argument over OVERLORD, Churchill had made the concession.

And then there was the problem of Turkish entry into the war, left over from Teheran. For months Churchill and Eden had labored to bring Turkey into the war. Turkish entry appealed to the British because if the Allies could move into Turkey, they would have air bases at their disposal from which to bomb German installations in Greece, Rumania, and Bulgaria. They would then dominate the Dardanelles, and the Bosphorus, neutral under the Montreux Convention, would be denied to the Germans. After Turkey had become an ally, American and British supplies could be shipped in bulk to southern Russia instead of using Iran which necessitated lengthy transshipment; the dangerous convoy route to Murmansk would no longer be necessary. Moreover, an Allied presence in Turkey would force the Germans to divert troops to southeast Europe and away from the beachheads in France. Churchill also wanted to reestablish British influence in the eastern Mediterranean and in the Middle East after the war. Turkish entry on the Allied side would help his postwar plans. Here, then, was the clear appeal for Churchill.

Balanced against these prospects were the actual conditions in Turkey. The armed forces needed modern equipment which the Allies would be obliged to supply. Any Allied preparations would somehow have to be hidden from the German diplomats in Turkey, who were headed by the sly Franz von Papen. German forces were closer to Turkey than were the Allied forces. Finally, there remained the Turkish leaders, who had to choose between Germany and Soviet Russia.

When Roosevelt and Churchill had invited the leaders to come to Cairo, the wily President Ismet Inönü insisted on preconditions before accepting the invitation. The discussion would be one between equals—he would not just be informed of the decisions that had been reached at Teheran concerning Turkey. Both Churchill and Roosevelt sent the desired assurances. Roosevelt dispatched his son-in-law, Major John Boettiger, to accompany Inönü to Cairo. Churchill dispatched his son, Randolph, on a similar mission, but Inönü flew with Boettiger, arriving in Cairo on December 4. The British, American, and Soviet ambassadors also came to the second Cairo Conference with Inönü. The notorious Andrei Vyshinsky had been expected, but he missed the conference because of alleged communications problems. The Soviet ambassador, Sergei Vinogradov, had come to Cairo as the guest of Inönü, but when he realized that there were no instructions awaiting him and that Vyshinsky was supposed to represent the Soviet government, he refused to attend a single meeting. To the Turks, Vyshinsky's absence indicated Soviet disinterest in having them fight alongside an Anglo-American expeditionary force.

In two days of meetings with Roosevelt and Churchill, Inönü sought to be as neutral as possible, to obtain the maximum amount of armaments, and to prepare for whatever demands might come from the Russians. Inönü held his tongue, refusing to tell Roosevelt and Churchill that he regarded Soviet power as the principal threat to Europe and that he wanted Turkish military power strengthened and conserved for that day when Anglo-American forces would have to be dispatched to save the Balkans from Soviet armies.

Churchill and Roosevelt tried to woo the Turkish leader, but he proved a shrewd negotiator, more than equal to their combined efforts. Throughout the talks, Churchill carried the heavier load in seeking to persuade Inönü that Turkey should join the war. Hinting that Turkey would improve relations with her Russian neighbor, Churchill stated that Stalin had authorized them to say that should Bulgaria march against Turkey after she had entered the war, then Soviet Russia would declare war on Bulgaria—a prospect that did not reassure Inönü.

He reminded his audience that so long as Turkey remained out of the war, she would not be in danger. Moreover, Turkey was alone and unprepared. She had asked for planes and tanks but not until her minimum requirements were met could she be useful to the Allies. Once the Germans thought Turkey would enter the war, they would move quickly to bomb Turkish cities and attempt to seize Istanbul. So far Inönü had not been encouraged by the meager supplies furnished by Britain and the United States. He blamed the British for failing to ship promised equipment, and reminded Churchill that the airplanes which had been sent, Hurricanes and Beauforts, were outdated. Churchill huffed and puffed, trying to evade this accusation by claiming that the Turks were receiving antiquated equipment because of the needs of the British forces in the campaign in Italy.

Then the argument turned to Allied plans. After six weeks of preparations, Allied aircraft would arrive in Turkey, but Inönü feared that their arrival would set off an immediate declaration of war by Germany. Roosevelt and Churchill, evasive as could be, would only mutter that Allied planes flying into Turkish airfields would not necessarily produce a German declaration of war. They hoped that the Turks would enjoy peace until war preparations were completed. Inönü demanded to know how soon help would come after the first German attack. The answer was not reassuring: The arrival of Allied help would depend on the extent of the preparations! As is so often the case, when a problem becomes unsolvable, turn it over to a committee.

So Anthony Eden, Harry Hopkins, and Numan Menemencioğlu, the Turkish foreign minister, along with the British and American ambassadors to Turkey, and other British officers were now obliged to wrestle with the problem. The British tried to explain how they would infiltrate approximately two thousand technicians into Turkey without tipping the Germans off to an impending invasion. But Menemencioğlu switched the discussion, complaining about the small amount of equipment Turkey had received, only 4 percent of that promised by Churchill. Eden blamed the shortage of equipment on Turkish railroads, but Menemencioğlu could not be so easily pacified. As Turkey lacked everything, he demanded a list of minimum requirements that would be needed if she became involved in the war. But his demands did not concern the Americans and the British, who desired Turkey to enter the war by February 1944. To that end, Harry Hopkins made an impassioned plea for her to do so "willingly and wholeheartedly," promising that she would receive all possible aid from the Allies. In the end, however, Menemencioğlu vowed that Turkey would not take any action leading to war with Germany until she had the necessary supplies. That evening at dinner, Churchill pressed Inönü, pleading, almost threatening the Turkish president to enter the war. Once again Churchill failed.

On December 6, the day on which Roosevelt had planned to leave Cairo, he had to remain while the argument continued. But again Churchill and Roosevelt failed to sway the Turks. Nor could they quiet Inönü's fears that Germany would attack Turkey while preparations were in progress and before Allied aid would be available in substantial quantities. The meeting ended with Inönü uncommitted to bringing Turkey into the war.

After Roosevelt had left Cairo on December 7, Churchill once more tried to pin Inönü down to a date: February 15, 1944. By then, assuming preparations were completed and the Turkish government approved, fifteen Allied fighter squadrons would fly into Turkish airfields. But Inönü found enough excuses to avoid committing Turkey to war by that date. Churchill could not win him over even by preaching on the text that if Turkey joined the United Nations, she would be associating with Russia, "one of the strongest military powers in the world, if not the strongest, at any rate in Europe and Asia."[5]

When the Turkish delegation left Cairo, Churchill and Eden went to the airfield to bid them goodbye. There Inönü embraced Churchill before entering the plane for the flight back to Turkey. "Did you see, Ismet kissed me," exclaimed Churchill as they drove away from the airfield. But Eden complained that the kiss was all they had gained from fifteen hours of hard argument. That night, Churchill said to his daughter, Sarah, "Do you know what happened to me today, the Turkish President kissed me. The truth is I'm irresistible. But don't tell Anthony, he's jealous."[6]

Later the Turkish leaders came to understand why the Russians had been so cool toward Turkey entering the war armed and supported by the Anglo-Americans. The Soviet Union preferred to join in an agreement of "mutual assistance," which the Turks feared would mean Soviet forces on Turkish soil from which they might never leave. The Turks also could never get the Allies to commit themselves to any kind of a Balkan campaign because all their resources were soon to be committed to OVERLORD. Consequently, Turkey never went to war against Germany and only severed diplomatic relations on August 2, 1944.

The Turks were wise to avoid joining the Allied side without guarantees of adequate aid from either the British or the Americans. In the talks with the Turks, Roosevelt had appeared aloof, not wholly committed to the Turkish cause. Never would he and the Joint Chiefs of Staff disperse American military power through a landing on the shores of Turkey; their goal was OVERLORD. Had an Anglo-American force entered Turkey, Stalin would have been given an excuse to dispatch Soviet troops into Turkey in pursuit of German soldiers. He really did not care for an Allied military force landing in that part of Europe. For his part, Churchill had few resources to spare for the Turks. He was trying to trick them into war, so eager was he to get any operation under way in the eastern Mediterranean. He had been dreaming about Turkey entering the war and now the dream had ended.

Early on the morning of December 7, with Churchill at the airport to see him off, Roosevelt left Cairo on his way back to the United States. All day his plane carried him and his party across Egypt and Libya, over the scenes of bloody battles between the Afrika Korps and the British Eighth Army. That evening Roosevelt wrote in his diary:

> Here I am again, back at the Carthage Villa—after an all day trip the whole length of the British advance last winter—Over el Alamein & Benghazi & Tripoli—most interesting to see it all from the air—endless desert, but much of it broken country with a good lot of tanks & other equipment not yet picked up—In another year or two there will hardly be a trace—for even the shell hles [sic] & foxholes will be filled up— What a march that was! Over 1,000 miles—with fight-

ing practically all the way. But at the end, with the advance of Montgomery into Tunis from the south we and the British struck from the west—all of No. Africa was in our hands together with 300,000 prisoners.

Eisenhower met the President when he left his plane at Tunis, and riding with him from the airfield to the Villa Casa Blanca, he learned that he would command OVERLORD—a result of the Teheran Conference. Marshall would not have the appointment he so much desired. As Roosevelt told him, "Well, I didn't feel I could sleep at ease if you were out of Washington." That evening at the villa, Roosevelt entertained Eisenhower, officers from Elliott Roosevelt's squadron, and General Carl Spaatz, commander of the Allied Air Forces in North Africa, at a dinner served by Italian prisoners of war, whom Roosevelt noted in his diary "like $9/10$ of all the wops are crazy to come to the U.S. for 'good.' "

Roosevelt wanted to fly to Naples, but Eisenhower would not be responsible for his safety and would only permit the flight if given a direct order by the President. Reilly, with the help of Admiral Leahy, finally talked Roosevelt out of the trip. He settled for a flight to the island of Malta, escorted by P-38 fighter planes.

On December 8, Roosevelt arrived in Malta, where Lord Gort and his staff received him, and from a jeep, he reviewed the British forces guarding the island. Roosevelt presented a scroll to Gort citing the islanders for their heroism. A broken hydraulic pump in the President's plane meant a delay for repairs, so Gort took Roosevelt on a tour of the harbor. Then from Malta Roosevelt flew to Palermo, Sicily, where he met General Mark Clark, commander of the U.S. Fifth Army, and some other officers, including General George S. Patton. During the Sicilian campaign, Patton had received an official reprimand from Eisenhower because he had slapped a soldier who had been hospitalized for battle fatigue. After Roosevelt had called Patton over and talked with him, there were tears in his eyes.

From Sicily, Roosevelt returned to Tunis and the Villa Casa Blanca. Early on the morning of December 9, the President and his party left Tunis for Dakar:

* * *

By daylight we are nearly through the Atlas Mts. where
they "peter off" on their Eastern end. Then hour after
hour of desert—It is bad enough to fly at all but over
desert or ocean I am so bored I could shriek. Instead
of that I relapse into an awful vacuum—for I can't talk
or read, or play solitaire. At last we saw the Atlantic
& the good old *Iowa* in the outer harbor.

After *Iowa* had left Oran in November, she had been sent
to Brazil and then from there to Freetown, Sierra Leone,
where she remained until ordered to Dakar to pick up the
President. The Free French, who controlled the port of Dakar,
insisted that a French ship should be given the honor of
transporting Roosevelt from the dock to the battleship. All
explanations about his crippled condition were waved aside;
the French proposed to move Roosevelt from the upper bridge
of a Free French destroyer to the quarterdeck of *Iowa*. So
the President was hoisted aboard in a fancy boatswain's chair
by eight side boys to the tune of the boatswain's pipe just as
admirals in the days of sailing vessels. A narrow gangplank
with a standing line was put out to the French ship and the
remainder of the President's party used it to board the *Iowa*.
After carefully studying the situation, Harry Hopkins chose
to crawl aboard across the plank accompanied by the roar of
presidential laughter.

Within an hour after the President boarded *Iowa*, the
battleship was under way, escorted by a task group. The
crossing was smooth until *Iowa* and her escorts encountered
a storm on December 15. By nightfall, visibility was zero.
Near midnight the task group encountered a merchant vessel on a course that could have brought a collision. Radar
picked up the ship, and *Iowa* and her escorts had to turn on
their running lights to avoid colliding. The next morning,
when the *Iowa* reached the entrance to Chesapeake Bay,
Roosevelt dispatched a message by radio to Stephen Early,
his press secretary, announcing that he had returned to the
United States. Roosevelt entered in his diary:

A completely uneventful voyage under escort of destroyers all the way & of aircraft also for the last 3 days.

Marvellous warm weather & no sea up to yesterday noon when we hit a sudden storm from the coast, & from 60 it dropped last night to 20. And this morning early we came in through the Capes. Now we are steaming up Chesapeake Bay. We are all packed up— I am writing in the big room & the boys are having a final game of Gin Rummy.

The little "Potomac" has loomed 6 miles ahead at the mouth of the River and at 4:30 I will transfer to her, after first making a speech to this crew.

And tomorrow morning we should get to the Navy Yard in Washington at 9:30 & soon afterwards I will be at the W.H. & using the telephone. So will end a new Odyssey.

For his speech, *Iowa*'s crew had been mustered on the after deck, where a platform had been erected. Roosevelt talked to the crew for about twenty minutes, joking with them and discussing his trip and the progress in the war.

"I had a wonderful cruise on the *Iowa*—one that I shall never forget," he said. "I think that all my staff behaved themselves pretty well, with one or two lapses. When we came on board from that little French destroyer, I was horrified to note that Major General Watson and Mr. Hopkins came over the rail on all-fours. However, landlubbers like that do have lapses." All of the passengers had been well cared for. "You had a happy lot of visitors, fellow shipmates." He found *Iowa* a happy ship. "And having served with the Navy for many years, I know and you know, what that means."

Becoming serious, he explained that he had gone abroad to have "conversations with other nations, to see that this war that we are all engaged in shall not happen again." They had to "eliminate from the human race nations like Germany and Japan." They must also eliminate the possibility that Germany and Japan could ruin the lives of other nations. "Obviously it will be necessary when we win the war to make the possibility of a future upsetting of our civilization an impossible thing." At the Teheran Conference, the three leaders "all had the same fundamental aim—stopping what has been going on in these past four years, and that is why I believe from the viewpoint of people—just plain people—this trip has been worthwhile."

Looking back on the events since Pearl Harbor, he believed that "we are making real progress . . . from being on the defensive—very definitely so—two years ago, from being in the process of building things up to a greater strength a year ago, to where we are today, when we have the initiative in every part of the world.

"And now I have to leave you for the U.S.S. *Potomac*. When I came out on deck quite a while ago and saw her about a half mile away I looked and decided how she had shrunk since I had been on the *Iowa*.

"And so good-bye for a while. I hope that I will have another cruise on this ship. Meanwhile, good luck, and remember that I am with you in spirit, each and every one of you."[7]

It was not the greatest speech Roosevelt ever made, but to the officers and sailors on the after deck of the *Iowa* it meant a great deal on that rainy, cold December day.

Roosevelt spent the night on the *Potomac*, and the next morning docked at the Navy Yard in Washington. When he arrived at the White House, the full cabinet, alerted by Early, greeted him. At that point, Roosevelt had traveled 17,442 miles, farther than any other President had ever traveled while in office.

17
"The Greatest Event of Our Times"

BEFORE THEY HAD EVEN LEFT Teheran, the story of a meeting between Roosevelt, Churchill, and Stalin had begun to slip past the censors. Japanese Foreign Minister Mamoru Shigemitsu by November 29 had received "an irrefutable report that Stalin is somewhere in the south with Molotov, I don't know whether in Russia or not." The British and American ambassadors had also traveled south. Shigemitsu had heard rumors "that the big wigs of the three countries would meet." This must be the meeting.[1]

The New York Times carried a report from London on December 3, datelined Istanbul, reporting that Roosevelt, Churchill, and Stalin were conferring in Teheran and drafting an ultimatum for Germany to surrender unconditionally or suffer destruction from Allied bombers. The paper also printed the report of Senator Connally's speech in Fort Worth, announcing that the three leaders were conferring in the Middle East. Another report on December 4 said that Stalin had left the Kremlin to confer with Roosevelt and Churchill.

By December 5 so many rumors were floating about in Berlin that Propaganda Minister Paul Joseph Goebbels made a diary entry about the "conference of the Big Three to decide on military plans of great magnitude against Germany." He noted: "The Anglo-Americans have asked Stalin for airports within the territory of the Soviet Union so as to be able to bombard Germany from the east also. Churchill intends to cede all of eastern Germany to the Poles as an equivalent for the Soviets' laying claim to eastern Poland." He could not imagine that "the leading English statesmen are so stupid and shortsighted as to put that sort of an estimate on Bolshevism. Stalin won't think of fulfilling obligations entered upon with England and America." On December 6, the information coming out about the conference was "quite mysterious," according to Goebbels. As there had not yet been any lengthy communiqué, "we are still groping in the dark." By that evening he had heard that "a committee in Teheran was working on an appeal to the German people." Where was it?

On the morning of December 7, those on the inside of Nazi politics were still ignorant of what had happened at Teheran, according to Goebbels. "Everybody is tense and full of expectation. As a result there is very little news, because the entire world news machinery is geared to the Teheran communiqué." That evening, when the communiqué at last appeared, Goebbels found it "neither fish nor fowl." He recorded in his diary: "One might expect that a little more would result from three days of conference, but apparently Stalin could not agree to the plans of Churchill and Roosevelt. Stalin undoubtedly was the guiding spirit of the Teheran Conference." Goebbels had expected an Allied appeal to the German people, but thought it had been dropped because of the counter propaganda campaign which he had mounted against the expected communiqué. That evening, Goebbels and Hitler discussed the communiqué over the telephone and decided that it was so innocuous they could let the German people read it.[2]

Originally the news of the Teheran Conference had been scheduled for release at 1 P.M. Washington time, 8 P.M. Moscow time, on December 6. But on December 3, Radio Moscow announced: "A few days ago, in Teheran, a conference took place between the leaders of the three Allied powers, President Roosevelt, Prime Minister Churchill and Premier Stalin. Diplomatic and military representatives took part in the conference. At the Conference, questions on the conduct of the war against Germany were discussed as well as a number of political questions."[3]

The Soviet news scoop infuriated American newsmen and reporters who had been waiting until the agreed release time.

Their anger was doubly bitter because the Reuters News Agency had also beaten them by releasing the story of the first Cairo Conference ahead of the agreed time of release on November 30. Molotov defended the Soviet action on the grounds that Senator Connally had mentioned the meeting in his Fort Worth speech and Reuters had predicted the conference. He claimed that TASS, the Soviet News Agency, had to release the story in order to end rumors.[4] The full release came as scheduled on December 6, appearing in the morning newspapers the next day.

Opinions on its significance varied from ecstatic to suspicious. From Rio de Janeiro, *O Radical* compared Roosevelt, Churchill, and Stalin to the Three Wise Men "who saw the star which conducted them to the humble cradle of truth— heralds of new life, a better world, a lasting peace."[5] The Philadelphia *Evening Bulletin* declared: "Hitler will not mistake the significance of Teheran. It means more than the wrecking of his present Third Reich. For if the parties to the new compact stick to their engagements no new power of aggression will be permitted to rise in Europe." The Washington *Star* complained about the official communiqué from Teheran because it told "disappointingly little of the most significant war council of modern times." The Washington *Times-Herald* criticized the conferences because they would stiffen the Axis will to fight to the bitter end. "Why not, when you have nothing to gain by quitting? However, this is the policy of our four leaders in this war, Messrs. Chiang, Churchill, Roosevelt and Stalin. There seems to be nothing their people can do about it but string along behind the leaders. So it looks as if we are still in for a long, bloody and costly war." The Washington *News*, on the other hand, felt that criticism of the Teheran Conference was "understandable but superficial. What mattered was that Marshal Stalin, Prime Minister Churchill and President Roosevelt have been able to make far-reaching commitments for victory, which no other persons on earth could make and which Stalin would not make except face to face." According to the New York *Daily Worker*, the Teheran meeting overwhelmed the imagination. "To the beasts of fascism . . . the Roosevelt-Stalin-Churchill handclasp is the seal of doom. . . . The sinister conspiracies of influential reactionary forces must now be completely defeated." And the London *Daily Worker*, which had run a regular feature demanding the second front, proclaimed: "Let the declaration be read from the housetops, let it echo on every hand. Never before has there been such grand inspiring news to lift up the heart and rally workers and soldiers alike for the last fight."

As for the columnists, Ernest Lindley writing in *The Washington Post* commented that "in his efforts to find ground for a long time understanding with the Soviet Union, the President has been tenacious and patient . . . [he] steadfastly has tried to break down the wall of misunderstanding between the Soviet Union and the West. In some respects getting Stalin to leave the Soviet Union to confer with him and Churchill may be the President's greatest single achievement in that direction." David Lawrence of the Washington *Star* declared: "For the American people the agreement represents a milestone of human progress. . . . The Teheran declaration is God-guided statesmanship. It has the restraint and objectivity which only the leaders of free men, conscious of the rightness of their cause, can truly proclaim." And Hanson Baldwin wrote in *The New York Times:* "Very clearly, 1944 is to be the year of decision in Europe. . . . To say that Premier Stalin dominated the Teheran Conference, as he did, means probably that the western European invasion will be the main effort of Britain and the United States, for the Russians have long defined 'second front' as a land front across the Channel."

But Edgar Ansel Mowrer, in the *New York Post*, sounded more critical:

> Even though based upon the dubious foundations of personal friendship, solidarity between the U.S., Britain, and the Soviet Union for war and peace is the essential foundation for victory. . . . Political questions have been scantily treated. . . . The result is a declaration Russian in form, Kremlinesque in phraseology and Oriental in obscurity. . . . It will hardly satisfy the Americans. And unless I miss my guess, it will not satisfy the British. The sooner Roosevelt and

Churchill return to their respective haunts and begin explaining all the things left unexplained at Teheran, the happier everyone will be.[6]

The Soviet press, so critical of Britain and the United States before the Teheran Conference, now overflowed with praise. Any note of caution which had appeared following the Moscow Conference now had vanished because Stalin had taken a very personal role in this conference. *Izvestia* announced:

> For four days, at a round table meeting, the most important statesmen of our time got together, exchanged views and took decisions. They achieved complete agreement on the questions relating to the conduct of the war and on the most important problems of the postwar world order. All the peace-loving peoples awaited this meeting with hope. Our enemies were terrified of such a meeting. . . . The leaders of the Three Powers express their confidence that the existing cooperation between Allies will guarantee an enduring peace.

Pravda's leading article stated: "The whole world was thrilled by the news of the historic meeting of the leaders of the three Allied powers, Stalin, Roosevelt, and Churchill, in Teheran." Never before had there been such precise and concrete planning of military operations by the Allies. The conference had surveyed the problems of the future and through the declaration confirmed that their task would be to assure cooperation and friendship among all nations whose people struggled for liberty against tyranny. *Pravda* regarded the Declaration on Iran as an example of the relation of the three powers to the small states. The declaration expressed the wish of the three governments to maintain the independence, sovereignty, and territorial integrity of Iran, "which, as is well known, was encroached on by bandit Hitlerite imperialism." The conference had "deepened the mutual understanding between the three great powers and strengthened their friendship," and the meeting of the three leaders was "in itself an event of first class significance."

At the meetings in Soviet factories and collective farms, spokesmen hailed Stalin for leaving Russia for the first time since the Russian Revolution, and for returning from Teheran with great benefits for the Soviet people. Among these were a new understanding with the United States and Britain to end the war quickly, recognition that the Soviet Union was a world power of great importance, and the promise of a secure future in a world that would be friendly to the Russian people. In a ball-bearing plant, the chief of one of the departments declared: "My department, after hearing the Declaration [of Teheran], promised to complete the December program ahead of schedule." The workers of the No. 4 Stalin Oil Refinery in Baku, the largest in Russia, in response to the decisions of the Teheran Conference, promised to work even more efficiently and to send to the front in December six trainloads of gasoline over and above their planned quota.

Meetings were held in detachments of the Red Army, where it was announced that Russia was not alone—"We have faithful allies." Sailors and officers of the Red Banner group of motor patrol boats of the Black Sea Fleet were reported to be greatly satisfied by the results of the Teheran Conference. Senior Lieutenant Zolotov said: "The decisions of the conference fill us with confidence in early victory over bloodthirsty German Fascism. All our efforts and skill are devoted to speedy defeat of the enemy." Members of collective farms, on hearing of the declaration by the three leaders at Teheran, decided to give the Red Army two rams, 200 liters of milk, 40 kilograms of rusks (hard, crisp bread), 12 kilograms of makhorka, 20 liters of vodka, and 40 pairs of warm socks and mittens. Leaders of the Academy of Sciences of the USSR, in a message broadcast by Radio Moscow stated: "Soviet scientists learned with tremendous satisfaction of the decisions of the conference of leaders of the three Allied powers Stalin, Roosevelt and Churchill. . . . These conference decisions fill us with still greater confidence in the speediest victory over the hated enemy. . . . Soviet scientists, together with the whole of our people, are delighted with the wise policy and the skill and genius in military leadership of our great Stalin."

Mikhail Kalinin, chairman of the Presidium of the Supreme Council of the Soviet Union, a type of figurehead president, gave the official Soviet pronouncement on the Teheran Conference. In his New Year's message, Kalinin proclaimed the conference to be "in reality the greatest event of our times, a historical landmark in the struggle with the German aggressor. All efforts of the Germans to separate freedom loving nations failed. The leaders of the three powers reached full agreement on questions of war and peace."[7]

In the United States, groups of civilians wrote their President about their feelings on learning of the Teheran Conference. The business manager, Local 1250, Department Store Workers of New York, wrote:

On behalf of 2500 department store workers we wish to state that the agreement reached at Teheran between Marshal Stalin, Prime Minister Churchill, and yourself is most joyous and exciting news for all freedom loving people. Agreement reached on questions of military actions against the enemy with reiterations of the principles of the Atlantic Charter is a guarantee that the world will be one and in the shortest possible time.

The crew of the S.S. *George Woodward* telegraphed the President their support of the Teheran Conference. "Stupendous task you, our President, Prime Minister Winston Churchill, and Premier Stalin have undertaken to obliviate [sic] the Fascist powers will be immortalized in the future pages of history." In Philadelphia, the secretary of the Machine, Tool, and Die Local 155 wrote:

Dear Mr. President: the membership of Local #155, United Electrical Radio and Machine Workers of America, comprising some 700 war workers . . . has discussed the recent conference at Teheran at its last meeting. We greet with joy the decisions of that conference which spells quick and decisive victory for the forces of the United Nations within a short time. . . . We pledge to you, as our Commander-in-Chief, to

maintain our splendid records of uninterrupted production, as we have done for the entire period since
the attack on Pearl Harbor, and we will exert ourselves even more to produce the materials needed for
victory. We hail you as our Commander-in-Chief and
leader of the progressive forces of the world.

From the crew of the S.S. *Robert Luckenbach* came the
message:

Dear Mr. President: We American seamen have
watched with anxiety the personal risks that you, our
Commander-in-Chief have taken going to the far
reaches of the world. And there in conference with
the leaders of our great allies have concluded agreements which shall destroy our enemies and those of
mankind—German Nazism and Japanese Fascism. The
6,000 American seamen who have died so that our
nation and freedom shall live, have been assured in
the historical pacts of Teheran that their sacrifice was
not in vain. For this, Mr. President, we thank you.[8]

In an era when the "summit conference" has become a
highly publicized media event designed to make the current
President of the United States appear presidential on the six
o'clock television news, the sentiments of the Soviet and
American people may appear corny. But in its way, the Teheran Conference was a media event, an effort to show the
world that Allied leaders were striving for a united front
against the enemy. Surely this conference would produce
military operations that would bring the Allied nations closer
to final victory.

As for Soviet citizens, they were probably more surprised
than their American counterparts at Stalin's trip out of the
Soviet Union to confer with western capitalists. His was a
forbidden deed. At the height of the Great Purge, and even
during the war, a Soviet citizen conferring secretly with foreigners—capitalists at that—in a foreign country would have
risked swift arrest, imprisonment, and perhaps execution
unless he had very high-level official permission. By doing

what millions of Soviet citizens dared never attempt, Stalin seemed to signal a momentous change in Soviet future policy. Consequently to people in the Allied nations, also, the news of the Teheran Conference marked a new era, one filled with hope for the future, in which the hatred and mistrust that had brought about the terrible war would disappear and the hated enemy would be forever defeated.

Before the results of the Teheran Conference had been announced, German commentators had been expecting a major propaganda appeal in the form of an ultimatum or manifesto to the German people demanding unconditional surrender. This was about all the people had been told about the conference until the official news release. The Declaration on Iran surprised the Nazis because they had been stressing Russian domination of Iran. When the Nazi commentators realized that no ultimatum would be issued from the Teheran Conference, they chose the line that the three leaders had dropped the ultimatum because they realized that it was useless. The Nazi newspapers, filled with scorn and defiance, labeled the "Declaration of the Three Powers" as a failure. German newspapers headlined the Teheran Conference as "Complete Political Failure," "Empty," "Dud from Teheran," "Under the Shadow of the OGPU," "Conference of War Criminals," "Mendacious List of Wishes from Teheran," and "Fiasco Before the World."[9]

A confidential German report circulated in high government quarters that Roosevelt and Stalin had had a strong difference of opinion at the conference over the Far East. The report alleged that for the first time Roosevelt discovered secret arrangements between the Russian and the Japanese over mutual supply of war materials. In addition, there had been no agreement on concrete matters, and the Teheran Conference represented a worsening of relations between the western Allies and Soviet Russia.[10]

To the Arabic world, Berlin broadcast the line that the results of the Teheran Conference were completely useless. Churchill had traveled all the way from Britain and Roosevelt from the United States to meet Stalin in Teheran. "This proves," claimed Radio Berlin, "that both the British and

American leaders have bowed to Stalin just as we have said before. . . . Both the British and American leaders are now obeying Stalin's order, who wants to Bolshevize Europe and the Near East." Roosevelt and Churchill, the Arabs were told, had territorial ambitions but would give countries in Europe and the Middle East to Stalin. The choice of Teheran as the meeting place, Radio Berlin declared, showed that Stalin had the upper hand at the conference. Roosevelt and Churchill were doing all that they could to win Stalin's sympathy. Roosevelt's energy was explained by his ambition to win the presidential election in 1944. The Teheran Conference proved one thing: "the incompetence of the Allies as well as their low morale."[11]

Even as the Nazi radio broadcasters damned the Teheran Conference, information on its contents was coming to Berlin from a unique source: the spy "Cicero," who worked in the British Embassy in Istanbul. Elyesa Basna, who was given the cover name "Cicero" by his German employers, had been a small-time thief, ex-convict, locksmith, taxi driver, and a "kavass," or servant, at foreign embassies in Ankara. He answered an advertisement for a driver for the first secretary of the British Embassy in Ankara in April 1943. From his new mistress, the nurse for the first secretary's children, he learned of an opening for a valet for the ambassador, Sir Hughe Knatchbull-Hugessen, a seasoned diplomat who had served in China, Persia, and Belgium.

Basna began his career as a spy for the Third Reich by reading a document placed in an unlocked desk drawer by the first secretary. From other documents Basna learned about the amount of armaments the Allies were shipping to the Soviet Union. When he discovered that a foreign ministers' conference would be held in Moscow in October 1943, Basna invested in the spy business. After purchasing a camera, he constructed a tripod for it in order to photograph documents kept in a safe in the ambassador's residence and in a dispatch box in his bedroom. Sir Hughe had developed the habit of bringing documents home from the embassy office and working on them at night. Using wax impressions, Basna had keys made for the safe and the dispatch box. He contacted the Germans on October 26, 1943, offering them fifty-six photographs of documents for £20,000. His offer was accepted with little haggling because the Germans were paying him in counterfeit pounds sterling manufactured in the Sachenshausen concentration camp. Whenever Cicero had documents to turn over to the Germans, he telephoned Ludwig Moyzisch, the local representative of the German Foreign Intelligence Agency. "What about a game of bridge tomorrow?" meant that Cicero had to see Moyzisch that same evening at ten o'clock at a spot in the city agreed upon at their previous meeting. Moyzisch would pick Cicero up at the appointed street corner, and after driving through the streets to throw off anyone tailing them, Cicero exchanged the photographs for cash.

Among the documents which Basna turned over to Moyzisch were summaries of conversations at Cairo and at Teheran. Through these documents, Berlin learned that an invasion of France would come some time in the spring of 1944 and that the code name would be OVERLORD. The plenary meeting at which the decision was announced concerning the timing of OVERLORD was never part of the information included in the summaries sent to Knatchbull-Hugessen. The documents seemed to point to a British and American push into southeast Europe through the involvement of Turkey in the war. When the British telegrams to Knatchbull-Hugessen showed that the possibility was being considered of erecting radar stations in Turkey to guide American bombers against Rumanian oil fields, Von Papen hurried to the Turkish Foreign Ministry to register a protest, claiming that he had heard about the proposal from neutral sources who had learned of it from the British air attaché. Sir Hughe, of course, soon heard about Papen's protest, and advised London: "Papen knows more than is good for him." Early in January 1944, American intelligence sources discovered that Papen had come into possession of documents which he considered of great value and "which, seemingly were secured from the British embassy in Ankara by an important German agent." Roosevelt informed Churchill, who assured him that the British intelligence services were investigating the matter.

Basna continued to photograph documents as spring approached. Moyzisch, his contact with the German government, hired a new attractive secretary who had lived in the United States and had contacts with the OSS. She may even have been an OSS agent; at least Basna became convinced of that. When he saw her in a cocktail lounge with a young man from the American Embassy who had chased Moyzisch and Basna one night when they were driving through the city, Basna hurried home, smashed his equipment, and in April left Ankara, retiring from the profession of espionage.

In Berlin, an argument raged on the highest levels as to whether Cicero was genuine. The information from the "Cicero" documents did not convince Hitler to strip the eastern Mediterranean of all German forces. Sufficient information appeared in the documents hinting at a "threat" to the Germans in the eastern Mediterranean, the very strategy which the American chiefs of staff so strongly opposed at the second Cairo Conference.

The information turned over to his German employers happened to fit into the deception plan first known as JAEL and later as BODYGUARD. It would make them believe that southeastern Europe was threatened by Allied forces. Was Basna being used by the British? Were they deliberately feeding him information they wished him to have as part of the deception plan? Cicero never obtained documents that would jeopardize the impending Allied invasion of France. The code word OVERLORD referred to the overall plan. NEPTUNE referred to the actual invasion itself, a word not found in the Teheran or Cairo documents. Ironically, the Germans may have learned more about the Teheran Conference sooner than the people in the Allied countries, but except for the details on Allied policy toward Turkey, they learned little that would undermine Allied plans and operations.[12]

Roosevelt returned to Washington feeling that there had been great distrust on Stalin's part when they had first met in Teheran. When he left he still had no idea if the distrust had been dissipated. To his wife, Eleanor, he announced his intention to see "that we kept our promises to the letter." He hoped "Britain would be able to do so and he would do all to help them do it. He felt that by keeping our word we could build the confidence of this leader, whose people, though fighting on our side, still did not trust us completely."[13]

On December 17, back in the Oval Office, Roosevelt gave his impressions of the Teheran Conference to reporters—the first press conference since his return. The reporters, who found him in a jovial mood, asked for his personal impressions of Stalin.

"Well," said the President, "the actual fact of meeting him lived up to my highest expectations. We had many excellent talks. And I was extremely glad to meet with Generalissimo Chiang Kai-shek. And on the whole, the mere fact of getting to know those two world leaders, I think, is going to make for excellent relations in the future."

"How were the talks conducted? Was it an easy matter?" asked a reporter.

"Through an interpreter," replied Roosevelt, "which of course is not as easy as if I spoke Russian and Chinese and they spoke English, but still we got on all right."

"Facile at all?" asked another reporter.

"Oh, yes."

"Back and forth?"

"Oh my, yes, yes, yes," Roosevelt answered.

"Was it stodgy, or anything of that sort?"

"Not stodgy at all, except that the answer sometimes came before the translation was finished," he replied to the sound of laughter from the reporters.

"Did you find Stalin—all we know about him is that picture with a handle-bar mustache, which evidently is out of date."

"Yes," said the President, "that is rather out of date."

"What type would you call him? Is he dour?"

"I would call him something like me—he is a realist."

Pressed to explain himself more fully, Roosevelt turned aside the question, claiming that he did not write a social column.

"Sir, does he share your view that there is hope of preventing another war in this generation?"

"Very definitely, if the people who want that objective will back it up," declared the President. "We figured out that the governments and associated nations that were on our side represented between two-thirds and three-quarters of the entire population of the world, which I thought was rather a significant fact."

"Mr. President, what did you call Mr. Stalin?"

"I told him it was a beautiful day."

"What did you *call* him. How did you address him?"

"Marshal."

"Mr. President, is there anything you can tell us about the methods of your travels?"

"Well, I think I can put it this way, mostly that when I— well, I couldn't put it that way because it might disclose something else." He laughed along with the reporters. "I went to Teheran in a plane. You can't go there by water."

"Did you go anywhere by water, sir?"

"Oh, now you are asking questions. That's different."

"That's what I get paid for," replied the reporter as his colleagues laughed.

"Well, one thing that irks me just as much as anything else, on these voyages," said the President. "The Secret Service and the Army and Navy are on my neck all the time for what they call security reasons; the reason is when you leave a place and issue a statement, it is obvious you are going away. Well, I would give the thing out right away, if I had my choice, but some places it isn't considered in the best interests of security because then they would know that you were leaving, and throughout the whole distance, you are practically under the range of German planes. And it's like shooting a duck sitting on the water for a German pursuit plane to go after a transport plane without any guns on it.

"Well, for instance, I don't put much stock in this, but when we got to Teheran I went to the American Legation, which is about a mile from the Russian—they have an embassy there—a compound—a high wall. And next door to them is the British Embassy.

"And that night, late, I got word from Marshal Stalin that they had got word of a German plot.

"Well, no use going into details. Everybody was more or less upset, Secret Service, and so forth. And he [Stalin] pleaded with me to go down to the Russian Embassy—they have two or three different buildings in the compound—and he offered to turn over one of them to me, and that would avoid either his, or Mr. Churchill's or my having to take trips through the streets, in order to see each other.

"So the next morning I moved out, down to the Russian compound. I was extremely comfortable there, and it was just another wall from the British place, so that none of the three of us had to go out on the streets, for example.

"But of course, in a place like Teheran, there are hundreds of German spies, probably, around the place, and I suppose it would make a pretty good haul if they could get all three of us going through the streets. And, of course, if your future plans are known, or if they can guess the time because of departure from one place, they can get German pursuit planes over the transport plane very easily."

Then one reporter asked: "Did you attend one of those dinners where they have forty-five toasts?" The other reporters standing about his desk laughed, awaiting Roosevelt's answer.

"Well, I can tell you this. We had one banquet where we had dinner in the Russian style. Very good dinner, too. Russian style means a number of toasts, and I counted up to three hundred and sixty-five toasts. And we all went away sober. It's a remarkable thing what you can do, if you try." Again the reporters laughed at his story.

"I made one glass of vodka that big," said the President indicating a two-inch width with his fingers, "last for about twenty toasts—just about"[14]

Roosevelt's only press conference about the Teheran meeting broke up in gales of laughter. But the reverberations from this conference were soon felt in Teheran. The story of the plot to assassinate the three leaders, picked up by the wire services, appeared in newspapers around the world. The Iranian foreign minister summoned Richard Ford, the American attaché in Teheran, to the foreign ministry to receive a diplomatic scolding for his President on December 22. The foreign minister read an official statement formally denying Roosevelt's story. At no time during the conference, before or after, declared the minister, had the Iranian government received any statement from the three

Allies of Iran regarding the existence of preparations for a plot against the three men. Iranian security officials had afforded every means of security and protection to their guests. Every precaution had been taken and no unpleasant incident had occurred, declared the minister. Washington made no reply when Ford reported this meeting.

The news story created a problem for the Reuters correspondent in Teheran. Should he comment on the story? Bullard, the British ambassador, advised him to say nothing, and the Foreign Office concurred. Bullard assumed that Roosevelt had revealed the story to explain why he had stayed at the Soviet Embassy instead of the American legation. It would have been embarrassing for Roosevelt if the British security authorities had to state, in answer to a Reuters dispatch, that they had no information about the plot. Bullard surmised that the Russian security personnel had invented the plot because the credit for unraveling the German intrigues in Iran had been accomplished by the British. The Russians had told the British nothing about any plot—only Roosevelt and the American Secret Service.[15]

Berlin picked up the story and ridiculed it as a "fantastic invention in the Hollywood style." The Germans agreed with Bullard that Roosevelt intended his statement as an explanation of his reasons for staying at the Soviet Embassy.[16]

Months later, Secret Service agent Guy H. Spaman, following instructions of the chief of the Secret Service, sent in his report on the security arrangements for Roosevelt's trip to Cairo and Teheran. Commenting on the reasons for the President's move from the American legation, Spaman stated: "Stalin sent word to the President that he was very much concerned about this situation because it was well known that the city of Teheran was filled with Axis sympathizers; it had been under complete German control only a few months before and the risk of assassination of Mr. Churchill and Marshal Stalin while coming to visit the President was very real." Spaman omitted any comment about a plot because there was no plot for him to report.[17]

The plot report served its purpose for Roosevelt by deflating Republican complaints that he should have stayed in the American legation instead of accepting Soviet hospitality. Most important of all, the plot report enabled him to show that a capitalist leader trusted Stalin and the Soviet Union so much that he was happy to sleep and eat within the walls of the Soviet Embassy.

Eager to maintain the close personal relations begun in the Soviet Embassy in Teheran, Roosevelt hastened to keep up his correspondence with Stalin. Soon after reaching Cairo, on December 3, Roosevelt informed Stalin of his safe arrival. He considered the conference "a great success and I am sure that it was an historic event in the assurance not only of our ability to wage war together but to work in the utmost harmony for the peace to come. I enjoyed very much our personal talks together and particularly the opportunity of meeting you face to face." He looked forward to meeting Stalin again.

Stalin, in replying, expressed a wish to meet Roosevelt again and agreed that the Teheran Conference had been a great success. He only hoped that their common enemy, Hitler Germany, would feel the importance of their meeting. "Now there is certainty that our peoples will cooperate harmoniously, both at present and after the war."

Remembering his manners, Roosevelt sent Stalin a "bread and butter" note which did not arrive until December 18 although it had been dated December 3. In it Roosevelt thanked the Marshal for his thoughtfulness and hospitality in providing quarters in the Soviet Embassy. "I was not only extremely comfortable there but I was very conscious of how much more we were able to accomplish in a brief period of time because we were such close neighbors throughout our stay." He looked back on "those momentous days of our meeting with the greatest satisfaction as being an important milestone in the progress of human affairs." In his reply, Stalin did not find the Teheran Conference the equivalent of a Roosevelt "milestone." He merely "attached great importance" to the meeting on the problem of accelerating victory "and establishing lasting peace among the nations." [18]

The difference in the tone of the messages exchanged reflected the weight given by both men to the first encounter between the President of the United States and the Soviet ruler. While Roosevelt valued personal meetings, Stalin had no wish for intimacy because it might undermine his image as the leading Soviet genius. He could not maintain this image by continually consorting with capitalist leaders. The supreme hero of the Soviet proletariat had no desire to sully himself by personal meetings with such imperialists because if the deals with them went sour that could reflect on Stalin's genius, as in the 1939 pact with Hitler. Stalin probably preferred that his underlings meet with Roosevelt; for himself, he regarded the meeting as an unpleasant but necessary task which he did not intend to make a habit.[19]

Despite hours of private talk, drinking and dining together, Stalin did not trust either Roosevelt or Churchill. In the spring of 1944, he exclaimed to Milovan Djilas: "Churchill is the kind who, if you don't watch him, will slip a kopeck out of your pocket. By God, a kopeck out of your pocket! And Roosevelt? Roosevelt is not like that. He dips in his hand only for bigger coins."[20] To Stalin, they were simply a pair of pickpockets. Obviously Roosevelt's effort to put as much distance as possible between himself and Churchill at Teheran had failed. Stalin had still classed him with that British imperialist.

What then had "the greatest event of our times" produced? And what were the mistakes, the defaults, the errors? As for Stalin, he returned from the Teheran Conference in "a particularly good frame of mind," according to his daughter.[21] After all, he had met privately with the two most important capitalist leaders and discovered that they could not unite against him. Roosevelt even appeared to crave Stalin's support in opposition to Churchill. Moreover, Roosevelt's stratagem did not hide any capitalist trickery. Such tactics must have amused Stalin, who had often played the reverse game with his rivals: seeming to be friendly when he was plotting to send them to his executioners.

Even before the conference had begun, Roosevelt and Churchill had given Stalin an advantage by failing to draft and to insist on an agenda. Keeping to a strict agenda could have been embarrassing to Stalin because he would have been forced to object to discussing unpleasant topics. Without an agenda, he had only to wait until the others introduced topics for discussion. If he found a topic unsuitable, no one objected if he changed it.

The lack of an agenda also distorted the timetable of the conference. Nothing was more wasteful than for Roosevelt and Churchill, after traveling so great a distance with their staffs, to argue about launching OVERLORD in the presence of Stalin for three days and to push important political questions off until the last day of the conference. If possible, it would have been better to have discussed the political questions first and then inform Stalin about OVERLORD. But such a procedure required an agenda—which Roosevelt had vetoed.

In four days, approximately thirty-five hours were devoted to meetings and discussions at meals. Approximately eighteen hours were taken up with OVERLORD. Of the four plenary sessions, three concerned OVERLORD, while approximately sixteen hours were spent in meals and banquets, and only eleven hours in a more or less serious discussion of global matters. The imbalance in the discussions was not only Roosevelt's fault but also Stalin's.

For months he had berated the Allies for their delays in launching the second front while alleging that the Soviet people were bearing the entire burden of the war. Such tactics created deep guilt feelings in the hearts of his western allies while adding to their fears that after making a deal with Hitler, he would take the Soviet Union out of the war. But once Stalin had reached Teheran and discovered disunity on the question of OVERLORD, he seized the advantage by insisting that the opening of the second front was a pledge of good faith required before any serious negotiation. Until OVERLORD had been settled, Stalin skillfully blocked all discussions of other questions in order to prevent a tradeoff of OVERLORD for something about Poland.

After three days of arguing and delay, Stalin obtained agreement by the Combined Chiefs of Staff, Roosevelt, and Churchill that OVERLORD would be launched during the month of May 1944. Moreover, he received the promise that a commander for OVERLORD would soon be designated, and that a second landing would take place in the south of France in conjunction with OVERLORD. Roosevelt and Churchill promised OVERLORD without any conditions attached.

In addition, Stalin was promised Königsberg and the northern half of East Prussia. As for the Far East, Stalin indicated his desire that Dairen would be a free port. He demanded the southern half of the Sakhalin Islands as well as the Kuriles without any opposition or bargaining by Churchill or Roosevelt. Stalin also obtained the promise of one-third of the Italian fleet to be delivered to the Soviet Union at the end of January 1944. As for Finland, despite statements from Roosevelt and Churchill, Stalin retained freedom of action.

A bargain had been struck at the Teheran Conference over the eastern Polish frontier. It would follow in general the Curzon Line, which adhered to the frontier drawn by Ribbentrop and Molotov in 1939 after the defeat of Poland. For Poland it was a symbol of defeat because it meant surrendering territory to Soviet Russia. This concession was given Stalin without any consultation with the Polish Government-in-Exile in London. It signaled to him that Roosevelt and Churchill had no wish to support the Poles in opposing a frontier unacceptable to them. On the vital aspect of internal Polish politics, Stalin still had freedom of action. There was no challenge of his demand for a "friendly" government.

In return for these promises, the Soviet Union would join the war against Japan as soon as the Nazi defeat had been completed. Stalin assented to a collective security organization that would be founded on a worldwide basis, and he accepted Roosevelt's idea of breaking up Germany. He agreed that the European Advisory Commission could develop policy concerning Germany.

Stalin had the better part of this bargain. He retained a free hand and gained territory while giving his allies vague promises. His allies, after refusing to accede to his demands on the Polish frontier question for two years, conceded without insisting on any quid pro quo from him. The deal concerning war with Japan gave him another advantage. He exchanged in advance an action of which he was the sole master—declaration of war on Japan—against territories which Soviet armies would soon occupy. It was not an equal bargain. Moreover, the lack of any decision concerning Poland's future government represented a favorable decision for Stalin. More than either Roosevelt or Churchill, he realized the long-range consequences of the Polish decisions at Teheran.

At the moment when Soviet forces were on the verge of spreading out over eastern Europe, Stalin maneuvered so as to avoid giving any precise guarantees. He made no explicit engagement that would limit his freedom of action in the areas which the Soviet armies would soon enter. The failure to be more precise about the future of eastern Europe at Teheran became advantageous for Stalin. The Teheran Conference was the time to explore his ideas about the future of eastern Europe, yet little definite was decided about Germany's future. Except for the Polish frontiers, eastern Europe was a gaping void as far as decisions were concerned, for there Stalin retained a free hand. Any implication that the Atlantic Charter would apply to eastern Europe meant nothing to him. Had Roosevelt and Churchill met these questions head on, they could have created obstacles to Stalin's ambitions and plans. A serious discussion of these problems could have disclosed something of the nature of Stalin's aims by forcing him to reveal more details. But such a discussion was avoided because too much time was taken up with debating OVERLORD.

Roosevelt's policy of striving to prove to Stalin that there was no cause for suspicion and that he ought to work with the western Allies in the postwar world revealed only Roosevelt's profound ignorance both of the Soviet Union and of Stalin's nature. The President's hope that talking with Stalin and poking fun at Churchill would lead to greater understanding had failed.

In hindsight it is easy to blame Roosevelt and Churchill for failing to bargain more vigorously with Stalin. Churchill, however, had become the junior partner in the alliance, and Roosevelt, because of his beliefs, personality, and knowledge, preferred accommodation to argument. The information available in Washington about Stalin and his policies simply would not support a tough bargaining position at the time of the Teheran Conference. The best available source of information in Washington concerning the Soviet Union, the Office of Strategic Services (OSS), ancestor of the CIA, was cautious and certainly not hostile. Serious study indicated that the Soviet Union might not collaborate with Britain and the United States unless they recognized the basic Soviet interests. These included the 1941 eastern frontiers, friendly governments along these frontiers (Poland in particular), and a position of equality in a system in which the three powers had a major share of world control. Moreover, because Moscow had ordered the dissolution of the Communist International in 1943, it was theorized that hereafter Soviet Russia would be concerned more with national security than with fomenting world revolution. If the British and the American governments did not bring Soviet Russia around to cooperating, Stalin might revert to independent action—a prospect frightening to Roosevelt. The OSS warned that the Soviet Union could not be left out of the postwar arrangements for peacekeeping as in 1919. This time Russian influence would be felt and it would be directed toward enhancing Soviet power and security. Undoubtedly Moscow would reject collaboration with its western Allies unless the minimal conditions were accepted by them.[22]

But now the foreign leaders, their admirals and generals had left Teheran. Determination of the real success or failure of "the greatest event of our times" lay in the future.

18
Success and Failure

IN ITALY, the fighting was heavy all along the Winter Line; it was made worse by rain, mud, and cold. From Berlin came the announcement that Field Marshal Erwin Rommel would command the German forces deployed along the Channel and Atlantic coasts in anticipation of the allied assault on Fortress Europe. Washington announced on December 24 that Eisenhower had been appointed Supreme Commander, Allied Expeditionary Force. Both generals would play a major role in the failure or success of OVERLORD. The three Allied leaders, meanwhile, had returned from the summit conference in Teheran, Stalin quietly to Moscow, Roosevelt to Washington; but Churchill was less fortunate.

Originally he had planned to visit Eisenhower's headquarters and there to meet with General Eisenhower, Harold Alexander, and Bernard Montgomery. He got only as far as Tunis when the strain of the conferences, the effects of his head cold and sore throat, plus general exhaustion combined to bring him down. In the early morning hours of December 11, Brooke was awakened from sleep by a voice crying, "Hulloo, Hulloo, Hulloo!" Opening his eyes, he discovered Churchill in his dressing gown wandering about the bedroom seeking his physician, Lord Moran. Brooke led him to Moran, who put him back to bed. The next morning Churchill was running a temperature of 101 degrees; Moran summoned nurses and a pathologist from Cairo. By December 13, Moran diagnosed Churchill's malady as pneumonia, dan-

gerous for a man of his age. Moran advised informing the War
Cabinet and Mrs. Churchill, who arrived in Tunis on December 15.

Churchill's condition became graver when he complained of his heart, "It feels to be bumping all over the
place." Moran knew that "we were right up against things."
The heart was fibrillating and did not resume regular beating for four hours. The next day, December 16, Moran believed that the worst was over as the congestion in Churchill's
chest began to clear. Within days he had enough energy to
argue with his doctors. For the second time in a year he had
defeated pneumonia. Because he needed two weeks con-
valesence, it was decided to move him to Marrakesh where
he could continue his recuperation until strong enough to
return home to London. Consequently he had to attempt to
direct the government from North Africa, which he could only
find frustrating.[1]

Roosevelt returned to Washington, tired after the long
journey but confident that by his trip and his talks he had
accomplished more for the nation and for world peace. But
in Washington already rumors were afloat that he had given
much away at Teheran which Hull had secured at the Moscow Conference. Columnist Drew Pearson wrote that at
Teheran there had been much friction between Roosevelt and
Churchill. The British Embassy heard that the President had
gotten on much better with Stalin than with Churchill. According to Czech sources, Stalin had been unimpressed with
Roosevelt.[2]

In a Christmas Eve fireside broadcast from Hyde Park, the
President announced Eisenhower's appointment, and reported to the American people on the progress of the war and
on the Teheran Conference:

> There we met with Marshal Stalin. We talked with
> complete frankness on every conceivable subject
> connected with the winning of the war and the estab-
> lishment of a durable peace after the war. Within three
> days of intense and consistently amicable discus-
> sions, we agreed on every point concerned with the
> launching of a gigantic attack upon Germany. . . . But

on the basis of what we did discuss, I can say even today that I do not think any insoluble differences will arise among Russia, Great Britain, and the United States. . . . To use an American and somewhat ungrammatical colloquialism, I may say I "got along fine" with Marshal Stalin. He is a man who combines a tremendous relentless determination with a stalwart good humor. I believe he is truly representative of the heart and soul of Russia; and I believe that we are going to get along very well with him and the Russian people—very well indeed.[3]

As for Stalin, soon after returning to Moscow he met with Eduard Beneš, president of the Czechoslovak Government-in-Exile, who had traveled to Moscow to sign a treaty of alliance and friendship that would eventually help transform Czechoslovakia into a Soviet satellite state. In their talks, Stalin quizzed him about the Poles because "we want to reach an agreement with Poland." He asked Beneš, "Where can one find any Poles one could talk to?" Beneš had little good to say for the Poles because of past disputes over territory which both nations claimed. As for the Teheran Conference, Molotov reported that "the conversations were quite uninhibited there, even about the most sensitive issues and the atmosphere was that of complete trust and friendship." The second front problem had been solved, and everyone agreed that Germany would be dismembered. The Curzon Line had been settled. But in questioning Beneš, Stalin seemed to doubt his allies. Did they intend to pursue the war to the end? What were their intentions about invading Europe? Beneš reassured him; however, he had no doubts about Stalin when he talked later with Harriman. "Great satisfaction in the new relationships with the United States and Great Britain was expressed to Beneš by Stalin," Harriman reported, "who had been much impressed with the President and who felt that complete agreement on all questions, not of course in detail but in approach, had been reached with him at Teheran."[4]

Not everyone in Europe was thrilled by the new relationships. From inside Europe, OSS sources reported the widespread impression that Soviet Russia would become the dominant force in the future. The Teheran Conference had dispelled any idea of a German-Soviet deal to take the Red Army out of the war. Europeans believed that Soviet Russia had laid plans for the Europe she wanted and no force could block her progress. A fear of Russian domination of Europe was growing, similar to that which had surfaced after the fall of Napoleon in 1815.[5]

In Washington, the Teheran Conference was judged a great success. Hopes were high that the conference marked the first step in breaking down Soviet suspicion and hostility toward western countries. Now that Stalin had met Roosevelt face to face, with an opportunity to unburden himself of all his complaints against the leading capitalist power, distrust would vanish. Differences in political and economic philosophies would be overcome because two men had eaten and drunk together and had talked in the Soviet Embassy in Teheran. An improvement in Soviet-American relations would soon be seen as Soviet doors closed to American and British officers now opened. What had been secret would be revealed. The success of the Teheran Conference would be marked by close Soviet-American cooperation, not only in fighting the war but in winning the peace. However, cooperation between Moscow and Washington did not in fact follow automatically after the Teheran Conference.

The military proposals made to Stalin at Teheran did not bring about immediate action after he had returned to Moscow. More than a month after the conference, Harriman found that Soviet officials with whom the Americans had to work were cordial and friendly, but that although some proposals were approved in principle, "we have had a complete runaround in getting action on or even detailed discussion of these proposals." After discussing the problem with members of the American mission in Moscow, Harriman concluded that the bottleneck was located in the Kremlin, and that "the spirit of Teheran has not percolated to lower echelons." Unless he blasted this open, he feared that the United States would receive only a minimum of value from the cooperation which Stalin had agreed on at Teheran. Early in January 1944, on the 10th, General John Deane, chief of the

United States military mission, was suddenly called to the Soviet General Staff where a few matters were disposed of in the meeting. But Deane learned that despite the spirit of Teheran, Soviet military leaders were not yet ready to consider topics submitted to Stalin at the Moscow and Teheran conferences. Although encouraged, Harriman realized that he faced a fight to obtain the cooperation with Moscow to which he felt the United States was entitled.[6]

Abruptly the Moscow press, which had been treating the Americans and British to a series of compliments, turned nasty with a story that "two leading British personalities" had been discussing a separate peace with Ribbentrop in a Spanish coastal town. The story came from *Pravda*'s correspondent in Cairo, but there was no such correspondent and British censors would never have let it through. The hoax was so blatant that Churchill made a personal protest to Stalin. His defense was lame: The significance ought not to be over-rated and Churchill should not question the right of *Pravda* to print rumors.[7] Such a story in *Pravda*, however, signaled to Soviet readers that despite the spirit of Teheran, the capitalist Allies could not be fully trusted. Cooperation could not go too far.

Next came the turn of the Americans. Another *Pravda* article attacked Wendell Willkie, the former presidential candidate, for an article published fifteen months earlier in *Life* describing his meeting with Stalin and in which he had raised questions about Soviet policy regarding the Balkans, the Baltic States, Poland, and Finland. *Pravda* assailed Willkie for interfering in matters that would be decided directly by the Soviet Union and the countries concerned. Here was another signal to the West to leave eastern Europe to the Soviet Union, despite vows of friendship made at Teheran.

At the Teheran Conference Stalin had promised action on the shuttle bombing plan, but none came until Harriman met with Stalin early in February. At last the logjam was broken, and, at Stalin's order, three airfields were rushed to completion within four months in preparation for receiving American bombers flown from air bases in Britain and Italy. During the summer seven missions were carried out, but after the Allied forces had landed in Normandy and begun pushing toward the east, the Soviet authorities found less need for the bases and signaled that they wanted the project ended. When the Warsaw uprising broke out in the summer of 1944, there was one last shuttle mission to drop supplies to the Polish fighters. The Soviet government, unwilling to have foreign troops inside its borders, gradually forced the closing of the bases.

An attempt to coordinate air operations by exchanging liaison officers between the Anglo-American air forces and the Soviet air force never got started. There was limited success in improving the exchange of weather information and enemy intelligence, but the effort always came from the British and the Americans, never from the Soviet government, which regarded such requests and proposals with suspicion: What were the capitalists up to now? Roosevelt's talks with Stalin had not quieted distrust of American policies.[8]

Months passed—the Allied armies landed in Normandy and swept across France. By September 1944, a frustrated Harriman complained to Harry Hopkins over Soviet indifference to American interests. The Kremlin, ignoring his letters, refused to discuss pressing problems while demanding increased American aid through Lend-Lease. The Russians wanted items that were in short supply in the United States but refused to justify their requests—if the Russians wanted something, that was justification enough. "The general attitude seems to be that it is our obligation to help Russia and accept her policies because she has won the war for us," Harriman complained. He confessed that "the job of getting the Soviet government to play a decent role in international affairs is however going to be more difficult than we had hoped."[9]

A judgment in Teheran came from General Deane a year after the conference. "I have sat at innumerable Russian banquets and become gradually nauseated by Russian food, vodka, and protestations of friendship. It is amazing how these toasts go down past the tongues in the cheeks," he wrote Marshall. "After the banquets we send the Soviets another thousand airplanes, and they approve a visa that has been hanging fire for months. We then scratch our heads to see what other gifts we can send, and they scratch theirs to see what else they can ask for." The Russians wanted as little to do with foreigners as possible, Americans included. All requests were regarded with suspicion. "They simply cannot understand giving without taking, and as a result even our giving is viewed with suspicion." Unhappy because of the Soviet failure to respond in equal measure to Anglo-American generosity in yielding military information, Deane wanted a tougher attitude in dealing with the Russians. If proposals for collaboration received no answer, then "we should act as we think best and inform them of our action." The Americans should stop pushing themselves on the Russians and make the Russians come to the Americans, who could then be friendly and cooperative.[10]

Although three Allied leaders had joined in toasts in Teheran, their conviviality did not mean that the Soviet General Staff would give the American and British military missions the Soviet order of battle, or information on Soviet operations, reserves, casualties, and munitions. Nor would pledges of friendship over glasses of vodka mean that British and American officers would at least observe the Soviet army in action. For Stalin had no intention of giving his allies information about the Soviet armed forces or of permitting them to observe the Red Army in battle lest they learn about Soviet military weaknesses. By keeping the Allies ignorant of the true capabilities of the armed forces, he would preserve the mystique of Soviet military power: the unstoppable Russian "steamroller," which crushed everything in its path. Because Stalin feared that any close examination would threaten that mystique, his allies would remain in ignorance.

Perhaps Stalin would be more open in his dealings with the Allies if they were generous to him. Certainly, such a belief influenced Roosevelt in the question of dividing up the Italian fleet. Nevertheless, the President's generosity did not stop Stalin from haggling with him over the Italian ships just like a Russian peddler.

At the Moscow Conference in October 1943, Molotov had presented a Soviet demand for the immediate transfer of Italian naval vessels to the Soviet Union. A battleship, a cruiser, eight destroyers, and four submarines were to be dispatched to northern Soviet ports; in addition, the Soviet government wanted 40,000 tons of Italian merchant shipping. Molotov justified the request on the grounds that Italy's participation in the war had done incalculable damage to the Soviet merchant and naval fleets. Other than this statement, Molotov offered no further reason for his demand.

Roosevelt did not agree immediately to hand over the Italian ships but accepted the arrangement in principle. By the time he sailed for North Africa in November 1943, he favored turning over one-third of the Italian ships to the Soviet Union as a token of goodwill, but there would not be any transfer of title. The Allies should use the ships for the prosecution of the war; after they had finished using them, then they could discuss the question of title.

At the December 1 meeting in Teheran, Molotov asked for a reply to the Soviet request. Stalin knew, he said, that the United States and the United Kingdom needed ships, but he was not asking for much. Roosevelt saw it as a simple matter: The three nations would use the ships during the war and then afterward distribute them by title. Until then, those would use the ships who could use them best. Although agreeable to the transfer, Churchill asked for time to work out the arrangements. At Stalin's suggestion, they agreed that the Italian ships would pass to Soviet control at the end of January.

By mid-December, Harriman had to remind Roosevelt about the promise because if they waited until Moscow began to pressure them, the delay would infer laxness on their part in carrying out the commitments made at Teheran. Roosevelt was prepared to turn over one-third of the Italian fleet to Stalin until reminded that Stalin did not really covet that many ships. Then the Combined Chiefs of Staff threw cold water on the deal. Italian naval vessels were being used in the Mediterranean and in the Atlantic as blockade patrols; Italian submarines were scheduled to be trained for antisubmarine work. If the transfer alienated the Italian officers and men, replacements could be found only at the expense of the British and American fleets already preparing for operations OVERLORD and ANVIL, which could then be in jeopardy.

The entire refitting program under way in Italian shipyards could be threatened if Italian workers resented the transfer. Such news could precipitate sabotage and scuttling of the ships. Until after the Allied armies were firmly established in France, the risk involved in transferring the ships was simply too great. The gain from the transfer would be minimal because the Italian ships would have to undergo extensive alterations before they would be suitable for duty in the northern waters. Maintenance would require spare parts and ammunition that were already in short supply; the Soviet crews would require time for shakedown, and as a result, the ships would not be actively employed for warfare.

Realizing the wisdom of the Combined Chiefs' objections, Roosevelt and Churchill proposed to Stalin that a British battleship, H.M.S. *Royal Sovereign*, recently refitted in the United States with radar for gun control, and an American light cruiser would be made available to the Soviet Union. Russian crews could take the ships over at British ports and sail them to Soviet ports where they could be altered for Arctic conditions. These vessels would fly the Soviet flag until Italian ships could be made available. Until Italian merchant shipping could be obtained without endangering OVERLORD and ANVIL, both governments would make available a total of 40,000 tons of Allied merchant shipping. The Soviet government could make use of these ships earlier than under the former proposal.

To their proposal, Stalin expressed only objections and no gratitude. Nevertheless, he would accept the two ships. But he wished to know about the eight Italian destroyers and the four submarines which had been promised at Teheran. The proffered battleship and cruiser would be powerless unless accompanied by destroyers. Since the entire Italian navy lay at the Allies' disposal, it would be easy for them to transfer eight destroyers and four submarines to the Soviet navy. However, he consented to accept American or British destroyers and submarines in place of the Italian vessels. The transfer of the destroyers and submarines should occur at the time agreed on at the Teheran Conference. When Churchill forwarded this message to Roosevelt, he wrote: "What can you expect from a bear but a growl?"

To appease the Russian bear, and to avoid a mutiny in

the Italian fleet, Churchill was prepared to loan Stalin eight British destroyers until the Italian ships could be turned over. But the destroyers would be those over-age ships given to Britain by Roosevelt in 1941, which could be used as training ships for Soviet crews until the Italian vessels were handed over and refitted. He expected Stalin to reproach his allies for the quality of the ships. Finding four submarines would be difficult and new British submarines could not be spared. Could Roosevelt supply them? Roosevelt replied that American submarines could not be spared in view of operations in the Pacific, and asked Churchill to find them. The four submarines would have to come from the Italian navy, which had thirty. If the request were to be presented as diplomatically as possible, Roosevelt thought the Italian government would not have any valid objection to joining in a common effort.

Roosevelt offered Stalin two American merchant ships, S.S. *Harry Percy* and the S.S. *John Gorrie*, both already in British ports, and the cruiser U.S.S. *Milwaukee*, which would arrive in Britain soon. Upon learning that he would receive antiquated destroyers, Stalin complained as Churchill had predicted. He saw no reason why Britain and the United States could not transfer modern destroyers instead of old ones. Russia had lost a substantial part of her destroyers during the Italian and German military operations, and it was most important for that loss to be made up by the British and American navies.

Roosevelt and Churchill continued to seek to pacify Stalin. Wishing to be frank with him, Churchill had the British ambassador reveal the age of the destroyers, which were serviceable vessels, quite efficient for escort duty. In the entire Italian fleet there were only seven fleet destroyers and they were unsuited for work in the north without much refitting. It would be more convenient to hand over the British destroyers at that time. New destroyers could not be spared because two had recently been lost in a Russian convoy and forty-two destroyers would be needed for close-in fighting in the OVERLORD landing when a large proportion might be lost. The Anzio campaign, convoy work in the Atlantic and in the Pacific, convoys to Russia, and OVERLORD all required every available vessel. Roosevelt and Churchill promised to deliver the Italian ships as agreed at Teheran but only after consulting the Italian government. But Stalin retorted that Russia needed destroyers for combat operations other than escort duty.

Roosevelt helped confuse the problem more when he announced in a press conference on March 3 that Italian warships would be sent to the Russian navy and that discussions were in progress regarding the transfer of one-third of the Italian fleet to Russia. His announcement offended the Italians, who considered that because they were now Allies against Nazi Germany their navy ought not to be taken from them. German propaganda seized on Roosevelt's gaffe to denounce the Allies as exploiters and destroyers of Europe, not liberators.

An angry Churchill reminded Roosevelt that he had never agreed to a division of the Italian fleet nor had the Russians asked for so much. If there were to be such a division, what about other nations who had fought Italy? Greece, for example. In such a division, British losses had to be considered because Britain had fought Italy alone from 1940 until American forces entered the war in the Mediterranean in November 1942. Moreover, relations with the Italian government had to be considered. "A prisoner of war is one thing but once you accept a man's services and he fights at your side against the common enemy, a different status and relationship are established." He would have to make a statement in Parliament.

In the end, Stalin received his warships in May. Only one came from the U.S. Navy; the remainder, thirteen in all, came from the Royal Navy because of the potential repercussions from the Italian people and their navy. Neither Roosevelt nor Churchill wrote Stalin when the transfer came. "It is for the Russians to show gratitude rather than for us to show deference. . . . Not one word of thanks has ever been expressed to us for this transfer of ships," Churchill wrote the First Sea Lord. In the affair of the Italian warships, Stalin had his way. Allied ships had to be transferred to Russia to appease him even though the Anglo-American forces were preparing for the landing in France. Churchill and Roosevelt too were

obliged to squander time and energy because at Teheran they
had promised the warships without considering the impact
on the Italians, who now enjoyed the status of Allies, not
prisoners of war.[11]

While Churchill and Roosevelt had been arguing with
Stalin over Italian ships, millions of Allied officers, soldiers,
and sailors had been training in preparation for the invasion
promised at Teheran. When the Supreme Allied Commander, Eisenhower, arrived in London to take over command of the OVERLORD assault, he had to grapple with another
promise made at Teheran to launch an attack on the south of
France at the same time as OVERLORD. To fulfill the promise, he must overcome a shortage of landing craft and troops.
Since the promise had been made, General Bernard Montgomery, the cocky little victor of El Alamein, the commander of the British 21st Army Group, who would also
command the assault phase of OVERLORD, had demanded that
the invasion front be widened from twenty-five to forty miles
and that the assault force be increased to five divisions. An
increase in the size of the OVERLORD assault force would require additional landing craft, which were in short supply.
At the same time, the invasion of southern France, code-
named ANVIL, would require landing craft that could be used
to carry the additional troops demanded by Montgomery for
OVERLORD.

The Allied troops assigned to ANVIL would have to be
taken from the forces available for the fighting in Italy, which
seemed to be bleeding the German army. Consequently,
Churchill and his chiefs of staff, now wholeheartedly in support of OVERLORD, wanted to cancel ANVIL. They argued that
if ANVIL were launched in conjunction with OVERLORD, the
forces available would be insufficient to attempt both of these
operations while maintaining the pressure on the German
armies for more troops in Italy. The British, in charge of the
Mediterranean theater of operations, believed the Italian
campaign would draw more German troops from OVERLORD
than would a small-scale invasion of southern France. However, cancelation of ANVIL would be contrary to the promise
given to Stalin at Teheran. Moreover, any change in the plans
agreed to at Teheran with Stalin deeply troubled Roosevelt.

It would become one more in a series of broken promises that would embitter the suspicious Soviet ruler.

The ANVIL problem led the Joint Chiefs of Staff to request a meeting with the President on February 21, 1944. They reported that the British wanted to cancel ANVIL because of the difficulties being encountered by the forces fighting in Italy. The Joint Chiefs opposed cancellation. Roosevelt made it final, pointing out that it had taken three days at Teheran to get the British to agree to ANVIL. "The Russians were then 'tickled to death' in that their suggestion had been accepted," said Roosevelt. "The Russians would not be happy even if we told them the abandonment of ANVIL would mean two or more divisions for OVERLORD." He felt "we are committed to a third power," but he "did not feel we have any right to abandon this commitment for ANVIL without taking up the matter with the third power." Roosevelt was unwilling to discuss the abandonment of ANVIL with the Russians at that time because "we had made previous promises to the Russians which we had not been able to meet. . . . We have given up promises in the past and had better not do it again."

Despite Roosevelt's opposition to any change, he had to heed the wisdom of the supreme commander and his staff. By March 21, an ANVIL operation simultaneous with OVERLORD was postponed in order to strengthen both the cross-Channel assault and the Italian campaign. But Stalin was not informed.[12]

Another problem arose in connection with OVERLORD: the timing. The Teheran promise that OVERLORD would take place during May gave the supreme commander until May 31 to launch the invasion. By January 1944, the OVERLORD planners realized that a June invasion date would give additional time for preparations and for the construction of landing craft. Moreover, the timing of the landing would depend on tides and weather and the June tides would be more favorable. When Churchill mentioned the possibility of a June OVERLORD, Roosevelt begged him not to communicate anything about this subject to "Uncle J."

Early in April the American military mission in Moscow reminded Washington that at Teheran Stalin had committed the Soviet army to offensive action timed to help OVERLORD. The moment was approaching when the decisions had to be made to ensure a coordinated effort among all the forces, but the Soviet General Staff could not plan an attack timed to coincide with OVERLORD unless they received a clearer indication of that date than simply "during May." This information was needed for the Soviet General Staff to start preparing their troop concentrations for the offensive. Could not instructions be issued to the British and American missions in Moscow to pass along the necessary information?

Soon Deane and General Burrows were instructed to inform the Soviet General Staff that in accordance with the agreement reached at Teheran, it was the firm intention to launch OVERLORD on the agreed date. They were also to pay a "handsome tribute to the magnificent progress of the Soviet armies." They asked the Soviet General Staff to confirm that the promise would be fulfilled, which Stalin had given at Teheran, to organize a great offensive that would assist OVERLORD by containing the German armies in the east. All of that meant little unless Stalin were informed.

From Churchill and Roosevelt came the message on April 18. "Pursuant to our talks at Teheran, the general crossing of the sea" would take place around the date which Deane and Burrows would transmit. The date they transmitted was May 31, with the understanding that it might have to be shifted two or three days before or after depending on tides and weather. Stalin replied that he was "gratified to learn that in accordance with the Teheran agreement the sea crossing will take place at the appointed time."[13] But he had not yet learned about the postponement of ANVIL in the south of France.

Finally, on May 10, Roosevelt and Churchill told him that because of the need of landing craft in the English Channel and the necessity to use troops in Italy, the landing in southern France would not occur in conjunction with OVERLORD. This time there were no recriminations from Stalin—"You can best decide how and in what way to allocate your forces. The important thing of course is to insure complete success for OVERLORD."

On June 6, 1944, in the early morning hours, Anglo-

American forces began landing on five beaches on the shores of Normandy. The pledge made to Stalin at Teheran had been kept; the debacle which Churchill feared never occurred. He informed Stalin: "Everything has started well. The mines, obstacles, and land batteries have been largely overcome. The air landings were very successful and on a large scale. Infantry landings are proceeding rapidly and many tanks and self propelled guns are already ashore." In his reply, Stalin called this news "a source of joy to us all and of hope for further success," adding that the Soviet summer offensive was timed for mid-June, to develop by stages.[14]

Stalin, however, waited to make sure that OVERLORD would be successful, not another Dieppe, and that the Anglo-American armies would not be driven into the sea. On June 22, the third anniversary of the German attack on Russia, the promised Soviet offensive opened along a 450-mile-front where the attacking forces outnumbered and outgunned German troops.

All of the parties had fulfilled the bargain made at Teheran. As a result, the great Allied assault on Hitler's Fortress Europe had commenced at last in 1944. The decision made at the Teheran Conference to concentrate on OVERLORD in 1944 and to avoid distraction by sideshows had saved lives. Any delay in launching OVERLORD that year would only have given the Germans more time to strengthen their defenses against the Allies and it would also have meant more casualties for the invading forces.

One last promise still remained from the Teheran Conference: ANVIL. Should the postponed invasion of southern France be carried out because of a promise to Stalin? This operation now became a source of bitter argument between Churchill and Roosevelt.

After Rome had fallen on June 4 and the Allied troops had secured a bridgehead in Normandy, the British opposed ANVIL, claiming that landing in southern France would only result in acquiring a port—Marseilles—whereas just as useful a port could be seized in northwestern France. Troop movements up the Rhône Valley would be slow; the Germans could easily block their advance. These troops would of course mean a reduction in the forces that could be used in Italy. The British wanted to move on north through Italy and into the valley of the Po, and then to turn eastward through the Ljubljana Gap. There, the Allied troops could join up with the Yugoslav Partisans and eventually form another front with the Russians approaching from the east. If divisions were taken from Italy to be used in the ANVIL operation, then the Italian campaign would be slowed down, relaxing the pressure on the Germans.

Eisenhower and the American chiefs of staff advocated ANVIL because it would mean the seizure of Marseilles and more direct support to the OVERLORD campaign by increasing the assault on Germany while at the same time maintaining a holding operation in Italy. The Americans believed that ANVIL would open up additional ports more quickly while also drawing off German troops.

Churchill and Roosevelt took up the argument. Churchill appealed to the President to reject the recommendation of the Joint Chiefs of Staff to withdraw troops from Italy for AN-VIL and to launch the operation in mid-August. He begged Roosevelt to examine the matter in detail because he found the tone of the American chiefs of staff "arbitrary." He reminded Roosevelt that at the Teheran Conference he had talked about Istria. To strengthen his case, Churchill sent Roosevelt a long memorandum in which he argued for the continuation of the drive through Italy and the cancellation of ANVIL. He feared that they would "ruin all hopes of a major victory in Italy and all its fronts and condemn ourselves to a passive role in that theater, after having broken up the fine Allied army which is advancing so rapidly through the peninsula for the sake of ANVIL, with all its limitations."

But Roosevelt stuck to the Teheran decision: OVERLORD, advance in Italy, assault on southern France, combined with a Soviet drive from the east. He would not accept Churchill's argument that withdrawing troops from Italy would weaken the Allied campaign there. Even if troops were withdrawn, enough would remain to drive the Germans north of the Po River and to contain them there. At best not more than six divisions could be deployed beyond the Ljubljana Gap. "I cannot agree to the employment of United States troops against Istria and into the Balkans," he wrote firmly.

Roosevelt went on to remind Churchill that because the ANVIL operation had been agreed on at Teheran, he would not accept any course of action that meant abandoning AN-VIL without first consulting Stalin. If they could not agree on launching ANVIL at the earliest possible date, then they had to communicate with Stalin. They would also have to discuss this with the French, who were to supply troops for AN-VIL. "At Teheran we agreed upon a definite plan of attack. That plan has gone well so far. Nothing has occurred to require any change. . . . My dear friend, I beg you to let us go ahead with our plan." For "purely political considerations over here," he could never survive the slightest setback in OVERLORD if it became known that large forces had been diverted to the Balkans.

Roosevelt's rejection of Churchill's argument "deeply grieved" the prime minister. The splitting of the Mediterranean campaign into two operations was "the first major strategic and political error for which we two have to be responsible." He claimed that at Teheran, Roosevelt had emphasized to him the possibilities of a move eastward after Italy had been conquered and had mentioned Istria. "No one involved in these discussions has ever thought of moving armies into the Balkans." He feared that the forces advancing up the Rhône Valley could easily be blocked by a smaller German force. It would be a "cul-de-sac into which increasing numbers of United States troops will be drawn."

Concerning the President's threat to place the matter before Stalin if Churchill persisted in seeking to change the Teheran agreement about ANVIL, the prime minister backed off, preferring to settle the problem with Roosevelt. He did not know what Stalin might say if the issue were to be placed before him. Churchill thought he might show great interest in the movement of the Allied armies eastward, which would profoundly affect forces in the Balkans. Then, taking a more political view, Churchill argued that Stalin might prefer that American and British forces concentrate on the heavy fighting in France and allow eastern, central, and southern Europe to fall under his control.

If the President insisted on pressing the British to accept

the withdrawal of U.S. forces from Italy for ANVIL, "His Majesty's government on advice of their chiefs of staff, must enter a solemn protest." It was with the greatest sorrow that he wrote to Roosevelt.

But the President still would not concede, insisting that the correct course of action was to launch ANVIL at the earliest possible date with the Allied commanders in Italy continuing on with the forces left to them. At Teheran he had been thinking only of a series of raids in force in Istria if the Germans began a general retreat, which had not yet occurred. The terrain and the weather in the area would create difficult conditions for fighting during the winter; much worse than southern France, in his opinion.[15]

Shortly before ANVIL—now retitled DRAGOON—was launched, Churchill tried without success to convince Eisenhower and Roosevelt to switch the target from southern France to Bordeaux. Once more Churchill's pleas were rejected. On August 15, three American divisions and seven French divisions plus an Anglo-American airborne division landed in southern France, and by September 11 linked up with the forces that had swept across France from Normandy. The Teheran plan had been completed.

Churchill had given way because Roosevelt controlled the larger forces. But he was much affected by the argument over ANVIL, according to Gilbert Winant, the American ambassador in London. "I want you to know how deeply the Prime Minister has felt the differences that have ended in his accepting your decision," Winant informed the President on July 3. "I have never seen him as badly shaken. He believed completely in the program he was supporting. It was only his great friendship for you, the personal consideration you showed him in your exchange of messages, the knowledge of the greater contribution we were making in the campaign and a recognition that time was pressing that prevented continued resistance on his part. . . ."[16]

When the ANVIL-DRAGOON landings occurred, Churchill was in Italy visiting commanders and their troops. To show his interest in the operation, he flew to Corsica and there boarded a British destroyer which sailed in among the invasion fleet, allowing him to watch the landing craft ferrying

American troops to the shores of southern France. Despite his arguments with Eisenhower over ANVIL-DRAGOON, he hastened to send his congratulations. "All I have learnt here makes me admire the perfect precision with which the landing was arranged and the intimate collaboration of British-American forces and organizations."

Later, writing in his memoirs, Churchill insisted that by the date ANVIL-DRAGOON had been launched, none of the reasons presented at the Teheran Conference had any relation to what was done. The operation, he wrote, did not affect OVERLORD, nor did it compel the German High Command to disperse any of the troops in northwestern France. The reverse was true: Anglo-American forces beginning to sweep across France threatened the rear of the German units retreating up the Rhône Valley and forced many to surrender. Churchill thought a very heavy price had been paid for this success: "The army of Italy was deprived of its opportunity to strike a most formidable blow at the Germans, and very possibly reach Vienna before the Russians, with all that might have followed there." [17]

The Teheran record shows that Roosevelt did not mention Istria as he maintained. But on November 28 he definitely spoke about "a possible operation at the head of the Adriatic to make a junction with the Partisans under Tito and to operate northeast into Rumania in conjunction with the Soviet advance from the region of Odessa." (The Istrian peninsula is at the head of the Adriatic.) According to the Combined Chiefs of Staff minutes of the same meeting, he spoke about an entry through the northeastern Adriatic in order to launch offensive operations against Germany "in the direction of the Danube." According to the British minutes, he reminded Churchill "of the further project of moving up to the northern Adriatic and then north-east to the Danube." The Soviet minutes show Roosevelt suggesting the possibility of a landing in the northern part of the Adriatic, "when the Soviet armies approach Odessa." Churchill did not take up the subject, but Stalin twice asked for more information about the operation in the Adriatic area. Neither Roosevelt nor Churchill answered him. [18]

Yet Roosevelt's comments about the Adriatic surprised

Hopkins. He passed a note to Admiral King: "Who's promoting that Adriatic business that the President continually returns to?" And King answered: "As far as I know it is his own idea." [19] He was correct, but as early as November 19, Roosevelt had mentioned the Adriatic in a meeting with the Joint Chiefs of Staff on board *Iowa*. Then he had wondered if Stalin might ask the British and the Americans for help from the Adriatic area when the Soviet armies reached Rumania. He was thinking, as he later told Churchill, in terms of commando raids to help Tito. But something in Stalin's reactions to his comments about the Adriatic at Teheran led him to drop the proposal. Stalin had never asked for aid by way of the Adriatic. Instead, he wanted only OVERLORD and an invasion of southern France. After Roosevelt agreed to these operations, he refused to abandon either of them without consulting Stalin. Moreover, by the summer of 1944 Roosevelt would do nothing to arouse Stalin's suspicions, particularly by permitting an Anglo-American force to confront Soviet armies in the Balkans.

The Teheran promise of a combined assault on the German forces was now a fact. Although it was causing the Germans severe casualties, it would mean armies spreading across Europe exerting a great political impact on the future of eastern and central Europe, as Churchill had warned. No nation would experience this impact more forcibly than Poland.

19
The Polish Riddle

POLAND'S HISTORY HAS been a tragic one. Once a great state dominating central and eastern Europe, she succumbed to powerful neighbors in the eighteenth century, being divided among Austria, Prussia, and Russia. Following World War I, after the defeat of Russia, Germany, and Austria-Hungary, an independent Poland emerged, but she would survive only as long as her more powerful neighbors left her in peace. Poland's independence required weak neighbors; when their strength revived, Poland was doomed. In 1939, Nazi Germany and the Soviet Union secretly made a pact to divide Poland between themselves. After defeating the Polish armies, they carried out their plot. Only Hitler's attack on Soviet Russia in June 1941 so altered the political relationship in eastern Europe that a revival of an independent Poland seemed possible. However, the more powerful neighbor intended to influence Poland's political future even before the war had ended.

At the Teheran Conference the Polish riddle had been posed, but only briefly. The answer had not been supplied. The Polish Government-in-Exile had yet to accept the decisions reached concerning Poland's future. Consequently, during 1944, while Churchill and Roosevelt wrangled with Stalin over dividing up the Italian fleet and Anglo-American forces prepared for the Normandy invasion, they also had to confront the riddle left over from the Teheran Conference: Poland. It would be a test case, proving whether Roosevelt

had succeeded in talking Stalin out of his suspicions and had
converted the Soviet ruler into cooperating wholeheartedly
with the western Allies.

At the heart of the problem was the western frontier of
the Soviet Union, which Stalin regarded as "the main question for us in the war."[1] It could strongly influence Soviet
support in the remainder of the war and, most important of
all, in the future international peace arrangements. The task
of resolving the frontier question would be complicated by
Stalin's antipathy toward the Polish Government-in-Exile in
London.

Immediately after the Teheran Conference, Churchill and
Eden took up the task of finding the answer to the riddle
through a compromise between Stalin and the London Poles.
It would be arduous because they must satisfy Stalin's demands while quieting the fears of the Poles. In addition, they
had to work without Roosevelt's help since he had left the
task of seeking a compromise up to them. He had no desire
to become entrapped in sticky negotiations during a presidential election year. He, too, had fallen victim to the paral-
ysis that sets into American policy making during presidential
election campaigns—even one held during a world war.
Taking sides on such an issue could provide the Republicans with a useful, headline-making controversy. At the same
time, Roosevelt probably hoped to improve his standing with
Stalin by staying out of the argument. Consequently, he preferred that Churchill, the imperialist, become the target of
Stalin's complaints and Polish anger. Better that Churchill
become the center of controversy than the Democratic presidential candidate seeking reelection for his fourth term.

Not only would Churchill lack Roosevelt's full support,
he had another handicap: Time was on Stalin's side. Daily,
Soviet troops moved closer to the old 1939 frontier between
Poland and the Soviet Union. After the soldiers had crossed
the line, the Polish government would lose whatever leverage it possessed. If at all possible, the Poles should have
signed a treaty with Stalin when German troops were deep
within Soviet territory. Since it was now too late for that,
Churchill had to solve the Russo-Polish question as quickly
as possible.

At Teheran, Churchill and Roosevelt had handed Stalin an advantage when they had promised the second front without any conditions. At the time there seemed to be no alternative because when the Normandy invasion began, the Anglo-American forces would need the Soviet offensive, launched from the east, to prevent Hitler from shifting troops to France. Churchill and Roosevelt dreaded pushing Stalin too far in any negotiation over Polish frontiers. At the Teheran Conference he appeared to have received a promise of Anglo-American backing in solving the Polish problem. If now they reneged on their pledges, the promised Soviet offensive might be delayed or even canceled. Any such delay by the Soviet armies in launching their offensive could result in very heavy casualties on the Normandy beaches.

In December 1943, after the second conference at Cairo was over, Churchill had flown to Tunis. There, because of his exhausted condition, he became ill and developed pneumonia. While recuperating at Marrakesh, Churchill instructed Eden to open the Polish frontier question with the Poles, which he would have done himself except for his illness. Eden should show the Poles the Teheran formula for the new frontiers and stress that in the west they would receive "a magnificent piece of country," 300 to 400 miles in width, and over 150 miles of seashore. The Poles ought to put themselves into the hands of their British and American friends, who would try to turn this formula into reality. Eden could sweeten the pill by picturing the inclusion in Poland of German territories up to the Oder River. The Poles would be creating a homeland for themselves that would be secure and solid. But if the Poles threw out these proposals, Churchill could not see how his government could press the Soviet Union for anything more for them. Within a matter of months the Soviet armies would be crossing the Polish frontiers; before that happened, there ought to be a friendly recognition of the Polish government by the Soviet Union and a broad agreement on the postwar frontiers.[2]

Commencing with the Polish ambassador on December 17 and then with Polish Premier Stanislaw Mikolajczyk on December 29, Eden gave the first reports of the results of the Teheran Conference. He told them that Stalin had complained about the Polish Government-in-Exile instructing its supporters in Poland to resist Russian partisans; he had even accused the Poles of collaborating with the Germans. In reply to the Poles' denials, Eden asked for a statement to pass on to Stalin that there had been no contact between the Poles and the Germans. To strengthen his argument, Eden read aloud from the Teheran minutes Stalin's accusations, which Mikolajczyk denied. "No Poles had ever cooperated with the Germans and they were unchangeable in their resistance to them."

When the discussion came to the question of Polish frontiers, Eden tried to blur Stalin's demands by using such phrases as "our general impression" and "broadly speaking." According to Eden, "the idea had emerged that the future territory of Poland would lie between the Curzon Line and the Oder." Stalin was prepared to give Poland compensation in East Prussia and to extend the western frontiers to the Oder River. But to Mikolajczyk, giving up this territory, including Lvov and Vilna, to the Soviet Union would not be offset by the land in the west. Eden assured him that according to Churchill if he would agree to this proposal, there would be a good chance of reaching an agreement with Russia that would make Poland independent and stronger than she had been before the outbreak of the war.

Mikolajczyk saw no possibility of settling the frontier question. Instead, he would accept Roosevelt's invitation to visit Washington which had been postponed because of the Teheran Conference. Eden balked, preferring that Mikolajczyk see Churchill when he returned to Britain. He would ask the White House to postpone Mikolajczyk's planned visit. The Poles left, complaining that even Iran received a guarantee from the three powers, but Poland who had made such sacrifices had received none. "Believe me," Eden replied, "I am utterly devoted to your cause and I am eager to render service to it."[3]

Churchill, tipped off by Eden, recommended to Roosevelt that the trip be postponed until an agreement could be reached with Stalin. Otherwise he feared that Mikolajczyk might become "the center of Polish enthusiasm, much of which is likely to be anti-Russian and may this not cost them dear?" Roosevelt, eager to conceal his role at Teheran, agreed absolutely that the trip should be postponed.[4]

With the coming of the new year, the negotiations in London over the Polish question speeded up after Soviet armies crossed the old 1939 frontier on January 3. Following the Soviet forces had come a seamy character, Boleslow Bierut, former NKVD agent, who headed an unofficial Communist government in the town of Lublin.

The Poles in London took up the challenge by issuing a declaration on January 5 staking out their position. They declared that because of sacrifices in the war, Poland expected justice and redress as soon as she had been liberated, including reestablishing Polish sovereignty in the liberated territories and protecting the life and property of Polish citizens. The Polish government expected the Soviet Union to respect the rights and interests of the Polish Republic and its citizens. Accordingly, the Polish government had instructed the underground in Poland to continue intensifying its resistance against the Germans and to avoid all conflict with the Soviet armies entering Poland in their war against Germany.[5]

Although drafted and revised with the approval of the Foreign Office, the declaration infuriated Stalin because the Poles insisted on regarding themselves as a genuine government strong enough to bargain with him. If he were to accept the argument that this government represented Poland, whose independence was confirmed by the Atlantic Charter, which he hated, he might never obtain the Curzon Line as the eastern frontier of the Soviet Union. The Poles soon had an answer to their challenge of Stalin.

Shortly after midnight on January 11, Molotov summoned Averell Harriman to the Kremlin, where he kept him waiting for about fifteen minutes before receiving him with an apology for the delay, claiming that the declaration he was giving him had just been completed. Molotov hoped the statement relating to Poland "would be found to conform to the spirit of the conversations at Teheran with President Roosevelt and Prime Minister Churchill." He added that because everyone was talking about Poland, it would be wrong to remain silent.

The statement was aimed at correcting the declaration issued by the exiled Polish government. "As is well known, the Soviet constitution established the Soviet-Polish frontier in accordance with the will of the population of the western Ukraine and western White Russia, expressed in the plebiscite conducted on a broad democratic basis in 1939." The plebiscite corrected the injustice in the Riga Treaty forced on the Soviet Union in 1921. Instead of injuring Poland, the entry of the western Ukraine and western White Russia into the Soviet Union had created the basis for more permanent friendship between both countries. The Soviet government desired "to establish friendship between the USSR and Poland on the basis of firm good neighborly relations and mutual respect and, if the Polish people so desire, on the basis of an alliance for mutual assistance against the Germans." The new Polish state should be reborn not by seizing Ukrainian and White Russian lands but by the return to Poland of the lands taken by the Germans. Only in this way could confidence and friendship be established between these peoples.

Poland's eastern boundaries could be fixed by agreement with the Soviet Union. Moreover, the 1939 boundaries were not unchangeable. "The Soviet-Polish boundary might follow approximately the so-called Curzon Line, which was accepted by the Supreme Council of the Allied Powers in 1919 and which envisaged the incorporation of the western Ukraine and western White Russia in the Soviet Union." But the exiled Polish government was incapable of establishing friendly relations with the Soviet government. Nor could it organize the struggle against the German invaders of Poland. Its incorrect policies had only played into the hands of the German occupiers. The interests of Poland and the Soviet Union lay in establishing friendly relations.

Molotov's statement did not tell all of the truth. The plebiscite held in 1939 came only after the Soviet armies had defeated the Polish army, occupied the western Ukraine and western White Russia (the area to the east of the Curzon Line), and forcibly removed hundreds of thousands of people, transporting them to Soviet prison camps from which they never returned. The Curzon Line had never been accepted by the Supreme Allied Council in 1919; rather, Lord Curzon, the British foreign secretary, had proposed such a line as an armistice line, not a final frontier. As to Molotov's comment that the declaration conformed to the spirit of the Teheran conversations, Harriman did not challenge Molotov on that basis because the demands for the Curzon Line and for a "friendly" Polish government had indeed been stated at Teheran without challenge from either Churchill or Roosevelt. In addition, the Soviet declaration inferred that Poland had been offered a generous concession; but if so favorable an offer were to be declined, it could only mean that the Polish reactionaries had rejected a "fair" proposal.

In their reply, on January 14 toned down by Eden, the Poles announced that they would not accept unilateral decisions because they desired a Polish-Soviet agreement on terms just and acceptable to both parties. Consequently, the Polish government would approach the British and the Americans to ask them to act as intermediaries in the discussions and even to participate in the negotiations. By this tactic, the Poles sought allies in the negotiations with the Soviet government.

Moscow viewed the Polish reply as a rejection of the Curzon Line. Moreover, the Soviet government could not negotiate with a government with whom diplomatic relations had been broken because the Poles had joined "in the hostile anti-Soviet slander campaign of the German occupants concerning the Katyn murders."[6]

As the Polish government had asked the American government to participate as a mediator, Roosevelt and Hull had to draft a reply. On January 15, they begged Stalin to consider favorably the Polish offer to discuss outstanding questions since a friendly solution of the differences between the two nations would have far-reaching effects on world opinion. If the Soviet government found it agreeable and desirable, the United States government would be glad to extend its good offices to arrange for the initiation of the discussions.[7]

Of course no hint had been given that at Teheran Roosevelt had sat quietly by during the Churchill-Stalin colloquy on the Curzon Line. Now he volunteered to serve as a mediator! His services, however, would not be needed because Molotov informed Harriman that Moscow would not deal with the Polish government. Moreover, the time had come to form a new government of honest men, untainted by fascism and well disposed toward the Soviet Union. The only basis for the resumption of diplomatic relations would be the acceptance of the Curzon Line by a Polish government. Molotov had issued "non-negotiable demands."

The resolution of these differences fell to Churchill, who returned to London on January 18, pale and unsteady on his legs as a result of the medication he had been taking. Roosevelt, hiding behind the impending presidential election, left to Churchill the chore of finding a compromise on the Polish-Soviet frontiers. Churchill did not shirk his duty and took up the matter with the Poles soon after his return. With preparations for the invasion of France accelerating, he did not want an argument with the Poles to undermine efforts aimed at ensuring Soviet cooperation. A Polish frontier was not worth it.

On January 20, he met with Mikolajczyk, Tadeusz Romer, the Polish foreign minister, and Count Eduard Raczynski, the Polish ambassador, for the first of a series of stormy meetings. Churchill asked them at least to accept the Curzon Line in principle because it was the best they could hope to obtain and because it was a fair solution. He warned that it was unthinkable that Britain would go to war over this frontier, and the United States would certainly never do so either. Mikolajczyk, however, would only consider a revision of the Riga agreement which had determined the Polish-Soviet frontier that lasted from 1921 until 1939. To use the Curzon Line as the basis for negotiations, argued Mikolajczyk, would be to the advantage of the Soviet Union.

Churchill, in return, wanted the Poles to look to the west, where the extension of the Polish frontiers at Germany's expense would mean for Poland "the high duty of standing guard against future German aggression with the guarantee of the three great powers." He reminded Mikolajczyk that "Britain alone could never have restored Poland to independence. It was the Russian army that had done that and had made possible the rebuilding of a strong and independent Poland." Churchill saw little room for negotiation. Moreover, it would be better to make this adjustment now than to wait until the Soviet army had marched into Poland. Churchill's vision of Poland on guard against German attack did not end Mikolajczyk's worry over Polish losses in mines, oil fields, and valuable farmland suffered because of the Curzon Line. The meeting ended with Mikolajczyk promising to get back to Churchill after considering the question with the members of his government.[8]

The Polish cabinet backed Mikolajczyk's position in the meeting with Churchill. Angry over the attempt to pressure them into accepting the Curzon Line, yet fearful of losing Allied support, the Poles sought to learn how far London and Washington were prepared to go in supporting Poland's cause. They wished to know about the administration and occupation of Poland after she had been freed of the Germans. Would Britain and the United States guarantee Poland's political independence? Would any one of the powers who had conferred in Teheran wish bases in Poland? If Poland ceded territory, would it be final? Would Germany be compelled to take the German-speaking population from the land turned over to Poland? Would Polish citizens living in the Soviet Union be repatriated?

None of these questions had been considered at the Teheran Conference. So Eden, answering for the British government, claimed that they could not be decided by Britain alone. An agreed settlement between Poland and the Soviet Union would provide the best safeguard for Poland, Eden maintained.

Before the Poles met again with Churchill, he reported to Stalin on the progress of the negotiations with the Poles. He had told them that "I believed from what had passed at Teheran that the Soviet government would be willing to agree to the easterly frontiers of Poland conforming to the Curzon Line." He had advised them to accept this line as the basis for discussion. For Poland's protection from Germany, he thought the three powers would provide a guarantee. The Poles should settle on this basis, and at the peace conference, Britain would support such a settlement.[9]

In talks with the British and American ambassadors in the Kremlin and in his reply to Churchill, Stalin had demanded, as "the first essential," changes in the Polish government and acceptance of the Curzon Line. In addition, at Teheran he had told both Churchill and Roosevelt that he claimed the northeastern part of East Prussia and Königsberg for the Soviet Union. To Harriman, he insisted that he had expressed his point of view clearly at Teheran. In pondering these reports, Churchill came to the conclusion that "we would make the best bargain we could for our unreasonable clients and let the clients know that if at the proper time they do not accept it we would withdraw from the case."[10]

Churchill met his clients again on February 6, hoping to hammer out an agreement satisfactory to Stalin that would follow the Teheran formula. Speaking for the clients, Mikolajczyk announced that the Poles were determined to preserve Poland's territorial integrity. Accepting the Curzon Line as the starting point constituted accepting dictated terms and ruled out a genuine negotiation. Churchill's reply was blunt. "In that case the situation was hopeless. No agreement could be reached on such a basis and the Soviets having occupied the whole of your country will impose their will." If he could not reach an agreement with the Poles, he would have to come to an understanding with the Russians.[11]

While Churchill had been arguing with the Poles over the frontier accepted at Teheran, little had been heard from the third party present at the Teheran Conference when the Curzon Line had been discussed. Roosevelt held Poland less important than the Soviet connection. Certainly the Curzon Line to him mattered far less than Soviet cooperation in the international organization to keep the peace which he hoped to form after the war. He feared this organization would fail unless he could obtain Stalin's cooperation; it was for this purpose that he had traveled to Teheran. A question such as the Polish frontier problem might antagonize Stalin, kindle his suspicions, and so anger him that he would veto Soviet membership in the United Nations.

For Roosevelt, debating future frontiers before the war ended made bad politics. Such prickly questions ought to be postponed until they required decision. When the decisions were eventually forced on him, who knew how the political landscape would appear? This philosophy had colored his thinking when Churchill and Stalin debated in Teheran. Some of his views about determining Polish frontiers can be found in a draft of a message to Churchill in March 1944 that was never sent:

> In regard to the general Polish situation I am inclined to think that the final determination of matters like boundaries can well be laid aside for awhile by the Russians, by the Polish government and by your government.
>
> In other words, I think that on these particular matters we can well let nature take its course. The main current problem is to assure the cooperation of the Polish guerrillas and the population with the Russians as they advance into Poland. Most certainly we do not want any Polish opposition to the Russian armies.
>
> In the meantime we will learn much more about Polish sentiment and the advisability of continuing or not continuing to let the Polish government in London speak for the Poles. It is entirely possible that as the Russians advance they may recognize some other organization as more representative of the people of Poland.
>
> The advancing Russian army will doubtless find many local Poles who will aid them as they proceed westward. This is essentially a military occupation. *I still think the future government and matters like boundaries can be put on ice until we know more about it. This, in line with my general thought that we ought not to cross bridges till we come to them.* [My italics] [12]

Roosevelt steadfastly refused to commit himself on either side of the Curzon Line debate as long as possible, fearing that the political fallout would not be worth the cost and that he would be trapped in a position which later would be costly to defend. His tactics reflected a political practice he had long followed: pushing unpleasant political decisions into the future as far as possible. Continuing this practice with Stalin, Roosevelt assumed that the Soviet dictator differed little from

American politicians whom he knew so well. However, there were marked differences between Stalin and the members of Tammany Hall.

Already Stalin's actions had puzzled Hull after the friendly words and lengthy toasts exchanged at the conferences in Moscow and Teheran. He complained to Harriman that Stalin's unilateral actions over Poland undermined "the broad principles of international cooperation laid down at the Moscow and Teheran conferences." Stalin's policies dampened the "spirit of hope and confidence which was born with the Moscow Conference and stimulated and confirmed at Teheran." [13] Hull may have thought that Stalin had reverted to his old ways of suspicion; but Stalin had not changed. He was implementing Teheran as he understood it, and so far Roosevelt had not dared challenge his understanding.

Late in January, the Polish Government-in-Exile tried to learn what help it might expect from Roosevelt by sending him three questions. His answers were very general so that he would not be trapped in the Polish-Soviet quarrel. In answer to the question did the U.S. government believe it advisable at that time to commence discussions on the final settlement of European territorial problems, Roosevelt said that he approved in principle but he would not rule out an accord between two countries with mutual territorial problems. As for the U.S. government participating in achieving such settlements and guaranteeing them, there could be no guarantee, but the United States would offer its good offices to help the Poles reach a settlement by facilitating discussions between governments. Finally, as to the U.S. government supporting Churchill's plan that the Poles accept the Curzon Line as the basis for discussion, Roosevelt would commit himself only to supporting Churchill in reestablishing friendly relations between the Polish and Soviet governments on the basis of a friendly solution of outstanding problems. There would be no guarantees by the United States government.[14] Once more Roosevelt had been careful to conceal his role at the Teheran Conference lest Polish-American voters learn what he had done.

At last he had dared to enter the Polish-Soviet squabble, taking this step, as he explained to Churchill, because "our primary concern is the potential dangers [sic] of this situation to the essential unity which was so successfully established at Moscow and Teheran." On February 7 he communicated with Stalin about "your relations with Poland . . . on the basis of our conversations at Teheran," but he would never suggest, much less advise him on where Russian interests lay in this question. "The overwhelming majority of our people and Congress, as you know, welcomed with enthusiasm the broad principles subscribed to at the Moscow and Teheran conferences, and I know that you agree with me that it is of the utmost importance that faith in these understandings should not be left in any doubt." Consequently, he wanted to see a solution that would satisfy Stalin's desire for a friendly, independent Poland as well as protect Soviet interests but not harm the cooperation "so splendidly established at Moscow and Teheran." Roosevelt recommended that Churchill's proposal for a "clean cut acceptance" by Mikolajczyk of the territorial changes desired by Stalin become the basis for the negotiations. Then they could decide on the composition of the Polish cabinet, leaving it to Mikolajczyk to make the changes so that it would appear as though he had made them under outside pressure from a foreign government. By reminding Stalin about the Teheran Conference, Roosevelt tried to place the Polish question on a more personal level. The camaraderie and the vows made at Teheran all meant for Roosevelt closer Soviet-American ties. Negotiations over a mere frontier and the composition of a Polish cabinet must not weaken the personal bond he believed had been established with Stalin at Teheran.[15]

Roosevelt's calls for Stalin to remember the Teheran Conference did not move him. Replying to Roosevelt's plea on February 16, he was brief and curt. The Soviet government had given up the 1939 frontier for the Curzon Line, and because this was a considerable concession on the part of the Soviet Union, the Poles must state that the Curzon Line had been accepted as their new frontier just as the Soviet government had done because the Poles would not budge from the Riga Treaty of 1921. As for the Polish government, it contained "pro-fascist imperialist elements," and could not establish friendly relations with the Soviet government. Not a word here about the cooperation "so splendidly established at . . . Teheran."[16]

On February 15, the Poles announced their refusal to negotiate on the basis of the Curzon Line. The next day, employing all of his eloquence, Churchill tried to sway them. But Mikolajczyk and his colleagues, fearing condemnation as traitors if they accepted the Curzon Line, would only propose a demaracation line running to the east of the Curzon Line. Churchill argued that the Curzon Line was just, and that it was the only solution satisfactory to Stalin. He would support the line at the peace conference, but he must have some agreement with Stalin before the Soviet armies occupied Poland. It was pointless to anger the Russians and to drive them to set up a puppet government in Warsaw. He assured Mikolajczyk that "there was no reason to suppose that Russia would repeat the German desire to dominate all Europe." But Churchill's histrionics could not move Mikolajczyk.[17]

With the Polish prime minister's approval, Churchill tried a new tactic. He informed Stalin that the Polish government would declare the Riga frontier no longer realistic; they were now prepared to discuss a new frontier with the Soviet government. For the present, the Polish government could not announce publicly its readiness to cede territory because the announcement would appear one-sided and would create dissatisfaction among Poles living abroad and fighting in the underground. The territorial settlement would have to await the final, general territorial arrangement in Europe. He asked Stalin to assist the return of the Polish government to liberated Poland and to help in establishing civil administration in the liberated districts. After the Polish government had entered into diplomatic relations with the Soviet Union, "none but persons fully determined to cooperate with the Soviet Union would be in the Polish government."[18]

In all his discussions with the Poles and in his correspondence with Stalin, Churchill had carefully omitted Roosevelt's name. Now he asked the President to do whatever he could to gain Stalin's acceptance of this proposal. In response to Churchill's request, Roosevelt's reply was short, bland, and devoid of any commitment. He would only say that Churchill's suggestion would go a long way toward furthering the prospects for victory. He recommended that Stalin give the proposal "favorable and sympathetic consideration."[19]

Stalin shot this down, dismissing Churchill's proposal with a snicker. When the British ambassador assured him that the Poles would not recant, he sneered: "Is that serious? How handsome of them!" After rejecting all of Churchill's suggestions, Clark Kerr asked Stalin what he wanted. All he wanted was the Curzon Line and the reconstruction of the Polish government. If the Poles meant business they should openly accept the Curzon Line; the reconstruction of their government could not await the recapture of Warsaw. Clark Kerr failed to change Stalin's mind—"This dreary and exasperating conversation lasted for well over an hour. No argument was of any avail."[20]

Churchill persisted in seeking for the formula that would bridge the gap between Stalin and the Poles. To Stalin he maintained that his proposals would give the Russians de facto control of the territories lying to the east of the Curzon Line. He hoped that Stalin would not close the door to a working arrangement with the Poles, but if that proved impossible, the British government would still recognize the Polish government. Soon he would have to make a statement in Parliament about the break in his efforts to arrive at an arrangement between the Soviet and the Polish governments. He begged Stalin not to let the breakdown between them over Poland "have any effect upon our cooperation in other spheres where the maintenance of our common action is of the greatest consequence." Here he dropped his guard, revealing fears that the squabble over Poland might harm Allied cooperation in preparing for the invasion of France.[21]

Suddenly on March 23 Stalin lashed out at Churchill, accusing him of sending messages bristling with threats and implying that the Soviet Union was resorting to a policy of force in seeking to implement the Curzon Line. Churchill had described the Curzon Line as unlawful and the struggle over it unjust. "I must point out that at Teheran you, the President and myself were agreed that the Curzon Line was lawful." Did Churchill now mean that he no longer recognized the agreement at Teheran? Was Churchill ready to violate the Teheran agreement? If Churchill had persevered in his Teheran stand, the trouble with the Poles would now have been settled. As for Stalin, he and his government would adhere to the Teheran agreement. Because the Soviet Union was not waging war against Poland, he refused to postpone the solution of the Soviet-Polish frontier problem until the peace conference. And as for Churchill telling Parliament that Britain could not recognize any forcible transfers of territory, that made the Soviet Union sound as if it were hostile to Poland and not fighting to liberate the Poles. This statement would be regarded in the Soviet Union as an "unjust and unfriendly act." Such intimidation and defamation would not benefit Allied cooperation.[22]

Stalin sent a copy of this message to Roosevelt, who neither commented nor acknowledged the message. Stalin considered that the three leaders had made an agreement over Poland at Teheran. If this were not the case, why did Roosevelt keep silent on the matter? He may have thought, as did Churchill, "that the bark may be worse than its bite and that they have a great desire not to separate themselves from their British and American allies."[23] By letting this statement pass unchallenged, Roosevelt strengthened the Soviet belief that when Churchill and Stalin had negotiated the Polish question on December 1 at Teheran, his silence signaled agreement. Roosevelt had yet to learn the lesson which Molotov finally taught Harriman: "Molotov has on a number of occasions indicated to me that he considered that after they had put us on notice of a Soviet policy or plan and we did not at that time object, we had acquiesced in and accepted the Soviet position."[24]

Since Stalin seemed intent on finding fault and picking a quarrel with Churchill on every issue, the War Cabinet saw no point in continuing the correspondence on Poland. The topic ought to be dropped until after the invasion of France, when the possibility of influencing Stalin might be greater. In the immediate future too many British and American lives were at stake to justify replies and counter replies. Nothing could stand in the way of OVERLORD, already accepted at Teheran.

The message came to Stalin on April 18 that the "general crossing of the sea" would take place about May 31. In fact, delays postponed the Anglo-American assault until June 6, when Allied troops landed on five Normandy beaches. But the pledge made to Stalin at Teheran had been kept and the debacle Churchill had feared did not take place. However, the fierce fighting did not produce a swift breakout from the Normandy beachhead. German resistance only made the promised Soviet offensive more vital. Nothing must stand in the way of launching the new Soviet offensive that would relieve the pressure on the British and American forces—not even Poland.

Even as the Allied fleets were moving into their final positions before launching the invasion, Prime Minister Mikolajczyk had set out for Washington, arriving on June 5 for his often postponed meeting with Roosevelt. Early in April, Churchill had suggested that Roosevelt invite Mikolajczyk in order to show Stalin the interest the United States had in the future of Poland. Hull recommended that the President see Mikolajczyk before rather than after the presidential election campaign had begun. By meeting Mikolajczyk, Roosevelt could calm Polish-American groups anxious over the Soviet advance into Poland. Their vote, so it was believed, would be of great importance in the states of Illinois, Michigan, Pennsylvania, New Jersey, and New York. As for Mikolajczyk, he hoped that by visiting the President of the United States he would strengthen his hand in the negotiations with Stalin.

At eighteen years of age, Stanislaw Mikolajczyk, the son of a Polish farmer, had joined the Polish army, fought the Germans to enforce the provisions of the Treaty of Versailles, and then battled the Russians until wounds forced him to be mustered out of the army. After returning to farming, he became active in politics in the new Polish Republic, and by 1937 he headed the Peasant party, pro-French and democratic in orientation. In 1939 he fought as a private until the Polish army had been defeated by the Germans and the Russians. Escaping to Hungary, he then made his way to France, where he joined the Polish National Council formed to replace the Polish Parliament. He became deputy vice-chairman, succeeding Chairman Ignace Jan Paderewski at his death. When France fell, he escaped to London, becoming deputy prime minister and minister of the interior in the Polish Government-in-Exile, which was headed by General Wladyslaw Sikorski. After the general's death in a plane crash on July 14, 1943, Mikolajczyk became prime minister.

At the first of their four meetings, on June 7, Roosevelt regaled Mikolajczyk and Jan Ciechanowski, the Polish ambassador, with his impressions of Stalin during the Teheran Conference. Stalin had struck Roosevelt as a "realist who was neither an imperialist nor a communist." Although very suspicious, he appreciated a good joke. Conferring with him was not easy because if he was unwilling to be drawn into discussing a particular subject, he simply let the matter drop. Roosevelt was pleased that he could more easily understand Stalin's sense of humor "than my poor friend Churchill." As an illustration of Stalin's humor, Roosevelt told the prime minister the story of Stalin's toast at Teheran to the death of at least fifty thousand German officers. Churchill, laughed Roosevelt, missed the joke, displeasing Stalin, who gave Churchill "a dirty look"; but Roosevelt claimed that he had smoothed it over by changing the wording of the toast to "death in battle of forty-nine and a half thousand German officers."

As for the Curzon Line, neither he nor Stalin had suggested it as a final frontier. When Churchill brought up the subject, Stalin took advantage of the opportunity. "I want you to know," Roosevelt told Mikolajczyk, "that I am still opposed to dividing Poland with this line and that eventually I will act as a moderator." He claimed not to know the best method to adopt in the Soviet-Polish conflict, but it was indispensable for Poland to reach an understanding with the Russians. "When a thing becomes unavoidable one should adopt oneself to it."

Mikolajczyk replied that Stalin's demands were irreconcilable with Poland's independence and sovereignty. But Roosevelt advised him to remember that "there are five times more Russians than Poles and Russia was a neighboring power which could swallow up Poland if she could not reach an understanding on her terms." He did not believe that

Russia wanted to destroy Poland because Stalin knew that the U.S. government and American public opinion would be opposed to such a solution. Roosevelt recommended that Mikolajczyk enter into personal conversations with Stalin, or at least Molotov.

The prime minister admitted that he had been thinking about such a move, but without Roosevelt's support, he felt Stalin would insist on certain conditions as a preliminary to negotiations. Speaking as if he were taking Mikolajczyk into his confidence, Roosevelt explained that as a politician he would understand that for the time being, in the President's "political year," he could not officially begin a new intervention with Stalin on the Polish problem or propose mediation on his part. However, Roosevelt proposed to act as a moderator, interpreting ideas and views and facilitating an understanding.

That evening there was a full dress state dinner at the White House in Mikolajczyk's honor. Roosevelt's toast, really an impromptu speech, greatly moved the Polish prime minister. The President spoke of Poland's history, geographical position, partitions, political rights, the achievements of the Polish army, navy, and air force, and of the necessity to ensure Poland's independence in a future peaceful world. After dinner, he took Mikolajczyk into his study for more talk about the Polish problem. He proposed to send a telegram to Stalin urging him to talk man-to-man with Mikolajczyk. But such a meeting troubled the prime minister because he feared Stalin would press him to agree to the Curzon Line. Roosevelt admitted that he was probably correct, but direct conversations were necessary if he expected genuine collaboration to materialize. Before the evening was over, Roosevelt promised to do what he could in getting talks started. "We left the President at midnight," wrote Ciechanowski, "definitely under his spell."

At the next meeting, on June 12, Roosevelt urged Mikolajczyk to engage in direct conversation with Stalin without delay. The prime minister must face up to the emergency and be prepared to make concessions, particularly over the government. Roosevelt reminded Mikolajczyk that the Polish nation was numerically smaller than Russia; it could not ef-

fectively resist Soviet pressure. If he were in such a situation, Roosevelt said, he would unhesitatingly agree to make
concessions if he considered them unavoidable. If personal
contact could be satisfactorily established with Stalin and a
more friendly atmosphere created, Roosevelt thought that
Stalin would be less insistent in his territorial demands. If
the personal relationship could be established, then Stalin
would help Poland obtain territories including East Prussia,
Lvov, Drohobycz, Silesia, and even Königsberg, which he
thought Stalin did not really want.

When Mikolajczyk again voiced his fears that Stalin would
lay down preliminary conditions before agreeing to see him
at all, Roosevelt countered that he must be realistic. "You
must remember what I told you before. There are five times
more Russians than Poles, and you cannot risk war with
Russia. What alternative remains? Only to reach agreement." By the word "agreement," Roosevelt explained frankly
that Mikolajczyk must change the composition of the Polish
government. After all, Stalin only wanted four men removed. If Roosevelt found himself in such a situation, he
would not hesitate to alter the composition of the government if he could thus win the confidence of a stronger ad-
versary and open the door to understanding.

When Mikolajczyk left the final meeting with Roosevelt
on June 14, the President, grasping him by the hand, declared: "I want you to rest assured that I will watch over the
matter and will do all I can to help you."[25]

Once more the Roosevelt charm had overcome fears and
hesitations. Mikolajczyk left the White House caught up in
the spell cast by the President, believing that in Washington
Poland had a powerful friend who would moderate Stalin's
demands. Mikolajczyk need only talk man-to-man with Stalin and make a few changes in the Polish government and
Stalin's territorial demands would be curtailed. He had assurances from Roosevelt that Stalin did not want to destroy
Poland; moreover, Stalin knew that the American government and the American people would oppose such a solution to the Polish-Soviet problem.

Roosevelt, hiding behind the upcoming presidential
election, had not been candid with Mikolajczyk because he
wanted to maintain the Soviet connection so vital to him in

the prosecution of the war and in his plans for the postwar world. At the same time he had to overcome any suspicion of a deal over Poland made in Teheran, which was already making the rounds of the embassies in Washington. An honest admission by Roosevelt that he would not oppose Stalin might have spurred Mikolajczyk and his colleagues to seek the best arrangement they could with Stalin over the frontier problem. But such an admission would not have remained secret, and Roosevelt feared the resulting domestic political repercussions. He may have imagined that after the Anglo-American contribution to the defeat of Germany in the form of armies landing in France, he could wangle a better deal with Stalin. But he allowed Mikolajczyk to leave Washington strengthened in his resolution to resist Stalin's territorial demands.

Mikolajczyk's visit to Washington could easily fuel Kremlin suspicions of a Polish-American conspiracy against Stalin and the Teheran agreement. Before Mikolajczyk arrived in Washington, Roosevelt had briefed Harriman, home for consultations, on allaying Stalin's fears. Upon his return to Moscow, Harriman assured Molotov that Roosevelt and Hull "were firm in their determination to carry out the understandings reached at Moscow and Teheran for solidarity in Soviet-American relations and that no minor difficulties would affect this determination to work out agreements on all questions." To the Polish premier, Roosevelt would stress the importance of establishing cordial relations between Poland and the Soviet Union. Roosevelt "remembered what Stalin had said to him on this question at Teheran." Because the Polish-Soviet question must not become an issue in the presidential campaign, the President felt it best to remain quiet on the Polish issue. Mikolajczyk, too, would make no public speeches while he was in the United States. Interrupting Harriman, Molotov asked if Roosevelt's attitude was still the same as he had expressed at the Teheran Conference. "Of course," replied Harriman. Pleased at the reply, Molotov promised to inform Stalin, who would be gratified. When Harriman next saw Molotov, he reported Stalin's pleasure at learning Roosevelt's attitude was the same as expressed at Teheran.

When Harriman finally saw Stalin on June 10, he assured

him that Roosevelt regarded relations between the two men "in the atmosphere of Teheran." Roosevelt had full confidence that Stalin would carry out the policies regarding the Polish people which had been discussed at Teheran. Stalin assured Harriman that Soviet policy had not changed since Teheran. After talking with Stalin, Harriman reported to Washington that it had been the "first friendly talk I have had with Stalin about the Poles and I got the feeling that he saw a solution in the making which would be acceptable all around."[26]

Stalin could well be happy. Roosevelt had not changed his position since Teheran, although Mikolajczyk had been talking with him. Even after Stalin's arguments with Churchill and the London Poles, Roosevelt had not taken up the cause of Mikolajczyk and his government. The Allied landings in Normandy meant that Churchill and Roosevelt needed a Soviet offensive sweeping through eastern Europe to draw on Germany's reserves of manpower. Churchill had been pressing the Poles for a negotiated settlement, and Roosevelt, as he had promised Stalin in Teheran, remained quiet over Poland because of the election.

Stalin was doubly pleased because Allied troops had landed in France without any demands being made on him by Churchill and Roosevelt. Since they had not imposed conditions prior to giving the order for the landings, after the Allied soldiers were ashore, Churchill and Roosevelt had lost their leverage with Stalin. He would not have to pay any price for Allied help through concessions, particularly in Poland. Had Churchill and Roosevelt been inclined to bargain with Stalin over Poland, that bargaining would have had to come before D-Day. By adhering to the pledges made at Teheran without imposing any conditions on Stalin, Churchill and Roosevelt sacrificed whatever advantage they once had.

In July, Soviet troops had crossed the Curzon Line and Moscow had recognized the Polish Committee of National Liberation, headed by the Communist Bierut, as the administrator of the Soviet-occupied areas of Poland. Eventually Mikolajczyk received an invitation to visit Moscow. But even as his plane flew toward Moscow on July 29, in Warsaw the Polish Home Army, supported by his government, prepared to seize control of the city before Soviet troops entered. Then Moscow would be forced to come to terms with the London Poles. Poorly prepared, lacking weapons and supplies, the uprising failed. Stalin refused the Poles aid because he wanted to destroy the Polish Home Army and discredit Mikolajczyk's government. Not only did Stalin succeed, but Mikolajczyk's mission to Moscow failed as well. He could not convince Stalin either to help Warsaw or to resume diplomatic relations with the London Poles.

As the Warsaw uprising came to its tragic, bloody end, Churchill and Eden, worried over the Polish-Soviet problem and troubles in the Balkans, journeyed again to Moscow in October. Mikolajczyk also received an invitation to join them in their meetings with Stalin. In a Kremlin meeting on October 13, the Curzon Line again became the focus of the argument. Mikolajczyk refused to accept the line, rejecting a cession of territory to the Soviet Union without the approval of the Polish people. Churchill countered that he had to accept the Curzon Line as a de facto line of demarcation, with the final settlement coming at the peace conference. He and the British government were committed to the Curzon Line. Both Churchill and Stalin promised to support the Polish claims in East Prussia up to the line of the Oder River in the west. Suddenly Molotov exclaimed, "But all this was settled at Teheran!" He claimed that all three major powers supported the Curzon Line because at Teheran Roosevelt had accepted the Curzon Line as the Polish-Soviet frontier and considered it a just solution but could not for the time being make public his position. Molotov could not remember any objection by Roosevelt to the Curzon Line. He paused dramatically, looking at Eden, Churchill, and Harriman, who was also present, waiting to see if they would challenge his statement. They were silent.

Later, Harriman claimed that he had remained silent because any attempt to correct Molotov would have made the situation worse. After dinner that evening when he talked with Churchill about Molotov's statement, the prime minister recalled that Roosevelt showed interest in hearing his views and Stalin's about the boundary question but he had expressed no opinion one way or the other at Teheran about the Curzon Line. When Churchill queried Stalin about Roosevelt expressing agreement with the Curzon Line, Stalin recalled a private conversation with the President in which he had agreed to the Curzon Line as the Soviet-Polish boundary.[27]

Molotov's statement at the Kremlin meeting and the silence of Churchill, Eden, and Harriman shook Mikolajczyk's faith in Roosevelt. He had left Washington thinking that Roosevelt had not consented to the Curzon Line as the Polish-Soviet frontier at Teheran. Moreover, Roosevelt had told him that this dispute ought not to be settled on the basis of the Curzon Line, and that at an appropriate time he would help Poland retain the eastern area. The President had appeared opposed to the settlement of territorial problems before the end of the war. Harriman's explanation did little to restore Mikolajczyk's confidence in the Americans. The American ambassador, claiming that Roosevelt had not agreed to the Curzon Line, asked Mikolajczyk not to inform his London colleagues about Molotov's statement.

No alternative remained for Mikolajczyk but to seek from Roosevelt an explanation about the events at Teheran. After returning to London from Moscow, he waited until October 26 before writing to ask for the truth from Roosevelt. Wisely he did not demand an explanation of the Teheran discussions, but instead reminded Roosevelt of assurances given during their conversations in Washington: "The memory of these assurances had not been dispelled even by Mr. Molotov's onesided version about your attitude in Teheran, which he gave me during the last conversations in Moscow. I have no doubt that in your attitude, Mr. President, purely objective arguments have played the most important part." Mikolajczyk described to the President the pressure on him to concede to Stalin's demands. To grant the territory would destroy Polish confidence in Mikolajczyk and in his government. He asked Roosevelt to support him by making a personal appeal to Stalin to settle the frontier question in such a way that Lvov and the East Galician fields would remain within Poland. If the President would undertake this personal initiative, Mikolajczyk believed that a Polish-Soviet understanding would be possible.[28]

Mikolajczyk's plea arrived at an unpleasant time for Roosevelt, for he was in the midst of a presidential election campaign in which the Polish-American vote could be vital. Political analysts in the Democratic party thought that the great majority of the Polish-American voters supported the Polish government in London. In May the Polish-American Congress had urged Roosevelt to back the London Poles and to oppose territorial changes in Poland achieved by force. Because the Polish-American vote appeared so significant, Roosevelt received a delegation from the Polish-American Congress on October 11. Avoiding all commitments in their discussion, he agreed that Poland had to be reconstituted as a great nation, and he permitted photographs of the delegation meeting with him in front of a large map of Poland on which the prewar boundaries were marked in heavy ink. During the remainder of the presidential campaign, the photograph was featured in Polish-language newspapers.

When Mikolajczyk's message reached him, Roosevelt delayed answering because the election loomed ahead. Instead, he met with Charles Rosemarek, chairman of the Polish-American Congress, in Chicago on October 28 on a campaign tour in the closing days of the campaign. While refusing Rosemarek's demand for a tougher stand with the Soviet Union over Poland, Roosevelt implied that he knew how to handle Stalin and would stand behind Poland when the peace conference finally met. To the press, Rosemarek announced that he would vote for Roosevelt. His endorsement, widely noted in the Polish-American press, helped Roosevelt's victory in the November election.

Roosevelt still held back from replying to Mikolajczyk until prompted by the Acting Secretary of State, Edward R. Stettinius, who finally drafted the letter which Roosevelt signed on November 17, with the election safely passed. Once more the platitudes were repeated of supporting a strong, free, and independent Poland. But as for the frontiers of Poland, there would be no objection to a mutual agreement between the governments. No United States guarantee of any specific frontier would be given. Instead, the United States was working toward establishing a world security organization which would assume responsibility for the general security of all frontiers. The United States would have no objection to transferring national minorities into and out of Poland. The letter closed with a carefully guarded promise to help with postwar economic reconstruction, subject to legislative authority.[29]

Here was the official answer to the Curzon Line and the events at Teheran. Soon after receiving Roosevelt's message, Mikolajczyk gave up the struggle and resigned as prime minister.

On December 31, the Soviet-sponsored Lublin Committee, led by Bierut, proclaimed itself the Provisional Government of Poland; he styled himself temporary president of Poland. On January 5, 1945, Moscow recognized the new political arrangement in Poland. In this manner, Stalin had gained his Teheran demands: He had achieved a "friendly" government that would accept the Curzon Line.

Roosevelt would not now join a united front against Stalin as some in the State Department had begun to urge him to do. The reason for his refusal can be found in the record of his meetings with Mikolajczyk, which reveal much of the basis for his policy. Poland was small, weak, and the Soviet Union was large—"there are five times more Russians than Poles." Realistically, the Poles had to reach an understanding with Stalin. It was unavoidable.

Although Roosevelt had won the presidential election for the fourth time, he still would not risk damaging the arrangement he believed had been made at the Teheran Conference. Too much was at stake. He refused to destroy the Grand Alliance and wreck his plans for a future peaceful world because of Poland. The Soviet connection was too vital. Moreover, as victory finally approached in Europe, another victory remained yet to be won in the Pacific theater, and there it was believed Soviet help would save Allied lives. If Poland ceded some territory and changed politicians, so be it. The complete answer had not yet been found to the Polish riddle. For Roosevelt there would be another chapter to the Teheran story, and it would be played out at Yalta, where he would once again confront the Polish riddle.

NOTE: For further reference, see the map on page 518.

20
The Yalta Connection

THE NAME "YALTA" has aroused as much condemnation as the policies associated with the word "Munich." The site of Roosevelt's last meeting with Stalin became a source of bitter controversy. It has been labeled a "sell-out" to Stalin, a conspiracy to divide eastern Europe, a betrayal of Poland, and the beginning of the Cold War. However, much that was debated at the Yalta Conference had first been discussed at Teheran, some issues almost in outline form. There is a good deal of the Teheran Conference in Yalta. It cannot be understood without pondering the results of the earlier conference held in the Soviet Embassy in Teheran.

Both conferences are connected. Yet the Yalta Conference, held in the Livadia Palace on the shores of the Black Sea, remains the most notorious of the wartime conferences. The sordid reputation of Yalta can be traced to the secret agreements signed there, the arguments over interpreting the Yalta Agreements, the sudden death of the President soon after the conference, and the presence at Yalta of Alger Hiss who would later be convicted of being a Soviet agent. Because the Teheran Conference lacked these features, historians have tended to neglect it, except for the pioneering work of Herbert Feis, and a few other historians.[1] In some ways, Yalta completed the work begun at Teheran.

The need for the three leaders to meet again developed from the swift progress of the war. By the summer of 1944 the problems related to the final defeat of Germany, the war against Japan, the future of the United Nations, and as always Poland, seemed to demand another meeting of the Big Three. Consequently, in the aftermath of the ANVIL-DRAGOON debate, Churchill suggested to Roosevelt that the three men meet again soon, and he proposed Invergordon in Scotland, with each leader using his own battleship as headquarters. The President immediately undertook the task of negotiating with Stalin over arrangements.

Once the taboo of meeting with Stalin had been broken, arranging for another meeting ought to have been easy after the experience of preparing for Teheran. It would not prove to be so.

In July, Roosevelt proposed to Stalin that they meet in September in Scotland. Stalin claimed, however, that the Soviet armies were fighting on so wide a front he could not leave the Soviet Union and be away from directing the war for any length of time. In September, when Harriman talked with Stalin, he maintained that he had to postpone the meeting because his health was so poor that his doctors forbade him to travel. After returning from Teheran, his ears had troubled him for two weeks. His recent illness, he claimed, resulted from a trip to the front. (A most interesting illness because Stalin did not visit the front.)

Back in Washington, Hopkins told the President there was no chance of getting Stalin out of Russia. They had best make up their minds to travel to a convenient place there, preferably the Crimea. Roosevelt, however, thought it unwise to make such a journey until the presidential election was over. After Roosevelt had won reelection, Hopkins informed Gromyko that they wanted to arrange a conference with Stalin. Was there any place in the Crimea where such a conference could be held? Upon learning that he would not have to leave the Soviet Union, Stalin's health immediately improved. He would welcome a meeting in the Crimea. "The three of us," he informed Roosevelt, "could meet late in November to examine the questions that have piled up since Teheran."[2]

Under pressure from some of his advisers—Hopkins was the exception—Roosevelt tried to sell Stalin other sites. On the advice of his doctors, Stalin declined, promising only to travel as far as the Crimea. Next it was Roosevelt's turn to postpone the trip until after his inauguration in January 1945. However, because Stalin remained adamant, Roosevelt and Churchill, accompanied by a large assortment of aides, clerks, generals, admirals, and other personnel, agreed that they would meet him in Yalta and confer in the Livadia Palace, once the summer home of the czars.

Again it had been a repeat of the Teheran scenario for arranging a conference with Stalin. Despite all pleas and arguments, he would travel only to a site suitable to himself. Consequently a dying President would be obliged to make a long journey by ship and by plane in wartime. Churchill, too, had to accommodate Stalin. Once again he had forced the capitalists to come to him—to meet him on his own turf. Just as at Teheran, before the conference had opened, he had won an advantage.

Again the bargaining over the meeting place had been between Stalin and Roosevelt, with Churchill playing a secondary role, a sign of the change in the balance of power. Churchill observed wryly: "If we had spent ten years on research, we could not have found a worse place in the world than Yalta."[3]

Again as in Teheran, Roosevelt at Yalta would stay in quarters prepared by the Soviet government, and probably surrounded by NKVD officers disguised as servants who could eavesdrop for their master. Churchill too had to live in similar quarters; his was an old palace, attractive but very deficient in plumbing. It would have been possible to have installed listening devices in both of these palaces because both required extensive repairs as a result of the destruction caused by the German occupation.

And finally, just as in the case of Teheran, the joint Anglo-American preparations for the Yalta meeting were inadequate, deliberately so in order that no whisper of concerted action might reach Stalin's ears. Consequently, Roosevelt and Churchill once more entered a conference with Stalin lacking any joint agreement on how they would deal with the important issues they were to discuss with him.

Between the conference at Teheran and the one at Yalta, however, there would be one major difference: Roosevelt would no longer be operating on his own. Accompanying him was a State Department delegation, including the new Secretary of State, Edward Stettinius. No longer would Roosevelt depend on his own resources, with Harry Hopkins as his sole adviser. Moreover, for this conference State Department briefing books had been prepared, setting forth the government's positions on important issues that might arise. In view of the President's deteriorating physical condition, there is doubt as to how closely he studied the briefing books, if at all; nevertheless, even the preparation of these materials signaled a change from Teheran.

At Yalta, just as at Teheran, the Anglo-American need for Soviet help would overshadow the conference. At Teheran, Churchill and Roosevelt had been much concerned about the impending Operation OVERLORD and the necessity of a Soviet offensive to hold German troops in eastern Europe when the British and American troops would be invading France. At Yalta, too, they were mindful of the necessity of Soviet aid when the time came to invade Japan. Once more their need provided Stalin with leverage in the talks because they would need his help more than he would need theirs.

And, just as at Teheran, one of Roosevelt's chief aims had been to have face-to-face meetings with Stalin, with only interpreters present. At Yalta, he continued the practice established at Teheran of private conferences with the Soviet ruler. In general, the Teheran format was repeated: Stalin waited for Roosevelt to bring up topics for discussion. Yet to Roosevelt, this was a meeting of old friends who had met previously and corresponded ever since. At Yalta, they were only renewing personal contacts.

In their first talk, on February 4, Roosevelt maintained the views originally expressed at Teheran concerning Germany and Charles de Gaulle. After remarking on the enormous destruction he had observed in the Crimea, he asked Stalin to again propose a toast to execute fifty thousand German officers, as he had done at Teheran to Churchill's discomfiture. Stalin replied that the Germans were bloodthirsty and savage as well as sadistic. The President agreed with this description. After mentioning the progress of the fighting on the western and eastern fronts, Roosevelt asked Stalin how he had fared with Charles de Gaulle when they had negotiated a treaty in Moscow late in 1944. Stalin replied that he had found him unrealistic but not very complicated. (In truth, he had found de Gaulle a hard-nosed negotiator, who did not hesitate to leave one of Stalin's banquets when he decided there was no point in remaining.) Roosevelt described his talk with de Gaulle at which the general had compared himself with Joan of Arc. Then, admitting that he was being indiscreet, Roosevelt told Stalin that the British were attempting to build France up into a strong power to hold the eastern frontier while the British assembled a large force. "The British," he said, "were a peculiar people and wished to have their cake and eat it too."[4]

Turning to the question of the tripartite zones of occupation of Germany, Roosevelt confessed that he was having trouble with the British because he wanted the Americans to have the northwestern zone so that lines of communication would not run through France. According to the President, the British seemed to believe that the Americans should restore order in France and then hand political control over to the British.

Stalin asked if Roosevelt thought France should have a zone of occupation in Germany. The President admitted that it was "not a bad idea, but he added that it was only out of kindness."[5] Stalin and Molotov agreed.

Once again Roosevelt had followed the Teheran model: Denigrate the French and put down the British. He seemed to be signaling that in the future the Soviet Union and the United States would be the only powers who carried any weight.

The President's remark about executing fifty thousand German officers may again have been made in jest, but it seemed to imply that he would still be tough in dealing with Germany's future. At Teheran, he had urged dismembering Germany. At Yalta, Germany's future had to be settled. Consequently, when the German question came up before the three leaders, Stalin seized on Roosevelt's statement at Teheran favoring dismemberment to argue that dismemberment should be included in the surrender terms. Since Teheran, Churchill had lost his enthusiasm for dismembering Germany, and so he battled to keep a blanket statement about this issue out of the surrender terms. But Stalin, relying on Roosevelt's emphatic statement at Teheran that Germany should be broken up into five states, forced them to accept a statement in the surrender terms that the three powers would take steps to dismember Germany.

The main purpose of the second private talk between Roosevelt and Stalin, on February 8, was to complete a task left over from Teheran: settling on the price for Soviet entry into the war against Japan. Stalin explained that he wanted his political terms met because, as he alleged, he must explain to the Soviet people why the Soviet Union had to go to war against Japan. The two men quickly agreed on the conditions for Soviet entry but left the drafting of the final agreement to Harriman and Molotov. A short meeting on February 10 completed the deal.

The terms, first discussed at Teheran, were now committed to paper with one addition: The status quo of Outer Mongolia would be preserved. Within two or three months after Germany's defeat, the Soviet Union would enter the war against Japan on the basis of certain conditions, which included the return of the southern part of the Sakhalin Islands and the Kurile Islands to the Soviet Union, the internationalizing of the port of Dairen, the lease of Port Arthur as a Soviet naval base, and the joint operation of the Manchurian Railway by the Soviet Union and China.

This deal was not sprung on a naïve, unsuspecting President. He had not come to the conference ignorant of the price Stalin was demanding. The basic demands had been made first at Teheran, and since then, Harriman and Stalin had discussed the terms in Moscow. Roosevelt knew what he was doing.

Before concluding this bargain with Stalin, however, Roosevelt had not consulted with another ally, Chiang, whom he intended to keep in the dark. Roosevelt excused this omission on the grounds of poor security at Chiang's headquarters. Chiang never learned about the deal until after Roosevelt's death.

The deal begun at Teheran and completed at Yalta profoundly altered the balance of power in the northwestern Pacific area. By obtaining the southern Sakhalin and the Kurile Islands, the Soviet Union would have the means to bar access to the Sea of Okhotsk and to turn it into a Soviet preserve. Ultimately, Moscow made this body of water a vital link in Soviet naval power—vessels operating from this Russian sea could threaten Japan and the United States.

The issue of Poland dominated much of the conference. It had become so important that Roosevelt could no longer talk about it privately only with Stalin. At Yalta, unlike Teheran, he had to debate it with Churchill and Stalin. His excuse for remaining silent was no longer valid because the presidential election had produced another victory for him. No longer would he have to fear the reactions of Polish-American voters in the polling booths. But there had been a marked change in the politics of Poland because now Soviet armies occupied much of the area and the Soviet-backed Provisional Government had recognized the Curzon Line. At last Stalin had found the friendly Poles for whom he had been seeking.

At Teheran, Stalin had argued for the Curzon Line and for a friendly Polish government. Now he wanted recognition of both. He made Roosevelt and Churchill raise the question. Roosevelt confessed that he accepted the Curzon Line; Churchill did not debate it. But on the question of the "friendly" government, there was much argument. Roosevelt pointed out that American opinion did not support the Lublin government because it represented only a small portion of the Polish people. Together with Churchill, he proposed an interim government in Poland until free elections could be held. Stalin, however, would not give up his "friendly" government, the Lublin Poles. Eventually Roosevelt and Churchill had to accept a compromise. The Provisional Government (Polish Communists at Lublin) would be reorganized on a broader "democratic" basis by including "democratic" leaders from within Poland and from abroad. Molotov, Harriman, and Clark Kerr would consult with the various Polish groups on the reorganization. This Polish Provisional Government of National Unity would be pledged to hold free and unfettered elections as soon as possible. In those elections all democratic and anti-Nazi parties would have the right to participate and put up their respective candidates.

The Anglo-American interpretation of this compromise was that a new government would emerge from the reorganization. However, the Soviet interpretation was different—the basis for the new government would be the current Provisional Government, made up of the Lublin Communists. Any reorganization involving adding Poles from London could be blocked by Molotov, and that he ultimately did exceedingly well. In this way Stalin achieved the friendly Polish government he had called for at Teheran. He would also win out in the battle of interpreting the agreement. "Democratic" meant Communist and Communist sympathizers, while "anti-Nazi" meant parties supportive of the Soviet Union. Any party that did not support the Soviet Union must be Nazi. And so it went.

Once he had a friendly Polish government, Stalin would be well on the way to achieving his demands on the frontier with Poland which he had been seeking since 1941. In the Yalta Agreements, the Curzon Line—with some digressions of five to eight kilometers in favor of Poland—was accepted by the three leaders. But on the western frontier there was limited agreement. Stalin had wanted them to advocate the Oder River and the Neisse River as the frontiers. He had argued for the Oder at Teheran. Instead, Roosevelt and Churchill would only agree that Poland should have territory in the west. The final frontier should await the peace conference.

For Roosevelt and Churchill, it was the best they could do as far as Poland was concerned. The foundation had been laid at Teheran when they failed to reject the Curzon Line and agreed with Stalin's ranting about the unfriendly London Poles. The arguments over Poland during 1944 indicated to Stalin how weak the London Poles really were when both Washington and London failed to support their claims. By the time the three leaders sat down in the Livadia Palace to consider Poland, it was too late for Churchill and Roosevelt to do any effective bargaining. At Teheran, because of

OVERLORD, they had allowed Stalin to stake out his claims regarding Poland; at Yalta, OVERLORD had already succeeded and the Russian troops controlled most of Poland. Moreover, because they believed in the need for Soviet assistance in overthrowing Japan, they would not undo the results of Teheran. Further, Roosevelt would not now undo the Polish agreements because he wanted the Soviet Union to join in founding the United Nations at San Francisco. So Poland would have to pay the price.

Both conferences were evidence of the sloppy use of words. Much of the quarreling over the results of the Yalta Conference would stem from the meaning of words. "Roosevelt never was much of a stickler for language," wrote Harriman. "Even at Teheran, when his health was better, he didn't haggle with Stalin over language. It was my impression that as long as he could put his own interpretation on the language, he didn't much care what interpretations other people put on it."[6]

In the end, Yalta became more notorious because this conference produced written documents which seemed to prove betrayal of Poland, a deal with Stalin over eastern Europe, and a written secret pact over the Far East that changed the balance of power. Nevertheless, the Yalta Conference ratified much that had been accepted at Teheran concerning eastern Europe. As for the Far East, the Yalta Conference completed a deal which had been considered briefly in the Soviet Embassy in Teheran. Stalin's promise at Teheran to bring the Soviet Union into the war against Japan meant that such a deal was inevitable. He would have to be paid off. It seemed a small price to pay if American and British lives could be spared when the Allied forces invaded the Japanese home islands in 1945 and 1946 according to plans already being prepared. No one could know that the atomic bomb would make such an invasion—as well as the deal with Stalin—totally unnecessary.

21
Summing Up

When the State Department released documents dealing with the Yalta Conference in 1955, the event produced newspaper stories, books, angry editorials, and denunciations of Franklin D. Roosevelt by politicians who probably had not read the Yalta papers. In contrast, when the Teheran papers were released in 1961, little interest was shown either by the press or by the politicians. In their ignorance, they did not realize that the Teheran Conference in its own way was just as significant as the Yalta Conference. Yet one historian wrote: "Except for the development of the atomic bomb, it was probably the most important event in the Second World War. By acts of commission and omission, it has shaped nearly three decades [in 1972] of postwar history."[1]

In ignoring the Teheran Conference, journalists and politicians missed an opportunity to study an American President handling negotiations with the leading world Communist by himself, without briefing books or State Department advisers. Moreover, those who overlooked this conference did not realize that the roots of the Yalta Agreements could be found in the Teheran Conference.

The results of the Teheran meeting cannot be dismissed as insignificant. The three Allied leaders there agreed on a basic plan which ultimately defeated Hitler's armies and ended Nazi domination of Europe. In addition, at Teheran Stalin obtained the Curzon Line as the frontier between the

481

Soviet Union and Poland which at the same time brought Moscow that much closer to the heart of central Europe. The Teheran Conference also helped Stalin obtain that "friendly" government in Poland. At Teheran, the three leaders considered dismembering Germany, and there the United States entered into an agreement that would tie it closely to the fate of the shah of Iran. Moreover, at Teheran steps were taken to involve the Soviet Union in the war against Japan by considering Stalin's price for going to war. Finally, in this conference Roosevelt tried to interest Stalin in cooperating with him in maintaining peace in the postwar world.

If there is any one symbol of Teheran, it is the Polish-Soviet frontier—a line drawn on a map by Stalin in red crayon. This action symbolized the shift in politics and power in eastern Europe. Nothing else could so clearly illustrate the future impotence of the Polish people and the new power of Soviet Russia. No more could the Soviet ruler be ignored in the councils of Europe because at one stroke his crayon redrew national frontiers.

At Teheran, however, both sides saw the Polish issue from opposite viewpoints. To Stalin, Poland's Government-in-Exile represented a threat to his hold on the Soviet Union. He believed that unless Soviet power dominated Poland, the latter could undermine Soviet security. Stalin still dreaded another June 22, 1941, when German armies invaded Russia from Polish soil. His fear made the frontier vital to his security. As he told Eden in December 1941, he considered the question of the USSR's western frontiers "as the main question for us in the war."[2] If the Polish frontier followed the Curzon Line, Soviet armies would be that much closer to the heart of Germany. Moreover, only a "friendly" government would accept such a change, and a government that accepted such a change would not be inclined toward the West. It was necessary for Stalin to achieve the goals of the Curzon Line and the friendly government before the war ended and before he lost his leverage with Churchill and Roosevelt.

From the West, the view of Poland was different. London and Washington wanted the Soviet armies to continue to fight the Wehrmacht and to mount an offensive in connection with OVERLORD. To that end, Britain and the United States would sacrifice men and ships to supply the Soviet armed forces. Any sacrifice by any country, even Poland, seemed necessary to keep Russia in the war. If a mere frontier change and a friendly government helped the Soviet Union remain an ally, so be it. Here was the leverage Stalin used in the Teheran Conference.

Stalin surely believed that Roosevelt and Churchill had given him the green light to establish the Curzon Line as the western frontier and to find a friendly government for Poland. At the same time, the pledge to create a second front would give greater impetus to his drive into eastern Europe. In 1943 no one could realize how much British and American opinion would change once it became aware of the actual meaning of the Curzon Line and the "friendly" government of Poland.

During his third talk with Roosevelt at Teheran, Stalin perceived a fundamental weakness in the work of the Teheran Conference. Roosevelt had indicated his acceptance of the Soviet annexation of Estonia, Latvia, and Lithuania, and jokingly had said that he had no intention of going to war with the Soviet Union over this issue. He urged some expression of the will of the Baltic people to satisfy American public opinion. Stalin saw no need for such a procedure. Roosevelt replied that "the public neither knew nor understand."[3] Then Stalin advised him that they ought to be informed and that some propaganda work should be undertaken. Roosevelt failed to follow Stalin's advice.

Roosevelt permitted his fellow Americans to believe that there would be no territorial changes in Europe and Asia until a final peace conference met. However, at Teheran he had accepted territorial changes demanded by Stalin. Neither Roosevelt nor Churchill had opposed the demands. By allowing Stalin to rearrange eastern Europe and to acquire pieces of Asia, Roosevelt accepted a great change in the balance of power. In the future, the reality of Soviet power would not be ignored. One day the United States would be forced to come to terms with this reality, and in doing so, adjustments would be necessary. Yet Roosevelt did not attempt to explain the ramifications of these adjustments to the American people. He had time to commence the task, but he never did so. His failure can be traced to his fear that telling the world about the future reality of Soviet power would alarm not only the American voters but also Europeans. The revelation would give Hitler the means of arousing the German people and much of Europe against the Allied armies even before they had landed in Normandy.

If the idea of informing the world about the future reality of Soviet power ever crossed Roosevelt's mind, he dismissed it, probably because he imagined that the future might very well take care of itself. He would try, as he had before, to postpone explaining this unpleasant truth as long as possible. Presumably he imagined that when the time at last came to explain the reality, he could bring it off as he had in the past, relying on his exalted position and his personality. Stalin, however, had sensed the inconsistency between Roosevelt's conduct at Teheran and his public pronouncements, filled with Wilsonian idealism and based on strong support for the principles of the Atlantic Charter. Consequently, he urged "propaganda work" to acquaint the American people with the reality of Soviet power as exercised at the Teheran Conference.

Roosevelt had come to Teheran believing in a Stalin that never existed. "Uncle Joe" was not the wise, paternal, kindly Russian politician who wished only the best for all of the Russian people. He was a deceitful, paranoid murderer, a conniver whose mistakes had cost the lives of millions of Soviet men, women, and children. He was a man who had intentionally sent millions of his fellow citizens to Soviet prison camps, there to work themselves to death. To protect his grasp on political power, he had had untold numbers of Russian people executed by his secret police. Nor had he, thanks to the war, suddenly been converted into a liberal of the type that Roosevelt and Hopkins knew so well. Nothing was further from the truth than Hopkins's verdict on the Teheran Conference: "The President knows that Stalin is 'getatable' and that we are going to get along fine in the future."[4]

At Teheran, Roosevelt had hoped to establish a close relationship with Stalin that would continue after the war and solidify the peace settlement. To attain this goal, he relied on his own personal experience because in his many years in politics, he had successfully convinced many men and women to work wholeheartedly for him. They had even become devoted to him. The Roosevelt charm had always seemed to work with most Democrats and even with some Republicans. But it would not be so with Stalin because his ideological beliefs, his personality, and his political sense were all alien to Roosevelt's. Finally, how could Stalin conceive of such a close, personal relationship? He had his friends of one day executed the next day. Stalin did not perceive politics as being based on close personal relationships. He only understood raw power sufficient to frighten his fellow citizens.

In assessing the Teheran Conference, it is easy to denounce Roosevelt and Churchill for negotiating with Stalin; but they had no other person in the Soviet Union with whom to discuss the basic strategy of the war. Their military staffs required information from the Soviet High Command, yet because of Stalin's dictatorship no one dared release such information. Consequently, the President and the British prime minister had to meet with Stalin. It was to their credit that they dared make such a journey in wartime in the cause of victory and peace. Most certainly Stalin would never have made such a journey.

But in their negotiations with Stalin, Roosevelt and Churchill labored at a great disadvantage. Very few foreigners who were not devoted Communists had ever really met Stalin face to face and talked with him for any length of time. The British and American ambassadors had had little personal contact with Stalin. Of course Roosevelt had talked at length with Litvinov, who surely reported to Stalin on the strengths and weaknesses of the President, as Molotov also must have done. Much the same can be said for Churchill in his relations with Maisky, the Soviet ambassador.

The printed sources of information on Stalin were limited, and neither Roosevelt nor Churchill had the time to research his life and times. In contrast to the Soviet press, the American press delighted in analyzing and criticizing the weaknesses and errors of Roosevelt. In the Soviet Union, no one dared criticize Stalin publicly or privately, because he was after all the "genius of all times and peoples."[5] Both Churchill and Roosevelt had to endure gibes and attacks from political opponents in public and in private; those who indicated less than enthusiastic support of Stalin could well be denounced and shipped off to the GULAG. Consequently, both Churchill and Roosevelt operated in ignorance of the true nature of Stalin. The ignorance was probably greater on Roosevelt's part since he preferred not to hear those such as William Bullitt who criticized the Soviet dictator. There were Russian experts in the State Department who could have advised him about Stalin, but critics of the Soviet Union were out of favor in the White House, particularly if they hailed from Foggy Bottom.

Roosevelt and Churchill erred in failing to agree on the details and date of OVERLORD as well as the strategy in the Mediterranean before meeting Stalin. He would not have been surprised to hear from them an agreed plan on dates and strategy. Their failure gave him an advantage which he hastened to exploit.

As three days of debate were spent on OVERLORD, the political discussions were pushed back until the final day. Yet even if there had been more time to debate political matters, probably little would have changed given Roosevelt's determination not to antagonize Stalin or drive him into a corner. Throughout the conference, Roosevelt aimed at convincing Stalin that he could trust this American President and that he was not like those tricky British. Only by establishing such a relationship, Roosevelt believed, would Stalin trust him and work with him in the future. It followed then that a searching examination of Stalin's political goals in eastern Europe might have undermined that trust. Yet had there been such a discussion, perhaps Roosevelt might have learned rather more about the real Stalin. As it was, given the character of the talks, his strategy failed.

In meeting with Stalin, Roosevelt had other concerns which overshadowed the future of eastern Europe. He realized that final victory demanded that Stalin be brought in from the cold, into the inner circle of Allied leadership. If the Grand Alliance were to be as strong and effective as possi-

ble, only one man could guarantee Soviet military cooperation in the final assault on Nazi Germany: Joseph Stalin. He
was simply too important to be left out of another Roosevelt-
Churchill meeting. Through his repeated invitations and his
entreaties, Roosevelt sought to show Stalin that he took him
seriously and wanted him to join the Allied leaders. He must
not feel left out of the Allied councils, and the best method
of satisfying the feeling of being wanted would be some type
of personal meeting.

Although Soviet cooperation after the Teheran meeting left
much to be desired, without the personal meeting it could
have been much worse. As it was, the Teheran Conference
paid off with the Soviet offensive after D-Day which forced
Hitler to divide his forces.

Teheran fixed the final strategy of the war in Europe. The
meeting made OVERLORD definite as far as Britain and the
United States were concerned. It can be argued that if it had
been left up to Churchill, OVERLORD might well never have
occurred or most certainly would have been delayed because of his fear of heavy casualties and another disastrous
defeat. At the same time, by everyone agreeing on OVER-
LORD from the west, eastern Europe would be open to Soviet conquest and occupation.

Teheran also resolved the basic quarrel over strategy.
British concentration on a Mediterranean campaign could
have brought not only a postponement of OVERLORD but also
a shift of American energies, manpower, and supplies to the
Pacific theater of the war. Churchill's fixation on the Mediterranean had so antagonized the American chiefs of staff that
they could have opted to withdraw American power from the
Mediterranean area. This was a choice that Roosevelt did not
want to face. But at Teheran any danger that the Americans
might consider concentrating on the Pacific operations ended.

In addition, until Teheran, Operation ANVIL did not form
a significant part of Allied strategy. But once Stalin urged a
landing in southern France and Roosevelt had promised him
that landing, he would not permit cancelation at any cost.
They must all be true to the pledges made to Stalin at
Teheran.

Roosevelt had shocked the British at Teheran when he

lined up with Stalin on the OVERLORD issue. Yet earlier in Cairo, Hopkins had warned: "Sure we are preparing for a battle at Teheran. You will find us lining up with the Russians."[6] By coming down on Stalin's side, Roosevelt had tried to separate himself from Churchill. He hoped that this tactic would place him in a more favorable light with Stalin, who would then be more inclined to work with the President after the war.

Roosevelt proved wise to join with Stalin in forcing Churchill to stop delaying a decision on a specific date for OVERLORD. Further adventures in the Mediterranean could well have postponed the Normandy landings and given Von Rundstedt and Rommel more time to improve the Atlantic Wall. Such delay would have been to Hitler's benefit.

That Roosevelt and Stalin would prevail over Churchill in the OVERLORD debate should not have been unexpected because it reflected the new political reality. Soviet Russia possessed the manpower and the armies which had already defeated German armies at Stalingrad and Kursk; without Soviet might, the final defeat of Germany could not be achieved. Equally, the United States possessed the resources in equipment, ships, supplies, money, manpower, and manufacturing capacity to determine Allied policy and strategy. In contrast, Britain was limited in manpower, short on supplies, and using all available industrial resources. Her future was mortgaged to the hilt.

Churchill's junior position reflected Roosevelt's belief that Britain was a declining power. In the future, he expected that Soviet Russia would exert greater influence on international politics. The best intelligence estimates confirmed his opinion, which was why he had done all that he could to court Stalin at Teheran.

But at the Teheran Conference there was no sadder figure than Winston Churchill. Certainly he realized that his friend Roosevelt was making fun of him in order to gain Stalin's friendship. Both Roosevelt and Stalin had agreed on the basic OVERLORD timing and plan, which frightened Churchill because he knew that failure of OVERLORD would wipe out Britain's army. He would also find his political career devastated. Finally, and worst of all, at Teheran it became apparent to Churchill that he had become the junior partner in the Grand Alliance.

As for the Polish riddle—for that was exactly what it must have seemed to Roosevelt—the President had resolved long before Teheran not to allow Poland to come between himself and Stalin. His vision of the future could not be wrecked by Polish politicians squabbling over frontiers. That was not an issue important enough to warrant breaking with Stalin.

To Roosevelt it was more important that the Teheran Conference had set the strategy that would bring final victory in Europe and help end the war in the Pacific. Thanks to Roosevelt's insistence on having this meeting and making these decisions, there would be no turning back: OVERLORD would be mounted from the west, ANVIL aimed at the south of France, and a great Soviet offensive from the east. The Anglo-American debate over strategy had ended, and Churchill and his chiefs of staff would labor for victory.

At the same time, Teheran finished the threat of secret negotiations between agents of Stalin and Hitler. Any chance of another Nazi-Soviet deal disappeared. But the success of the plans agreed on at Teheran would determine the political map of Europe for generations to come. The conquering armies would decide European politics. In the words of Stalin, "This war is not as in the past; whoever occupies a territory also imposes on it his own social system. Everyone imposes his own system as far as his army can reach. It cannot be otherwise."[7]

The Teheran Conference marked the first time that an American President conferred personally with a Soviet ruler. In so doing, Roosevelt established a tradition of traveling to meet the Soviet leader even though the journey was long, grueling, and dangerous.

By meeting Stalin, Roosevelt hoped to break down the barriers between an American President and the world's leading Communist. After the meeting, the Republic still stood. As communications and travel have made it easier to arrange these meetings, other "summit conferences," as they are now called, have occurred. These conferences between the current Soviet ruler and the President of the United States have become important aspects of Soviet-American relations.

Roosevelt's "Odyssey" began a practice which his successors in the White House have followed, some with more enthusiasm than others. As a result of the precedent he established, every President since Roosevelt has had a personal meeting of some type at least once with the Soviet ruler.[8] The events have assumed a significant position in presidential diplomacy.

Unlike Stalin, who had to be enticed to such meetings, Soviet leaders since then have accepted summit conferences as regular diplomatic procedure because of the benefits derived from meeting with American Presidents. The conferences have ranged from clearing up problems left over from World War II to arguing over the Cold War, to simply getting acquainted, exchanging gifts, and bragging about grandchildren.

The change in attitude among Soviet leaders is related to the new way in which these meetings are presented to the world, bringing worldwide attention, with television coverage and extensive reporting on radio and in newspapers. Summit conferences have become media events, offering both Soviet and American leaders a marvelous opportunity to appear before the entire world as global statesmen. The conferences offer trips at the taxpayers' expense to far-off cities, glamour, excitement, splendid banquets, and the best possible red carpet treatment.

It all began with Roosevelt's "Odyssey." But one question remains unanswered: By these trips and conferences, how much has been learned about the other side? Have relations between both nations have improved and suspicions lessened as Roosevelt hoped they would? Historians are still seeking the answer.

Notes

Prologue

1. "Draft Memoirs of Admiral John L. McCrea," Franklin D. Roosevelt Library.

2. "Trip of FDR to Cairo and Teheran, Nov. 12–Dec. 15, 1943," Official File 200, Franklin D. Roosevelt Library.

Chapter One

1. Winston Churchill, *The Grand Alliance* (Boston, 1950), p. 605.

2. *The Public Papers and Addresses of Franklin D. Roosevelt,* edited by Samuel I. Rosenman (13 vols.; New York, 1938–50), 1940, p. 93.

3. Raymond H. Dawson, *The Decision to Aid Russia, 1941. Foreign Policy and Domestic Politics* (Chapel Hill, N.C., 1959), p. 121; Churchill, *The Grand Alliance*, p. 372.

4. Robert E. Sherwood, *Roosevelt and Hopkins An Intimate History* (New York, 1948), pp. 321–33.

5. *Ibid.*, p. 343.

6. Roosevelt to Stalin, December 16, 1941, *Stalin's Correspondence with Roosevelt and Truman, 1941–1945* (hereafter cited as *Stalin's Correspondence*; New York, 1965), p. 17.

7. Churchill, *The Grand Alliance*, p. 630.

8. Churchill to Roosevelt, March 7, 1942, *Roosevelt and Churchill. Their Secret Wartime Correspondence*, edited by Francis L. Loewenheim, Harold D. Langley, and Manfred Jonas (New York, 1975), p. 196.

9. Halifax to the Foreign Office, March 13, 1942, Premier Files, Prime Minister Winston Churchill Manuscripts, 3/399/8, Public Record Office (hereafter cited as PREM and PRO), London. There is no record of this conversation in the State Department files.

10. Roosevelt to Churchill, March 18, 1942, *Roosevelt and Churchill. Their Secret Wartime Correspondence*, p. 196.

11. Foreign Office to Washington, March 26, 1942, FO 954/25, PRO.

12. Welles Memorandum, March 30, 1942, *Foreign Relations of the United States. Diplomatic Papers, 1942* (hereafter cited as *FRUS 1942*). Vol. III (Washington, D.C., 1961), pp. 536–38.

Chapter Two

1. Roosevelt to Churchill, April 1, 1942, *Roosevelt and Churchill. Their Secret Wartime Correspondence*, p. 200.

2. Roosevelt to Stalin, April 11, 1942, *FRUS 1942*, Vol. III, pp. 542–43.

3. Stalin to Roosevelt, April 20, 1942, *Stalin's Correspondence*, p. 24.

4. Standley to Hull, April 24, 1942, *FRUS 1942*, Vol. III, p. 545.

5. Watt to Churchill, April 24, 1942, FO 954/25, PRO; Eden to Churchill, April 28, 1942, *ibid.;* Churchill to Eden, May 14, 1942, *ibid.*

6. "First Meeting with the Soviet Delegation at No. 10 Downing Street at 11:30 A.M. on May 21, 1942," *ibid.*

7. Raymond Clapper, Personal File, Memoranda 1942–43, Container 23, June 2, 1943, Manuscripts Division, Library of Congress.

8. David Dilks, ed., *The Diaries of Sir Alexander Cadogan, 1938–1945* (New York, 1972), p. 454.

9. Samuel Cross memoranda, May 30, June 1, 1942, *FRUS 1942*, Vol. III, pp. 577, 582–83.

10. Cf. Joseph L. Strange, "The British Rejection of Operation SLEDGEHAMMER, an Alternative Motive," *Military Affairs*, Vol. XLVI, no. 1 (February 1982), pp. 6–14.

11. W. Averell Harriman and Elie Abel, *Special Envoy to Churchill and Stalin, 1941–1946* (New York, 1975), p. 160.

12. Winston Churchill, *The Hinge of Fate* (Boston, 1950), p. 502.

13. Roosevelt to Stalin, November 19, 1942, *Stalin's Correspondence*, pp. 39–40; Stalin to Roosevelt, November 27, 1942, *ibid.*, p. 41; Roosevelt to Churchill, November 25, 1942, *Foreign Relations of the United States: The Conferences at Washington, 1941–1942, and Casablanca, 1943* (Washington, D.C., 1968), pp. 488–90; Churchill to Roosevelt, November 26, 1942, *ibid.*, pp. 490–91; Roosevelt to Churchill, December 2, 1942, *ibid.*, pp. 494–95; Churchill to Roosevelt, December 3, 1942, *ibid.*, pp. 495–96.

14. Roosevelt to Stalin, December 2, 1942, *Stalin's Correspondence*, p. 42; Stalin to Roosevelt, December 6, 16, 1942, *ibid.*, pp. 43–44.

15. Andrew Rothstein, ed., *Soviet Foreign Policy During the Patriotic War* (London, n.d.), Vol. I, p. 49.

16. Peter Kleist, *The European Tragedy* (Isle of Man, 1965), p. 140.

17. Stalin to Roosevelt, January 13, 1943, *Stalin's Correspondence*, p. 50.

Chapter Three

1. Quentin Reynolds, *The Curtain Rises* (New York, 1944), pp. 86–88; Standley to Hull, March 9, 1943, *Foreign Relations of the United States. Diplomatic Papers, 1943* (Washington, D.C., 1963), Vol. III, pp. 631–32.

2. Harriman and Abel, *Special Envoy*, p. 198; Clark Kerr to Eden, March 10, 1943, FO 371/37005, PRO.

3. Alexander Werth, *Russia at War, 1941–1945* (New York, 1964), p. 628.

4. Much of this chapter is based on the diaries, journals, and memoranda of Joseph E. Davies in the Manuscript Division of the Library of Congress. Davies made notes of his conversations with Roosevelt and Stalin, and others soon after the events. Later he polished the entries. There is no other record extant of his talks with Roosevelt, Hopkins, and Stalin. Davies intended to publish another book on his wartime travels; the manuscript of that book, in the Library of Congress, is currently unavailable to researchers. Because there are so many citations from this one collection, I have not noted them.

5. Anthony Eden, *The Memoirs of Anthony Eden, Earl of Avon*. Vol. II, *The Reckoning* (Boston, 1965), p. 433.

6. Halifax to the Foreign Office, March 16, 1943, FO 371/36991, PRO.

7. William H. Standley, *Admiral Ambassador to Russia* (Chicago, 1955), p. 366.

8. Standley to Hull, May 22, 1943, *FRUS 1943*, Vol. III, pp. 651–53; Reynolds, *The Curtain Rises*, pp. 83–84; Clark Kerr to Cripps, May 31, 1943, FO 800/301, PRO. Of Davies's apology to the news correspondents, Quentin Reynolds said, "That is the first time I have had my ass licked before I had time to take my trousers down." His object in going after Davies had been "to puncture the inflated ego of this pompous ass," whom he considered to be "a very bad American and a very dangerous one." (Clark Kerr to Cripps, May 31, 1943, FO 800/301, PRO.)

9. Standley to Hull, May 25, 1943, *FRUS 1943*, Vol. III, pp. 653–55; Clark Kerr, May 31, June 3, 1943, FO 800/301, PRO; Reynolds, *The Curtain Rises*, p. 83.

10. Clark Kerr, May 31, 1943, FO 800/301, PRO.

11. Standley, *Admiral Ambassador to Russia*, p. 380.

12. Davies to Roosevelt, May 29, 1943, *FRUS 1943*, Vol. III, pp. 657–60.

Chapter Four

1. Maurice Matloff and Adwin M. Shell, *Strategic Planning for Coalition Warfare, 1941–1943* (Washington, D.C., 1953), p. 124.

2. Stalin to Roosevelt, June 11, 1943, *Stalin's Correspondence, with Roosevelt and Truman* (Moscow, 1957), pp. 70–71.

3. Churchill to Stalin, June 19, 1943, *Stalin's Correspondence with Churchill and Attlee* (Moscow, 1957), p. 133.

4. Churchill to Clark Kerr, June 16, 1943, PREM 3/333/5, PRO.

5. Stalin to Churchill, June 24, 1943, *Stalin's Correspondence with Churchill and Attlee*, p. 138.

6. Kleist, *The European Tragedy*, pp. 145–46; Vojtech Mastny, *Russia's Road to the Cold War* (New York, 1979), pp. 79–80.

7. Churchill to Roosevelt, June 12, 1943, *Roosevelt and Churchill*, pp. 340–41.

8. Churchill to Roosevelt, June 25, 1943, *Foreign Relations of the United States: The Conferences at Cairo and Teheran, 1943* (hereafter cited as *FRUS Cairo and Teheran;* Washington, D.C., 1961), pp. 10–11; Roosevelt to Churchill, June 28, 1942, *ibid.*, pp. 11–12.

9. Churchill to Roosevelt, June 29, 1943, *ibid.*, p. 13.

10. Roosevelt to Stalin, July 15, 1943, *ibid.*, p. 16.

11. Davies's diaries, July 24, August 4, 1943.

12. Stalin to Roosevelt, August 8, 1954, *FRUS Cairo and Teheran*, pp. 17–18.

13. Stalin to Churchill, August 9, 1943, *Stalin's Correspondence with Churchill and Attlee*, p. 142.

14. Roosevelt and Churchill to Stalin, August 18, 1932, *FRUS Cairo and Teheran*, pp. 20–21.

15. Roosevelt to Stalin, September 6, 1943, *Stalin's Correspondence with Roosevelt and Truman*, pp. 8–89.

16. Stalin to Roosevelt, September 8, 1983, *ibid.*, pp. 90–91.

17. Stalin to Roosevelt and Churchill, August 22, 1943, *ibid.*, p. 84.

Chapter Five

1. Roosevelt to Stalin, September 9, 1943, *FRUS Cairo and Teheran*, p. 24.

2. Churchill to Stalin, September 10, 1943, *Stalin's Correspondence with Churchill and Attlee*, p. 161.

3. Churchill to Stalin, September 27, 1943, *ibid.*, pp. 165–66; Stalin to Churchill, October 3, 1943, *ibid.*, p. 171.

4. Davies journal, September 25, 1943.

5. Davies diary, September 27, 1943. He also mentioned the talk with Roosevelt in the journal entry for May 13, 1945.

6. Davies diary, September 30–October 2, 1943.

7. Davies journal, May 13, 1945, detailing a conference with President Harry Truman.

8. Davies diary, October 6, 1943.

9. Eden to the Prime Minister, March 16, 1943, FO 371/36991/0475, PRO.

10. Churchill to Roosevelt, October 14, 1943; Roosevelt to Churchill, October 14, 1943, *FRUS Cairo and Teheran*, pp. 30, 32.

11. Roosevelt to Stalin, October 14, 1943, *ibid.*, pp. 31–32.

12. Churchill to Roosevelt, October 27, 1943, *ibid.*, pp. 47–48.

13. Code name for the invasion of northwestern Europe in the spring of 1944.

14. Deane to Joint Chiefs of Staff, November 9, 1943, RG 319, envelope #3, item #15, Moscow Conference Topics.

15. Roosevelt to Hull, October 21, 1943, *FRUS Cairo and Teheran*, pp. 35–37.

16. Hull to Roosevelt, October 26, 1943, *ibid.*, pp. 45–46.

17. Eden to Churchill, October 22, 1943, PREM 3/136/1, PRO.

18. Eden to Churchill, October 31, 1943, *ibid.*

19. Arnold memorandum for Hopkins, October 24, 1943, Hopkins Papers, Box 331, Roosevelt Library.

20. Churchill to Roosevelt, October 29, 1943, *FRUS Cairo and Teheran*, pp. 49–50.

21. Roosevelt to Churchill, October 29, 1943, *ibid.*, p. 50.

22. Churchill to Roosevelt, October 30, 1943, *ibid.*, pp. 54–55.

23. Memorandum of conversation, Molotov and Hull, October 29, 1943, *ibid.*, pp. 52–53.

24. Hull to Roosevelt, October 31, 1943, *ibid.*, pp. 57–58.

25. Eden to Churchill, November 1, 1943, PREM 4/74/2, PRO.

26. Eden to Churchill, October 31, 1943, PREM 3/136/1, PRO.

27. Eden to Churchill, November 2, 1943, *ibid*

28. Churchill to Roosevelt, November 2, 1943, *FRUS Cairo and Teheran*, pp. 60–61.

29. Quoted in Dilks, ed., *The Diaries of Sir Alexander Cadogan*, p. 488.

30. Elliott Roosevelt, *As We Saw It* (New York, 1946), p. 359.

31. Barbara W. Tuchman, *Stilwell and the American Experience in China, 1911–1945* (New York, 1971), p. 397.

32. Roosevelt to Chiang, October 27, 1943, *FRUS Cairo and Teheran*, p. 47.

33. Stalin to Roosevelt, November 5, 1943, *ibid.*, pp. 67–68.

34. Harriman to Roosevelt, November 7, 1943, *ibid.*, pp. 70–71.

35. Roosevelt to Stalin, November 8, 1943, *ibid.*, pp. 71–72.

36. Roosevelt to Churchill, November 11, 1943, *ibid.*, pp. 79–80.

37. Memorandum by Bohlen, November 9, 1943, *ibid.*, pp. 74–76.

38. Roosevelt to Churchill, November 11, 1943, *ibid.*, pp. 79–80.

Chapter Six

1. Admiral McCrea memoirs, Roosevelt Library; U.S.S. *Iowa* Action Report, December 22, 1943, Operational Archives, U.S. Naval History Division; E. D. H. Johnson, "Trip to Oran with President Roosevelt," June 1945, *ibid.*; H. H. Arnold, *Global Mission* (New York, 1949), p. 455; Ernest J. King and Walter Muir Whitehill, *Fleet Admiral King: A Naval Record* (London, 1953), p. 292; William H. Rigdon, *White House Sailor*

(New York, 1962), p. 64; Robert Goralski, *World War II Almanac 1931–1945* (New York, 1981), p. 289.

2. Johnson, "Trip to Oran with President Roosevelt."

3. Gerald Pawle, *The War and Colonel Warden* (New York, 1963), p. 261.

4. Lord Moran, *Churchill. Taken from the Diaries of Lord Moran* (hereafter cited as *Diaries;* Boston, 1966), p. 139.

5. Arthur Bryant, *Triumph in the West, 1943–1945* (London, 1959), pp. 47–49.

6. John Ehrman, *Grand Strategy* (London, 1956), Vol. V, *August 1943–September 1944*, pp. 109–11.

7. Alanbrooke Diary, November 20, 1943, Liddell Hart Centre for Military Archives, King's College, London.

8. Henry Stimson Diary, August 10, 1943, microfilm, George C. Marshall Library.

9. Memorandum, August 8, 1943, OPD, 381 sec VIIIA PA 2 Case 217, National Archives (NA).

10. "Minutes of the President's Meeting with the Joint Chiefs of Staff, November 15, 1943," *FRUS Cairo and Teheran*, p. 195.

11. "Minutes of the President's Meeting with the Joint Chiefs of Staff, November 19, 1943," *ibid.*, pp. 248–61.

12. Memorandum of Wallace Murray, November 15, 1943, *ibid.*, pp. 89–90.

13. Early memorandum to Hull, Stimson, Knox, and Wilson, November 16, 1943, *ibid.*, pp. 90–91.

14. Roosevelt to Eisenhower, November 17, 1943, *ibid.*, p. 96; Churchill to Roosevelt, November 18, November 19, 1943, *ibid.*, pp. 98–99; Roosevelt to Churchill, November 19, 1943, *ibid.*, p. 99.

15. *F. D. R. His Personal Letters, 1928–1945* (New York, 1950) Vol. II, p. 1469.

Chapter Seven

1. Quoted in Bryant, *Triumph in the West*, p. 53.

2. Joseph W. Stilwell, *The Stilwell Papers* (New York, 1948), p. 245.

3. Bryant, *Triumph in the West*, p. 55.

4. Eden, *The Reckoning*, p. 491.

5. Minutes of the meeting of the Combined Chiefs of Staff with Roosevelt and Churchill, November 24, 1943, *FRUS Cairo and Teheran*, pp. 329–34.

6. "The President's Log at Cairo," *ibid.*, p. 299.

7. Bryant, *Triumph in the West*, p. 57.

8. *Ibid.*

9. Roosevelt to Stalin, November 22, 1943, *FRUS Cairo and Teheran*, pp. 373–74; Stalin to Roosevelt, November 25, 1943, *ibid.*, p. 415.

10. Louis L. Dreyfus, "Memorandum Re. the President's Visit at Te-

heran, November 27–December 2, 1943," RG 84, Entry 59A543, Teheran Embassy, Box 2242, NA.

11. Hurley to Roosevelt, November 26, 1943, *FRUS Cairo and Teheran*, p. 440.

12. Michael P. Reilly, *Reilly of the White House* (New York, 1947), pp. 175–76.

13. To accommodate the expected party of Americans and be for the conference, suitable refreshments had been ordered sent to the British legation:

4 bottles of liqueur brandy
2 dozen champagne
1 dozen each sherry and port
4 dozen whiskey
2 dozen gin
cigars
6 tins of clams
2 tins of marmalade
5 pounds of tea
7 pounds of coffee
6 tins of sausage
12 pounds of sugar
12 tins of orange juice
2 hampers of fresh fruit

Hankey to Martin, November 24, 1942, PREM 4/74/1/04775, PRO.

Chapter Eight

1. Dreyfus, "Memorandum Re. the President's Visit at Teheran, November 27–December 2, 1943," RG 84, Teheran Embassy, Box 2242, NA. The treatment inflicted on Dreyfus reflected Hopkins's opposition to him. "The man just won't get along with anyone. We have enough problems on our backs as it is at this conference without adding trouble by having Dreyfus around," said Hopkins. Don Lohbeck, *Patrick J. Hurley* (Chicago, 1956), p. 212.

2. Winston Churchill, *Closing the Ring* (Boston, 1951), pp. 342–43.

3. Eden, *The Reckoning*, p. 494.

4. Donald N. Wilber, *Reza Shah Pahlavi: The Resurrection and Reconstruction of Iran* (Hicksville, N.Y., 1975), p. 200.

5. Intelligence summary, August 16, 1943, WO 208/1568, PRO.

6. Reilly, *Reilly of the White House*, p. 178.

7. "Axis Agents in Iran—to August 15, 1943," USA Forces in the Mid-East, RG 165, G-2 Regional, Iran, Box 1832, NA; "Review of Developments in Iran Covering the Period August 15 to September 25, 1943," U.S. Army Forces in the Middle East, RG 226, G-2, Office of Strategic Services, 46077, NA; "Iran/Iraq. Enemy Fifth Column and Other Activities Therein," Naval Intelligence Report, October 13, 1943, RG 165, G-2 Re-

gional, Iran, Box 1844, NA; "General Summary for December and Press Summary December 16–31, 1943," Office of Strategic Services, 57620.

There is an important file on Franz Mayer in the Public Record Office which is still closed. Other sources: Bullard to the Foreign Office, November 11, 1942, PREM 3/237/1, PRO; War Office Intelligence Summaries, WO 208, 1568, 1585, 1588, 1588B, PRO; "Case of Franz Mayer, November 14, 1943," FO 371/35077, PRO; Bullard to the Foreign Office, July 28, 1943, FO 371/350721 file 38/34, PRO; Bullard to the Foreign Office, August 5, 1943, FO 371/35073/38/34, PRO; and Bullard to Eden, August 29, 1943, FO 371/35076, PRO.

8. Bullard to Baxter, December 24, 1943, FO 371/40180, PRO.

9. Dreyfus to Hull, August 20, 1943, RG 165, G-2 Regional, Iran, Box 1832, NA.

10. Harriman and Abel, *Special Envoy to Churchill and Stalin, 1941–1946*, p. 264.

11. Reader Bullard, *The Camels Must Go: An Autobiography* (London, 1961). p. 255.

12. See London *Times*, December 20, 1968. Laslo Havas, *Hitler's Plot to Kill the Big Three* (New York, 1967) is not to be trusted.

13. Cavendish Bentick minute, Meeting Joint Intelligence Committee of the War Cabinet, December 28, 1943, FO 371/35077, PRO.

14. Henry H. Adams, *Harry Hopkins. A Biography* (New York, 1977), p. 343; Dilks, ed., *The Diaries of Sir Alexander Cadogan*, p. 579; Hastings Ismay, *The Memoirs of General Lord Ismay* (New York, 1960), p. 337.

15. Rigdon, *White House Sailor*, p. 89.

Chapter Nine

1. In addition to the official Churchill biography, Randolph S. Churchill and Martin Gilbert, *Winston S. Churchill*, Vols. I–V (Boston 1966–77), I have relied on Violet Bonham Carter, *Winston Churchill: An Intimate Portrait* (New York, 1965); Winston S. Churchill, *My Early Life: A Roving Commission* (New York, 1930); Ronald Lewin, *Churchill as Warlord* (New York, 1973); John W. Wheeler-Bennett, ed., *Action This Day: Working with Churchill* (New York, 1969); and A. J. P. Taylor, et al., *Churchill Revised: A Critical Assessment* (New York, 1969).

2. Churchill, *A Roving Commission*, p. 83.

3. Robert Rhodes James, *Churchill, A Study in Failure* (New York, 1970), p. 139.

4. Churchill and Gilbert, *Winston S. Churchill*, Vol. V, p. 290.

5. Material on Stalin's life can be found in Adam E. Ulam, *Stalin: The Man and His Era* (New York, 1973); A. Montgomery Hyde, *Stalin: The History of a Dictator* (New York, 1971); Ronald Hingley, *Joseph Stalin: Man and Legend* (New York, 1974); Robert C. Tucker, *Stalin as Revolu-*

tionary, 1879–1929. A Study in History and Personality (New York, 1973); Nikolai Tolstoy, *Stalin's Secret War* (New York, 1891).

6. Tucker, p. 240.

7. Basil Dmytryshyn, *USSR. A Concise History* (New York, 1965), p. 158.

8. Robert Conquest, *The Great Terror. Stalin's Purges of the Thirties* (New York, 1973), pp. 699–713.

9. Quoted in Ulam, p. 259.

10. Anthony Eden, *The Memoirs of Anthony Eden, Earl of Avon*, Vol. I, *Facing the Dictators* (Boston, 1962), p. 171.

11. Tolstoy, pp. 50–57.

12. Among the biographical sources for background on Franklin D. Roosevelt are: James MacGregor Burns, *Roosevelt: The Lion and the Fox* (New York, 1956), and *Roosevelt: The Soldier of Freedom* (New York, 1970); Robert Dalleck, *Franklin D. Roosevelt and American Foreign Policy, 1932–1945* (New York, 1979); Joseph P. Lash, *Roosevelt and Churchill, 1939–1941, The Partnership That Saved the West* (New York, 1976); Joseph Alsop, *FDR 1882–1945* (New York, 1982).

13. Paul F. Boller, Jr., *Presidential Anecdotes* (New York, 1981), pp. 262–63.

14. Rosenman, ed., *The Public Papers and Addresses of Franklin D. Roosevelt*, Vol. 1940, p. 517.

15. Lash, p. 402.

16. Bullitt to Roosevelt, January 29, 1943, in Orville Bullitt, ed., *For the President. Personal and Secret. Correspondence Between Franklin D. Roosevelt and William C. Bullitt* (Boston, 1972). pp. 575–99.

17. Frances Perkins, *The Roosevelt I Knew* (New York, 1946), pp. 85–86.

18. Hugh DeSantis, *The Diplomacy of Silence* (Chicago, 1980), p. 25.

19. Ross T. McIntire, *White House Physician* (New York, 1946), p. 171.

20. Quoted in Sherwood, *Roosevelt and Hopkins*, p. 343.

21. *Ibid.*, pp. 641–43.

22. Churchill, *The Hinge of Fate*, p. 492.

23. Djilas Milovan, *Conversations with Stalin* (New York, 1962), p. 73. Cf. Robert H. McNeal, "Roosevelt Through Stalin's Spectacles," *International Journal*, Vol. 18 (1963), pp. 194–206.

Chapter Ten

1. Charles E. Bohlen, *Witness to History, 1929–1969* (New York, 1973), p. 133.

2. There are two records of this conversation: Bohlen minutes, *FRUS Cairo and Teheran*, pp. 483–86, and Robert Beitzell, ed., *Teheran, Yalta, Potsdam. The Soviet Protocols,* hereafter cited as *Protocols* (Hattiesburg, Miss., 1970), pp. 338–40.

3. Elliott Roosevelt, *As He Saw It*, pp. 174–76.

Chapter Eleven

1. Joint Chiefs of Staff minutes, *FRUS Cairo and Teheran*, pp. 477–82.

2. Alanbrooke diary, November 28, 1943, Liddell Hart Centre for Military Archives, King's College, London.

3. Churchill minute, "Future Operations in the European and Mediterranean Theater," PREM 3/136/12/04775, PRO.

4. Cornelius H. Bull diary, September 12, 1943, Thomas Buell/Walter Whitehill Collection, U.S. Naval War College.

5. A. H. Birse, *Memoirs of an Interpreter* (New York, 1967), p. 155.

6. There are four records of this meeting, and the quotations come from these sources: Bohlen minutes, *FRUS Cairo and Teheran*, pp. 487–97; Combined Chiefs of Staff minutes, *ibid.*, pp. 497–508; *International Affairs* (Moscow, July 1961), pp. 136–39; PREM 3/136/5, PRO.

7. Moran, *Diaries*, p. 145.

8. Quoted in *The Diaries of Sir Alexander Cadogan*, p. 582.

9. *Ibid.*

10. Bryant, *Triumph in the West*, pp. 60–61.

11. Cf. Bernard Fergusson, ed., *The Business of War. The War Narrative of Major-General Sir John Kennedy* (New York, 1957), pp. 305, 307.

12. Bohlen, *Witness to History*, p. 143.

13. For the record of the conversations during and after dinner on November 28, consult Bohlen minutes, *FRUS Cairo and Teheran*, pp. 509–12; Bohlen memorandum, *ibid.*, pp. 523–14; PREM 3/136/8, PRO. Churchill, *Closing the Ring*, pp. 359–62, is helpful; also *Protocols*, pp. 343–47.

14. Eden, *The Reckoning*, p. 495.

Chapter Twelve

1. For the accounts of this meeting, see *FRUS Cairo and Teheran*, pp. 514–28; *Protocols*, pp. 10–19; PREM 3/136/5/8311, PRO.

2. Moran, *Diaries*, p. 146.

3. Sherwood, *Roosevelt and Hopkins*, p. 784.

4. For the record of this meeting, see *FRUS Cairo and Teheran*, pp. 529–33; *Protocols*, pp. 340–43.

5. William D. Leahy, *I Was There* (New York, 1950), p. 207.

6. For the records of this meeting, see *FRUS Cairo and Teheran*, pp. 533–52; *Protocols*, pp. 19–31; PREM 3/136/5/8311, PRO.

7. Leahy, *I Was There*, p. 245.

8. Quoted in Alanbrooke Diary, November 29, 1943, Liddell Hart Centre for Military Archives, King's College, London.

9. Arnold Journal, "Trip to Sextant, November 11, 1943–December 15, 1943," Manuscripts Division, Library of Congress.

10. Ismay, *The Memoirs of General Lord Ismay*, p. 338.

11. Bryant, *Triumph in the West*, p. 62.

12. Forrest C. Pogue, *George C. Marshall: Organizer of Victory, 1943–1945* (New York, 1973), p. 313.

13. Andrew B. Cunningham, *A Sailor's Odyssey: The Autobiography of Admiral of the Fleet Viscount Cunningham of Hyndhope* (New York, 1951), p. 587.

14. Cornelius H. Bull diary, December 12, 1943; Glenn Perry to Edmond Bartnett, December 20, 1943, Thomas Buell/Walter Whitehill Collection, U.S. Naval War College.

15. Bohlen, *Witness to History*, p. 147.

16. Churchill, *Closing the Ring*, p. 374.

17. Elliott Roosevelt, *As He Saw It*, p. 190.

18. Moran, *Diaries*, pp. 152–53.

19. Bohlen minutes, *FRUS Cairo and Teheran*, p. 555.

20. Bohlen memorandum, December 1943, *ibid.*, p. 837.

21. Elliott Roosevelt, *As He Saw It*, p. 191.

22. George Greenfield, "An Observer at Teheran," in *History of the Second World War* (April 1974), p. 1525.

23. Moran, *Diaries*, pp. 149–51.

24. Arnold Journal, November 30, 1943, Manuscripts Division, Library of Congress.

Chapter Thirteen

1. For the record of this meeting, see Combined Chiefs of Staff minutes, November 30, 1943, *FRUS Cairo and Teheran*, pp. 555–64.

2. Ford memorandum to Dreyfus, November 26, 1943, RG 84, Entry 59A543, Teheran Embassy, Box 2242, NA.

3. Dreyfus memorandum, "The President's visit at Teheran November 27–December 2, 1943," RG 84, Entry 59A543, Teheran Embassy, Box 2242, NA; Mohammed Reza Shah Pahlavi, *Mission for My Country* (New York, 1961), p. 80.

4. For the record of this luncheon meeting, see Ware minutes, November 30, 1943, *FRUS Cairo and Teheran*, pp. 568–75; "Record of a conversation between the Secretary of State for Foreign Affairs, M. Molotov and Mr. Hopkins on the 30th November," PREM 3/136/8, PRO.

5. "Record of a Conversation between the Prime Minister and Marshal Stalin at the Soviet Embassy 12:45 P.M. November 30, 1943," PREM 3/136/11, PRO.

6. "Record of a Conversation between the Prime Minister, President Roosevelt and Marshal Stalin at luncheon on the 30th November," PREM 3/136/8, PRO; Bohlen minutes, November 30, 1943, *FRUS Cairo and Teheran*, pp. 565–68.

7. Bohlen minutes and the Combined Chiefs of Staff minutes, November 30, 1943, *FRUS Cairo and Teheran*, pp. 576–81; "Minutes of the Third Plenary Meeting held at the Soviet Embassy, Teheran on Tuesday, 30th

November, 1943 at 4:00 P.M." PREM 3/136/5, PRO; *Protocols*, pp. 32–34.

8. Djilas, *Conversations with Stalin*, p. 114.

9. Fergusson, ed., *The Business of War: The War Narrative of Major-General Sir John Kennedy*, pp. 305, 312–14. This source has often been overlooked.

10. Georgi K. Zhukov, *The Memoirs of Marshal Zhukov* (New York, 1971), p. 493; Vojtech Mastny, "The Beneš–Stalin–Molotov Conversations in December 1943: New Documents," *Jahrbücher für Geschichte Osteuropas*, Vol. 47, no. 3 (1975), p. 399.

11. Greenfield, "An Observer at Teheran," pp. 1525, 1529; Joan Bright Astley, *The Inner Circle: A View of War at the Top* (Boston, 1971), pp. 123–24.

12. Bryant, *Triumph in the West*, p. 69.

13. Birse, *Memoirs of an Interpreter*, pp. 159–60.

14. The events and comments during dinner are based on Churchill, *Closing the Ring*, pp. 384–88; Boettiger minutes, November 30, 1943, *FRUS Cairo and Teheran*, pp. 582–85; Bohlen memorandum, December 1943, *ibid.*, p. 837; "President's Log at Teheran," *ibid.*, pp. 468–69; and Bryant, *Triumph in the West*, pp. 68–69.

Chapter Fourteen

1. Perkins, *The Roosevelt I Knew*, pp. 83–84.

2. For the record of this meeting, see Bohlen minutes, December 1, 1943, *FRUS Cairo and Teheran*, pp. 585–93; PREM 3/136/8, PRO; and *Protocol*, pp. 34–38.

3. Bohlen minutes, December 1, 1943, *FRUS Cairo and Teheran*, pp. 594–96. The Soviet record of this talk has never been published.

4. Roosevelt to Churchill, February 29, 1944, *Roosevelt and Churchill*, p. 456.

5. Harriman to Roosevelt, October 14, 1944, *Foreign Relations of the United States: The Conferences at Malta and Yalta* (Washington, D.C., 1955), pp. 202–203.

6. Quoted in Dalleck, *Franklin D. Roosevelt and American Foreign Policy, 1932–1945*, pp. 436–37.

7. Robert I. Gannon, *The Cardinal Spellman Story* (New York, 1962), p. 223.

8. "Memorandum of a Conversation with President Roosevelt," October 5, 1943, *Foreign Relations of the United States. Diplomatic Papers, 1943* (Washington, D.C., 1963), Vol. I, p. 542.

9. J. H. Burns, "Memorandum for Mr. Hopkins," August 10, 1943, *Foreign Relations of the United States: The Conferences at Washington and Quebec, 1943* (Washington, D.C., 1970), pp. 624–27. Burns, chief of Army Ordnance, apparently was a close adviser of Hopkins. See also Eden to Cadogan, August 19, 1943, FO 371/36992/04775, PRO.

10. Bohlen minutes, December 1, 1943, *FRUS Cairo and Teheran*, pp. 596–604; PREM 3/136/8, PRO; *Protocols*, pp. 38–44.

11. Cf. Tony Sharp, "The Origins of the 'Teheran Formula' on Polish Frontiers," *Journal of Contemporary History*, Vol. 12 (1977), pp. 381–93.

12. Eden memorandum, "Possible Lines of a Polish-Soviet Settlement," CAB 66/43/04911, PRO.

13. Eden to Nichols, June 15, 1943, in Antony Polonsky, ed., *The Great Powers and the Polish Question, 1941–1945. A Documentary Study in Cold War Origins* (London, 1976), p. 133.

14. "Soviet attitudes towards Poland," September 4, 1943, OSS file 44339, Record Group 226, NA.

Chapter Fifteen

1. Memorandum by Wallace Murray, February 11, 1943, *FRUS 1943*, Vol. IV, pp. 330–36.

2. George V. Allen to Hull, November 4, 1943, *FRUS Cairo and Teheran*, pp. 400–405; Dreyfus to Hurley, November 29, 1943, *ibid.*, pp. 619–20; Draft Declaration, *ibid.*, pp. 623–25; Iranian aide-memoire, December 1, 1943, *ibid.*, pp. 627–28.

3. "Declaration of the Three Powers Regarding Iran," December 1, 1943, *ibid.*, pp. 646–47; Jernegan to Henry, December 3, 1943, *ibid.*, pp. 648–49; Bohlen memorandum, December 1943, *ibid.*, p. 838; Dreyfus to Hull, December 9, 1943, *ibid.*, pp. 840–43; Harriman memorandum, November 13, 1944, *ibid.*, pp. 885–86; Roosevelt to Hull, December 8, 1944, *FRUS 1944*, Vol. V, p. 483. Cf. Bruce R. Kuniholm, *The Origins of the Cold War in the Near East: Great Power Conflict and Diplomacy in Iran, Turkey, and Greece* (Princeton, 1980), pp. 148–78.

4. Hurley to Roosevelt, December 21, 1943, *FRUS 1943*, Vol. IV, pp. 420–26.

5. Pahlavi, *Mission for My Country*, p. 80; Ford to State Department, February 18, 1944, Record Group 165, G-2 Regional (Iran), Box 182, NA; PICME Political and General Intelligence Summary, December 14, 1943, February 22, 1944, *ibid.*

6. "Military Conclusion of the Teheran Conference," *FRUS Cairo and Teheran*, pp. 651–52.

7. Bohlen memorandum, December 1943, *ibid.*, p. 838.

8. Communiqué, December 1, 1943, *ibid.*, pp. 634–41.

9. Dreyfus to Hull, December 10, 1943, Record Group 84, Entry 59A 543, Teheran Embassy, Box 2242, NA; "Memorandum Re. the President's Visit at Teheran November 27–December 2, 1943," *ibid.*; Dreyfus memorandum, December 6, 1943, *ibid.*; Lohbeck, *Patrick J. Hurley*, p. 212.

10. Bullard to Churchill, December 12, 1943, PREM 4/74/1/04775, PRO; Memorandum to Prime Minister, February 23, 1944, *ibid.*; Bullard to Baxter, November 27, 1944, *ibid.*; Bullard to Eden, December 12, 1944, *ibid.*

Chapter Sixteen

1. Quoted in Bryant, *Triumph in the West*, p. 72.
2. Rosenman, *Working with Roosevelt*, p. 407.
3. Combined Chiefs of Staff minutes, December 3, 4, and 5, 1943, *FRUS Cairo and Teheran*, pp. 668–74, 675–81, 705–11; Churchill, *Closing the Ring*, pp. 408–12.
4. *FRUS Cairo and Teheran*, pp. 725–26.
5. Minutes of the Tripartite meetings, December 4, 5, and 6, 1943, *ibid.*, pp. 690–98, 711–18, 726–33, 740–47; Edward Weisband, *Turkish Foreign Policy, 1943–45. Small State Diplomacy and Great Power Politics* (Princeton, 1973), pp. 201–15.
6. Eden, *The Reckoning*, p. 497.
7. "USS Iowa Action Report, 22 December, 1943."

Chapter Seventeen

1. MAGIC Summary #615, December 1, 1943, NA.
2. Louis P. Lochner, ed., *The Goebbels Diaries, 1942–1943* (New York, 1948), pp. 542–44.
3. Hull to Harriman, December 4, 1943, *FRUS Cairo and Teheran*, p. 642.
4. Harriman to Hull, December 6, 8, 1943, *ibid.*, pp. 644–45.
5. Caffery to Hull, December 7, 1943, State Department Decimal File 740.0011 European War 1939/32355, NA.
6. Press Digests, Official File, Container 4675, Roosevelt Library.
7. "Soviet Monitor," FO 371/37064/04911, PRO; Harriman to Hull, January 3, 1944, *FRUS 1944*, Vol. IV, pp. 801–802.
8. Official File 4675, Roosevelt Library.
9. Federal Communications Commission, Foreign Broadcast Intelligence, "Reactions to the Teheran Conference," December 9, 1943, RG 165, G-2 Regional File, USSR, Box 3442, NA.
10. OSS Dispatch, Berne, December 18, 1943, State Department Decimal File 740.0011 European War 1939/32738, NA.
11. "Axis Broadcasts in Arabic for the period December 1–7, 1943," State Department Decimal File 740.0011 European War 1939/32517, NA.
12. David Kahn, *Hitler's Spies* (New York, 1978), pp. 340–46, 369–70; Elyesa Bazna, *I Was Cicero* (New York, 1962), pp. 509–18; Franz von Papen, *Memoirs* (New York, 1953), pp. 509–18; "Memorandum for the President," G. Edward Buxton, January 10, 1944, Roosevelt to Churchill, January 14, 1944, Churchill to Roosevelt, January 19, 1944, Map Room, Container 5, Roosevelt Library.
13. Eleanor Roosevelt, *This I Remember* (New York, 1949), pp. 315–16.
14. Presidential News Conference, December 17, 1943, *The Public Papers and Addresses of Franklin D. Roosevelt*, Vol. 1943, pp. 549–53.

15. Ford to Hull, December 22, 23, 1943, State Department Decimal File 740.0011 European War 1939/323430, 32436, NA; Bullard to Foreign Office, December 20, 1943, FO 371/35077/PO6565, PRO.

16. RG 165, G-2 Regional File 1933–44, U.S.S.R. 3850, Box 3442, NA.

17. Spaman to Wilson, June 28, 1945, Secret Service file, Roosevelt Library.

18. Roosevelt to Stalin, December 3, 1943, *FRUS Cairo and Teheran,* p. 785; Stalin to Roosevelt, December 6, 20, 1943, *Stalin's Correspondence with Roosevelt and Truman,* pp. 112, 114.

19. Cf. McNeal, "Roosevelt Through Stalin's Spectacles," pp. 194–206.

20. Djilas, *Conversations with Stalin,* p. 73.

21. Svetlana Alliluyeva, *Twenty Letters to a Friend* (New York, 1967), p. 134.

22. "The Bases of Soviet Foreign Policy," September 1, 1943, O.S.S., RG 165, G-2 Regional File 1933–44, U.S.S.R., Box 3442, File 3850, NA.

Chapter Eighteen

1. Bryant, *Triumph in the West,* pp. 81–82; Moran, *Diaries,* p. 159–67.

2. H. G. Nicholas, ed., *Washington Dispatches, 1941–45. Weekly Political Reports from the British Embassy* (Chicago, 1981), pp. 287–88, 295.

3. *Public Papers and Addresses,* Vol. 1943, pp. 553–62.

4. Vojtech Mastny, "The Beneš–Stalin–Molotov Conversations in December 1943. New Documents," *Jahrbücher für Geschichte Osteuropas,* new series Vol. 20 (September 1972), pp. 376–79, 397; Harriman and Abel, *Special Envoy,* p. 288.

5. OSS memorandum, "Central and Western Europe: Prospects of Russian Dominance," January 11, 1944, Map Room, Container 73, Roosevelt Library.

6. Harriman to Hull, January 9, 11, 1944, *FRUS 1944,* Vol. IV, pp. 802–803.

7. Churchill to Stalin, January 24, 1944, *Stalin's Correspondence with Churchill and Attlee,* pp. 188–90.

8. John R. Deane, *The Strange Alliance* (New York, 1947), pp. 107–61.

9. Harriman to Hopkins, September 10, 1944, *FRUS 1944,* Vol. IV, pp. 988–90.

10. Deane to Marshall, December 2, 1944, Marshall Library.

11. There is an enormous correspondence on the argument over the Italian ships. I offer only a sampling. "Assignment of Ships Surrendered to the Allies," Combined Chiefs of Staff 448, 448/1, December 24, 25, 1943, Map Room, Container 35, Roosevelt Library; OSS memorandum, "Unfortunate Consequences for the United States of an Announcement Concerning the Italian Fleet," March 7, 1944, Map Room, Container 73, Roosevelt Library; Churchill and Roosevelt to Stalin, January 23, February 24, March

9, 1944, *Stalin's Correspondence with Churchill and Attlee*, pp. 186–87, 197–98, 208; Stalin to Churchill and Roosevelt, January 29, February 26, 1944, *ibid.*, pp. 190, 206; Stalin to Churchill, February 19, 1944, *ibid.*, pp. 204–205; Churchill to Stalin, February 22, 1944, *ibid.*, p. 205; Roosevelt to Churchill, January 8, February 17, February 23, March 3, 1944, *Roosevelt and Churchill*, pp. 412–13, 427, 437–39, 448, 458; Churchill to Roosevelt, January 9, January 21, February 1, February 3, March 7, 1944, *ibid.*, 413, 416–17, 423–26, 462–63.

12. Matloff and Snell, *Strategic Planning for Coalition Warfare, 1943–1944* (Washington, D.C., 1957), pp. 413–22; "Minutes of meeting between the President and the Joint Chiefs of Staff held in the White House on Monday 21 February 1944 at 1400," Map Room, Roosevelt Library.

13. Burrows to Chiefs of Staff, April 4, 1944, PREM 3/342/10/04796, PRO; Churchill to Ismay, March 31, 1944, *ibid.;* Churchill to Roosevelt, April 14, 1944, *Roosevelt and Churchill*, p. 486; Roosevelt to Churchill, April 16, 1944, *ibid.*, pp. 488–89; Roosevelt to Stalin, April 18, 1944, *Stalin's Correspondence with Churchill and Attlee*, p. 214; Stalin to Roosevelt and Churchill, April 22, 1944, *ibid.*, p. 215. Suspicions of the British and the American Allies, however, grew each time it was necessary to report that the date had been postponed. This happened three times during May.

14. Roosevelt to Churchill, May 10, 1944, *Roosevelt and Churchill*, p. 495; Roosevelt and Churchill to Stalin, May 14, 1944, *Stalin's Correspondence with Churchill and Attlee*, pp. 217–18; Churchill to Stalin, June 6, 1944, *ibid.*, p. 223; Stalin to Churchill, June 6, 1944, *ibid.*, p. 224.

15. Churchill memorandum, "Operations in the European Theatres. The Attack on the South of France," *Triumph and Tragedy*, pp. 716–21; Roosevelt to Churchill, June 29, 1944, *ibid.*, pp. 721–23; Churchill to Roosevelt, June 25, July 1, 1944, *Roosevelt and Churchill*, pp. 524, 544–48; Roosevelt to Churchill, June 28, July 1, 1944, *ibid.*, pp. 545–46, 438–49.

16. Winant to Roosevelt, July 3, 1944, Map Room, Container 33, Roosevelt Library.

17. Churchill to Eisenhower, August 18, 1944, *Triumph and Tragedy*, p. 96.

18. *FRUS Cairo and Teheran*, pp. 493, 503; PREM 136/5/8133, PRO; Beitzell, p. 7.

19. Sherwood, *Roosevelt and Hopkins*, p. 780.

Chapter Nineteen

1. Eden memorandum to War Cabinet, "Western Frontiers of the U.S.S.R.," PREM 3/355/4/04796, PRO.

2. Churchill to Eden, December 20, 1943, PREM 3/355/6, PRO.

3. Roberts to O'Malley, December 17, 1943, FO 371/34590/04953; Eden to Churchill, December 20, 1943, PREM 3/355/6/04730, PRO.

4. Hull memorandum, December 27, 1943, *FRUS 1943*, Vol. III, p. 494;

Churchill to Roosevelt, December 27, 1943, *ibid.*, pp. 494–95; Roosevelt to Churchill, December 28, 1943, *ibid.*, p. 495; Hull to Schoenfeld, December 29, 1943, *ibid.*, p. 496.

5. Schoenfeld to Hull, January 5, 1944, *FRUS 1944*, Vol. III, pp. 1216–17.

6. Harriman to Hull, January 11, 16, 1944, *ibid.*, pp. 1217–20, 1229–30; Schoenfeld to Hull, January 14, 1944, *ibid.*, p. 1226.

7. Hull to Harriman, January 15, 1944, *ibid.*, pp. 1228–29.

8. "Agreed record of a conversation between M. Mikolajczyk, M. Romer, Count Raczynski, Mr. Churchill, Mr. Eden and Sir Alexander Cadogan on the revision of the Treaty of Riga and prospects of compensation in the West, January 20, 1944," General Sikorski Historical Institute, *Documents on Polish-Soviet Relations, 1939–1945* (London, 1967), Vol. II, pp. 144–49.

9. Churchill to Stalin, February 1, 1944, *Stalin's Correspondence with Churchill and Attlee*, pp. 192–95.

10. Churchill to Clark Kerr, February 5, 1944, PREM 3/355/8, PRO.

11. "Record of a meeting held at Chequers on Sunday February 6, 1944 at 3 P.M.," PREM 3/355/8/04796, PRO.

12. Roosevelt and Churchill Strays, #5, Map Room, Container 7a, Roosevelt Library.

13. Hull to Harriman, January 25, 1944, *FRUS 1944*, Vol. IV, pp. 1234–35.

14. Eden to Churchill, February 3, 1944, PREM 3/355/8/04796, PRO.

15. Roosevelt to Churchill, February 7, 1944, *Roosevelt and Churchill*, pp. 429–31.

16. Stalin to Roosevelt, February 16, 1944, *Stalin's Correspondence with Roosevelt and Truman*, pp. 120–21.

17. "Note on the conversation between M. Mikolajczyk and Mr. Churchill," February 16, 1944, *Documents on Polish-Soviet Relations*, pp. 186–87.

18. Churchill to Stalin, February 20, 1944, *Stalin's Correspondence with Churchill and Attlee*, pp. 201–204.

19. Roosevelt to Stalin, February 22, 1944, *FRUS 1944*, Vol. III, p. 1264.

20. Churchill to Roosevelt, February 29, 1944, Map Room, Roosevelt Library.

21. Churchill to Stalin, March 21, 1944, *Stalin's Correspondence with Churchill aand Attlee*, pp. 211–12.

22. Stalin to Churchill, March 23, 1944, *ibid.*, pp. 212–13.

23. Churchill to Roosevelt, April 1, 1944, *Roosevelt and Churchill*, pp. 477–78.

24. Harriman to Hull, September 20, 1944, *FRUS 1944*, Vol. IV, pp. 992–93.

25. Jan Ciechanowski, *Defeat in Victory* (New York, 1947), pp. 291–310.

26. Harriman to Hull, June 7, June 12, 1944, *FRUS 1944*, Vol. IV, pp. 1276–77, 1282–83.

27. Harriman to Roosevelt, October 14, 1944, *FRUS 1944*, Vol. III, pp. 1322–23; Churchill to Roosevelt, October 18, 1944, *ibid.*, pp. 1325–26; Stanislaw Mikolajczyk, *The Rape of Poland: Pattern of Soviet Aggression* (New York, 1948), pp. 96–97.

28. Ciechanowski to the Acting Secretary of State, October 29, 1944, *FRUS 1944*, Vol. III, pp. 1328–30.

29. Roosevelt to Mikolajczyk, November 17, 1944, *ibid.*, pp. 1334–35.

Chapter Twenty

1. Cf. Louis Fischer, *The Road to Yalta: Soviet Foreign Relations, 1941–1945* (New York, 1972); Robert Beitzell, *The Uneasy Alliance: America, Britain, and Russia, 1941–1943* (New York, 1972); and Herbert Feis, *Churchill, Roosevelt, Stalin: The War They Waged and the Peace They Sought* (Princeton, 1957).

2. Stalin to Roosevelt, October 19, 1944, *Stalin's Correspondence with Roosevelt and Truman*, p. 165.

3. Hopkins to Roosevelt, January 24, 1945, *FRUS Malta and Yalta*, pp. 39–40.

4. Minutes of the Roosevelt-Stalin meeting, February 4, 1945, *ibid.*, p. 572.

5. *Ibid.*, p. 573.

6. Harriman and Abel, *Special Envoy*, p. 399.

Chapter Twenty-One

1. Robert Beitzell, *Uneasy Alliance: America, Britain, and Russia, 1941–1943* (New York, 1972), p. 378.

2. Eden memorandum, "Western Frontiers of the U.S.S.R.," October 5, 1943, PREM 3/355/4/4796, PRO.

3. *FRUS Cairo and Teheran*, p. 531.

4. Moran, *Diaries*, p. 153.

5. William Taubman, *Stalin's American Policy. From Entente to Detente to Cold War* (New York, 1982), p. 94.

6. Moran, *Diaries*, p. 142.

7. Djilas, *Conversations with Stalin*, p. 114.

8. At this writing no arrangements have been announced for a summit conference involving Ronald Reagan and his opposite number in the Soviet Union.

Bibliography

Manuscript Sources

UNITED STATES

National Archives, Washington, D.C., and Suitland, Md.
  Teheran Embassy Files, record Group 84
  Regional File USSR, Record Group 165
  G-2 Regional File, Iran, Record Group 165
  War Department Plans and Operations, Record Group 165
  Records of the United States Joint Chiefs of Staff, Record Group 218
  Office of Strategic Services Files, Record Group 226
  Records of the United States Army Staff, Record Group 319
  Department of State Serial Files 740.0011 European War 1939–1945
Library of Congress Manuscripts Division, Washington, D.C.
  Joseph Alsop Papers
  Henry H. Arnold Papers
  Raymond Clapper Papers
  Joseph E. Davies Papers
  Cordell Hull Papers
  William D. Leahy Papers
George D. Marshall Library, Lexington, Va.
  George C. Marshall Papers
Franklin D. Roosevelt Library, Hyde Park, N.Y.
  Map Room Papers
  Official File
  President's Personal File
  President's Secretary's File
  John Boettiger Papers
  Harry Hopkins Papers
  John L. McCrea Papers
Naval Historical Collection, Naval War College, Newport, R.I.
  Buell/Whitehill Collection

United States Naval History Division, Washington, D.C.
	Operational Archives

GREAT BRITAIN
Public Record Office, London
	Prime Minister's Operational Files, PREM 3
	Prime Minister's Confidential Files, PREM 4
	Foreign Office Political and Diplomatic Files, FO 371
	Inverchapel Papers, FO 800
	Avon Papers, FO 954
	War Cabinet Conclusions and Minutes, CAB 65
	War Cabinet Memoranda, CAB 66
	Chiefs of Staff (COS) Memoranda, CAB, 80
	Directorate of Military Intelligence, WO 208
Winston S. Churchill Library, Cambridge
	Halifax Papers

Articles

Berezkov, V. M. "The Teheran Meeting: From the Diplomatic History of
	World War II," *New Times* (1967), no. 48, pp. 16–21; no. 49, pp. 27–
	32; no. 50, pp. 30–34.
Brugel, J. W. "Teheran, Jalta und Potsdam aus sowjetischen Sicht," *Eu-
	ropa-Archiv*, Vol. 21 (1966), pp. 803–10.
Charlton, Michael. "The Eagle and the Small Birds: I The Spectre of Yalta,"
	Encounter, Vol. LX, no. 6 (June 1983), pp. 7–28.
Davis, Forrest. "What Really Happened at Teheran," *Saturday Evening
	Post*, Vol. CCXVI (May 13, 1944), pp. 13 ff.; (May 20, 1944), pp. 22 ff.
Field, Henry. "How FDR did His Homework," *Saturday Review of Lit-
	erature*, Vol. 44 (July 8, 1961), pp. 8–10.
Franklin, William. "Yalta Viewed from Tehran," in *Some Pathways in
	Twentieth Century History*, edited by David R. Beaver (Detroit, 1969),
	pp. 253–301.
Greenfield, George. "An Observer at Teheran," *History of the Second
	World War* (April 1974), pp. 1524–26.
Koch, H. W. "The Specter of a Separate Peace in the East: Russo-German
	'Peace Feelers,' 1942–44," *Journal of Contemporary History*, Vol. 10
	(1975), pp. 531–47.
Lahedy, Leopold. "Under Western Eyes. The Spectre of Yalta," *Encoun-
	ter*, Vol. LVIII, no. 10 (December 1981), pp. 92–96.
MacLean, Elizabeth Kimball. "Joseph E. Davies and Soviet-American
	Relations, 1941–1943," *Diplomatic History* (Winter 1980), pp. 73–93.
Mastny, Vojtech. "The Beneš–Stalin–Molotov Conversations in Decem-
	ber 1943: New Documents," *Jahrbücher für Geschichte Osteuropas*,
	Vol. 47, no. 3 (1975), pp. 367–402.

————. "Soviet War Aims at the Moscow and Teheran Conferences of 1943," *Journal of Modern History*, Vol. 47 (1975), pp. 481–504.

————. "Spheres of Influence and Soviet War Aims in 1943," in *Eastern Europe in the 1970s*, edited by Sylvia Sinanian, Istvan Deak, and Peter D. Ludz (New York, 1972), pp. 87–120.

McNeal, Robert. "Roosevelt Through Stalin's Spectacles," *International Journal*, Vol. 18 (1963), pp. 194–206.

Sharp, Tony. "The Origins of the 'Teheran Formula' on Polish Frontiers," *Journal of Contemporary History*, Vol. 12 (1977), pp. 381–93.

Strange, Joseph L. "The British Rejection of Operation SLEDGEHAMMER, an Alternative Motive," *Military Affairs*, Vol. XLVI, no. 1 (February 1982), pp. 6–14.

Takayuki, Ito. "The Genesis of the Cold War. Confrontation over Poland, 1941–44," in *The Origins of the Cold War in Asia*, edited by Yonosuke and Akira Iriye (New York, 1977), pp. 147–202.

Urban, George. "Was Stalin (the Terrible) Really a 'Great Man'?" *Encounter*, Vol. LVIII, no. 9 (November 1981), pp. 20–38.

Books

Adams, Henry H. *Harry Hopkins: A Biography*. New York, 1977.

Alliluyeva, Svetlana. *Twenty Letters to a Friend*. New York, 1967.

Alsop, Joseph. *FDR 1882–1945*. New York, 1982.

Arnold, H. H. *Global Mission*. New York, 1949.

Astley, Joan Bright. *The Inner Circle: A View of War at the Top*. Boston, 1971.

Avery, Peter. *Modern Iran*. New York, 1963.

Bailey, Thomas A. *America Faces Russia: Russian-American Relations from Early Times to Our Day*. Ithaca, N.Y., 1950.

Barker, Elizabeth. *Churchill and Eden at War*. New York, 1978.

Bazna, Elyesa. *I Was Cicero*. New York, 1962.

Beitzell, Robert, ed. *Teheran, Yalta, Potsdam. The Soviet Protocols*. Hattiesburg, Miss., 1970.

————. *The Uneasy Alliance: America, Britain, and Russia, 1941–1943*. New York, 1972.

Birse, A. H. *Memoirs of an Interpreter*. New York, 1967.

Bohlen, Charles E. *The Transformation of American Foreign Policy*. New York, 1969.

————. *Witness to History, 1929–1969*. New York, 1973.

Boller, Paul, Jr. *Presidential Anecdotes*. New York, 1981.

Brown, Anthony Cave. *Bodyguard of Lies*. New York, 1975.

Bryant, Arthur. *Triumph in the West, 1943–1945*. London, 1959.

————. *The Turn of the Tide*. New York, 1957.

Buell, Thomas B. *Master of Sea Power: A Biography of Fleet Admiral Ernest J. King*. Boston, 1980.

Bullard, Reader. *The Camels Must Go. An Autobiography*. London, 1961.

Bullitt, Orville E., ed. *For the President: Personal and Secret: Correspondence Between Franklin D. Roosevelt and William C. Bullitt.* Boston, 1972.

Burns, James MacGregor. *Roosevelt: The Lion and the Fox.* New York, 1956.

———. *Roosevelt: The Soldier of Freedom.* New York, 1970.

Butcher, Harry C. *My Three Years with Eisenhower.* New York, 1946.

Campbell, Thomas M., and Herring, George C., eds. *The Diaries of Edward R. Stettinius, Jr., 1943–1946.* New York, 1975.

Carter, Violet Bonham. *Winston Churchill: An Intimate Portrait.* New York. 1965.

Cassidy, Henry. *Moscow Dateline.* Boston, 1943.

Churchill, Randolph S., and Gilbert, Martin. *Winston S. Churchill.* Vols. I–V. Boston, 1966–77.

Churchill, Sarah. *Keep on Dancing.* New York, 1981.

Churchill and Roosevelt. The Complete Correspondence. Edited by Warren F. Kimball. 3 vols. Princeton, 1984.

Churchill, Winston S. *Closing the Ring.* Boston, 1951.

———. *The Grand Alliance.* Boston, 1950.

———. *The Hinge of Fate.* Boston, 1950.

———. *My Early Life: A Roving Commission.* New York, 1930.

Ciechanowski, Jan. *Defeat in Victory.* New York, 1947.

Clemens, Diane Shaver. *Yalta.* New York, 1970.

Coakley, Robert W., and Leighton, Richard M. *Global Logistics and Strategy, 1943–1945.* Washington, D.C., 1968.

Conquest, Robert. *The Great Terror: Stalin's Purges of the Thirties.* New York, 1973.

Cunningham, Andrew B. *A Sailor's Odyssey: The Autobiography of Admiral of the Fleet Viscount Cunningham of Hyndhope.* New York, 1951.

Dalleck, Robert. *Franklin D. Roosevelt and American Foreign Policy, 1932–1945.* New York, 1979.

Davis, Lynn Etheridge. *The Cold War Begins: Soviet-American Conflict over Eastern Europe.* Princeton, 1974.

Dawson, Raymond H. *The Decision to Aid Russia, 1941: Foreign Policy and Domestic Politics.* Chapel Hill, N.C., 1959.

Deane, John R. *The Strange Alliance: The Story of Our Efforts at Wartime Co-operation with Russia.* New York, 1947.

De Santis, Hugh. *The Diplomacy of Silence: The American Foreign Service, the Soviet Union, and the Cold War, 1933–1947.* Chicago, 1980.

Dilks, David, ed. *The Diaries of Sir Alexander Cadogan, 1938–1945.* New York, 1972.

Divine, Robert A. *Foreign Policy and U.S. Presidential Elections, 1940–1948.* New York, 1974.

———. *Roosevelt and World War II.* Baltimore, 1970.

Djilas, Milovan. *Conversations with Stalin.* New York, 1962.

Dmytryshyn, Basil. *USSR. A Concise History.* New York, 1965.

Eden, Anthony. *The Memoirs of Anthony Eden, Earl of Avon.* Vol. I, *Facing the Dictators.* Boston, 1962.

―――. *The Memoirs of Anthony Eden, Earl of Avon.* Vol. II, *The Reckoning.* Boston, 1965.

Eisenhower, Dwight D. *Crusade in Europe.* New York, 1948.

Ehrman, John. *Grand Strategy.* Vol. V, *August 1943–September 1944.* London, 1956.

Eubank, Keith. *The Summit Conferences, 1919–1960.* Norman, Okla., 1966.

Farnsworth, Beatrice. *William C. Bullitt and the Soviet Union.* Bloomington, Ind., 1967.

Feis, Herbert. *Churchill, Roosevelt, Stalin: The War They Waged and the Peace They Sought.* Princeton, 1957.

Fergusson, Bernard, ed. *The Business of War: The War Narrative of Major-General Sir John Kennedy.* New York, 1957.

Filene, Peter G. *Americans and the Soviet Experiment, 1917–1933.* Cambridge, Mass., 1967.

Forbis, William H. *Fall of the Peacock Throne. The Story of Iran.* New York, 1980.

Fraser, David. *Alanbrooke.* New York, 1982.

Gaddis, John Lewis. *The United States and the Origins of the Cold War.* New York, 1972.

General Sikorski Historical Institute. *Documents on Polish-Soviet Relations, 1939–1945,* 2 vols. London, 1961, 1967.

Goralski, Robert A. *World War II Almanac, 1931–1945.* New York, 1981.

Harriman, Averell, and Abel, Elie. *Special Envoy to Churchill and Stalin, 1941–1945.* New York, 1975.

Harrison, Gordan A. *Cross-Channel Attack.* Washington, D.C., 1951.

Harvey, John, ed. *The War Diaries of Oliver Harvey, 1941–1945.* London, 1978.

Hentsch, Guy. *Staline négociateur. Une diplomatie de guerre.* Neuchâtel, 1967.

Hingley, Ronald. *Joseph Stalin: Man and Legend.* New York, 1974.

Hollis, General Sir Leslie. *One Mariner's Tale.* London, 1956.

House of Representatives. *Appendix to Committee Report on Communist Takeover and Occupation of Poland: Polish Documents Report of the Select Committee on Communist Aggression.* Report 2684, pt. 4, 83rd Congress, 2nd Session, pp. 106–46. Washington, D.C.

Howard, Michael. *Grand Strategy.* Vol. IV. *August 1941–September 1943.* London, 1972.

―――. *The Mediterranean Strategy in the Second World War.* New York, 1968.

Hoyt, Edwin P. *The Shah. The Glittering Story of Iran and Its People.* New York, 1976.

Hull, Cordell. *The Memoirs of Cordell Hull,* 2 vols. New York, 1948.

Hyde, Montgomery H. *Stalin: The History of a Dictator.* New York, 1972.

Ismay, Hastings. *The Memoirs of General Lord Ismay.* New York, 1960.

Issraelian, Victor. *The Anti-Hitler Coalition: Diplomatic Cooperation Be-*

tween the USSR, USA and Britain During the Second World War, 1941–1945. Moscow, 1971.

James, Robert Rhodes. *Churchill: A Study in Failure.* New York, 1970.

Kahn, David. *Hitler's Spies: German Military Intelligence in World War II.* New York, 1978.

Kennan, George F. *Memoirs, 1925–1950.* Boston, 1967.

King, Ernest J., and Whitehill, Walter Muir. *Fleet Admiral King: A Naval Record.* London, 1953.

Kleist, Peter. *The European Tragedy.* Isle of Man, 1965.

Kohler, Foy D. *Understanding the Russians: A Citizen's Primer.* New York, 1970.

Kuniholm, Bruce R. *The Origins of the Cold War in the Near East: Great Power Conflict and Diplomacy in Iran, Turkey, and Greece.* Princeton, 1980.

Lane, Arthur Bliss. *I Saw Poland Betrayed.* Indianapolis, 1948.

Lash, Joseph P. *Roosevelt and Churchill, 1939–1941: The Partnership That Saved the West.* New York, 1976.

Leahy, William D. *I Was There.* New York, 1950.

Leasor, James. *The Clock with Four Hands: Based on the Experiences of General Sir Leslie Hollis, K.C.B., K.B.E.* New York, 1959.

Lenczowski, George. *Russia and the West in Iran, 1918–1948: A Study in Bi-Power Rivalry.* Ithaca, N.Y., 1949.

Lewin, Ronald. *Churchill as Warlord.* New York, 1973.

Lochner, Louis P., ed. *The Goebbels Diaries, 1942–1943.* New York, 1948.

Lohbeck, Don. *Patrick J. Hurley.* Chicago, 1956.

Lukas, Richard C. *Eagles East: The Army Air Forces and the Soviet Union.* Tallahassee, Fla., 1970.

———. *The Strange Allies: The United States and Poland, 1941–1945.* Knoxville, Tenn., 1978.

McIntire, Ross T. *White House Physician.* New York, 1946.

McNeill, William H. *America, Britain, and Russia: Their Cooperation and Conflict, 1941–1946.* New York, 1953.

Martel, Lieutenant General Sir Giffard. *An Outspoken Soldier: His Views and Memoirs.* London, 1949.

Mastny, Vojtech. *Russia's Road to the Cold War.* New York, 1979.

Matloff, Maurice, and Snell, Edwin M. *Strategic Planning for Coalition Warfare, 1941–1942.* Washington, D.C., 1953.

———. *Strategic Planning for Coalition Warfare, 1943–1944.* Washington, D.C., 1957

Mikolajczyk, Stanislaw. *The Rape of Poland: Pattern of Soviet Aggression.* New York, 1948.

Millspaugh, Arthur C. *Americans in Persia.* Washington, D.C., 1946.

Moran, Lord. *Churchill. Taken from the Diaries of Lord Moran. The Struggle for Survival, 1940–1965.* Boston, 1966.

Motter, T. A. Vail. *The Persian Corridor and Aid to Russia.* Washington, D.C., 1952.

Nicholas, H. G., ed. *Washington Dispatches, 1941–1945: Weekly Political Reports from the British Embassy.* Chicago, 1981.

Pahlavi, Mohammed Reza Shah. *Mission for My Country.* New York, 1961.

Papen, Franz von. *Memoirs.* New York, 1953.

Pawle, Gerald. *The War and Colonel Warden.* New York, 1963.

Perkins, Frances. *The Roosevelt I Knew.* New York, 1946.

Pogue, Forrest C. *George C. Marshall: Ordeal and Hope, 1939–1942.* New York, 1966.

———. *George C. Marshall: Organizer of Victory, 1943–1945.* New York, 1973.

Polonsky, Antony, ed. *The Great Powers and the Polish Question, 1941–1945: A Documentary Study in Cold War Origins.* London, 1976.

Potter, Neil, and Frost, Jack. *The Queen Mary.* New York, 1961.

Ramazani, Rouhollah K. *The Foreign Policy of Iran. A Developing Nation in World Affairs, 1500–1941.* Charlottesville, Va., 1966.

———. *Iran's Foreign Policy, 1941–1973. A Study of Foreign Policy in Modernizing Nations.* Charlottesville, Va., 1975.

Reilly, Michael F. *Reilly of the White House.* New York, 1947.

Reynolds, Quentin. *The Curtain Rises.* New York, 1944.

Rigdon, William H. *White House Sailor.* New York, 1962.

Romanus, Charles F., and Sunderland, Riley. *Stilwell's Command Problems.* Washington, D.C., 1956.

Roosevelt, Eleanor. *This I Remember.* New York, 1949.

Roosevelt, Elliott. *As He Saw It.* New York, 1946.

———, and Brough, James. *A Rendezvous with Destiny: The Roosevelts of the White House.* New York, 1975.

Roosevelt, Franklin D. *F.D.R. His Personal Letters, 1928–1945.* Vol. II. Edited by Elliott Roosevelt. New York, 1950.

———. *The Public Papers and Addresses of Franklin D. Roosevelt.* Edited by Samuel I. Rosenman. 13 vols. New York, 1938–59.

Roosevelt and Churchill. Their Secret Wartime Correspondence. Edited by Francis L. Loewenheim, Harold D. Langley, and Manfred Jonas. New York, 1975.

Rosenman, Samuel I. *Working with Roosevelt.* New York, 1952.

Rothstein, Andrew, ed. *Soviet Foreign Policy During the Patriotic War.* Vol. I. London, n.d.

Rozek, Edward I. *Allied Wartime Diplomacy: A Pattern in Poland.* New York, 1958.

Sherwood, Robert. *Roosevelt and Hopkins: An Intimate History.* New York, 1948.

Smith, Gaddis. *American Diplomacy During the Second World War, 1941–1945.* New York, 1965.

Stalin, Josef. *Stalin's Correspondence with Churchill, Attlee, Roosevelt and Truman, 1941–1945.* 2 vols. Moscow, 1957.

Standley, William H. *Admiral Ambassador to Russia.* Chicago, 1955.

Steele, Richard W. *The First Offensive, 1942: Roosevelt, Marshall and the Making of American Strategy.* Bloomington, Ind., 1973.

Stilwell, Joseph W. *The Stilwell Papers.* New York, 1948.

Stimson, Henry L., and Bundy, McGeorge. *On Active Service in Peace and War.* 2 vols. New York, 1948.

Stoler, Mark A. *The Politics of the Second Front: American Military Planning and Diplomacy in Coalition Warfare, 1941–1943.* Westport, Conn., 1977.

Taubman, William. *Stalin's American Policy: From Entente to Detente to Cold War.* New York, 1982.

Taylor, A. J. P. *Beaverbrook.* London, 1972.

———, et al. *Churchill Revised: A Critical Assessment.* New York, 1969.

Thompson, Walter H. *Assignment: Churchill.* New York, 1955.

Tolstoy, Nikolai. *Stalin's Secret War.* New York, 1982.

Tuchman, Barbara W. *Stilwell and the American Experience in China, 1911–45.* New York, 1970.

Tucker, Robert C. *Stalin as Revolutionary, 1879–1929: A Study in History and Personality.* New York, 1973.

Tully, Grace. *F.D.R. Was My Boss.* New York, 1949.

Ulam, Adam B. *Stalin: The Man and the Era.* New York, 1973.

United States Department of State. *Foreign Relations of the United States: The Conferences at Cairo and Teheran, 1943.* Washington, D.C., 1961.

———. *Foreign Relations of the United States: The Conferences at Malta and Yalta.* Washington, D.C., 1955.

———. *Foreign Relations of the United States: The Conferences at Washington, 1941–42, and Casablanca, 1943.* Washington, D.C., 1968.

———. *Foreign Relations of the United States: The Conferences at Washington and Quebec, 1943.* Washington, D.C., 1970.

———. *Foreign Relations of the United States. Diplomatic Papers, 1942.* Vol. III. Washington, D.C., 1961.

———. *Foreign Relations of the United States. Diplomatic Papers, 1943.* Vols. II and III. Washington, D.C., 1963.

———. *Foreign Relations of the United States. Diplomatic Papers, 1944.* Vols. III and IV. Washington, D.C., 1965.

United States Senate. *Hearings before the Committee on Foreign Relations, United States Senate, 83rd Congress, 1st Session. The Nomination of Charles E. Bohlen to Be United States Ambassador Extraordinary and Plenipotentiary to the Union of Soviet Socialist Republics, March 2 and 18, 1953.* Washington, D.C., 1953.

Weil, Martin. *A Pretty Good Club: The Founding Fathers of the U.S. Foreign Service.* New York, 1978.

Weisband, Edward. *Turkish Foreign Policy, 1943–1945: Small State Diplomacy and Great Power Politics.* Princeton, 1973.

Werth, Alexander. *Russia at War, 1941–1945.* New York, 1964.

Wheeler-Bennett, John, ed. *Action This Day: Working with Churchill.* New York, 1969.

Wilber, Donald N. *Riza Shah Pahlavi: The Resurrection and Reconstruction of Iran.* Hicksville, N.Y., 1975.

Wilt, Alan F. *The French Riviera Campaign of August, 1944.* Carbondale, Ill., 1981.

Woodward, Llewellyn. *British Foreign Policy in the Second World War.* Abridged edition. London, 1962.

————. *British Foreign Policy in the Second World War.* Vol. II. London, 1971.

Wright, William. *Heiress: The Rich Life of Marjorie Merriweather Post.* Washington, D.C., 1978.

Yergin, Daniel. *Shattered Peace: The Origins of the Cold War and the National Security State.* Boston, 1977.

Zhukov, Georgi K. *The Memoirs of Marshal Zhukov.* New York, 1971.

Zowandny, I. K. *Death in the Forest: The Story of the Katyn Forest Massacre.* South Bend, Ind., 1962.

Newspapers

The Times (London)
The New York Times

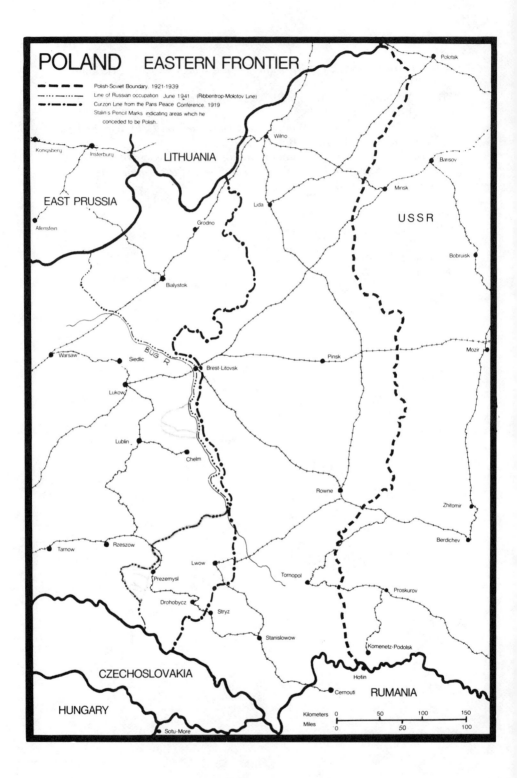

POLAND EASTERN FRONTIER

- - - - Polish-Soviet Boundary, 1921-1939
········· Line of Russian occupation, June 1941 (Ribbentrop-Molotov Line)
-··-··- Curzon Line from the Paris Peace Conference, 1919
●●●●● Stalin's Pencil Marks indicating areas which he conceded to be Polish.

LITHUANIA

Polotsk

Königsberg

Insterburg

Wilno

Barisov

EAST PRUSSIA

Minsk

Lida

USSR

Allenstein

Grodno

Bobruisk

Bialystok

BUG R.

Warsaw

Siedlce

Pinsk

Mozir

Brest-Litovsk

Lukow

Lublin

Chelm

Rowne

Zhitomir

Berdichev

Tarnow

Rzeszow

Lwow

Tornopol

Proskurov

Prezemysl

Drohobycz

Stryz

Stanislowow

Komenetz-Podolsk

CZECHOSLOVAKIA

Hotin

HUNGARY

Cernouti

RUMANIA

Sotu-More

Kilometers 0   50   100   150
Miles   0   50   100

Index

519